Theatre Props and Civic Identity in Athens, 458–405 BC

Also available from Bloomsbury

Costume in Greek Tragedy by Rosie Wyles
Greek Tragedy by Laura Swift
The Lost Plays of Greek Tragedy (Volume 1) by Matthew Wright
The Lost Plays of Greek Tragedy (Volume 2) by Matthew Wright
The Materialities of Greek Tragedy edited by Mario Telò and Melissa Mueller

Theatre Props and Civic Identity in Athens, 458–405 BC

Rosie Wyles

BLOOMSBURY ACADEMIC
LONDON • NEW YORK • OXFORD • NEW DELHI • SYDNEY

BLOOMSBURY ACADEMIC
Bloomsbury Publishing Plc
50 Bedford Square, London, WC1B 3DP, UK
1385 Broadway, New York, NY 10018, USA
29 Earlsfort Terrace, Dublin 2, Ireland

BLOOMSBURY, BLOOMSBURY ACADEMIC and the Diana logo are
trademarks of Bloomsbury Publishing Plc

First published in Great Britain 2020
This paperback edition published 2022

Copyright © Rosie Wyles, 2020

Rosie Wyles has asserted her right under the Copyright, Designs and Patents
Act, 1988, to be identified as Author of this work.

For legal purposes the Acknowledgements on p. ix constitute an extension of this copyright page.

Cover design: Terry Woodley
Cover image © Martin von Wagner Museum der Universität Würzburg, Foto: P. Neckermann.

All rights reserved. No part of this publication may be reproduced or transmitted in any form or by any
means, electronic or mechanical, including photocopying, recording, or any information storage or
retrieval system, without prior permission in writing from the publishers.

Bloomsbury Publishing Plc does not have any control over, or responsibility for, any third-party websites
referred to or in this book. All internet addresses given in this book were correct at the time of going to
press. The author and publisher regret any inconvenience caused if addresses have changed or sites
have ceased to exist, but can accept no responsibility for any such changes.

A catalogue record for this book is available from the British Library.

Library of Congress Cataloging-in-Publication Data
Names: Wyles, Rosie, author.
Title: Theatre props and civic identity in Athens, 458-405 BC / Rosie Wyles.
Description: London ; New York : Bloomsbury Acacemic, 2020. | Includes bibliographical references and
index. | Summary: "This book answers the question 'How did Athenian drama shape ideas about civic
identity?' through the medium of three case studies focusing on props. Traditional responses to the
question have overlooked the significance of props which were symbolically implicated in Athenian
ideology, yet the key objects explored in this study (voting urns and pebbles, swords, and masks) each
carried profound connections to Athenian civic identity while also playing important roles as props on
the fifth-century stage. Playwrights exploited the powerful dynamic generated from the intersection
between the 'social lives' (off-stage existence in society) and 'stage lives' (handling in theatre) of these
objects to enhance the dramatic effect of their plays as well as the impact of these performances on
society. The exploration of the 'stage lives' of these objects across comedy, tragedy, and satyr drama
reveals much about generic interdependence and distinction. Meanwhile the consideration of
iconography representing the objects' lives outside the theatre sheds light on drama's powerful interplay
with art. Essential reading for scholars and students of ancient Greek history, culture, and drama, the
innovative approach and insightful analysis contained in this volume will also be of interest to
researchers in the fields of Theatre Studies, Art History, and Cultural Studies"– Provided by publisher.
Identifiers: LCCN 2020022268 (print) | LCCN 2020022269 (ebook) | ISBN 9781350143975 (hardback) |
ISBN 9781350186477 (paperback) | ISBN 9781350143982 (ebook) | ISBN 9781350143999 (epub)
Subjects: LCSH: Theater–Greece–Athens–History–To 500. | Stage props. | Literature and society–
Greece–Athens–History–To 1500. | Greek drama–History and criticism. | Athens (Greece)–Civilization.
Classification: LCC PA3203 .W95 2020 (print) | LCC PA3203 (ebook) | DDC 792.02/509385–dc23
LC record available at https://lccn.loc.gov/2020022268
LC ebook record available at https://lccn.loc.gov/2020022269

ISBN:	HB:	978-1-3501-4397-5
	PB:	978-1-3501-8647-7
	ePDF:	978-1-3501-4398-2
	eBook:	978-1-35014399-9

Typeset by RefineCatch Limited, Bungay, Suffolk

To find out more about our authors and books visit www.bloomsbury.com
and sign up for our Newsletters

Contents

List of Illustrations	vi
List of Abbreviations	viii
Acknowledgements	ix
Introduction: Propping up Athens	1
I Objects and civic identity	1
II The 'social' and 'theatrical' life of objects	4
III Shaping the study	6
1 Casting Votes in Athens	9
2 Trialling Props on Stage	35
I The *Oresteia*'s appropriation of voting urns and ballots	35
II Dramatic retrials after 458 BC	43
3 A Weapon of Democracy	53
4 Swords Drawn on the Tragic Stage	75
I The *Oresteia*'s tyrant slayers	76
II *Ajax*'s battlefield *sphagia*	83
5 Swords Redrawn on Stage	97
I The comic redrawing of swords	97
II Swords redrawn again in *Phoenician Women*	109
6 The Mask in Hand	123
I Society	125
II Theatre	134
Conclusion: Evaluating Objects	149
Appendix: Clytemnestra's Sword in the *Oresteia*	153
Notes	159
Bibliography	241
Index	261

Illustrations

1. Bronze Greek *hydria*, c. 460 BC, J. Paul Getty Museum 73.AC.12. — 12
2. Attic red-figured *kylix* attributed to Brygos painter, c. 490–480 BC, British Museum 1843,1103.11. Side A. — 16
3. Underside of Attic red-figure cup attributed to the Stieglitz Painter, 470–460 BC. — 18
4. Side A of Attic red-figure cup attributed to the Stieglitz Painter, 470–460 BC. — 19
5. The casting of ballots on Side A of Attic red-figure cup attributed to the Stieglitz Painter, 470–460 BC. — 20
6. Seated figures on Side A of Attic red-figure cup attributed to the Stieglitz Painter, 470–460 BC. — 22
7. Fragment showing seated figure to left on Side A of Attic red-figure cup attributed to the Stieglitz Painter, 470–460 BC. — 23
8. Side B of Attic red-figure cup attributed to the Stieglitz Painter, 470–460 BC. — 24
9. Figures approaching the urns to the right of the composition on Side B of Attic red-figure cup attributed to the Stieglitz Painter, 470–460 BC. — 25
10. Figures to the left of the composition on Side B of Attic red-figure cup attributed to the Stieglitz Painter, 470–460 BC. — 26
11. Interior of Attic red-figure cup attributed to the Stieglitz Painter, 470–460 BC. — 29
12. Underside of the Attic Red-Figured Kylix, attributed to Brygos Painter, 490–480 BC, J. Paul Getty Museum 86.AE.286. — 31
13. Plaster cast copy of the tyrannicides group. Museo del Gessi. — 55
14. Attic red-figure *stamnos*, c. 470–460 BC, Martin von Wagner Museum 515. — 56
15. Fragment of fifth-century Attic red-figure bell-krater found in Athenian Agora LCT-59, reproduced with kind permission of the American School of Classical Studies, Athens: Agora Excavations. — 66

16	Grave *stele* showing two young hoplites *c.* 420 BC (Athens, Piraeus museum).	68
17	White-ground *lekythos* attributed to the Painter of New York 23.160.41 (*ARV*² 1241,6). Zürich, ex Hirschmann collection G 35. © Photo: Archäologische Sammlung der Universität Zürich, Silvia Hertig.	70
18	Depiction of battlefield *sphagia*. Fragments of Attic red-figure kylix, *c.* 490–480 BC, Cleveland Art Fund, Dudley P. Allen Fund 1926.242.	72
19	Interior of the Attic Red-Figured cup, attributed to Brygos Painter, 490–480 BC, J. Paul Getty Museum 86.AE.286.	92
20	Choregoi vase. Tarentine red-figure bell krater, 390–380 BC, formerly J. Paul Getty Museum 96.AE.29.	98
21	Attic red-figure *pelike*, dated to *c.* 440–430 BC.	126
22	Comic performer confronted with mask 'backstage'.	128
23	Performer holding satyr mask. Fragment of fifth-century Attic red-figure *chous* or *oenochoe*, dated to *c.* 440–420 BC.	130
24	Grave *stele* showing performer with mask, found on Salamis (Athens, Piraeus museum).	133
25	Fragment of illustrated papyrus showing Agave, E16449.	140

Abbreviations

FHG	C. Müller, *Fragmenta historicum graecorum*, Vol. 2. Paris, 1848.
*GHI*²	M.N. Tod, *A Selection of Greek Historical Inscriptions*. Oxford, 1946.
IG	*Inscriptiones Graecae*.
LIMC	*Lexicon Iconographicum Mythologiae Classicae*. Zürich, 1981–97.
LSJ	H.S. Jones and R. MacKenzie, *A Greek–English Lexicon*. Oxford, 1940.
OCD	S. Hornblower, A. Spawforth, E. Eidinow (eds) *Oxford Classical Dictionary*. Fourth edition. Oxford, 2012.
PCG	R. Kassel and C. Austin (eds) *Poetae Comici Graeci*. Berlin and New York, 1983–.
PMG	D.L. Page, *Poetae Melici Graeci*. Oxford, 1962.
TrGF	B. Snell, R. Kannicht, and S.L. Radt (eds) *Tragicorum Graecorum Fragmenta*. Göttingen, 1971–2009.

Acknowledgements

I owe a debt of thanks to the many individuals and institutions who have supported this project. I am grateful to audiences at King's College, London, the University of Reading, the University of Oxford, the University of Kent and the Classical Association conference (2017) for helpful feedback on some of the ideas presented here. I also appreciate the comments of the anonymous readers for the book's proposal and draft, all the work of the team at Bloomsbury (especially Alice Wright and Lily Mac Mahon and Merv Honeywood at RefineCatch).

Many of the images were made possible through the kind help of individuals at institutions; special mention must go to Martin Bürge (Archaeological collection at the University of Zurich), Aspasia Efstathiou (ASCSA), Joachim Heiden (DAI Athens), Daria Lanzuolo (DAI Rome), and Alex Pezzati (Penn Museum). I am very grateful to Jeff Rusten for his generosity in allowing me to use his photograph of the Phanagoria *chous*. The support of the School of European Culture and Languages at the University of Kent enabled me to travel to Dijon to examine the Stieglitz cup. I am indebted to the wonderful Madame Catherine Gras, then Conservateur at Museum des Beaux Arts, who took me behind the scenes at the museum, to Perry Holmes for his expert photography, and to the archivist, Madame Dominique Bardin-Bontemps.

Colleagues, past and present, and friends have shaped and supported the project. I am grateful to Anne Alwis, Sarah Alyn-Stacey, Paul Cartledge, Anna Dugdale, Laurel Fulkerson, Jon Hesk, Lucy Jackson, Matthew Leigh, Fiona Macintosh, Toph Marshall, Peter Olive, Ellen Swift, Oliver Taplin, and Mario Telò for their advice on various aspects of it. I am indebted especially to Edith Hall who has been an intellectual inspiration, an outstanding mentor, and a true friend. I appreciate more than I can say the encouragement of my mother, Lizzie Johnson, Susannah Rose, Alex Gwakyaa, David Holmes and other members of my family. My father, who is much missed by us all, was unstinting in his support. I am ineffably grateful to my husband, Perry Holmes, who brings me so much joy, and my daughter, Esme, who has been a source of amusement and delight.

This book is dedicated with love to my mother, Anne Wyles, who is awesome and who was the first to teach me to interpret material culture.

Introduction

Propping up Athens

Athenian civic identity was 'propped up' by objects invested with symbolic meaning. These objects could be, literally and conceptually, transported into the theatrical frame. As props in performance they functioned as intersections between civic life and the stage. The object's 'civic' symbolism could be exploited to dramatic effect, while its treatment on stage impacted upon its meaning in society. Theatre's handling of these props therefore contributed to the discourse of civic ideology that shaped citizen identity.[1] The negotiation, and renegotiation, of the object's meanings on stage, across different dramatic genres, reflects the complexity of that discourse and of theatre's contribution to it.[2] The examination of a selection of such objects that traverse the citizen experience sheds fresh light on the dialectic between theatre and civic ideology. The study simultaneously underlines the importance of taking intergeneric dynamics and iconography into account in the exploration of this dialectic.

I Objects and civic identity

The past forty years have witnessed significant developments in the study of fifth-century Athenian civic identity.[3] Chief amongst these has been the shift away from 'constitutional' and 'institutional' approaches to defining citizenship.[4] A wider lens on the citizen experience, an appreciation of citizenship's 'intangible qualities' (informing values and behaviour), the recognition of citizenship as a concept and ideological construct, and the awareness of the range of ways in which civic status might be 'performed' have now emerged.[5] The interrogation of the complex interrelation between political and social spheres in Athens and the recognition that categories might become blurred on the ground have further nuanced analyses.[6] The study of Athenian citizenship has profited from engagement with performance studies, sociology, structuralist theory, anthropology and political science.[7] Further gains can be made from the work outside the field of Classics that has established material culture's role in constructing, contesting and reaffirming identity at an individual and collective level.[8] By considering the role of objects/props, this discussion takes its lead from that work and intends to highlight the fresh contribution that its consideration can make to the understanding of civic identity in Athenian society.[9]

Textual evidence confirms material culture's role in asserting identity in Athens. Solon's sixth-century reforms already demonstrate an understanding of material culture's ability to display status and assert elite identity. The limitation of the number of *himatia* (cloaks/blankets) at burials exposes an awareness of their power as symbols.[10] The ongoing exploitation of objects to this end, despite Solon's measures, is evidenced by the iconic golden cicada hair clasps used by rich elderly Athenian males.[11] Beyond the differentiation between social strata, material culture claimed a place in framing collective civic identity in Athenian society. The symbolic status of the olive tree in Erechtheus' shrine on the Acropolis demonstrates this.[12] According to Herodotus, the Athenians claimed that Athena had set the tree there in her bid to become patron of the city.[13] His narrative couples this detail with the Athenian report that a fresh shoot had grown from the tree's trunk on the day after the Persians had burnt the shrine. These details reveal the prominent symbolic role played by this object in the construction of fifth-century Athenian identity and the importance of reaffirming that symbolism at a point of civic crisis.[14] Moreover, the emphasis on the Athenian propagation of these stories highlights the city's active participation in self-definition through material culture.

The same principle can be identified in operation in the construction and shaping of Athenian citizens' identity. Objects within the city's material culture that were invested with ideological significance could impact upon the citizen's sense of his civic identity.[15] The celebrated Athenian statue group of the tyrannicides, Harmodius and Aristogiton, is recognized to have functioned in this way.[16] This monument, discussed in Chapter 3, contributed to the ideologization of the pair's deed, trained the citizen in reading the democracy's visual codes and offered a concise means of expressing commitment to its values.[17] Yet it was not only landmarks that shaped citizen identity.[18] Objects that could be encountered close up and handled by the citizen also carried the potential to hold this symbolic sway. Euripides' exploration of civic identity through the recognition tokens in *Ion* exploits precisely this aspect of objects' operation within Athenian society.[19] Such objects, unlike a monument, can be easily overlooked in scholarship. In appearance, they can be unobtrusive and might seem, viewed in a museum display, quite ordinary (a water jar, a sword), yet under the citizen's gaze they were transformed by their symbolic associations. The acknowledgement that such objects had a part to play in the construction and affirmation of citizen identity forms the basis of this study.

An object-oriented approach builds further on the current understanding of citizenship as a dynamic construct, existing beyond strict legal or institutional parameters and including 'intangible qualities'.[20] A case could be made for a number of objects that meet with the criteria of being symbolically associated with citizenship. However, the objects considered in this study have been selected to offer insight into a range of identity's dimensions, bolstered by different values and experienced through diverse civic settings.[21] Voting urns and pebbles symbolically represented the citizen's right to act as a juror (and the value democracy placed on each citizen's view), swords embodied the citizen's obligation to protect the democracy, and masks symbolized the citizen's right to perform in a chorus (and the ideal of civic participation).[22] Each object gained symbolic traction through its association with the exercise of a citizen right. The encounter of them within 'institutional' settings (taken in a broad sense) invited reflection on citizen identity, while simultaneously reinforcing it.[23] The law court, battlefield, and theatre were locales within which citizenship could be performed.[24] The ideological importance of each activity to Athenian identity is confirmed in Thucydides' account of Pericles' Funeral Oration.[25] The collective and habitual nature of the activities with which the objects were symbolically associated (jury service, fighting, and performing theatre) heightened their potential to impact upon the citizen's sense of identity.[26] The communal gaze upon these objects in public settings with ideological significance contributed further to this effect.[27]

The consideration of a range of activities expressing civic ideology allows for a more nuanced account of the construction of citizen identity, and the role of objects in this, to emerge.[28] The selection of objects is valuable for the spectrum it represents in the complexity of the symbolism's construction. Voting urns and pebbles gained their symbolism primarily through association with their use in the law court. However, the sword gains meaning from its commemorated use by the tyrannicides, its display (in the panoply) at the Panathenaea and Dionysia, and its role in the battlefield *sphagia* ritual. This demonstrates that the objects functioned as repositories for values and concepts expressed across the breadth of civic experience and highlights the valuable access this approach grants to the 'intangible qualities' of citizenship.[29] Two further characteristics to the symbolism constructed for these objects reinforced their effectiveness as a means of expressing identity. The objects' symbolism could be embedded in cultural memory (through iconography and narrative) lending authority to the Athenian values that the objects represented through implying their longevity.[30] Meanwhile, the openness of the symbolism to reinterpretation created a dynamic force to the objects' role in identity's construct.[31] This allowed discourse on the object's meanings to become a means of reshaping as well as reaffirming citizen identity.

The objects themselves played a part in securing the efficacy of their role in shaping citizen identity. As physical presences in Athens, they could be encountered and handled by individuals in the city.[32] The haptic dimension to the experience of these objects endowed them with distinctive influence in forging identities – the physical act of dropping a ballot into a voting urn making for a more profound individual encounter with the symbols of Athenian ideology than looking up at the Parthenon's iconography.[33] The recognition that encountering objects may have enhanced the individual's sense of embodiment is significant for the construction of identity, as is the acknowledgement of the agency of objects.[34] The personal impact of objects plays into the dynamic between the individual and collective at the centre of civic identity.[35] While this study's approach is primarily semiotic rather than phenomenological, the materiality of the objects discussed is acknowledged to have reinforced the impact of their symbolism on the citizen's sense of identity.[36]

II The 'social' and 'theatrical' life of objects

The theatre's role in shaping Athenian citizens' sense of identity was made possible, in part, through the 'double' lives of its props.[37] The objects seen on stage were understood to have a 'social life', an existence (conceptual and concrete) outside the performance, alongside their 'theatrical' life.[38] While the concepts of the prop's 'social' and 'dramatic' life depend on modern critical writings, the ideas can already be found within ancient Greek drama.[39] In Aristophanes' *Acharnians*, performed in 425 BC, the audience is encouraged to think about the life of costumes and props outside the theatre as well as their 'dramatic' life.[40] Aristophanes' references to the manufacture of props, and stage mechanics, further expose the life of the objects outside the fictive world of the play.[41] Tragedy too, though less explicit in its mode, engages with the idea of its theatre objects' existence outside the action of the play. The dramatic effect of the Erinyes' new cloaks at the end of Aeschylus' *Oresteia*, for example, depends on awareness of the clothing's 'social life' and its use in a contemporary civic festival.[42] Athenian playwrights acknowledged and exploited the intersection between the 'social life' and 'dramatic life' of the objects populating their productions. This has ramifications for the question of drama's engagement with life outside the theatre in fifth-century Athens. Props have been almost entirely overlooked in assessments of this relationship, yet they function as intersections between the two spaces.[43] Moreover, the treatment of certain props on stage implicates their symbolism in civic life and vice versa. The identification of ideologically loaded language is a familiar tactic in discussions of Athenian drama's interaction with society.[44] Stage *objects* embedded with heightened civic significance merit the same consideration since they were equally capable of making demands on the audience to reflect on the relationship between the dramatic action and civic life.[45]

Athenian society asserts itself on the comic and tragic stage through a wide array of objects making up the fictive worlds presented there. Despite its near-default setting in the mythological past, the tragic stage is filled with objects familiar from the present: altars, garlands, torches, sticks, and writing tablets to name but a few.[46] Amongst these some carried specific symbolic meaning for Athenians, the dark red (or purple) costuming for the Erinyes chorus at the end of Aeschylus' *Eumenides*, for example, evoked the clothing worn by *metics* at the Panathenaea festival.[47] The interest of this study is in objects that resonated with Athenian audience members because of their symbolic association with civic identity and that as props boasted a significant 'dramatic' life. The requirement for the object to have become the dramatic focus of more than one stage production is generated from the concern to investigate props that become sites of contested meaning.[48] The negotiation of their symbolism across more than one production reveals their status in both theatrical and social discourse. The analysis of props that are significant as objects in civic life and have a notable stage past allows for the appreciation of the intersection between these two lives. The objects' civic symbolism informs their meaning, and dramatic effect, within the theatrical frame and their manipulation on stage impacts on the citizen's sense of identity. Voting urns and pebbles, swords, and masks meet the criteria of being symbolically significant to civic identity and the focus of dramatic attention across multiple plays and for more than one playwright.[49]

The 'dramatic life' of these selected objects determined the choice of plays discussed.[50] One of the advantages of this approach is that it challenges assumptions about which plays merit consideration. The prominent concern of Euripides' *Ion* with Athenian identity would ordinarily guarantee its inclusion in a study of the topic.[51] Yet the objects that become a focus of *Ion*'s stage action cannot claim to have the same extensive dramatic life as the voting urns or swords.[52] In other words, they are not a sustained subject in theatre's discourse on civic identity. Extant and fragmentary, tragic, satyric and comic, dating from certainly as early as 458 BC to *c.* 405 BC, the plays discussed are: Aeschylus' *Oresteia* and *Theoroi*; Sophocles' *Inachus* and *Ajax*; Euripides' *Electra*, *Phoenician Women* and *Bacchae*; Cratinus' *Seriphioi*; Aristophanes' *Acharnians*, *Knights*, *Wasps*, *Birds*, *Lysistrata* and *Thesmophoriazusae*; and Phrynichus' *Muses*.[53] The selection highlights the well-established principle that plays need not be set in Athens in order to resonate with Athenian identity.[54] The inclusion of tragedy, comedy and satyr drama in the list is a hallmark of this study's approach. Traditionally the theatre–society interface has been investigated for each dramatic genre separately.[55] That the distinctive parameters set by the generic frames of tragedy, comedy, and satyr drama result in each defining, negotiating and expressing their relationship to society in different ways is accepted. Yet the handling of objects that carried symbolic associations for Athenian audience members unites these genres.[56] The meaning(s) of these objects is contested across the dramatic genres so that a proper understanding of the theatrical and social discourse emerging from this can only be achieved through taking an intergeneric approach.[57] A study that considered the tragic treatment of the sword in isolation, and ignored the comic contestation of its meaning, would offer only a partial perspective of the theatrical impact on the object's civic status. It would also overlook the profound significance of that symbolic negotiation between genres. The interpretation and reinterpretation of props' meaning highlights the elastic capacity of the symbols that construct identity.[58] This mirrors the nature of the knowledge upon which the democracy depended, it too was 'flexible' and negotiated through discussion.[59] The intergeneric perspective demonstrates that at the same time as symbolizing aspects of the civic experience, these objects could invite reflection on democracy's operation.

III Shaping the study

The argument follows a case-study approach, focusing on voting equipment, swords and masks in turn.[60] The object's symbolic significance to civic identity is established in each case, before the consideration of its manipulation on stage. The order of the case studies is intended to allow a progressive narrative to emerge from the analysis. The opening case study allows for the principle to be established through objects connected to the most conventional setting for the expression of identity (the law courts). The claim of the symbolic association between voting urns and pebbles and Athenian values is not new. However, the case study is valuable in foregrounding the critical issues in the expression of those values

(Chapter 1) and role of theatre in negotiating them (Chapter 2). The weight given to iconographic evidence in Chapter 1 (discussing in detail the series of cups depicting a vote at the contest over Achilles' arms and the Stieglitz 'voting' cup (Dijon, CA 1301)) is programmatic.[61] Chapter 2 offers a model for analysis by assessing the complexities of the objects' function and effect in *Eumenides* and the subsequent interplay between comedy and tragedy expressed through their handling (setting the foundation for the discussion of intergeneric dynamics in Chapter 5). The book's major case study unfolds across three chapters allowing for the detailed exploration of its central concerns. The sword's richly faceted civic life and equally intense stage life make it a profound site of negotiation between theatre and society and between plays. The examination of this object's symbolic importance in Athens (Chapter 3), the manipulation of its civic resonance in tragedy (Chapter 4), and the reconfiguring of its significance on the comic and late fifth-century tragic stage (Chapter 5) establish the full potential of this approach. The final case study (Chapter 6) tests the limits of the study's premise by exploring a 'theatrical' object, the mask. In performance, this prop points to Athens (especially in tragedy in which it is an 'anachronistic' object).[62] Yet, its Athenian association and civic symbolism is entwined with the experience of theatre as an institution. This makes for a compact and complex case study that deliberately stretches the concept of the citizen's 'institutional' experience (it stands at the other end of the spectrum from the law court). It makes a critical contribution, also, at the study's close to the understanding of the intergeneric dynamics of such object's handling and the interplay with the iconographic representation of them (confirming principles touched upon in the earlier case studies).

The field of Classics has been slow to turn to object-oriented studies and yet the advantage of such an approach to the exploration of the interface between theatre and society should have become apparent.[63] While the study is much indebted to existing work in Classics, it also seeks to push beyond it through adopting this innovative approach.[64] The object's capacity to become a symbolic repository for Athenian values and a memory bank of past dramatic productions made it a powerful entity. It stood as an intersection between theatre and society, and between the production and the theatrical past. It is in the analysis of the dynamic tension in performance between meanings generated from society and those emerging from interplay with past productions that the prop's value to the understanding of theatre and its role in society becomes clear.

1

Casting Votes in Athens

Theatre's engagement in civic discourse through the handling of voting urns and ballots (explored in Chapter 2) depended on the symbolic meaning created for these objects in their social lives, specifically in the role that they played in reinforcing Athenian values when citizens voted. This opening case study delineates the objects' civic symbolism (through a focalized reassessment of the textual and iconographic evidence) to enable a thoroughgoing analysis of its dramatic exploitation (in Chapter 2) and to offer a framework of considerations, through these first two chapters, for the subsequent case studies.

Law courts, and their judicial process, formed a core aspect of Athenian identity in the fifth century BC.[1] The brilliantly absurd response of the comic character, Strepsiades, when presented with a map of the world by a pupil of Socrates (*Clouds* 206–8), plays on precisely this sense of the centrality of jurors to the city's identity:[2]

ΜΑΘΗΤΗΣ	αὕτη δέ σοι γῆς περίοδος πάσης. ὁρᾷς;
	αἵδε μὲν Ἀθῆναι.
ΣΤΡΕΨΙΑΔΗΣ	τί οὐ λέγεις; οὐ πείθομαι,
	ἐπεὶ δικαστὰς οὐχ ὁρῶ καθημένους.

Pupil:	And look, this is a map of the entire world. See?
	That's Athens right here.
Strepsiades:	What do you mean? I don't believe it;
	I don't see any juries in session.

This joke about Athenian litigiousness becomes a 'standby' of Aristophanes.[3] In 421 BC, he returned to it in his *Peace* and extends the observational comedy to the divine plane as Hermes explains to the Athenians why peace eludes them (503–5):[4]

| ΕΡΜΗΣ | καὶ τοῖς Ἀθηναίοισι παύσασθαι λέγω |
| | ἐντεῦθεν ἐχομένοις ὅθεν νῦν ἕλκετε· |

> οὐδὲν γὰρ ἄλλο δρᾶτε πλὴν δικάζετε.

Hermes And to the Athenians I say: stop hanging on to where you're now pulling from; you're accomplishing nothing but litigation.[5]

It emerges again in *Birds* in 414 BC, when Tereus fears that since Peisetaerus and Euelpides are from Athens, they must be jurors (108–11):

> ΤΗΡΕΥΣ ποδαπὼ τὸ γένος;
> ΠΕΙΣΕΤΑΙΡΟΣ ὅθεν αἱ τριήρεις αἱ καλαί.
> ΤΗΡΕΥΣ μῶν ἡλιαστά;
> ΕΥΕΛΠΙΔΗΣ μἀλλὰ θἀτέρου τρόπου, ἀπηλιαστά.
> ΤΗΡΕΥΣ σπείρεται γὰρ τοῦτ' ἐκεῖ τὸ σπέρμ';
> ΕΥΕΛΠΙΔΗΣ ὀλίγον ζητῶν ἂν ἐξ ἀγροῦ λάβοις.

Tereus What nationality?
Peisetaerus Where the fine triremes come from.
Tereus Not a couple of jurors, I hope!
Euelpides Oh no, the other kind: a couple of jurophobes.
Tereus Does that seed sprout there?
Euelpides You'll find a little in the country, if you look hard.[6]

Even while the pair of Athenians protest that they are a couple of jurophobes, Tereus' incredulity that such a category of person exists in Athens forces them to admit that they are in a minority.[7] *Birds* demonstrates the ongoing sense of the importance of this activity to Athenian identity (even if criticisms of that very practice appear later in the play).[8] In fact, Aristophanes had already alluded to the Athenian delight in law courts in *Knights* (1317), produced in 424 BC, demonstrating that this trait provided a running joke for at least ten years and suggesting that the Athenian characteristic remained of sufficient cultural prominence to support this sustained comic exploitation.[9]

While these jokes rely on references to jurors, the objects at the centre of the judicial process, the voting urns and pebbles or shells (the 'ballots'), were equally capable of acting as synecdochic representatives of law courts and the trials held in them.[10] In this capacity these objects were symbols of civic identity.[11] Voting in law courts in the fifth century took place as follows: each juror had a pebble or shell (his ballot) and dropped it into one of two urns (either the 'guilty' urn or the 'not guilty' urn).[12] The voting urns were *hydriai*, vessels that functioned primarily as water jars. Aspects of their design that made them suitable for carrying and pouring out water, however, proved equally valuable in the object's repurposed use.[13] Surviving evidence shows that *hydriai* could be made of terracotta or bronze, the latter creating an object of value that could serve as a prize at games. A representative example of such a bronze *hydria*, dating to *c.* 460 BC, offers insight to the design of such vessels in the period of the *Oresteia*'s production (Fig. 1).[14]

This *hydria* was most likely a prize and is more elaborate (in its decoration) than the voting urns shown on the Stieglitz cup (Fig. 5).[15] Nevertheless, its shape corresponds to those urns and it offers a helpful indication of the potential proportions of such vessels (it stands at 47 cm high). While the *hydriai* used for voting in the fourth century were bronze, this cannot be claimed with certainty for the fifth century.[16] The ballots (pebbles or shells, designated by the term ψῆφος) were objects supplied by nature rather than manufactured. Any surviving ballots remain anonymous (in contrast to fourth-century bronze ballots that are readily identifiable from their distinctive shape and official inscription).[17] The urns and pebbles, everyday objects from our perspective, acquired their significance from the framing context of their use and the symbolic meaning which Athenian society attached to them in that setting.[18]

The presentation of judicial participation as stereotypically Athenian implies the significance of this activity to civic identity.[19] Moreover, the existence of other Greek communities that also displayed commitment to justice and used voting urns and ballots to carry it out, highlights that the 'Athenianess' of this trait was a construct.[20] The deliberateness of its civic symbolism in Athens raises the stakes of reflecting upon the meaning that an Athenian citizen may have attached to the process of voting.[21] The act of casting a vote was delineated as a citizen activity in the first instance through the restriction of jury participation to male citizens over the age of thirty.[22] The significance of the action was more profoundly inscribed, however, through the idea that the pool of jurors (numbering 6,000 ordinary citizens, selected by lot annually) represented and acted on behalf of the entire citizen body.[23] The act of voting in the law court, already self-conscious as a performance of a citizen right (to serve in a jury), expressed the ordinary citizen's acceptance of the idea that his judgment was of equal merit to any of his fellow citizens (and could stand for them); in other words, it represented democratic ideology in action.

The form of the vote reinforced this since the procedure of assessing the judgment through ballots ensured that every vote counted.[24] This displayed the city's confidence in every citizen's capacity to judge and conferred a sense of individual responsibility on the voter.[25] This was in contrast to the alternative mode of expressing opinion used in Athenian democracy (in the Assembly and Boule), the show of hands (χειροτονία), that through its estimation of numbers minimized the sense of individual impact on the outcome.[26] The

Fig. 1 Bronze Greek *hydria*, dating to *c.* 460 BC, J. Paul Getty Museum 73.AC.12. Digital image courtesy of the Getty's Open Content Program.

responsibility incumbent on the juror was impressed upon him through the heliastic oath in which he swore to vote in accordance with the laws and decrees of the Athenian people and Council of the five hundred and, in matters with no laws, in accordance with his best judgment.[27] The abundance of legal proceedings in Athens suggests that those serving as jurors would engage repeatedly in the act of voting across the year.[28] This enabled the symbolic value attached to this action to become inculcated in the citizen, shaping his civic identity.[29]

The significance placed on this procedure of voting was reinforced through the circumstances of its use in the Assembly and Boule.[30] The use of voting urns and pebbles in these institutional bodies was the exception and not the rule (χειροτονία being the default procedure), heightening the self-consciousness of its deployment.[31] The nature of the cases employing this form of voting further suggests circumstances that prompted the citizen to reflect on democracy as he cast his vote on issues pertaining to: ἄδεια (immunity to discuss a forbidden topic), conferral of citizen rights and εἰσαγγελία (maladministration or treason).[32] Democracy, and its citizen body, was at stake in these cases. The carrying out of this procedure in the Assembly was 'cumbersome' given the numbers involved.[33] From the voter's perspective, however, the lengthy process gave far more time for reflection (both on his decision and the symbolic meaning of the action) than the usual raising of a hand; and this would have invited 'effortful' deliberation.[34] The numbers involved magnified the impact of the spectacle that also displayed the democratic principle in action through the participation of a broad demographic of citizens.[35] The awareness of the communal focus on the voting urns, as destined locus for the civic gesture, heightens the objects' ability to construct the citizen's sense of identity. He looks upon these objects that represent a civic ideal, he watches fellow citizens as they enact that ideal through voting, and, through his awareness of the gaze of others, he measures himself against this symbol's ideal.[36]

The experience allowed the citizen to see his place within the collective body of the demos. He could also recognize the individual role that his participation, embodied in the ballot he held and then cast, played within the functioning of that body.[37] His responsibility was symbolized in the pebble that would impact not only on the individual under judgment but also the community (i.e. the democracy). The use of this form of procedure, more familiar from the law court experience, in the democracy's governing institutions and the framing of jury service as acting on behalf of the demos, allowed for the collapse of the symbolic distinction between the use of the objects in the two contexts.[38] In the law court and the Assembly (and the Boule), the voting urns and pebbles represented democracy in action and the responsibility conferred on the citizen. In this respect these objects could embody the citizen's sense of who he was and the civic values he enacted as an Athenian.

The perception of the extraordinary power wielded by these objects is captured in the oath introduced in 410/9 BC on the proposal of Demophantus after the restoration of democracy (discussed further in Chapter 3). The striking turn of phrase at the opening of this oath elevates the ballot's status to that of a lethal weapon, as each Athenian citizen pledges to slay 'by word and by deed, by my vote and by my hand' anyone seeking to suppress the democracy.[39] The politically charged environment in which these words were spoken adds further to their weight and highlights the symbolic comfort sought in this small but mighty object within the democratic machinery. Its ideological standing allowed it to take this central place in the oath and its intended effect; the reassertion of this object's power at a time of crisis confirms its status as a symbol closely bound up with civic identity.[40] The latent power of these objects and their symbolic status is further demonstrated in a section of Xenophon's account of the controversial trial of the Athenian generals after the battle of Arginusae (406 BC).[41]

ἐντεῦθεν ἐκκλησίαν ἐποίουν, εἰς ἣν ἡ βουλὴ εἰσήνεγκε τὴν ἑαυτῆς γνώμην Καλλιξείνου εἰπόντος τήνδε· Ἐπειδὴ τῶν τε κατηγορούντων κατὰ τῶν στρατηγῶν καὶ ἐκείνων ἀπολογουμένων ἐν τῇ προτέρᾳ ἐκκλησίᾳ ἀκηκόασι, **διαψηφίσασθαι** Ἀθηναίους ἅπαντας κατὰ φυλάς· θεῖναι δὲ εἰς τὴν φυλὴν ἑκάστην **δύο ὑδρίας**· ἐφ᾽ ἑκάστῃ δὲ τῇ φυλῇ κήρυκα κηρύττειν, ὅτῳ δοκοῦσιν ἀδικεῖν οἱ στρατηγοὶ οὐκ ἀνελόμενοι τοὺς νικήσαντας ἐν τῇ ναυμαχίᾳ, **εἰς τὴν προτέραν ψηφίσασθαι**, ὅτῳ δὲ μή, **εἰς τὴν ὑστέραν**· ἂν δὲ δόξωσιν ἀδικεῖν, θανάτῳ ζημιῶσαι καὶ τοῖς ἕνδεκα παραδοῦναι καὶ τὰ χρήματα δημεῦσαι, τὸ δ᾽ ἐπιδέκατον τῆς θεοῦ εἶναι.

Then they called an Assembly, at which the Council brought in its proposal, which Callixeinus had drafted in the following terms: 'Resolved, that since the Athenians have heard in the previous meeting of the Assembly both the accusers who brought charges against the generals and the generals speaking in their own defence, they do now one and all **cast their votes** by tribes; and that **two urns** be set at the voting-place of each tribe; and that in each tribe a herald proclaim that whoever adjudges the generals guilty, for not picking up the men who won the victory in the naval battle, **shall cast his vote in the first urn**, and whoever adjudges them not guilty, shall **cast his vote in the second**; and if they be adjudged guilty, that they be punished with death and handed over to the Eleven, and that their property be confiscated and the tenth thereof belong to the goddess.'[42]

Callixeinus' proposal, with its embedded instructions about the vote, includes a striking repetition of terms for urns and the casting of votes (in bold). This emphasis may have formed part of a rhetorical strategy by Callixeinus to try to invest the proposal with legitimacy through normalizing references to familiar procedural elements.[43] At the same time, Xenophon's choice to record the proposal *verbatim* elevates the significance of these objects in his narrative and makes them the focal point of his account of this real-life episode in late fifth-century Athens.[44] More particularly, Callixeinus' proposal (and the report of it) invites both his and Xenophon's audience to consider the procedural actions relating to these objects: the setting up of the urns, each individual holding the pebble, the decision making over the choice of urns (guilty or not guilty), and finally casting the pebble into an urn. This highlights the communal focus on the objects, offering an implicit acknowledgement of the importance of this to their symbolic status for citizen identity. When it came to enacting these envisaged actions, it was a matter of life and death, as the pebbles cast in 406 BC graphically illustrate – the action resulted in the execution of the six generals who were present.[45] The 'emotional charge' of the objects, created through the purpose they serve and their ideological status, is exploited by Xenophon and reinforced by his narrative.[46] At the same time, their status as objects closely implicated in civic identity could be used to imply the rightness of taking action in this way (reflecting the ideals constructed through the Demophantus oath – a good citizen uses his ballot to assert democratic concern).

Iconographic evidence allows the significance of the voting process to Athenian civic identity and the pebble's status as a synechdochic object standing for the procedure's symbolism to be dated back to almost a hundred years before the Arginusae trial.[47] A series of Athenian vase paintings dated from between c. 500–480 BC depict the contentious judgment over the award of the armour of Achilles being decided by a vote.[48] The iconographic scheme of the scenes is broadly consistent across the eight cups (*kylikes*): Athena stands over a stone platform as the heroes approach from either side to place their voting pebbles on one of the two piles at either end of the platform.[49] A representative example of this iconography is offered by the Attic red-figured *kylix* attributed to Brygos painter in the British Museum (Fig. 2).

Though the cups' subject belongs to the mythological past, the iconography has been argued to be closely implicated in the expression of Athenian ideology. The format of the vote, with pebbles being brought forward as ballots to mark the decision of each voter, mirrors the newly introduced Athenian political procedure and legitimizes it through its mythologization.[50] The pebbles offer the link between the mythological past and present, they are the conduit for this

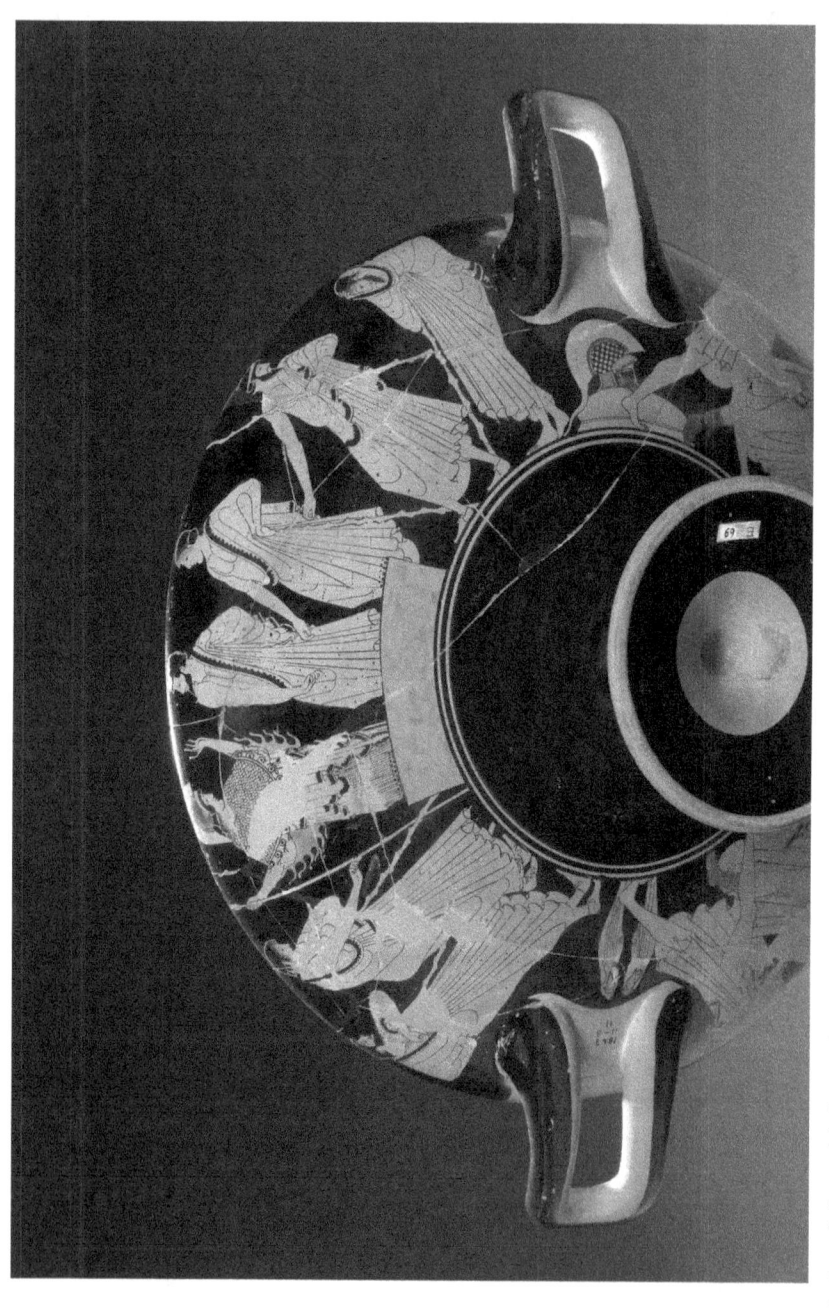

Fig. 2 Attic red-figured *kylix* attributed to Brygos painter, *c.* 490–480 BC, British Museum 1843,1103.11. Reproduced with kind permission of the Trustees of the British Museum.

glorification and, through it, they gain heightened symbolic status as objects used in the Athenian procedure. The contrast between the calm of those handling the pebble as they vote and the conflict shown on the other side of the cup highlights the benefits of this process and symbolically elevates this object further (implying a sense of agency through the pebble's apparent power to bring calm).[51] The impact of this celebration of the ballot would have been intensified if, as has been suggested, the images shown on the cups appeared as a pair of monumental wall paintings.[52] Even a reading of the iconography that lays greater emphasis on its ambivalence, must acknowledge the focal place given to the pebbles in the composition.[53] This is made especially clear in one of the cups from the series that focuses on the procedure of voting in its tondo too, directing the viewer to interpret this as the key subject.[54] The tondo image shows the male voter bending down to place his ballot at Athena's feet while she extends her right arm over his back, implying both divine support and supervision; the image thus expresses the voter's sense of responsibility discussed above. This series of images reflects, and reinforces, the status of the pebble as an ideological symbol in Athens.

The symbolic status of the voting urns and pebbles in Athenian society immediately before their manipulation on stage in the *Oresteia* can be gauged from the fifth-century Athenian red-figured cup, attributed to the Stieglitz painter by Beazley and dated to 470–460 BC.[55] Despite the centrality of voting to Athenian civic identity, this cup is remarkably the only surviving fifth-century vase painting to offer a direct representation of the activity.[56] The comparison between this cup and the earlier mythological series demonstrates the ways in which the Stieglitz painter draws on the existing iconographic tradition but also highlights the boldness of his arrestingly contemporary composition and the directness of its concerns. This important piece of evidence has gained only limited attention, perhaps due to its state of preservation which may also account for the absence of an accurate and detailed description of the cup's images in current scholarship.[57] The following discussion addresses this gap and highlights the overlooked significance of the tondo image, laying the ground for the consideration of what the composition reveals about the symbolic status of voting urns and ballots in this period.

The exterior images of the cup both depict male figures approaching voting urns along with seated male figures watching them (Fig. 3). The exterior image on Side A includes seven figures (four seated and three standing) in a composition set around two voting urns (Fig. 4). The standing figures approach the voting urns; at the composition's centre, a bearded man approaches the left-hand urn, while another bearded man (and a third damaged figure to the far right of the image) approach the voting urn on the right (Fig. 5). The damaged figure holds

Fig. 3 Underside of Stieglitz cup showing both exterior images (Side A and Side B). Musée des Beaux-Arts, Dijon, CA 1301. All photographs of this cup are © Perry Holmes and reproduced with his kind permission.

Fig. 4 Exterior image on Side A of the Sieglitz cup. Musée des Beaux-Arts, Dijon, CA 1301.

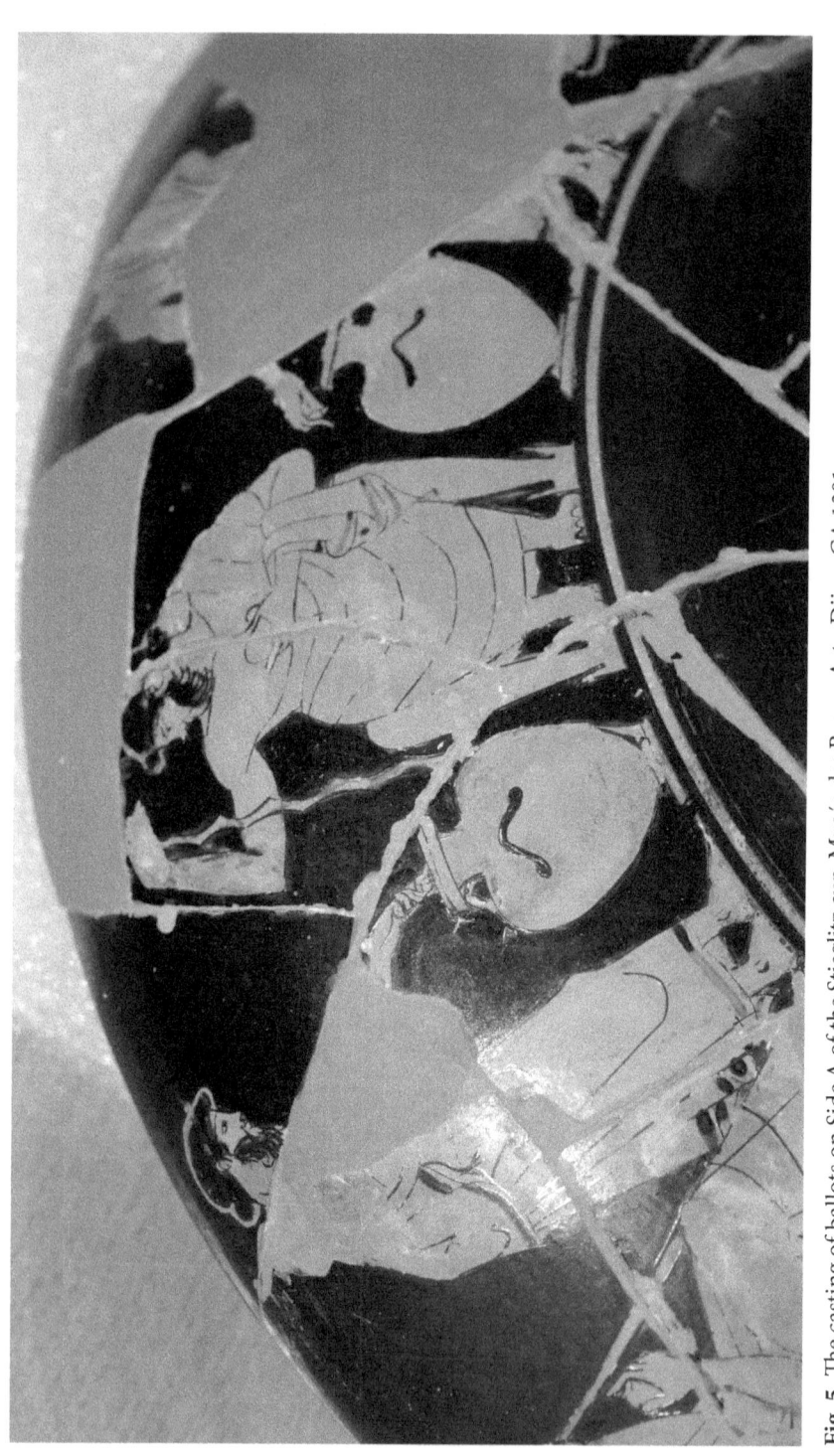

Fig. 5 The casting of ballots on Side A of the Stieglitz cup. Musée des Beaux-Arts, Dijon, CA 1301.

an object, perhaps a ballot, in his hand (just visible to the left of the damaged portion on the right-hand side of Fig. 4).[58] The bearded man, standing in front of the damaged figure, very clearly holds a ballot in his hand and leans down over the urn (although strangely he reaches just beyond the urn's mouth); he looks across towards the other standing bearded figure who is also casting a ballot. This other figure is shown leaning over the urn to the left, with his fingers curled round, presumably grasping his ballot as he casts it into the urn (Fig. 5). He looks down at the urn while the man sitting between the urns looks across in his direction, overseeing the action.[59]

The seated figure, shown in Fig. 5, holds a stave as do the other three seated figures on Side A (Fig. 6 and Fig. 7). The two seated figures closest to the urns and facing them (Fig. 5) also each hold a rounded object in the other hand. Schmidt first suggested that these hand-held objects might represent ψῆφοι (votes/ballots) and Neer has more recently argued that they represent the mussel shells used to vote; if so, then the proportions seem at odds with the object held by the figure casting his vote on the right (Fig. 5) although this might be explained by perspective.[60] The other two bearded and seated figures, far left, are turned towards each other in conversation (Fig. 6 and Fig. 7). The seated figure shown in Fig. 6 holds his slightly cupped hand towards himself in a conversational gesture and does not hold an object (other than his stave), while his interlocutor (Fig. 7) either mirrors this gesture or holds something in his right hand (paralleling the other seated figure facing right).[61]

The exterior image on Side B of the cup (Fig. 8) is even more packed, depicting nine figures (six standing and three seated) who are again set in a composition around two voting urns. To the right of the composition, two figures approach the voting urn on the right-hand side, a shorter figure stands (facing frontally) over it, while another figure leans down towards the urn on the left (Fig. 9). Standing behind this left-hand urn but facing sideways towards the left is another bearded figure. Though the cup is damaged, we can surmise that the man reaching towards the left-hand urn must almost overlap with the figure standing behind it. This man (with his back to the urns) is turned towards one of the seated figures and seems, from his gesture (his right hand turned upwards and outstretched), to be complaining or disputing (far right in Fig. 10). The seated figure has both hands raised suggesting that he is responding and perhaps offering a justification (Fig. 10).[62] Two figures on this side of the cup have been identified previously as problematically beardless: the figure leaning in towards the left-hand side urn and the figure to the far right of the composition (Fig. 9).[63] Close inspection of the vase reveals that the damaged figure, to the far right, was in fact depicted with facial hair.[64]

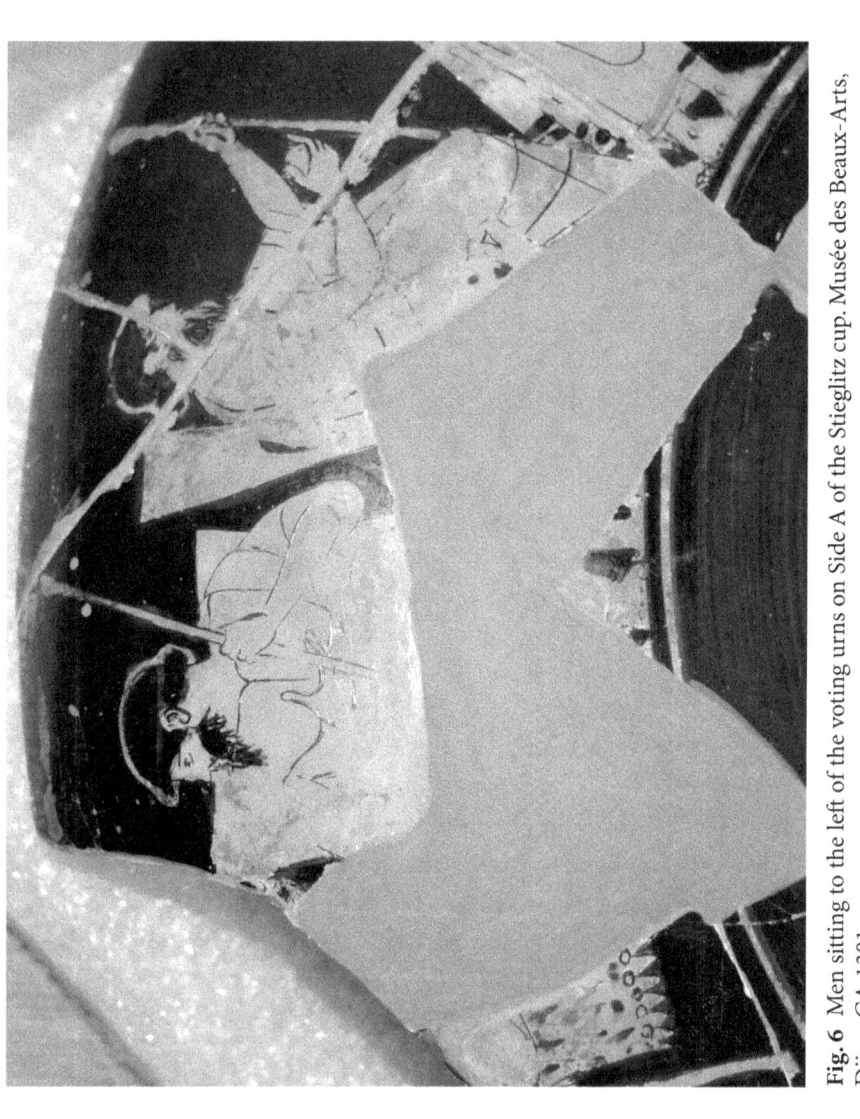

Fig. 6 Men sitting to the left of the voting urns on Side A of the Stieglitz cup. Musée des Beaux-Arts, Dijon, CA 1301.

Fig. 7 Seated man on fragment belonging to the far left of Side A of Stieglitz cup. Musée des Beaux-Arts, Dijon, CA 1301.

Fig. 8 Exterior image on Side B of Stieglitz cup. Musée des Beaux-Arts, Dijon, CA 1301.

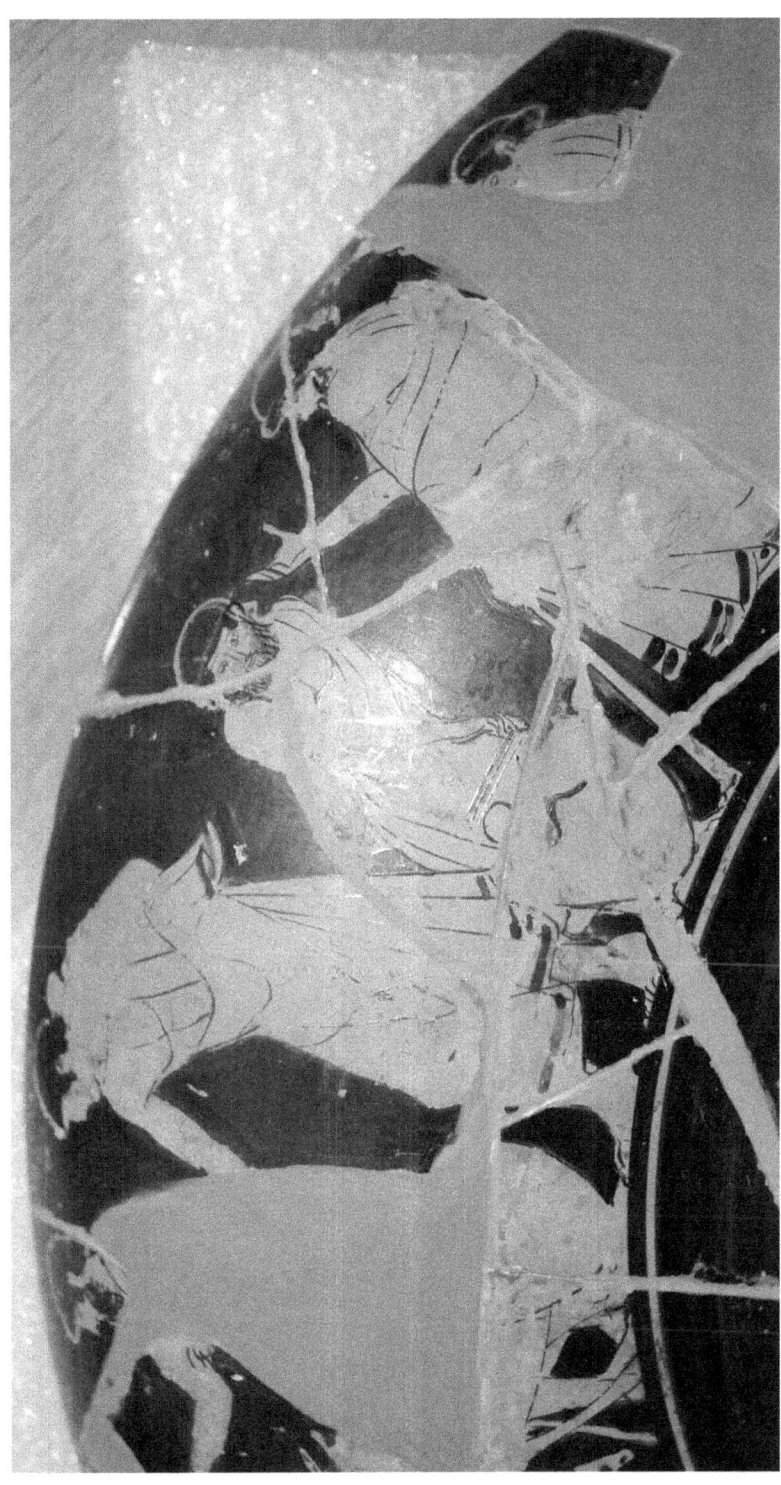

Fig. 9 Figures approaching the urns to the right of the composition on Side B of the Stieglitz cup. Musée des Beaux-Arts, Dijon, CA 1301.

Fig. 10 Figures to the left of the composition on Side B of the Stieglitz cup. Musée des Beaux-Arts, Dijon, CA 1301.

Further questions arise from the 'voter' hovering over the right-hand urn. He is shorter than the other figures and, unlike them, is positioned frontally standing behind the urn. His left hand is bound up in his *himation* (mantle), as almost every man's left hand is on the cup, and with his right hand he reaches awkwardly across the front of his body to grip the urn's mouth on its left-hand side.[65] At least two of his fingers rest on the outer rim of the urn's mouth in contrast to the voter by the left-hand urn on Side A (whose hand does not make contact with the urn, Fig. 5). It is just about possible to imagine that he has cast his ballot while holding onto the edge of the urn's mouth, but the gesture seems rather unnatural.[66] An alternative interpretation arises by taking his stature and the gesture of the figure beside him into account. The man standing to the right (from the viewer's perspective) of this figure seems to be declaiming in some way (he holds out his right hand in front of him, to reinforce his point). Though this figure is damaged, the angle of his head, bent forward, suggests that he is looking down at what the shorter figure is doing. It seems possible therefore that the taller of the two may be instructing the man behind the urn to reposition it (which explains his gripping of its rim).[67] If this is the case, then supervisory duties would not be restricted to seated figures and further layers would be added to the articulation of power dynamics on the vase.[68]

The three figures to the left of the composition (Fig. 10), behind the seated man, are in quite a poor state of preservation but two observations can be made. The figure standing in the centre of Fig. 10 seems to be supporting the seated figure (in front of him) in the dispute. His right hand is outstretched in a gesture that mirrors the seated figure's (the upturned hand with fingers slightly curled is clear and the trace of the raised thumb is just about visible despite the damage).[69] The positioning of this hand towards the shoulder of the seated figure suggests support of his view, which offers a further challenge to the assumed distinction in status between the seated and standing figures on this vase.[70] To the far left are two seated figures, both holding staves. The seat (*klismos*) of the right-hand seated figure in this pair is positioned frontally while the seat of the figure to the far left is depicted sideways-on, the composition thus mirrors the two seated figures to the far left of Side A (Fig. 6). There is a further indication of paralleling as the figure to the left faces towards the frontally seated figure who seems to be turned towards his companion in conversation.[71] The traces of this figure's gesture with his left hand also indicates engagement in discussion. The mirroring between the images on Side A and Side B is important since despite the apparent differences in the atmosphere within which the vote is depicted taking place on each side, there is also the assertion of continuity.[72]

The interior of the cup depicts two figures, one standing and one seated (Fig. 11). The standing figure is a woman. She is dressed in a Doric style *peplos* (indicated by its overfold), but it combines Ionic features through the multiple clasps securing its sleeves.[73] Her hairstyle, worn long though tied back at the nape of her neck, indicates her youth.[74] She also wears a headband (the faint traces of which can be made out especially with its looped bow at the back of her head) perhaps indicating status.[75] She plucks at the lower part of her *peplos* with one hand and with the other reaches out towards the seated figure. The damage to the vase does not allow us to determine the nature of the gesture, although from the relative heights of the figures in the composition it seems that the woman reaches out towards the head of the seated figure.[76] The seated figure is wrapped up in a *himation*, beneath which the pleats of a long Ionic *chiton* with dots patterning its border are depicted.[77] This Ionic style of chiton can be seen on earlier cups worn by both male and female figures and so in isolation it cannot determine the gender of this seated figure.[78] The case for reading the figure as female in this particular example, however, is strengthened by consideration that the male figures represented on the vase's exterior wear only *himatia* and by the parallel provided by a later tondo image by the Stieglitz Painter.[79]

If both figures depicted in the cup's tondo were female, then there would be a strong gender contrast marked between the interior and exterior of this cup with women adorning its inside and men the outside.[80] It is worth noting that while the men on the exterior only have their left arms confined by their *himatia*, the interior seated figure appears to be entirely wrapped up in the *himation* (reflecting a contrast in cultural expectations over the appropriate level of activeness for each gender). Resonances between the interior and exterior images invite comparisons and demand that the viewer should consider the dialectic between the two. These cues are as follows: the interior seated figure sits on a chair that is strikingly similar (including its patterned coverlet) to the chairs on the exterior, the composition explores the dynamic between a seated and standing figure (cf. exterior), the *himation* worn by the interior seated figure is decorated with the same simple border as the *himatia* worn by the men on the exterior, and the standing woman makes a significant gesture (the focus of the composition) with her right hand (cf. gestures on exterior, especially voting). The cup's exterior images are frequently reproduced to illustrate the process of voting but they are considered in isolation from this interior image.[81] Yet these visual cues point to the images' intentional juxtaposition by the painter. The inclusion of an image representing women on a cup that depicts, and celebrates(?), male civic participation in Athenian democracy is highly significant

Fig. 11 Stieglitz cup tondo: two figures in interior medallion. Musée des Beaux-Arts, Dijon, CA 1301.

for our understanding of the city's ideology and its citizens' self-definition (see below).

The images on the exterior of the Stieglitz cup invite the viewer to reflect on the political procedure of voting in an even more direct way than the series of cups showing the contest over Achilles' arms.[82] The Stieglitz painter foregoes the elevation generated from retrojecting the procedure into the mythological past, but there is recompense in the immediacy this grants to the cup's commentary. The process of casting ballots is aggrandized through its representation as the central action on both exterior images of the cup.[83] No matter which side of the cup faced out from the imbiber, the casting of ballots confronts the viewer. The framing of that action as the 'narrative nucleus', through the gaze lines of the internal spectators depicted on the cup, invite the viewer to reflect on his identity.[84] Even the agitation on Side B can be interpreted as contributing to the positive representation of the procedure.[85] It can be interpreted through the schema of the earlier series of cups that juxtaposed images of conflict (with swords drawn on the equivalent Side B of many of the cups, see Fig. 12) and order to show the calming impact of the vote.[86] The Stieglitz painter retains the contrast between sides but the 'conflict' has been civilized (avoiding the outbreak of violence) by extending the vote to Side B as well. The urns' placement within the composition, in pairs on each side, creates a sense of order through visual balance, reinforcing the expression of this procedure's calming power. The objects, and their symbolism within Athenian society, are thus celebrated through this composition.

The richness of this evidence lies, however, not only in the prominence given to the voting urns and ballots in the composition and the celebration of the values that they represent but also in the anxiety associated with the voting process that is articulated around them. These cues for disquiet confirm the importance Athenian society attached to the act of voting.[87] They also highlight the function of the voting urns and pebbles as objects that could become the locus for expressing both the significance of the action and concerns about its enactment. The agitation depicted on Side B (see above) indicates that rather than simply portraying an idealized view of voting, the Stieglitz painter is interested in exposing tension and prompting the viewer to reflect critically on the process. The inclusion of spectators watching the vote within the composition and the images' destined context (the symposium) reinforces the suggestion that the cup is intended to invite contemplation of civic identity.[88] The gaze lines within the composition focus attention on the voting urns and ballots while also revealing preoccupations associated with the vote (and projected onto these objects). The voter to the left on Side A (Fig. 5) looks down towards the urn as he

Fig. 12 Brygos cup (Getty 86.AE.286): exterior. Digital image courtesy of the Getty's Open Content Program.

casts his ballot into its mouth. His concentration on the action hints towards the solemnity and responsibility that is felt in its undertaking with the underlying awareness of each individual's view being taken into account through this system (see above). The casting of this vote under the watchful gaze of a fellow citizen highlights the necessity of such oversight to prevent corruption in the system and expresses anxiety over its potential occurrence (by contrast, an idealized portrayal of voting might choose to focus on the vote without drawing attention to this aspect of the process).[89] The parallel between the supervisory role of Athena in the mythological scenes of voting and the function of the seated figures in this composition perhaps suggests uneasiness over the democratization of competence (that asserted equality in citizens' capability to judge).[90] The parallel with Athena implies that the superintendants' influence extends beyond checking that only one ballot is cast, suggesting an iconographic attempt to assuage concern over this democratization.[91]

If the cup glorifies *isonomia*, it is also interested in expressing the complex power dynamics experienced in the principle's practice.[92] The seated figures are not the only ones to exert influence.[93] The gaze of the voter at the right-hand urn on Side A towards the voter who is casting his ballot in the other urn acknowledges the potential of peer pressure. It is significant that this voter (on the right) has not yet cast his vote, his hand (holding the ballot) extends beyond the urn's mouth. The image is deliberate in displaying that his decision is not yet made and allows concerns over his susceptibility to pressure to be confronted.[94] On Side B, the intervention of the figure to the right of right-hand urn (instructing the short bearded figure to adjust the urn's position or interfering with his vote?) points further to this engagement with the concern over the dynamics of influence (reinforced in the dispute that shows two figures siding against one).[95] The complexity of the power dynamics between the figures casting their ballots and the other figures on the cup problematizes the symbolism of the voting urns, as they are presented as the focal point for the exertion of influence and thus sites of tension. It is possible that this reflects a period of adjustment within society as the symbolic implications of the system, and its objects, settled; it is striking, however, that concerns over the potential for both influence and interference in the process of voting are still being explored in theatre decades after the production of this cup.[96] The Stieglitz painter's composition demonstrates that anxiety over the process was being addressed in the arts before the *Oresteia* and that its articulation centred on the objects used in voting.

The meaning of the voting urns and ballots in the images is further defined through the visual parallels between the cup's exterior and interior decoration (set out above) that assert the place of these objects in the construction of male civic identity. The choice to depict female figures on the cup's interior is one of the most significant elements to this vessel's engagement in civic discourse and yet it has been sidelined in scholarship.[97] The earlier set of cups depicting voting may again be relevant here since a parallel to this exterior and interior juxtaposition between male affairs and female roles can be found amongst them.[98] The Brygos painter's cup (Getty 86. AE. 286), dated to *c.* 490 BC, depicts the quarrel and vote over the arms of Achilles on its exterior (Fig. 12) and Tecmessa shrouding the corpse of Ajax in its tondo (see Fig. 19).[99]

This cup may therefore mark the initiation of this choice to define male engagement in voting by contrasting it to the social function performed by women.[100] The iconographic framing of male civic identity through opposition to female activity becomes even more pressing in the Stieglitz cup since here the mythological lens has been lifted and the voting depicted is contemporary. The Stieglitz painter's response to this strand in civic discourse (that had already been explored through the earlier composition by the Brygos painter) must have made a sharp impact on the viewer through its crystallization of this idea in a contemporary visual form. The syntax of the iconography, that juxtaposes the interior image with the exterior images, sets up the voting urns and ballots as objects of the male domain and recipients of male civic action (in contrast to the object which is the recipient of the standing female figure's gesture).[101] Through this contrast, the voting urns and pebbles become symbols of the male citizen's participation in democracy. This conceptualization of the objects resonates with the presentation of them as props in Aeschylus' *Oresteia* demonstrating that this cup, unique though it is, does not stand in isolation.[102] Yet this also highlights theatre's role in becoming the dominant medium through which the discourse on this element to civic identity continued. This is significant since it implies reflection by a broader demographic within the citizen body on the values and concerns embodied by these objects.[103]

The place of voting as an intellectual concept impacting on the city's self-definition is displayed in Herodotus' account of the debate before the battle of Marathon. The decision to engage, and so 'make history' through the creation of this defining moment for the construction of Athenian identity, depends on the action of one 'ballot-bearing' (ψηφιδοφόρος, Hdt. 6.109.2) man, the polemarch; his vote determines that the Athenians fight.[104] Herodotus' choice of language is designed to evoke the powerful ideological associations established for the Athenian voting process (by the time that he is writing) to frame the significance of this past event to the city's identity.[105] The textual and iconographic evidence ranging from the beginning of the fifth century to its end sets Herodotus' strategy in context, demonstrating the recurrent negotiation, within the city's cultural discourse, of voting's significance. The objects that stood for the process of voting offered a locus for the celebration, and definition, of the values inculcated by the action. The presentation of voting urns and pebbles at the centre of this collective civic activity – highlighted in the crowded composition of the Stieglitz cup and in Callixeinus' emphasis (as recorded by Xenophon) on tribes – hints towards a determining factor in the symbolic role they assumed; they forged civic identity as objects that were collectively encountered while also allowing, at the individual level, for the expression of citizen status through the casting of the ballot.[106] The importance of the procedure to civic identity is further indicated by the expression of anxiety, focalized on the voting urns and ballots, in the Stieglitz painter's composition and by the prominence given to these symbols of voting at times of crisis (displayed through the Demophantus oath and the Arginusae trial).[107] The elevated status of these objects within the city's ideological discourse, and the role which they played in the construction of citizen identity, raises the stakes for the import of their handling on stage. The following chapter explores the ways in which Athenian playwrights could profit from the civic symbolism of the props, exploiting them to dramatic effect, while also impacting upon citizens' perceptions of the objects' meaning in society; the efficacy of theatre as a medium through which to explore this dimension of civic identity is demonstrated by its dominance of the cultural discourse upon it.

2

Trialling Props on Stage

This chapter traces the 'stage life' of voting urns and pebbles from Aeschylus' theatrical appropriation of these objects in 458 BC through subsequent productions down to 405 BC. It examines the significance of this theatrical treatment to Athenian identity and the intergeneric dynamics to the props' manipulation.[1] The extensive dramatic engagement with these props, in settings that alluded to the experience of voting within society, suggests theatre's impact on the citizen's perception of these objects. In fact, their recurrent appearance on stage indicates theatre's dominant role in the cultural negotiation of voting's meaning for civic identity.[2] The theatrical impact of Aeschylus' focus on these objects in *Eumenides* is examined, alongside the contribution their dramatic treatment makes to the existing discourse on voting (continuing iconography's glorification and problematization of it). This analysis establishes the function of these props as sites of contestation that could be exploited to challenge and affirm civic ideals.[3] Moreover, the contextualization of Aeschylus' handling of these objects offers a fresh angle to assessing the trilogy's political stance. The exploration of the objects' stage life in subsequent productions demonstrates theatre's ongoing contribution to the discourse on this democratic procedure and highlights the complexity that the intergeneric dimension introduces to the negotiation of their civic symbolism.

I The *Oresteia*'s appropriation of voting urns and ballots

Aeschylus' *Eumenides*, the final play in the *Oresteia* trilogy which was first produced in 458 BC, is the earliest fully extant drama to feature voting urns and ballots as props.[4] While the importance of Aeschylus' 'court room drama' to theatre history has been noted in general terms, the full implications of this stage representation of voting have not been appreciated.[5] This analysis addresses shortfalls in critical attention in three ways: it acknowledges the civic symbolism of these focal props; it contextualizes this dramatization through considering earlier artistic explorations of voting's ideological status; and it reviews the legacy of Aeschylus' staging.[6] The discussion begins by setting out the scene before considering its dramatic effect, the meaning it constructs for the urns and pebbles, and the impact of this on civic identity.

The court scene in *Eumenides* presents a dramatization of the first ever trial held on the Areopagus hill in Athens, convened in the play by Athena to judge whether Orestes was justified in killing his mother.[7] The jury comprises Athenian citizens (selected by Athena, 482–9). After hearing from both sides (the chorus of Erinyes for conviction and Apollo in Orestes' defence), they stand up and cast their ballots into one of two urns. Athena votes last of all and then instructs the assigned jurors to cast the ballots out of the urns (to count them, 734–43).[8] Eight lines later, she announces the outcome (equal votes signifying Orestes' acquittal, 752–3).[9] Despite the well-known textual difficulties affecting *Eumenides*, the surviving text clearly indicates this scene's focus on the urns and pebbles and reasonable conjectures can be made about their handling and placement.[10] The urns, jurors, and pebbles must be on stage when Athena instructs the herald to make the proclamation to mark the convening of the court (566–9). Her instruction to the jury to rise to cast their votes (708–10) suggests that they are sitting on benches. The structure of the lines delivered while the vote takes place (711–33) seems designed to allow each of the eleven jury members to rise, approach the urns, and drop his ballot into one of them before Athena finally casts hers.[11] The jurors may have held their ballots from the beginning of the trial, or it is possible that Athena gives each a pebble as they approach the urns.[12] The likely outward appearance of these props can be surmised from the Stieglitz cup, discussed in Chapter 1, which offers a representation of voting urns and ballots (see especially Fig. 5) and is dated to the decade before the *Oresteia*.[13] The material used for the stage urns could have been terracotta or bronze.[14] It has been suggested that the urns may have been placed on a table.[15] However, even if they were not elevated, the verbal attention would ensure that they were still prominent.[16] The benches for the jurors, if they were brought on during the Erinyes' song (490–565), may have been placed just in front of the *skene* building so that the jurors sit looking towards the urns in front of them and towards the audience beyond.[17] This would place the urns as a central focus within the playing space, which is consistent with the verbal attention they receive.

References to the vote and speculation over its outcome ensure that the voting urns and ballots are the focus of the audience's attention from their arrival on stage to the trial's result (566–753). The props are a dominant presence for approximately a fifth of the surviving play.[18] The ten references to the vote have the effect of building dramatic tension over the critical interaction with these props (i.e. the stage action of voting):

(i) Athena anticipates instructing the jury to vote, *Eum.* 674–5:[19]

> ΑΘΗΝΑΙΑ
> ἤδη κελεύω τούσδ᾽ ἀπὸ γνώμης φέρειν
> ψῆφον δικαίας, ὡς ἅλις λελεγμένων;

> **Athena**
> Shall I now instruct these men to cast a vote in accordance with their honest opinion, on the ground that there has been sufficient argument?

(ii) Apollo anticipates the vote's outcome, *Eum.* 676–7:

> ΑΠΟΛΛΩΝ
> ἡμῖν μὲν ἤδη πᾶν τετόξευται βέλος,
> μένω δ᾽ ἀκοῦσαι πῶς ἀγὼν κριθήσεται.

> **Apollo**
> On our side every arrow has now been shot; I am staying to hear how the trial is decided.

(iii) The Chorus anticipate the jurors' casting of their vote, *Eum.* 679–80:

> ΧΟΡΟΣ
> ἠκούσαθ᾽ ὧν ἠκούσατ᾽, ἐν δὲ καρδίᾳ
> ψῆφον φέροντες ὅρκον αἰδεῖσθε, ξένοι.

> **Chorus** [to the judges]
> You have heard what you have heard; but when you cast your votes, gentlemen, have respect in your hearts for your oath.

(iv) Athena instructs the jurors to vote, *Eum.* 708–10:

> ὀρθοῦσθαι δὲ χρὴ
> καὶ ψῆφον αἴρειν καὶ διαγνῶναι δίκην
> αἰδουμένους τὸν ὅρκον. εἴρηται λόγος.

> Now you must rise, deliver your votes, and decide the case, respecting your oath. I have said my say.

(v) The chorus anticipate the vote's outcome, *Eum.* 731–3:

> ΧΟΡΟΣ

ἐπεὶ καθιππάζῃ με πρεσβῦτιν νέος,
δίκης γενέσθαι τῆσδ' ἐπήκοος μένω,
ὡς ἀμφίβουλος οὖσα θυμοῦσθαι πόλει.

Chorus
Since you are riding roughshod over me, the young over the aged, I am waiting to hear the decision of this case, being undecided whether to be angry with this city.

(vi) Athena anticipates casting her vote, *Eum.* 734–5:

ΑΘΗΝΑΙΑ
ἐμὸν τόδ' ἔργον, λοισθίαν κρῖναι δίκην·
ψῆφον δ' Ὀρέστῃ τήνδ' ἐγὼ προσθήσομαι.

Athena
This is now my task, to be the last to judge this case; and I shall cast this ballot for Orestes.

(vii) Athena instructs the ballots to be cast out, *Eum.* 741–3:

νικᾷ δ' ὁ φεύγων, κἂν ἰσόψηφος κριθῇ.
ἐκβάλλεθ' ὡς τάχιστα τευχέων πάλους,
ὅσοις δικαστῶν τοῦτ' ἐπέσταλται τέλος.

The defendant wins, even if the judges' votes on him are equally divided. Empty the ballots from the urns at once, you of the judges to whom this function has been assigned.

(viii) Orestes anticipates the vote's outcome, *Eum.* 744:

ΟΡΕΣΤΗΣ

ὦ Φοῖβ' Ἄπολλον, πῶς ἀγὼν κριθήσεται;

Orestes
O Phoebus Apollo, how will the verdict turn out?

(ix) Apollo advises on the count, *Eum.* 748–51:

ΑΠΟΛΛΩΝ
πεμπάζετ' ὀρθῶς ἐκβολὰς ψήφων, ξένοι,
τὸ μὴ ἀδικεῖν σέβοντες ἐν διαιρέσει.
γνώμης ἀπούσης πῆμα γίγνεται μέγα,
†βαλοῦσα† δ' οἶκον ψῆφος ὤρθωσεν μία.

Apollo
Count the emptied ballots correctly, gentlemen, scrupulously respecting justice in determining the outcome. Lack of good judgement can cause great harm, and a single vote can set an <afflicted> house on its feet.

(x) Athena announces the result, *Eum.* 752–3:

ΑΘΗΝΑΙΑ
ἀνὴρ ὅδ᾽ ἐκπέφευγεν αἵματος δίκην·
ἴσον γάρ ἐστι τἀρίθμημα τῶν πάλων.

Athena
This man stands acquitted of the charge of bloodshed. The votes have been counted, and they are equal.

This striking cluster of references to the vote and its outcome demands that the audience continually refocus their attention on the urns and pebbles. The effect is intensified by the prompts converging from all sides (from Athena, Apollo, the Chorus, and Orestes).[20] These verbal cues reveal the importance of these props within Aeschylus' dramaturgic design; the self-consciousness with which they are deployed raises the stakes in defining their dramatic meaning and function. Bakewell's insightful analysis of these props highlights the ways in which they realize the trilogy's insistent focus on the law and establish Athena's ballot as a symbol for a new type of justice.[21] If the urns were made of bronze, then this too would gain meaning within the trilogy's design. In their gleam, they would represent the progression from darkness to light and produce a corrective to the *Agamemnon*'s association of injustice with bad bronze.[22] The most impactful dimension to their effect and generation of meaning, however, comes from outside the bounds of the play, through their evocation of the Athenian experience of voting.

The elements Aeschylus 'borrowed from' contemporary society – the urns, the pebbles, and a jury made up of Athenian citizens – made this theatrical presentation particularly forceful.[23] In semiotic terms, the props present an exact equivalence between signifier and signified.[24] The lines between the 'performance' of legal proceedings in society outside the theatrical event and those being presented on stage were, therefore, blurred through the urns and pebbles, exploiting their dual status as both objects in society and theatrical props.[25] The framing of these objects through citizen experience is reinforced through the proceedings and language borrowed from the law courts.[26] While the Areopagus court is nominally represented in the play, it is framed through the lens of the law court experience.[27] The effect of these contemporary verbal terms is to 'zoom' the action to the present and to heighten the sense in which the props are simultaneously thought of as objects belonging to the citizen spectators' own experience.[28] However, unlike the transitory words, the props remain as concrete reminders of Athenian society on stage.[29] For almost 200 lines these props brought the Athenian present constantly into view in a bold fusion of the mythological with the civic experience. The theatre spectators sit on benches and look at two voting urns placed in front of them, just as they would have in the law court.[30] If certain lines were addressed directly to the audience, then the distance between the experience of the theatrical event and the audience's extra-theatrical experience of the law court may have collapsed at points during this scene.[31] The invitation to focus on the dramatic act of the jurors' voting prompts a self-conscious scrutiny of this action in society and the role that enacting it (and watching it enacted) played in forming a sense of citizenship.[32]

The significance of these objects to Athenian identity is displayed in, and retrojected into, the world of the trilogy. Athena's arrestingly explicit claim about the Areopagus court – that it is a bulwark such as no one else has, neither amongst the Scythians nor in the land of Pelops (*Eum.* 700–3) – marks that identity is at stake. The placement of these lines at the crucial point just before Athena instructs the jurors to cast their votes (708–10) forges the connection between the objects which represent the court and her claim of its distinctively Athenian nature. Further aspects cohere with the props' presentation as symbols of civic identity. When the voting urns and ballots appear on stage in *Eumenides*, a past (or biography) has already been established for them within the trilogy through the description of the divine vote on Troy's fate using precisely these objects (*Ag.* 813–17).[33] This elevates the status of the objects (within the *Eumenides* and in Athens) and strengthens their conceptualization as symbols of civic identity.[34] This framing is reinforced through the communal focus on these objects (prompted by the cluster of references to the vote) and soon after Athena's assertion, when they become recipients of collective activity as the jurors cast their votes.[35] Aeschylus' decision to draw attention to this aspect of the props' symbolism within his society heightens the importance of analysing their handing to understand the ways in which this play reflects on, and reinforces, voting's place within the cultural discourse on citizen identity.

The act of voting is glorified through its function within the trilogy; it serves as the means of resolving the cycle of violence afflicting the house of Atreus and is presented by Athena as a way forward in a risky situation (*Eum.* 471–89). The celebration of this procedure's ability to resolve conflict, marked by its role in the trilogy's progression from violence to order, gains force from the pre-existence of this concept within the cultural discourse on voting's significance. Approximately forty years before, the series of cups depicting the contest over Achilles' armour (discussed in Chapter 1) engages with this concept.[36] The audience may have been familiar with the iconographic schema of the cups from the pair of monumental wall paintings that are likely to have inspired them.[37] If so, then the audience could recognize that Aeschylus' trilogy corroborated the power attributed to voting pebbles within that iconography.[38] The agency of this object is given explicit articulation by Apollo's comment, *Eum.* 751 (passage ix above). His emphasis on a *single* vote's power draws attention to the weight given to each individual's view in this system of voting (on the ideological implications of this see Chapter 1) and highlights the responsibility this carried. The trust involved in allowing the voter to handle such a powerful object, and the anxiety this generated, is reinforced through the recurrent references to the importance of jurors respecting their oath.[39] Aeschylus invites the audience to connect this to contemporary concerns about the voting procedure through Athena's reference, at the oath's first mention, that she will set it up 'for all time' (*Eum.* 484). This link to the present gains further emphasis through the allusion to the oath sworn by Athenian jurors as Athena anticipates her instructions to the jury on voting (674–5).[40] The place of these preoccupations within the cultural discourse on voting is confirmed by the Stieglitz cup (see Chapter 1).[41] Aeschylus explores the theme further, however, by extending the concern over human agency to the count as well (748–9).

The centrality of the voting urns and ballots to the Stieglitz composition, as symbols of the process and as locus of concern, anticipates the stage focus Aeschylus offered to these props as well as the dramatic tension he built around interactions with these objects. The points of correspondence between Aeschylus' framing of the vote and previous artistic representations of this process confirms that the playwright was responding to an existing cultural discourse and that his drama contributed to it. The comparison also highlights the visual directness of Aeschylus' stage representation since, unlike the previous depiction of a mythologized vote (in the contest over Achilles' armour), *Eumenides* presented the contemporary form of voting (with ballots and urns) retrojected into the mythological past.[42] The staging's props bring it closer to the representation of voting on the Stieglitz cup and yet Athena's presence has the effect of elevating the action in the same way as she does on the earlier mythologized cups.[43] Aeschylus' presentation therefore shares elements with both previous artistic representations of voting but its effect is distinct from either. This engagement with the existing discourse on voting, and the continuity and difference from past representations of this process, takes on heightened significance when the historic context for this trilogy's production is taken into account.

The reforms to the Areopagus council's powers in 462 BC is a primary point of reference for the *Oresteia*'s reflections on the voting procedure. While the evidence for Ephialtes' reforms makes complete clarity over the events impossible, the resulting curtailment of the aristocratic Areopagus and establishment of the major role of the popular lawcourts is understood.[44] Aeschylus' intention to invite the audience to think about these events is made clear by his choice to make Orestes' case the first trial to be heard by the Areopagus, thus enabling Athena to set out its founding principles.[45] The exploration of *Eumenides*' implied political standpoint(s) has a long history in scholarship.[46] However, the significance of the artistic forerunners to Aeschylus' stage presentation of voting have not been taken into account in assessments of the production's political implications.[47] In broad terms, the purpose of those past artistic engagements might inform the audience's horizon of expectation when interpreting the *Eumenides*; if the series of cups with the contest over Achilles' armour (see above and Chapter 1) belonged to 'a process of legitimizing a novel political procedure', then this trilogy too might be understood to serve an equivalent function.[48] Audience members who identified ambivalence in the earlier iconographic schema would be primed to expect *Eumenides*' mediation of tension between democracy and the elite.[49] The stakes were arguably higher in 458 BC, lending the recognized elements to Aeschylus' representation of the voting process (its power to civilize conflict, the value it attributed to each individual, and the anxiety it generated) greater piquancy and placing more importance on their meaning. Simultaneously, Aeschylus' participation in this existing cultural discourse perhaps offered reassurance through the continuity it implied, while also bolstering the authority of the voting pebbles as symbols of civic identity by drawing attention to their past function in this role.[50]

Furthermore, the Stieglitz Painter's conceptualization of these objects, as symbols representing the civic activity of male citizens in contrast to the domestic activity of women (see Chapter 1), offers insight into the role of these props in framing the *Oresteia*'s response to the reforms. The conflict between male and female within the trilogy can be read through the conceptualization of citizen identity that informs the Stieglitz painter's composition.[51] This renders the appropriation of voting urns and ballots as the objects through which male superiority is asserted at the trilogy's close (through the acquittal of Orestes) all the more fitting. More importantly, if the voting urns and ballots presented in *Eumenides* are understood as symbols of male citizenship, then these props serve the role of promoting unity (as a symbolic possession of the Athenian male citizen irrespective of rank).[52]

Although the use of an Athenian court trial to break the cycle of violence afflicting the mythological house of Atreus may have depended on an existing tradition, Aeschylus' *staging* of this ending was destined to have a significant impact on both dramatic reworkings of the myth as well as the cultural discourse on the judicial dimension to citizen identity.[53] Moreover, the manipulation of the voting urns and pebble on stage is significant to our understanding of theatre more generally. From the point of view of the citizen spectator, these props blurred the lines between real life and theatre, perhaps even more powerfully than the probable use of *metic* robes, familiar from the Panathenaea festival, in the final procession of the chorus.[54] The acknowledgement of this presents a challenge to Taplin's position on tragedy's relationship with its audience.[55] It also suggests that while a movement towards 'realism' in performance style has been identified in the late fifth century (and was criticized in antiquity), in fact, the urns and pebbles offer a much earlier example of a facet in performance that invited the direct association between the imitation on stage with its real-life counterpart.[56] In political terms, the dramatic resolution's dependence on the machinery of democracy was pointed for the Athenian audience members and perhaps for allies as (future?) stakeholders in the Athenian justice system.[57] West describes the play as being 'composed for the express purpose of providing mythical backing to Athenian institutions'.[58] Yet the contemporary resonance of this scene's focal props and their influence on the drama's outcome simultaneously expresses the city's impact upon the past. This assertion of the objects' powers can be read as a direct response to the political crisis at the time of the production's staging; it affirms the ideals of the city shoring up a founding stone of civic identity (by revalorizing its symbols).[59] The results can be seen in the near non-existence of vase paintings depicting the process of voting in contrast to its prominent stage representation in both tragedy and comedy. This points to the *Oresteia*'s role in establishing theatre as the locus for negotiating the symbolic value of voting urns and pebbles to civic identity.[60]

II Dramatic retrials after 458 BC

The continuing role of theatre in negotiating the civic meaning of these objects is demonstrated by the subsequent re-emergence of the urns and ballots on stage through the remainder of the century.⁶¹ The props, which had been central to Aeschylus' engagement with contemporary politics and commentary on Athenian civic identity, re-emerge in Sophocles' *Inachus*.⁶² Amongst the surviving fragments are two that strongly suggest that a trial formed part of the dramatic action (fr. 288 and fr. 295):

κυαμόβολον δικαστήν
... a juror who throws in his voting bean⁶³

κημός
The funnel-shaped topper for the voting urn⁶⁴

The technical and prosaic language of these words suggest that they were intended literally and were part of a trial scene in the play.⁶⁵ Conjectures about this trial have been shaped by the debate on *Inachus*' dramatic genre. Calder, arguing for tragedy, made the case for the trial being held, with a chorus of Argos elders as jurors, to judge whether Inachus was correct to criticize Hera (who meted out punishments after Zeus' affair with Inachus' daughter Io).⁶⁶ Lloyd-Jones, however, preferring the supposition that *Inachus* was a satyr play, suggests that a musical contest between Argos (the guard of Io) and Hermes could have been judged by a jury of satyrs (the chorus).⁶⁷ Whether the play was a tragedy or satyr drama, the framing of the props has the same effect and stands in a relationship to Aeschylus' handling of them. In Sophocles' play, as in *Eumenides*, familiar technical language connects the mythological past with the judicial process of the Athenian present.⁶⁸ There is not an alternative type of voting, such as is displayed in the judgment of Achilles' armour cups (on which see Chapter 1), but the familiar contemporary Athenian mode of voting, which, in this play, is imagined to take place in mythological Argos.⁶⁹ While more of the play would need to survive to make an in-depth assessment of its relationship with the *Oresteia*, the use of props alone (which *can* be firmly established from the fragments) suggests interplay with the Aeschylean theatrical appropriation of these objects. By following Aeschylus in the transposition of these objects into the mythological past (this time into a different mythological sequence and location), Sophocles contributes further to the 'mythologization' of Athenian judicial practice and establishes the role of theatre in this process.⁷⁰ The projection of these symbols of Athenian civic identity into another city's past is indicative of the cultural 'imperialism' displayed in Athenian drama, while also operating to offer further authority to these objects.⁷¹ This layering of the props' theatre history also illustrates that by this time they were as much the property of the stage as of the real-life Athenian courts.

The comic stage played an equally important part in bringing the law courts' signature objects, along with their implications for civic identity, into the theatrical frame. Bakola argues that two comedies by Cratinus produced in the 420s may have responded to Aeschylus' *Eumenides*, and its trial scene in particular.[72] Unfortunately, the surviving fragments do not allow us to speculate further on the props that may have been used.[73] Similarly, a tantalizing fragment of Aristophanes' *Farmers*, also dated to the 420s, refers to an expression used by old men when sitting on a jury.[74] This demonstrates Aristophanic engagement in commentary on Athenian juries, even if it reveals nothing concrete about props.[75] Aristophanes' *Wasps*, however, produced in 422 BC, offers a spectacular example of the comic manipulation of props associated with the law courts (perhaps in response to the *agon* presented in Cratinus' *Pytine* the year before).[76] This comedy is a *tour de force* of engagement facilitated through the plotline which pivots around the central character's obsession with being a juror. I have argued elsewhere that this comedy intersects in important ways with Aeschylus' *Oresteia*, but of particular concern here is the stage life of Aeschylus' props (the urns and pebbles) and their fate in Aristophanes' hands.[77] If, as seems likely, a revival of the *Oresteia* took place in the years immediately before *Wasps*, then Aristophanes' transformation of the Aeschylean props would have been even more evident and pointed to the audience.[78]

In the play's mock trial, comic substitutes are found for the objects used in the law courts. In this comic setting, the voting urns are replaced by 'ladling cups' (ἀρύστιχος), which would have been used to serve soup.[79] The substitute props are, appropriately for comedy, domestic and connected to food.[80] A further comic aspect to their framing is created by scale. The voting urns used in the court were water jars (ὑδρίαι or κάδοι), suitable for drawing water from wells (see Chapter 1).[81] Here, the ladling cup is the equivalent to the water jar, sharing its function of drawing liquid but there is humour to the difference in scale (soup from its pot rather than water from a well). This, in turn, draws attention to the transformation of the jury in this parody of a court. Instead of the 200 or more jurors (as used in real trials), there is only Philocleon – the voting urns are accordingly downsized since they only need accommodate his one pebble.[82] The visually diminutive form, which debunks the grandeur of the voting urns, is reinforced linguistically. Even before the substitute is found for the court objects, it is possible that they are already diminished through the term Bdelycleon (Loathecleon) twice uses to describe them (καδίσκος), *Wasps* 852–5:[83]

ΒΔΕΛΥΚΛΕΩΝ   ἐς κόρακας. ὡς ἄχθομαι,
            ὁτιὴ 'πελαθόμην τοὺς καδίσκους ἐκφέρειν.

ΦΙΛΟΚΛΕΩΝ	οὗτος σύ, ποῖ θεῖς;
ΒΔΕΛΥΚΛΕΩΝ	ἐπὶ καδίσκους.
ΦΙΛΟΚΛΕΩΝ	μηδαμῶς·
	ἐγὼ γὰρ εἶχον τούσδε τοὺς ἀρυστίχους.
Loathecleon	Oh hell! How annoying, I've forgotten to bring out the voting urns.
Lovecleon	Hey you, where are you running off to?
Loathecleon	To get the urns.
Lovecleon	Don't bother, I've already got these soup ladles.[84]

Philocleon (Lovecleon) uses a further diminutive form to designate his proposed substitutes: ἀρύστιχος (soup ladling cups).[85] This emphasizes both the difference in scale between these objects (in contrast to ordinary voting urns), as well as their difference in status.[86]

The delay in bringing out these objects presents a further joke concerning status. The first case has almost been called (*Wasps* 851–2) when Bdelycleon suddenly remembers that they need voting urns (852). Up until this point there have already been a series of false starts as every object needed to 'recreate' a court is thought up and comic substitutes found.[87] Even the court railings are, on Philocleon's insistence (830–1), represented (by Hestia's pig pen, 844). Yet the most essential objects, those that were the central focus in *Eumenides*, are forgotten until line 852.[88] This delay creates humour as well as drawing special attention to the 'voting urns', which will, in a parallel to the *Eumenides*, become the focus of dramatic attention later in the scene (*Wasps* 986–94).[89] In that later part of the scene, when Philocleon votes on whether Labes is guilty or not, there is also emphasis on the voting pebble that he uses; Bdelycleon explicitly instructs his father to take his ballot using a deictic pronoun to draw attention to the prop: 'τηνδὶ λαβὼν τὴν ψῆφον' (*Wasps* 987).[90] This echoes the equivalent line spoken by Athena in *Eumenides* (735) and highlights Aristophanes' interplay with the Aeschylean voting scene through this prop.[91]

The comic construction of this scene and the manipulation of these props is designed not only to comment on Aeschylus' drama but also on the voting process in trials. In *Wasps*, the suspense over the trial's outcome is made to seem ridiculous since the audience have seen one voter approach two open receptacles and drop his pebble into one in plain sight (except, of course, for Philocleon himself who is somehow tricked over his choice of urn).[92] The anxiety over voting, explored by the Stieglitz cup and *Eumenides* (see above), and concern with secrecy is diffused through farce.[93] While there is brilliant comic distortion of the urns as objects, creating a pleasurable distance in semiotic terms between the signifier (ladling cups) and signified (voting urns), at the same time, the use of the voting pebble (an exact semiotic equivalent) and the legal terminology used throughout the scene intertwines familiar aspects of reality into the sublime farce of the dog trial.[94] *Wasps*' parody of the law courts thus invites the audience to reflect on their real-life experience of this significant institution in their society. The voting props play an important part in both prompting that reflection and articulating critique of the courts. *Wasps*, therefore, provides further evidence of the theatre's place in contributing to the discourse on law courts and use of voting props to do so. Aristophanes' dramatic (mis)representation of these objects threatens to destabilize the citizen's sense of identity as the playwright trivializes their symbolism and simultaneously critiques the integrity of the procedure they represent.

This scene's transformation and manipulation of these props also offers a comment on theatre (both Aeschylean and as an art form in general). The connection between this scene and *Eumenides*' court scene invites the reading of the voting equipment's distortion as a form of commentary on Aeschylus' play. The ladling cups are not only a comic substitute for the voting urns used in society; they also replace the props that Aeschylus used in his dramatization of that experience. Tragic theatre's grandeur is undermined here alongside the courts'.[95] The comic genre asserts itself and, in the process, can be argued to appropriate the role of commenting on this dimension of civic identity – the discourse is still taking place through theatre but it is now occurring on the *comic* stage.[96] The props' treatment also makes a broader comment about theatre. The metatheatrical aspect to this scene (setting up the court) and Bdelycleon's role as playwright/director in the play have been established in scholarship.[97] But the significance of the objects used in this metatheatrical episode has not been acknowledged. If setting up the court is taken to represent the way in which theatre sets a scene, then the origin of the 'props' used in the scene is important. They come from inside the *skene* – the stage building representing (in this play) Philocleon's house. The presentation of Euripides in his house surrounded by costumes in Aristophanes' *Acharnians* (425 BC) supports the implicit conceit here that Bdelycleon, as playwright/director, has props available inside the house.[98] Through the exaggeratedly domestic substitutes (a pig-pen for railings, ladling cups for voting urns) used for these props, however, Aristophanes draws attention to theatre's dependence on the objects of everyday life to create its illusion.[99] Bdelycleon's actions in setting up a court are equivalent to Aeschylus' appropriation of voting urns from the law courts to create powerful drama in his

Eumenides.[100] Aristophanes, however, deliberately selects props without the equivalent symbolic status to ridicule this strategy.[101] The episode acknowledges the difficulty in drawing the line between society and theatre while implying that it is comedy's, not tragedy's, prerogative to blur the line between the two.[102] The impingement on the meaning and status of the Aeschylean counterparts, effected by the comic substitutions, also draws attention to the mutability of objects' symbolism, highlighting an area of concern for identity's dependence on them.[103] The scene in *Wasps* therefore comments both on theatre's relationship with the world outside the performance as well as its capacity to prompt reflection on the symbols upon which the sense of civic identity in Athens depended.

Aristophanes reduces the grandeur of voting urns as civic symbols through their comic substitution and in the process critiques Aeschylus' dramatic exploitation of these objects. A related manipulation of the urn prop can be identified in Euripides' *Electra*. The importance of Electra's urn to the articulation of Euripides' engagement with Aeschylus' *Oresteia* has long been acknowledged but its potential relationship to the voting urns in *Eumenides* (and the ladling cups in *Wasps*) has, to the best of my knowledge, been overlooked.[104] The date of Euripides' *Electra* is uncertain and varies depending on the weight given to metrical analyses.[105] If it appeared on stage soon after *Wasps*, then the engagement of both plays with the *Oresteia* would have been striking.[106] Euripides' choice to rework the myth from a resolutely domestic (low) outlook could be argued to mirror Aristophanes' decision to parody the trial of *Eumenides* through a domestic court. From this perspective, the emphasis given to Electra's water jar in the opening part of the play merits reconsideration.[107] At her first entrance, Electra draws attention to the prop and her reason for carrying it (*El*. 54–9). The audience is invited to refocus on it when Orestes highlights it in his description of Electra (*El*. 107–11), and finally Electra refers to it again as she is setting it down (*El*. 140–2).[108] Hammond has already noted that visually, by carrying the water jar, Electra evokes her own past stage figure in *Choephori* and that her performance with it is used to ridicule Aeschylus' play.[109] The allusion is reinforced verbally as Electra uses the term τεῦχος when describing the vessel (*El*.140), the same term used in *Choephori* (*Cho*. 99). In fact, this verbal echo could evoke the voting urns of *Eumenides* (described using this term at *Eum*. 742). The recurrence of this term within Aeschylus' trilogy establishes a network of symbolic associations that arguably primed the audience of *Electra* to recognize this prop as an iconic symbol of two plays.[110]

This prop's evocation of *Eumenides* alongside *Choephori* enables the further development of Hammond's analysis.[111] The prop's allusion to the urns in the

Eumenides presents an elegant means of commenting on Aeschylus' aggrandizing of an object from Athenian society. It takes the same object that Aeschylus had appropriated from the law court, the symbol of male citizenship, and trivializes it by representing it on stage placed back into a lowlier everyday setting.[112] Euripides denies its symbolic *male* importance by framing it in a domestic setting. As a symbol of identity, the object switches from being an important marker of collective male civic participation to individual female domesticity.[113] This reconfiguration of the prop addresses gender's place in the framing of civic identity (as represented in the Stieglitz cup and *Oresteia*). It exposes the dangers of this mode of self-definition by highlighting the construct's instability (created by the multiple domains of the object's social life and the ease with which its symbolic association could be re-assigned to the opposite gender). Moreover, this dramatic exploitation of the prop creates further tension through disrupting the idea of the progressive transformation of that object within Aeschylus' trilogy.[114] In *Choephori*, the prop appears as a vessel from which to pour a libation (symbolizing Electra's grief and the limitations of her power), but later in the trilogy it reappears in a more positive iteration through the voting urns in *Eumenides*.[115] The Aeschylean transformation of this prop from a seemingly hopeless libation vessel to powerful voting urn is reversed in Euripides' play by the demotion of the τεῦχος to an emphatically mundane (and empty) water jar. Euripides, in this way, rivalled Aristophanes' comic transformation of this prop through an equally reductive and domestic reinvention of it on the tragic stage. This marks an important point in resisting generic assumptions about props: 'lowly' objects could appear on the tragic stage and the strategy of reductive reinvention was not solely comedy's domain. One of the major difference between the two theatrical treatments is that Aristophanes contributes to the discourse on civic identity by maintaining the props' symbolic association with the courts, whereas Euripides seems primarily concerned with the prop's theatrical status and its capacity to articulate his relationship to other playwrights. Yet, the handling of the urn in *Electra* still carries ramifications for its symbolic role in the construction of civic identity, revealing the intricate intermeshing of the object's theatrical and social life.

Voting urns continue to appear on the stage as props symbolizing the role of judicial activity in framing Athenian identity through the rest of the fifth century. They are used in Aristophanes' *Birds* (414 BC) to represent the litigious Athenian approach that Peisetaerus and Euelpides try to escape. An inspector appears with voting urns which suggest that he intends to set up an Athenian legal system in Cloudcuckooland.[116] Peisetaerus' resistance to Athenian officialdom is represented through his threat to smash these symbols of it.¹¹⁷ This stage appearance is important as it marks the objects' iconic status as symbolic representatives for the entire legal process or system as well as their association with Athenian identity. *Birds* demonstrates the theatrical economy of such props, which, by this time, offers an effective shorthand for commenting on Athenian activity in the law court as a marker of identity. Moreover, it is a powerful choice of prop in this play, which is concerned with civic identity and the ideals of citizenship.¹¹⁸ The presence of this ideologically laden object on stage embodies the thematic concerns of the dramatic action.

Theatre's ongoing discourse on this aspect of Athenian civic identity, expressed through these props, is demonstrated in the final decade of the fifth century in the fragmentary comedy Phrynichus' *Muses*, which was performed at the Lenaea festival in 405 BC and came second to Aristophanes' *Frogs*.¹¹⁹ One of the surviving fragments offers excellent evidence for both voting urns and pebbles being used in this play (fr. 33):

ἰδού, δέχου τὴν ψῆφον. ὁ καδίσκος δέ σοι
ὁ μὲν ἀπολύων οὗτος, ὁ δ' ἀπολλὺς ὁδί

Look, take the voting pebble, here is the voting urn,
this one for acquittal, that one for condemnation.¹²⁰

Though little is known of the context, the imperatives and deictic pronoun in these two lines emphasize the stage action, revealing that the vote, and the props (pebble and voting urns) used to enact it, was a central focus. There is a playful element to the engagement, as the double wordplay on the name Apollo in line 2 (drawing attention to his relationship to the courts) suggests.¹²¹ However, this does not prevent the props from yet again prompting (or insisting that) the audience reflect on the process of the law courts. This would be even more pointed in the aftermath of the trial of the Arginusae generals in which these very objects, now on the comic stage, had proved fatal in real life.¹²² This offers further evidence of comedy's response to this event, since the manipulation of these props could be viewed as the equivalent to the verbal allusions to Arginusae in Aristophanes' *Frogs* (performed in the same competition).¹²³ This example highlights the value of performance analysis, particularly in relation to props, to bring further insights into views within Athenian society. *Muses*, though fragmentary, offers a glimpse of the dialectic between society and theatre as Phrynichus could exploit both the stage history of these props and the audience's experience outside the theatre to generate meaning (and perhaps even palliative humour?) in his play.¹²⁴ If these props were used in a parody of real-life procedure, then this comic deflating of their power might be taken as a necessary part of the renegotiation of these symbols in the aftermath of their lethal use against the generals. For others, the symbolism of the voting objects may have been enhanced rather than tainted by the Arginusae trial (representing the will of the people enacted); in their case, this comic manipulation may have proved unsettling and unwelcome. The ways in which the handling of such objects on the comic stage reflects the broader function of comedy within society are explored further in Chapter 5. Phrynichus' engagement with these props demonstrates that over fifty years after Aeschylus' appropriation of these objects and iconic use of them in his trilogy, they were still being manipulated on stage and continued to contribute to the shaping of views on the aspect of civic identity which they represented.

What was the impact of this theatrical engagement with the process and objects of the law courts on the experience of those places? The influence of theatre on the performance of speeches in the law courts extended, as Hall has demonstrated, beyond the explicit references made to figures from tragedy.[125] It is my suggestion that the dramatic attention given to the power of the pebble and urns to determine fate (seen in *Eumenides*, *Wasps*, and *Muses*) must also have impacted on the jurors' experience of the law court.[126] This is strongly implied by the rhetoric used by Callixeinus at the trial of the generals who served at Arginusae and in Xenophon's account of it (see Chapter 1).[127] The 'charged' status of the voting equipment within the narrative is empowered by these objects' stage life.[128] The impact of the theatrical treatment of these props on the judicial experience presents another strand to the dialectic already identified by Hall between the law courts and the theatre.[129] The dialectic may have been highlighted within the frame of the theatrical festival itself through the probable use of water jars in the judges' vote at the end of the dramatic competition.[130] The importance of that judgment and its civic dimension would be conveyed by the objects' symbolic status in the law courts. The plays themselves, however, shaped the perception of that civic action (whether judging trial or decision making) through their treatment of those objects as props on stage. This encapsulates the complexity of the interplay between theatre and society situated in the symbolic negotiation of these objects. Voting urns and pebbles were not the only objects to operate in this way, however, as the subsequent case studies, which develop further the critical lines of analysis established here, demonstrate.

3

A Weapon of Democracy

This chapter argues that the sword offered a potent symbolic expression of the Athenian citizen's commitment to democracy. This symbolism is closely implicated in, and takes force from, the insistently negative presentation of tyranny in the fifth century that shaped Athenian civic identity.[1] Democracy's self-definition as the polar opposite of tyranny imposed upon the Athenian male citizen the 'civic duty' to oppose the restoration of tyranny or the rise of a would-be tyrant.[2] As has been noted by others, this facet of civic identity was bolstered on the political level through the practice of ostracism, the institutional swearing of oaths or curses against tyrants (by heliasts and at the start of meetings of the Boule and Assembly) and the passing of law.[3] It was further reinforced at the city's festivals through cult honours offered to the celebrated tyrannicides, Harmodius and Aristogiton at Panathenaea and the proclamation of reward for tyrant killing at the Dionysia.[4] The Panhellenic participation at both festivals raised the self-consciousness of these ideological statements by the city and heightened the impact on the individual citizen's sense of identity.[5] Outside of the festivals, the statue group commemorating the tyrannicides offered a prominent and permanent visual reminder to the citizen of the city's idealization, and indeed ideologization, of such action.[6] This powerful symbol of the citizen's expected ideological stance towards detractors of democracy, however, could be expressed through an even more eloquent semiotic shorthand, in a single object: the sword. This object, displayed in the tyrannicides' statue group and hoplite iconography, linked the ideals of imitating the tyrannicides to the citizen's commitment to fight on the battlefield.[7] Commemorated in the statue group, celebrated in song, paraded at the Panathenaea and Dionysia, carried by citizens in war, instrument of battlefield *sphagia*, and sworn to action against future tyrants, the sword embodied the civic commitment to defending Athenian democracy.[8] This chapter establishes the construction of the sword's symbolic status and examines the way in which it informed civic identity at home and abroad.

The sword's significance to civic identity was forged from the very beginning of the fifth century through its role in Athenian democracy's 'foundation myth'.

The tradition held that the city gained political equality through the 'tyrant killing' carried out by Harmodius and Aristogiton in 514 BC.[9] These tyrannicides became emblematic of the anti-tyrannicism that formed a central facet to the Athenian citizen's identity in the fifth century.[10] Importantly, the iconographic and poetic record leave no doubt that in the popular imagination the pair wielded swords; endowing this weapon with a specific ideological symbolism for Athenians and allowing it to become a tangible link between past and present.[11] The prominence of the swords in Critius' and Nesiotes' iconic bronze portrait group of the pair, set up in 477 BC, secured this symbolism. The impact of this monument was ensured by its positioning in 'superb isolation' in the Agora, the unusualness of such an honour and the monument's status as a symbolic assertion of Athenian resilience in response to Persian incursions.[12] It has been argued that the composition created a powerful mental image in the Athenian imagination.[13] From the surviving Roman copies, it can be ascertained that this sculpture presented the pair heroically naked, dynamically in action with one foot in front of the other and with swords held prominently; Fig. 13.[14]

Aristogiton holds his sword level in his right hand, the tension in his drawn-back right arm shows his readiness to strike. In his left hand, he holds the sword's scabbard in front of him drawing further attention to the weapon and conveying the immediacy of its unsheathing.[15] In a pose implying even greater imminent violence, Harmodius holds his sword aloft, bending his right arm over his head. The familiarity of the image of the pair wielding swords is further implied by iconographic evidence in other media from the fifth century BC.[16] Amongst the surviving vase paintings depicting the tyrannicides, the red-figure *stamnos* in the collection of the Martin-von-Wagner Museum, Würzburg and dating to c. 470–460 BC, is especially arresting for the central place given to the sword in its composition. The graphic rendering of Aristogiton's sword plunged into the body of the 'tyrant' takes up the centre of the image field, while the tyrant's gaze back towards Harmodius' raised sword draws further attention to the dynamic force of this object (Fig. 14); the image expresses that the killing is the act of the sword as much as the tyrannicides.[17]

The iconographic tradition reinforces the association in cultural memory between the sword and the tyrannicides' deed. The ideological significance of that action, and the sword's role in it, is indicated in one of four drinking

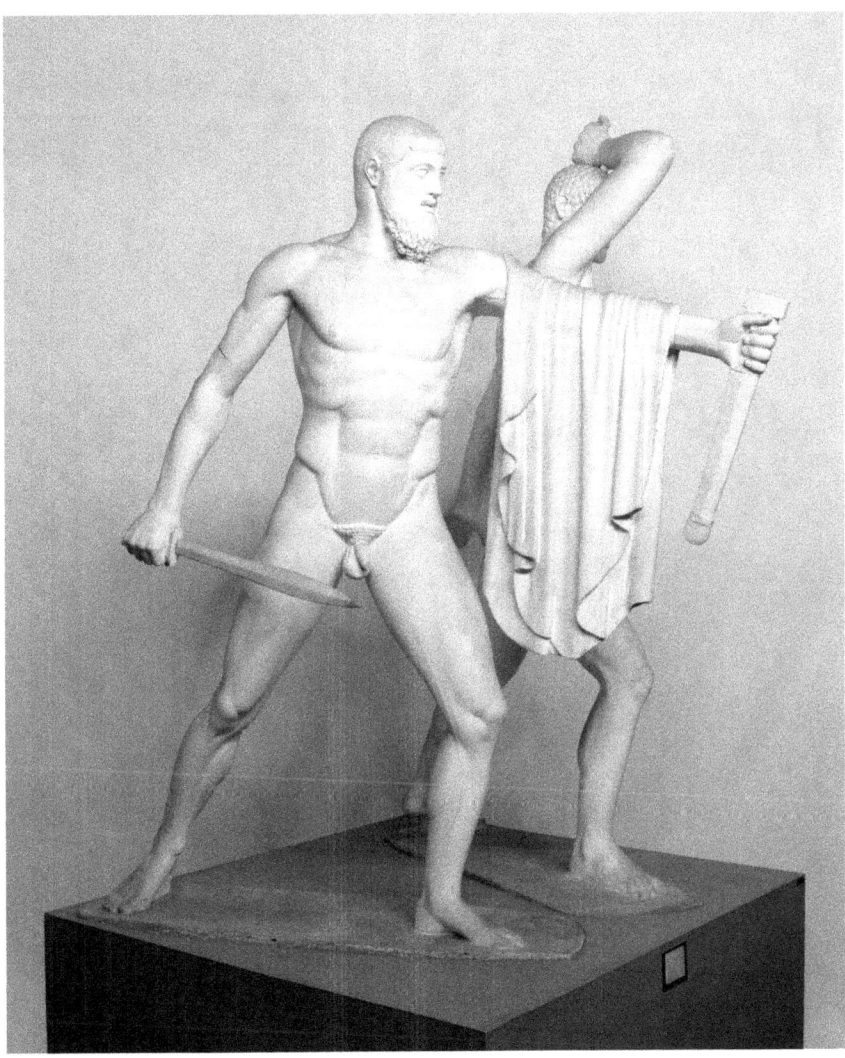

Fig. 13 Plaster cast of Roman marble copy of the tyrannicides group. Museo del Gessi, University of Rome. Photograph © Schwanke, Neg D-DAI-Rom 1984.3303, reproduced with kind permission of DAI Rome.

Fig. 14 Attic red-figure *stamnos*, c. 470–460 BC, Martin von Wagner Museum 515. Historic Collection/Alamy Stock Photo.

songs (*skolia*) that celebrate the supposed actions of the sixth-century BC tyrannicides.[18]

ἐν μύρτου κλαδὶ τὸ ξίφος φορήσω,
ὥσπερ Ἁρμόδιος καὶ Ἀριστογείτων
ὅτε τὸν τύραννον κτανέτην |
ἰσονόμους τ' Ἀθήνας ἐποιησάτην. (*PMG* 893)

In a myrtle branch I will bear my sword,
like Harmodius and Aristogiton
when they killed the tyrant
and made Athens a place of political equality (*isonomia*).[19]

The song highlights the perception of the sword's pivotal role in bringing *isonomia* (political equality) to the people of Athens. The original meaning of the song, imposed by the aristocratic context of the symposium, was transformed by the emergence of *isonomia* as a democratic term and evidence of the song's wider cultural familiarity.[20] The power of this commemorative song comes from its use of the first person (φορήσω) expressing not only the intended action but also, through the frequentative form, a commitment to repeat it. The singer styles himself after the tyrannicides through the tellingly emphatic adverb ὥσπερ (just as), implying his desire to persuade the audience.[21] The sword reinforces the claim through its status as an object that both the singer and the tyrannicides possess and experience. The implicit (fallacious) logic runs as follows: I have a sword, they had a sword, therefore I am like them. The past and present are brought together in the shared possession of this significant object. The second half of the song endows the sword with the symbolic associations of being the instrument of tyrant killing and the bringer of equality (*isonomia*). It is simultaneously a symbol of establishing democracy and a future icon, through the words sung about it, for defending it. The singer need not be imagined to have brandished a sword while singing, instead the song powerfully evokes both this object and its handling.[22] The prominence of the swords in the iconographic tradition, and therefore in the mental image of the tyrannicides in the cultural imagination, contributes to the effectiveness of the symbolic link forged through this song. The song in the symposium setting evokes both the swords assumed to have been used in the slaying as well as the swords owned by the drinkers.[23] Swords, past and present, are linked as symbols that define the defenders of prized Athenian values.[24]

Cultural familiarity with the 'tyrannicides' *skolia* is attested by Aristophanes' references to them in his comedies.[25] Particularly significant amongst these allusions is the one made in *Lysistrata* (630–35) that confirms broad knowledge of the conceptualization of the sword explored above. The leader of the semi-chorus of old men quotes the first line of this song in the 'parabatic debate' with the semi-chorus of old women:[26]

> ἀλλὰ ταῦθ' ὕφηναν ἡμῖν, ὦνδρες, ἐπὶ τυραννίδι.
> ἀλλ' ἐμοῦ μὲν οὐ τυραννεύσουσ', ἐπεὶ φυλάξομαι
> καὶ "φορήσω τὸ ξίφος" τὸ λοιπὸν "ἐν μύρτου κλαδί,"
> ἀγοράσω τ' ἐν τοῖς ὅπλοις ἑξῆς Ἀριστογείτονι,
> ὧδέ θ' ἑστήξω παρ' αὐτόν· αὐτὸ γάρ μοι γίγνεται
> τῆς θεοῖς ἐχθρᾶς πατάξαι τῆσδε γραὸς τὴν γνάθον.

> Actually, this plot they weave against us, gentlemen, aims at tyranny! Well, they'll never tyrannize over me: from now on I'll be on my guard, I'll 'carry my sword in a myrtle branch' and go to market fully armed right up beside Aristogiton. I'll stand beside him like this (posing like Aristogiton's statue): that way I'll be ready to smack this godforsaken old hag right in the jaw! (advances on the Women's Leader)[27]

Henderson's suggestion that the semi-chorus of old men take up the pose of Aristogiton is made attractive both by the comic effect to be won through such staging as well as the verbal cues in the text.[28] The phrasing of line 633 is designed to induce the audience to follow, in their mind's eye, the semi-chorus leader into the Agora where they are invited to picture the bronze statue group and imagine the old man beside (ἑξῆς) Aristogiton. The following line, 634, brings the audience abruptly back to the reality of the comic representation, with the deictic (ὧδέ) drawing attention to the pose being adopted on stage and the παρ' αὐτόν reinforcing the juxtaposition of this 'stage image' with the familiar one of the statues from the Agora. While the chorus' stripped *himatia* may go some way to shoring up the visual allusion, the incongruity of the comparison is the end goal.[29] The humour is generated not only from the failure of old men to imitate young men convincingly (as noted by Henderson), but also from the contrast between the idealized body in the statue group and the bulging silhouette of the comic chorus (displayed to full effect by this sideways stance).[30] This comic framing, however, does not detract from what the quotation of the drinking song and the likely imitation of the pose of Aristogiton here reveals about the symbolic status of the sword in 411 BC.[31] The words of the chorus are designed, as Henderson argues, to present a caricature of the clichés heard in the assembly and court.[32] They demonstrate the ongoing cultural currency of the tyrannicides' story. The staging parodies the equivalent visual cliché, since: 'Adopting the posture of a tyrannicide made it possible to express support for a whole set of democratic values and to do so with a great economy of formal means.'³³ The ideological framing of the event in oral memory, reflected in the drinking song quoted here, and the evocation of the imagery of the statues, reinforced the symbolic association of the sword with democratic patriotism and establishes it as a semiotic shorthand (when appropriately cued) for this aspect of civic identity.³⁴ Moreover, the comic sequence articulates the process by which this representation of an ideal constructs identity, namely through the conceptual juxtaposition of the citizen, under a communal gaze, beside it.³⁵

The symbolic association between the sword and the defence of democracy was reinforced across the fifth century whenever Athenian society looked back to the actions of the tyrannicides in moments of ideological crisis.³⁶ Thucydides offers evidence for this type of civic affirmation, when he notes that the people's response to the scandal of the Mysteries and Herms in 415 BC was mediated through their 'knowledge' of the putting down of tyranny approximately a century earlier.³⁷ He highlights both that this story was importantly influential, a root cause of fear and suspicion (Thuc. 6.53.3), and that it held a prime position within contemporary cultural discourse. The phenomenon is significant enough to occasion a digression to set out the 'real story' of Harmodius and Aristogiton.³⁸ The deeper purpose of Thucydides' excursus is debated but his explicit reason for it frames his account as an attempt to prove the inaccuracy of the Greek, and even Athenian, understanding of the incident (Thuc. 6. 54.1).³⁹ While Thucydides asserts that the value of his narrative lies in its accuracy over what happened, ironically for our purposes its usefulness in fact rests in what it can reveal about what people *thought* had happened and the tenacity of that tradition.⁴⁰ The enduring political value of the model provided by the tyrannicides, and its associated symbolism for the sword, in times of crisis is evidenced through the oath instituted (on the suggestion of Demophantus) in 410/409 BC, after the fall of the first oligarchy. Athenian citizens recited the oath before the Dionysia (either a day before or just prior to the plays) for at least a few years (it is presumed).⁴¹ The wording of the oath is recorded by Andocides in his speech *On the Mysteries* (delivered in 399 BC):

κτενῶ καὶ λόγῳ καὶ ἔργῳ καὶ ψήφῳ καὶ τῇ ἐμαυτοῦ χειρί, ἂν δυνατὸς ὦ, ὃς ἂν καταλύσῃ τὴν δημοκρατίαν τὴν Ἀθήνησι, καὶ ἐάν τις ἄρξῃ τιν'ἀρχὴν καταλελυμένης τῆς δημοκρατίας τὸ λοιπόν, καὶ ἐάν τις τυραννεῖν ἐπαναστῇ ἢ τὸν τύραννον συγκαταστήσῃ· καὶ ἐάν τις ἄλλος ἀποκτείνῃ, ὅσιον αὐτὸν νομιῶ εἶναι καὶ πρὸς θεῶν καὶ δαιμόνων, ὡς πολέμιον κτείναντα τὸν Ἀθηναίων, καὶ τὰ κτήματα τοῦ ἀποθανόντος πάντα ἀποδόμενος ἀποδώσω τὰ ἡμίσεα τῷ ἀποκτείναντι, καὶ οὐκ ἀποστερήσω οὐδέν. ἐὰν δέ τις κτείνων τινὰ τούτων ἀποθάνῃ ἢ ἐπιχειρῶν, εὖ ποιήσω αὐτόν τε καὶ τοὺς παῖδας τοὺς ἐκείνου καθάπερ Ἁρμόδιόν τε καὶ Ἀριστογείτονα καὶ τοὺς ἀπογόνους αὐτῶν. ὁπόσοι δὲ ὅρκοι ὀμώμονται Ἀθήνησιν ἢ ἐν τῷ στρατοπέδῳ ἢ ἄλλοθί που ἐναντίοι τῷ δήμῳ τῷ Ἀθηναίων, λύω καὶ ἀφίημι.

I will slay by word and by deed, by my vote and by my hand, if it be in my power, whosoever shall suppress the democracy at Athens, whosoever shall hold any public office after its suppression, and whosoever shall attempt to become tyrant or shall help to install a tyrant. And if another shall slay such an one, I will deem him to be without sin in the eyes of the gods and powers above, as having slain a public enemy. And I will sell all the goods of the slain and will give over one half to the slayer, and will withhold nothing from him. And if anyone shall lose his life in slaying such an one or in attempting to slay him, I will show to him and to his children the kindness which was shown to Harmodius and Aristogeiton and to their children. And all oaths sworn at Athens or in the army or elsewhere for the overthrow of the Athenian democracy I annul and abolish.[42]

It is striking that this pledge of allegiance is framed through reference to the tyrannicides.[43] The polysyndetic list of means through which the citizen pledges to dispose of anyone who poses a threat to the democracy is crowned with 'by my own hand'. This evokes the action of the tyrannicides and the taking up of swords.[44] The appeal to the tyrannicides' actions in the defence of democracy was, judging from the passage of *Lysistrata* explored above, apparently already a hackneyed trope and so in this pledge to act against any ideological detractors, the pair would not be far from the oath-taker's mind. This suggestion is reinforced by the explicit reference to the tyrannicides towards the end of the oath. The listing of other forms of action, alongside the one modelled on the tyrannicides' behaviour, serves multiple ends: it distances the oath from the drinking song (setting it instead within a serious frame); it celebrates the democratic machinery by including 'words' and 'the vote' as powerful weapons in the list; and it lends greater weight to the commitment (as every means possible will be undertaken).[45] Above all, however, they serve a euphemistic function mediating the call to arms by setting it within a democratic frame; the honouring of Thrasybulus with a gold crown for the assassination of oligarch Phrynichus at this same Dionysia highlighted the reality of the form of action required.[46] On a symbolic level, the oath's utterance by citizens, gathered in their military formation and in the Agora juxtaposed with the statue of the tyrant slayers, reinforced across the demos the association of the sword with the defence of democracy.[47] Even citizens who were too poor to own a sword might nevertheless share in the sense of identity that this 'instrument of democracy' bestowed through this powerful evocation of an image that belonged to them all.

Athenian civic ideology's exaltation of fighting in defence of the city and the importance of the hoplite experience to the formation of citizen identity are well established in scholarship.[48] The liability of all citizens, except *thetes*, to serve as hoplites or in the cavalry framed military service as a performance of citizenship and display of the civic ideal of participation.[49] The place of military duty within civic ideology was expressed and reinforced through the 'communal civic event' of the city's burial of its war dead and the public speech that accompanied the ceremony.[50] Pericles' Funeral Oration offers an explicit commentary on this aspect of civic ideology, highlighting the 'essential involvement of the democratic citizen in the military defence of the *polis*'.[51] In fact, the citizen's sense of military duty could be elided with the commitment to take action against tyranny. The treatment of the tyrannicides as Athenian war dead symbolically conflated fighting for political freedom from tyranny within Athens and the city's external military engagements. The placement of the tyrannicides' tomb in the Ceramicus and their styling as Trojan war heroes suggests that these 'martyrs of the fight against tyranny seem to have been treated like those fallen in Athens' "national" wars'.[52] Furthermore, Herodotus' account of the debate between the generals before the battle of Marathon attests that the Persian wars could be framed as a fight for freedom equivalent to, and even surpassing, the tyrannicides' celebrated deed (Hdt. 6. 109).[53] The sword, as an object wielded by both the tyrannicides and hoplites and symbol for the defence of democracy, reinforced this ideological equation, as Aristophanes' *Knights* (produced in 424 BC) hints. In the struggle against the slave Paphlagon (Cleon) to win Demos' favour, the Sausage-seller highlights his appreciation of Demos' past action of fighting for Athens with his sword at Marathon (781–7):[54]

ΑΛΛΑΝΤΟΠΩΛΗΣ
σὲ γάρ, ὃς Μήδοισι διεξιφίσω περὶ τῆς χώρας Μαραθῶνι,
καὶ νικήσας ἡμῖν μεγάλως ἐγγλωττοτυπεῖν παρέδωκας,
ἐπὶ ταῖσι πέτραις οὐ φροντίζει σκληρῶς σε καθήμενον οὕτως,
οὐχ ὥσπερ ἐγὼ ῥαψάμενός σοι τουτὶ φέρω. ἀλλ᾽ ἐπαναίρου,
κᾆτα καθίζου μαλακῶς, ἵνα μὴ τρίβῃς τὴν ἐν Σαλαμῖνι.

ΔΗΜΟΣ
ἄνθρωπε, τίς εἶ; μῶν ἔγγονος εἶ τῶν Ἁρμοδίου τις ἐκείνων;
τοῦτό γέ τοί σου τοὔργον ἀληθῶς γενναῖον καὶ φιλόδημον.

Sausage Seller

At Marathon you outduelled the Medes in defense of our country, and your victory bequeathed to our tongues matter for minting great phrases. But he doesn't care if you have to sit like that on the hard rocks, unlike me, who bring this cushion I've had made for you. Here, get up a moment; now sit back down comfortably, so you don't chafe what sat to the oar at Salamis.

Demos

Who are you, my man? You're not a descendant of Harmodius' famous family, are you? All I can say is, this act of yours is truly outstanding and Demos-spirited!

The verb διαξιφίζω, translated here as 'outduelled', lays specific emphasis on the role of the sword in Demos' defense of the country.[55] Demos here stands for all the 'Marathon fighters', the older generation of Athenians who were remembered not only for saving Greece but also for enabling Athens to become a powerful imperial city.[56] The sword in this passage is explicitly connected with a fight which was understood to have liberated Greece from the Persian invasion. This deed in turn is associated with the past actions of Harmodius by Demos' response to the Sausage-seller. While Demos uses the reference to Harmodius to highlight his recognition of the Sausage Seller's display of patriotism (further reinforced by the two adjectives in 788), at the same time the evocation of the past deed establishes a parallel between the two acts of liberty achieved through the sword.[57] The self-conscious concern of the play with Athenian identity, exemplified through the presentation of Demos as a central character, lends further significance to the linking of the ideas here.[58] The citizen defined himself through his sense of duty to defend the city, protecting it from external and internal threats. The sword offered a symbol for this aspect to his self-definition.

This symbolic association between the sword's role in fighting for political freedom and protecting the city from external threats was further reinforced at the celebration of the Panathenaea.[59] A series of amphorae, awarded as prizes at the city's annual festival in honour of Athena, depict the tyrannicides displayed on her shield as an apotropaic emblem.[60] The iconographic schema invites the viewer to see 'the tyrannicides forcefully advance with the goddess to protect her city and its democracy'.[61] This protection of the democracy is once again depicted as being achieved through swords, reinforcing this symbolic meaning for the weapon.[62] The likely ramifications of this for civic identity are corroborated by Shear's persuasive case for the Panathenaea's reinforcement of the connection between the Athenian citizen and the tyrannicides (whose cult honours, she argues, were included in the festival).[63]

The citizen's heightened awareness at this festival of the model of behaviour offered by the tyrannicides (as defenders of democracy and the city) seems likely to have informed their interpretation of the symbolic meaning to the visual spectacle of the festival's parade of panoplies (hoplite armour). The demand for a 'cow and panoply' to be brought by Athenian allies to the Greater Panathenaea festival is understood to have been introduced in the 440s.[64] Paraded in front of Athens by the allies at the city's command, the panoply could symbolize Athenian power over her allies as well as her military sway within the Hellenic world.[65] This procession enabled the panoply to become a symbolic possession for all Athenians (rather than holding meaning for only those who could afford to own one).[66] The sword included in these panoplies had the potential to carry particular symbolic meaning to the Athenian viewer at this festival.[67] The prominence of the tyrannicides at the Panathenaea ensured the sword's association with the past defence of democracy, while the parading of panoplies brought by members of the Delian league to Athens highlighted its continued importance in this role in the present.[68] Inscriptional evidence demonstrates that the notion of obedience to Athens could include an ideological commitment by league members to fight against tyranny within their own city.[69] The swords paraded in the panoplies were capable therefore of reminding the Athenian citizen both of his own commitment to fight tyranny as well as his city's power to impose this ideology on others.

The public display of the panoply at the Dionysia, a festival that was equally self-conscious in its projection of Athenian ideology, offered another occasion for reflection upon the sword's symbolic status as representing the ideal of defending the democracy and the city.[70] The communal gaze at both festivals reinforced the sword's capability, as the visual embodiment of this ideal, to influence the viewer's sense of identity.[71] The presentation of the war orphans in full hoplite armour was one of the pre-performance ceremonies in the Theatre of Dionysus, introduced probably from the mid-450s.[72] The self-consciousness of the war orphan ceremony and the 'political' potential of its symbolism was already recognized in antiquity.[73] It presented a display of Athenian power in a context in which the full weight of civic ideology was felt.[74] It is significant, for our understanding of the sword's symbolic status, therefore, that the war orphans' arrival to manhood was marked through the panoply rather than an oar, bow, sling or javelin.[75] The ceremony itself drew attention to the armour through the proclamation accompanying the presentation of the orphans; as Aeschines' retrospective account (*Against Ctesiphon* 3.154) reveals:[76]

τίς γὰρ οὐκ ἂν ἀλγήσειεν ἄνθρωπος Ἕλλην καὶ παιδευθεὶς ἐλευθερίως, ἀναμνησθεὶς ἐν τῷ θεάτρῳ ἐκεῖνό γε, εἰ μηδὲν ἕτερον, ὅτι ταύτῃ ποτὲ τῇ ἡμέρᾳ μελλόντων ὥσπερ νυνὶ τῶν τραγῳδῶν γίγνεσθαι, ὅτ᾽ εὐνομεῖτο μᾶλλον ἡ πόλις καὶ βελτίοσι προστάταις ἐχρῆτο, προελθὼν ὁ κῆρυξ καὶ παραστησάμενος τοὺς ὀρφανοὺς ὧν οἱ πατέρες ἦσαν ἐν τῷ πολέμῳ τετελευτηκότες, νεανίσκους **πανοπλίᾳ κεκοσμημένους**, ἐκήρυττε τὸ κάλλιστον κήρυγμα καὶ προτρεπτικώτατον πρὸς ἀρετήν, ὅτι τούσδε τοὺς νεανίσκους, ὧν οἱ πατέρες ἐτελεύτησαν ἐν τῷ πολέμῳ ἄνδρες ἀγαθοὶ γενόμενοι, μέχρι μὲν ἥβης ὁ δῆμος ἔτρεφε, νυνὶ δὲ **καθοπλίσας τῇδε τῇ πανοπλίᾳ**, ἀφίησιν ἀγαθῇ τύχῃ τρέπεσθαι ἐπὶ τὰ ἑαυτῶν, καὶ καλεῖ εἰς προεδρίαν.

For what Greek, nurtured in freedom, would not mourn as he sat in the theatre and recalled this, if nothing more, that once on this day, when as now the tragedies were about to be performed, in a time when the city had better customs and followed better leaders, the herald would come forward and place before you the orphans whose fathers had died in battle, young men **decked out in the panoply of war**; and he would utter that proclamation so honourable and so incentive to valour: 'These young men, whose fathers showed themselves brave men and died in war, have been supported by the state until they have come of age; and now, **fully armed in this here armour** by their fellow citizens, they are sent out with the prayers of the city, to go each his way; and they are invited to seats of honour in the theatre.'

Aeschines' interest in emphasizing that the war orphans were 'decked out in the panoply of war' can be explained by his rhetorical strategy of aggrandizing the past.[77] The wording of the reported proclamation, however, highlights the city's intentional emphasis on the armour at the ceremony too. The armour is given visual emphasis, as the deictic pronoun that implies the herald's gesture towards an orphan's panoply (καθοπλίσας τῇδε τῇ πανοπλίᾳ 'fully armed in this here armour') indicates.[78] This is reinforced verbally through the cognate verb καθοπλίσας (producing the deliberately emphatic polyptotonic phrase 'armed in armour'). The syntax sets up καθοπλίσας τῇδε τῇ πανοπλίᾳ as one of two opposing ideas (marked in the Greek through the particles: μὲν and δὲ): up until now (i.e. the past) the orphans have been cared for by the state, but *now* they are fully armed and ready to be sent on their way. The armour is the city's final gift to them, an act of generosity and protection (emphasized perhaps by the intensifying prefix of the verb *kata-* 'fully' armed); at the same time the implicit reciprocity here suggests that, by way of return, the war orphans will fight on behalf of the state (like their fathers).[79] This ceremony and proclamation at the City Dionysia, shows that the panoply, with its sword included, symbolized the virtue of the state in looking after its own at the same time as reinforcing the citizen ideal of fighting on behalf of that state.[80] The probable inclusion of the proclamation of rewards to tyrant slayers as one of the pre-performance ceremonies in the theatre, perhaps juxtaposed with the parade of war orphans, could prompt the simultaneous viewing of the sword in the panoplies through the filter of the tyrannicides as a symbol of the defence of democracy.[81] The self-consciousness of this Athenian perspective on the meaning of the object would be heightened by the citizen's awareness that these ceremonies were being performed in front of a Panhellenic audience.[82]

This symbolic meaning invested in the sword through these ideologically framed public displays, and reinforced at each festival, explains this weapon's place within the idealized image of the hoplite. The sword's inclusion in this iconography is notable since this weapon is argued to have played a limited role in hoplite fighting.[83] This points to the sword's symbolic importance to civic identity and reinforces it. The range of media considered highlights that the meaning of the sword, and the civic ideal it represented, was at once personal and public; reflecting the complex intertwining of the two in the construction of citizen identity.[84] The surviving fragment from a fifth-century Attic red-figure bell-krater found in the Athenian Agora (LCT-59, dated *c.* 440–430 BC) demonstrates the elevated status of the sword, given a central place within a heroized view of the hoplite fighter, Fig. 15.

The nudity of the figure primarily suggests the heroization of the hoplite, but also has the effect of drawing greater attention to his armour (as the few items which *are* being worn or carried): the plumed helmet, spear, shield and sword.[85] The composition is designed to communicate the dynamic force of the fighter in battle (expressed through the tension in the drawn back arm, his left leg bent in motion, and the shield's angle (suggesting its movement forward)). The composition is carefully balanced so that all four parts of the armour remain visible to the viewer; the sword, which could so easily have been covered by the shield, is deliberately included within the composition. While our interpretation of this figure is partly hindered by the loss of its full iconographic context, the medium upon which the image is placed carries its own significance.[86] Since this hoplite appears on a bell-krater, a vessel used as a mixing bowl for wine at the symposium, it suggests a target audience of the elite. The heroized figure of the hoplite reflects both on elite ideals as well as their shared civic identity that was reinforced through the communality of the symposium.[87] Further examples, in different shaped vessels,

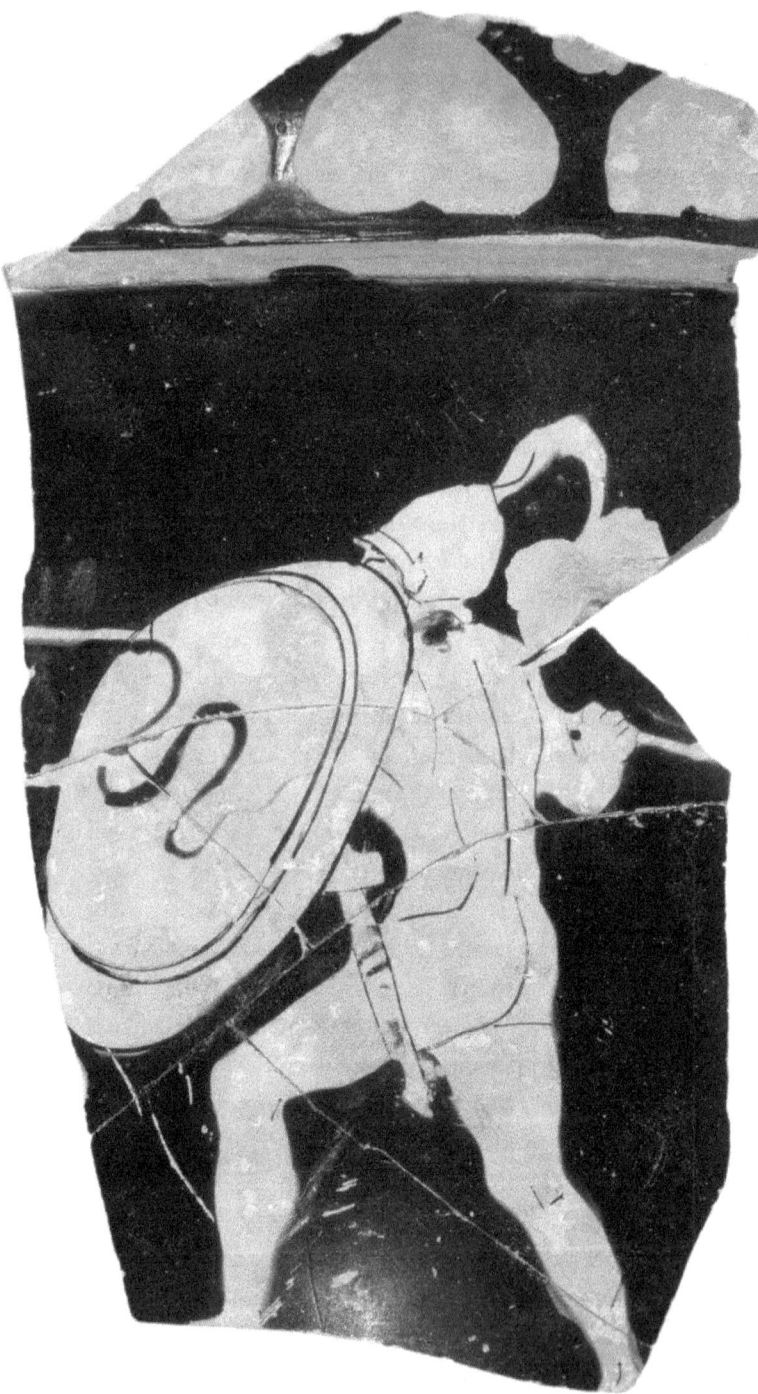

Fig. 15 Hoplite, fifth-century Attic red-figure bell-krater fragment, Agora Museum P 15837.

of this motif suggest that the sword enjoyed an established place as part of the image of the heroized hoplite.[88] For the Athenian viewer, this weapon within the iconographic schema, conveyed more than simply bravery on the battlefield, it suggested the ideal of the hoplite willing to fight for his city and its ideology.[89] The sword contributes to the sense in which this is not only an idealized but an ideologized image.[90]

The grave *stele* for two young hoplites, Chairedemos and Lykeas, dated to *c.* 420–410 BC, found on Salamis, and now in the Piraeus museum, further confirms the sword's persistent place in the iconographic schema for the idealized hoplite; Fig. 16.[91]

The hoplite to the left, Chairedemos, shares the heroic nudity of the hoplite on the bell-krater fragment (although this time a cloak is flung over one shoulder of the otherwise naked figure). The idealization of the figure is marked by its nudity and its stance (recalling Polykleitos' Doryphoros statue, representing the male ideal).[92] The nudity also again has the effect of emphasizing the weapons carried by the young hoplite: shield, spear, and sword (the hilt of which can be seen above the left hip).[93] The composition is designed to enable the inclusion of all these weapons as well as their careful framing: the inner rim of the shield encompasses them.[94] Both the individual and the figure of the hoplite in general are glorified here.[95]

The *stele* demonstrates the familiarity of this iconography in Athens and its vicinity (reinforced by its appearance across media; in pottery as well as grave relief) and also reveals the desirability of the motif as an expression of civic identity. The *stele* celebrates two real-life individuals, identified as Chairedemos and Lykeas (who died in fighting *c.* 410 BC).[96] The casualty list on which Lykeas' name is found reveals that he was a trierarch and yet he is represented on the *stele* as a hoplite.[97] For his family, or whoever commissioned this commemoration of Lykeas, therefore, the hoplite ideal was forceful enough to impose itself on the iconographic schema chosen for this relief.[98] The grave *stele* offers an example of individual identity and status being communicated through the pride felt in the civic role of fighting as a hoplite for Athens.[99] If, as Goette has argued, the iconography of grave reliefs such as this depended on state burial monuments, then its significance is even more profound.[100] This would offer a permanent public display of the hoplite sword's civic symbolism reinforcing its meaning in between the city's festivals. The sword's place in the iconographic schema of grave reliefs allows a statement to be made about an Athenian citizen's values, implicitly justifying (or compensating for) the death of that individual fighting for the city.

Fig. 16 Grave *stele*, c. 420–410 BC, Piraeus Archaeological Museum 385. Photograph © Perry Holmes and reproduced with his kind permission.

The pride in the values represented by the hoplite's sword (suggested in the above examples) is problematized by the iconography of white-ground *lekythoi* that use this same weapon to highlight the pathos of loss. Amongst the graveside scenes that dominated these funerary vessels from about 450 BC onwards, can be found the 'departing warrior' motif.[101] On an Attic white-ground *lekythos* attributed to the Painter of New York 23.160.41, a husband is shown leaving his wife and son as he goes to war.[102] The arrangement of the scene around a grave conveys that this departure operates on another level; this image commemorates a hoplite who did not return from battle. The scene is emotionally heightened, as Oakley notes, by the gaze that is exchanged between the hoplite and his young son who is shown sitting on steps of the grave.[103] The wider composition underlines this further through its representation of the 'insurmountable separation' between husband and wife, expressed through the failure of their eyes to meet.[104] The pathos is also intensified, however, by the depiction of the hoplite's wife and her handling of two pieces of his armour (Fig. 17).

Draped in a dark red *himation*, she gazes down towards an empty helmet that she holds in her left hand. In her right hand, she clutches a sword in its scabbard with its hilt pointing downwards (the angle of the sword mirroring her gaze). While her expression conveys a general sense of grief, the weapons offer a specific dimension to the loss. The empty helmet is, as she gazes at it, all that she has left. The scabbard's strap flaps down uselessly – highlighting the absence of the man who once wore it. The futility of these weapons is underscored by the placement of the sword in particular – sheathed and held upwards behind the body; it is far from being drawn in readiness to defend. This creates pathos for the woman who is left vulnerable as well as for the fallen dead whose sword could not save him. The tension to the woman's grip on the scabbard betrays the intensity of her emotion, conveying perhaps her desperation now that she is alone, or even anger at her loss?[105] Since, as Oakley notes, the composition fuses an arming-departure scene with a visit to the grave scene, it operates on both levels – commenting on both the feelings associated with soldiers parting for war as well as the emotional response to their failure to return.[106] The image therefore enables us to gain a sense of what the sword might have meant to those left behind, temporarily and permanently, and offers a more intimate perspective than the civic pride displayed by the *stele*.[107] This iconography highlights the capacity for an object's symbolic meaning to be changed by its framing and, in this case, focalization. The image invites the object to be viewed through the female gaze allowing for the generation of pathos that the male civic perspective of the sword cannot admit.[108] This offers further evidence for the way in which the male citizen could be defined through

Fig. 17 Attic white-ground *lekythos* attributed to the Painter of New York 23.160.41. Zürich, ex Hirschmann collection G 35. © Photo: Archäologische Sammlung der Universität Zürich, Silvia Hertig. Image reproduced with their kind permission.

contrast to the female.[109] The white ground *lekythos* points to a distinction between the public civic male perspective of the sword, encapsulated by its place in the idealized figure of the hoplite, and the female understanding of its meaning.[110] However, the hierarchy of meaning ensures that the dominant symbolism of the sword is the one associated with the public celebration of Athenian values, as exemplified by the tyrannicides' monument.

The symbolism for the sword established through the tyrannicides, and their residual presence within the city's collective political thought and self-definition, acted as a lens through which the Athenian citizen viewed this object displayed at festivals and presented as part of the idealized image of the hoplite.[111] It would also impact on his understanding of the significance of battlefield *sphagia*. In this rite, the sword was used to slit the throat of a sacrificial victim (ram or goat) to determine, by the way in which the blood flowed, whether the signs were propitious; victims continued to be slaughtered until the outcome was favourable.[112] The process was minimalist; dispensing with altar and fire, it required only the hoplite-seer, victim(s) and sword.[113] The impact of this was to focus on the action of the sword in killing and the flow of blood that resulted as these fragments of an Attic red-figure cup graphically depict (Fig. 18).[114] The sword is shown piercing through the victim's neck and added red paint, depicting the blood flowing down, draws the eye towards the wound it inflicts. The reciprocal gaze between the hoplite-seer and the victim invites further attention, reflecting on the communal focus on the deed and highlighting its role in empowering the rite's influence on identity.[115]

Importantly for this discussion, the hoplite-seer represented here 'kills with no special implement but the sword which he will shortly use in battle'.[116] This gave an elevated status to this object across the army since without it there could be no *sphagia* and without the rite's favourable outcome there would be no battlefield engagement. Herodotus' account of the Battle of Marathon demonstrates the principle in action (Hdt. 6.112.1):

ὡς δέ σφι διετέτακτο καὶ τὰ σφάγια ἐγίνετο καλά, ἐνθαῦτα ὡς ἀπείθησαν οἱ Ἀθηναῖοι δρόμῳ ἵεντο ἐς τοὺς βαρβάρους.

When they [the Athenians] had been set in battle array and the *sphagia* had come out favourably, at once the Athenians were released and advanced against the foreigners at a run.[117]

The engagement in this battle, which would prove so formative to Athenian cultural identity, depended on the favourable outcome of the *sphagia* as the structure of the sentence makes clear.[118] The syntax is further revealing since it

Fig. 18 Fragments of Attic red-figure kylix, *c*. 490–480 BC, Cleveland Museum of Art, Dudley P. Allen Fund 1926.242. Digital image courtesy of the Cleveland Museum of Art's Open Access Program.

pairs the ordering of troops quite naturally with the carrying out of *sphagia*, presenting both as a normal precursor to battle.[119] The rite, carried out in front of the army and critical to their action, must have been 'an intense focus of communal attention'.[120] The role of the sword as enactor of this powerful rite, which anticipated human slaughter on the battlefield, could impact the hoplite's understanding of his own sword's symbolism.[121] Through the *sphagia*, the sword represented the brutality of conflict but also the rightness of their action. For an Athenian, the rite's symbolic sanctioning of military action gained an ideological aspect through the sword's association with the tyrannicides.[122] The equation between the tyrannicides' act and fighting for the city (discussed above) symbolically linked the idea of the sword as a tool for defending democracy and the city; the *sphagia*, carried out by the sword, secured religious favour for the city's military endeavours and implied the rightness of their ideology.[123] This heightened the ideological ramifications of the hoplite experience that was already inherently tied to democratic identity.[124]

The depiction of *sphagia* on the Attic red-figure cup (Fig. 18) points to this symbolism extending beyond the battlefield and its importance to civic identity is implied by its inclusion within the setting of the symposium.[125] Moreover, the placement of the image in the cup's tondo reinforces this effect through the direct gaze between the drinker and this image.[126] The symbolism of the sword, perpetuated through the iconographic and poetic responses to tyrannicides' deed and reinforced at the Panathenaea and Dionysia, informs the understanding of the idealized hoplite and extends beyond the city to impact upon views of battlefield *sphagia* (which in turn finds its way back to the symposium). Through this nexus of symbolic associations and experiences the sword embodies the civic duty to defend democracy and the city, representing this core value of Athenian identity in the eloquent semiotic shorthand of a single object.

4

Swords Drawn on the Tragic Stage

The symbolic framing of the sword in its 'social' life, explored in Chapter 3, informed the experience of the Athenian spectator watching the exploitation of this prop and figure of the hoplite on the stage.[1] The Athenian theatre audience understood this prop as significant both in the past and present. The visual continuity between the depictions of the sword held by the tyrannicides, the prop wielded on stage by tragic heroes, and weapon used in battlefield *sphagia*, supported this connection.[2] Moreover, the Athenian 'sword of democracy' was retrojected into the mythological past as fifth-century depictions of Theseus demonstrate. In a striking phenomenon, artistic representations of the mythical Athenian king were influenced by the iconographic schema for the tyrannicides.[3] This sets Theseus' deeds, and his sword, within the framework of the ideologically charged actions of the celebrated pair; he becomes a mythological precursor for their action and for the fifth-century citizen aspiring to follow their example.[4] Thus Theseus, the tyrannicides, and the fifth-century citizen were connected through their shared ideals represented symbolically in a physical object: the sword. The dramatic effects generated from this connection in tragedy, and the impact of these stage moments on civic identity, are explored in this chapter through the examples of the *Oresteia* and *Ajax*. A focused examination of the sword in the *Oresteia* reveals the way in which its dramaturgy engaged with, and shaped, the ideological symbolism of the tyrant in Athens.[5] In *Ajax*, the sword's presentation as the instrument of a corrupted form of battlefield *sphagia* intersects uncomfortably with the Athenian hoplite experience, unsettling the ideological affirmation and cohesion associated with this object's ritual role. This enhances our understanding of Sophocles' dramatic technique, *Ajax*'s significance and effect, and the prop's potential to invite reflection on civic identity.

I The *Oresteia*'s tyrant slayers

Aeschylus' use of costume and props in the *Oresteia* to signal the intersection between its dramatic action and contemporary Athenian preoccupations is attested by the long-established example of the *metic* cloaks worn by the Erinyes and by the voting urns and pebbles that dominate *Eumenides* (see Chapter 2).[6] Building on this knowledge of the playwright's dramaturgic strategy in the trilogy, a strong case can be made for his exploitation of the sword prop to equivalent effect.[7] The example enhances our understanding of Aeschylus' technique, and the *Oresteia*'s design, since (in marked contrast to the *metic* cloaks and voting urns/pebbles) the appropriation of the sword's ideological symbolism is deployed to alarming effect. This symbol of civic identity is problematized within the dramatic action and only finds resolution at the end of the trilogy through the positive dramatic function of another powerful civic symbol (the voting urns and pebbles). A substantial part of the prop's dramatic force in the trilogy for the Athenian audience member is created through this exploitation of its civic symbolism. At the same time, through the dialectic between theatre and society, a significant portion of the *Oresteia*'s impact is generated from the effect of this prop's manipulation on the audience's perception of the object's ideological meaning.

Athenian society's preoccupation with the notion of tyranny played a vital role in its process of self-definition, resulting in the pervasiveness of the tyrannicides' exemplum in the civic experience. Fifth-century authors could be confident that: 'Hints and allusions would suffice to conjure up the whole picture and produce the expected reactions among the audience.'[8] Aeschylus cues the spectator's awareness of his trilogy's engagement with this nexus of ideas through the use of terminology familiar from fifth-century political discourse (τύραννος and τυραννίς).[9] The unusualness of this terminology of tyranny within the extant plays of Aeschylus suggests the careful deliberateness of its deployment here.[10] The contemporary associations of these trigger words are reinforced by the dramatic scenario: death being brought by the sword to those who are presented as ruling tyrannically. The verbal references combine with the visual allusion (made through the sword) to evoke the set of ideas associated with tyranny and the tyrannicides' actions, inviting the audience to view the dramatic action through this lens (and allowing the trilogy to reflect back on contemporary society).[11] The culmination of this engagement with the motif comes in *Choephori* when Orestes stands, most likely with sword in hand, over the corpses of Clytemnestra and Aegisthus and declares them tyrants (*Cho*. 973–4, extract iv below).[12] *Agamemnon*, however, offers careful preparation for this moment. Four explicit references to tyranny in the *Oresteia* work together to set up the implicit comparison between Orestes and the tyrannicides:

(i) *Ag.* 1354–5; the fourth chorus member to comment in the deliberation during Agamemnon's murder:

ὁρᾶν πάρεστι· φροιμιάζονται γὰρ ὡς
τυραννίδος σημεῖα πράσσοντες πόλει.

You can see that. Their first actions show the behaviour of men giving the signal that they mean to be tyrants of this city.

(ii) *Ag.* 1364–5; the ninth chorus member to comment in the deliberation during Agamemnon's murder (in response to the question of whether they should live under the new rulership):

ἀλλ' οὐκ ἀνεκτόν, ἀλλὰ κατθανεῖν κρατεῖ·
πεπαιτέρα γὰρ μοῖρα τῆς τυραννίδος.

No, it's intolerable, and it's better to die! That's a less bitter fate than living under tyranny.

(iii) *Ag.* 1633–5; Chorus to Aegisthus:

ὡς δὴ σύ μοι τύραννος Ἀργείων ἔσῃ,
ὃς οὐκ, ἐπειδὴ τῷδ' ἐβούλευσας μόρον,
δρᾶσαι τόδ' ἔργον οὐκ ἔτλης αὐτοκτόνως.

As though I'll let you be tyrant of the Argives – you who, when you'd planned the death of this man, didn't have the courage to do the deed with your own hands!

(iv) *Cho.* 973–4; Orestes' first words on being revealed after the murder:

ἴδεσθε χώρας τὴν διπλῆν τυραννίδα
πατροκτόνους τε δωμάτων πορθήτορας.

Behold the twin tyrants of this land, the murderers of my father and the ravagers of my house!

The allegations of tyranny at the end of *Agamemnon* (extracts i–iii) gain force from the presentation of Clytemnestra and Aegisthus engaging in characteristically tyrannical behaviour.[13] Both these earlier references and the presentation of the pair's behaviour help to corroborate the claim made by Orestes (extract iv).[14] Further justification for his action is implied by the combination of the ideologically charged language of tyranny and his stance, most likely with sword in hand, over the corpses.¹⁵ His demand that people should look upon the sight (ἴδεσθε, *Cho.* 973) adds to the self-consciousness of his pose in the tableau on the *ekkyklema* and evokes the experience of the public viewing of statues.¹⁶ The pose, assertion of tyrant slaying, and demand to look seem designed to evoke the statue of Harmodius (in the statue pair of tyrannicides in the Agora; Fig. 13).¹⁷ The triumphant mood of Orestes' utterance captures the spirit of the iconography and the attitude towards the act conveyed by it.¹⁸ The vibrant dynamic of the statue group offers no sense of hesitation or despair, the pair are purposeful.¹⁹ In this artwork celebrating the figures as heroes, there is no place for the ethical complexity of the *Oresteia*.²⁰ The appeal to it therefore has the impact of reinforcing the 'striking reversal' from jubilation to despair in this scene.²¹ Orestes starts with a confident appropriation of a positive Athenian ideological symbol, but the world of the *Oresteia* does not allow it to stand unsullied for long.²² Soon the realities and complexities of the situation undercut the projected image complicating the sword's symbolism.²³ While this highlights the difficulties of Orestes' position, it also, as a dialectic, has the potential to reflect back on the statues with the effect of pointing to the moral complexities of the tyrannicides' action that the public image of it sought to elide.²⁴ Furthermore, if, as Wilson suggests, the performances at the Dionysia was preceded with an announcement of rewards for the murder of aspiring tyrants, then the exposition of Orestes' complex position carries worrying implications for the audience.²⁵ The citizen ideal of being willing to take up a sword against tyranny, following the model of the tyrannicides, is unsettled by the contestation of the prop's positive symbolism.²⁶ Moreover, the process through which the tyrannicides' swords constructed identity (as representatives of an ideal subjected to a communal gaze) is problematized by its failed enactment here.²⁷

The outcome of the trial in *Eumenides* is critical to resolving this. There is more at stake than the celebration of Athenian justice, the saving of a mythological royal household, the championing of patriarchal hierarchy, or the aetiology of a political alliance.²⁸ If Orestes' action is seen through the lens of the Athenian tyrant slayers, then the acquittal validates violence in the correct circumstances and dispels the concerns raised in *Choephori*.²⁹ The 'newly-drawn' sword held by Orestes at the shrine of Delphi (*Eum.* 42), in semiotic limbo at the beginning of *Eumenides*, is redeemed as a symbol through the verdict.³⁰ In other words, Athenian ideology is celebrated through the framing of Orestes' sword in the trilogy as well as the voting urns and pebbles (on which see Chapter 2). Adopting the tyrannicide pose could be understood to 'express support for a whole set of democratic values and to do so with a great economy of formal means' in the fifth century.³¹ When Orestes first appropriates the motif, it is not clear that he appreciates those values or that his action could be tolerated by them, but by the end of the trial, the acquittal and Orestes' admirative gratitude reassure the audience on both points.[32] The approval of the violence perpetrated by Orestes' sword, however, seems particularly controversial given the claim that Ephialtes, attributed with introducing the reforms of the Areopagus was murdered.[33] The sources for this claim, both from later than the fifth century BC, do not give precise detail about either this violent deed's timing or the means of its enactment.[34] The possibility of politically motivated violence erupting, however, may explain the concern with exploring this theme and the desire to reinforce the parameters of the ideologically approved model for shedding blood. The destabilizing and reaffirmation of the sword's symbolism is critical to this agenda.

The example of Orestes, and his framing of his action as an act of tyrant slaying, stands in contrast to two engagements with the motif earlier in the trilogy. The comments of the chorus, extracts i–iii, set up the idea of the killers of Agamemnon as would-be tyrants, preparing the audience for the claim that Orestes makes at *Cho.* 973–4. The chorus' allusions to tyranny simultaneously, however, conjure up alternative narratives. The chorus member's suggestion that it would be better to die than to live under tyranny, *Ag.* 1364–5 (extract ii), advocates either suicide or death trying to bring down the tyranny.[35] The latter interpretation is reinforced by the words and actions of the chorus in response to Aegisthus, *Ag.* 1063–6 (extract iii) and *Ag.* 1652. The attribution of lines in the exchange within which *Ag.* 1652 appears is debated but the most persuasive interpretation sets out the dialogue as follows (*Ag.* 1649–52):[36]

ΑΙΓΙΣΘΟΣ
ἀλλ' ἐπεὶ δοκεῖς τάδ' ἔρδειν καὶ λέγειν, γνώσῃ τάχα.
εἶα δή, φίλοι λοχῖται, τοὔργον οὐχ ἑκὰς τόδε.

ΛΟΧΑΓΟΣ
εἶα δή, ξίφος πρόκωπον πᾶς τις εὐτρεπιζέτω.

ΧΟΡΟΣ
ἀλλὰ κἀγὼ μὴν πρόκωπος, κοὐκ ἀναίνομαι θανεῖν.

Aegisthus Well, since you think fit to act and speak like this, you will soon know the consequences. Ho there, my friends of the guard, your duty is close at hand here!

Captain Ho there, everyone, hold swords at the ready, hilt forward! [*The guards obey this order.*]

Chorus Well, I too am at the ready, and I do not refuse to die! [*They raise their staffs with a view to defending themselves.*]

This reading of the exchange is predicated on the assumption that neither Aegisthus nor the chorus of elders has swords.[37] The suggestion that Aegisthus is without sword in this scene is attractive given the logic of *Cho.* 1010–11 (that implies Clytemnestra used his sword) and the eloquent expression of the gender-inversion this creates.[38] The idea that the chorus do not carry swords here, but brandish their sticks, begs a greater question, though a reasonable case can be made in support.[39] The chorus describe themselves as πρόκωπος in line 1652.[40] The term is proper to swords (referring as it does to the hilt) and so, if they do not carry swords, it operates metaphorically to mean that the chorus is ready to fight. If they raise their staffs, as Sommerstein suggests, then the term can also be taken as a transferred epithet amounting to a semantic attempt to elevate the threat of the sticks by implying their figurative equivalence to the guards' swords (described using the same term, in the line before, *Ag.* 1651).[41] This stretches the limits of verbal manipulation to transform the meaning, or power, of the prop.[42] The staffs cannot 'become' swords, in part since the chorus themselves have earlier established the props as symbols of age and weakness (*Ag.* 72–82); it will instead take Clytemnestra's intervention to resolve the situation.[43] The implication of this is that the chorus cannot, even if they seem to aspire to the role, become tyrant slayers. The scene shows that the 'substitute' prop, explored in Chapter 2 (ladling cups for urns in *Wasps*) and assumed to belong to the domain of comedy, in fact has a place in tragedy, although the effect here is importantly different. In a moment of heightened tension, marked by the change in metre to faster-paced trochaic tetrameters, the chorus raise their staffs only to fall short of becoming Harmodius.[44] This offers visual articulation of their powerlessness in the situation and reinforces the sentiment expressed a few lines before that their only hope is Orestes (*Ag.* 1646–8). The difference from the attempt of the leader of the semi-chorus in *Lysistrata* to imitate Harmodius (see Chapter 3) is notable. In the comedy, the threat of tyranny posed by the women is not real and the attempt to become a tyrant slayer is deliberately debunked. Here, by contrast, the predominant feeling must be one of discomfort as the chorus try, and fail, to find a means to challenge the regime. Despite the differences to the situation, the motif of tyrant slaying lurks behind the dramatic action (thanks to the earlier utterances of the chorus) and comes to fruition in the figure of Orestes.[45] The ways in which the chorus fails to embody the model only serves to highlight how much closer the image of Orestes comes to it (and yet even his fulfilment of it is problematic).

There is, however, the further spectre of this image before Orestes embodies it in *Choephori*. The deliberate mirroring effect between the murder tableaus in *Agamemnon* and *Choephori* is well known.[46] The implications of this effect for the present argument, however, require further unpacking. Clytemnestra stands sword in hand over the dead ruler of the city (for her use of this weapon and her stage presentation with it, see the Appendix). The choice to allow her to adopt this pose, that implies such recent action, creates a stage image with the potential to evoke the tyrant slayers.[47] It is further significant that there are already hints towards this through the way in which she manipulates perceptions of Agamemnon before his death. While the chorus, in their deliberation, frame the murderers as would-be tyrants, in fact Clytemnestra has, through the careful staging of Agamemnon's homecoming, already implied the same of him. Amongst the rich layers of meaning to Agamemnon's stage action of walking over the purple cloth strewn on the ground before him is the reading of it as the action of a tyrant.[48] Clytemnestra makes Agamemnon behave like a tyrant before killing him and then appears in the pose of a tyrant slayer, sword in hand and fresh from the deed (representing the precise moment captured in the iconographic tradition for the tyrant slayers). Crucially, however, she falls short of making the claim that she has freed the land of its tyrant (in contrast to Orestes' bold proclamation, *Cho.* 973–4) and instead her focus is on the death of Iphigenia.[49] The tableaus are mirrored, but there is a critical difference to the ways in which the stage image is framed.[50] Orestes is styled as the righteous tyrant slayer, a position that will be further confirmed in *Eumenides*.[51]

Clytemnestra, nevertheless, plays with the image, appropriating it in a way that is likely to have proved as disruptive and disturbing as her usurpation of the male role in the killing.[52] For the Athenian audience members, her stance reinforces the audacity the chorus perceive in her words (*Ag.* 1399–400) and her sword takes on an alarming dimension. The Athenian symbol for the defence of democracy is wielded by a woman who has transgressed norms by killing her husband, by slaying the community-approved king and by taking a lover.[53] The role of gender categorization in the formation of male civic identity, suggested through the analysis of the Stieglitz cup in Chapter 1, makes this transgression all the more significant.

This image, however, will be 'righted' by Orestes, a young *male* slaying those who have been explicitly acknowledged by the community as tyrannical.[54] Moreover, Clytemnestra's act of appropriating an Athenian ideological symbol will be counterbalanced by the voting urns and pebbles introduced in *Eumenides* by Athena, a 'safe' female character with every right to be involved in Athenian matters.⁵⁵ This reassuring development disempowers the disturbing effect of Clytemnestra's attempts to tamper with the ideologically laden symbol of the sword. This demonstrates the trilogy's profound engagement with Athenian civic identity, explored and problematized through the sword, then restored through the voting urns and props (Chapter 2).⁵⁶ The handling of these objects on stage marks the renegotiation of identity in response to a crisis, a phenomenon discussed in Chapter 3, and evidences theatre's social function in this process.⁵⁷ The residual lesson, drawn from Clytemnestra's toying with the motif of the tyrannicides' sword, on the dangers of the misappropriation of ideological symbols resonates beyond the world of the *Oresteia*.⁵⁸ Moreover, the failed attempt of the elders to elevate their staves to the level of swords and to become tyrant slayers highlights the precarious nature of this symbol and its reliance on those with the strength and capability to empower it. Aeschylus' exploitation of this prop enables close reflection on the ideological concept of tyranny and its implications for the Athenian citizen in the politically tense period of this trilogy's production.⁵⁹

The theatrical impact of Aeschylus' evocation of, and engagement with, the tyrannicide statues in the *Oresteia* can be traced in subsequent dramatizations of the myth. Sophocles, in his *Electra*, allows Electra to evoke the statue group as she attempts to persuade her sister Chrysothemis to slay Aegisthus; Sophocles' *Electra* 973–85:⁶⁰

> λόγων γε μὴν εὔκλειαν οὐχ ὁρᾷς ὅσην
> σαυτῇ τε κἀμοὶ προσβαλεῖς πεισθεῖσ' ἐμοί;
> τίς γάρ ποτ' ἀστῶν ἢ ξένων ἡμᾶς ἰδὼν
> τοιοῖσδ' ἐπαίνοις οὐχὶ δεξιώσεται,
> Ἴδεσθε τώδε τὼ κασιγνήτω, φίλοι,
> ὢ τὸν πατρῷον οἶκον ἐξεσωσάτην,
> ὢ τοῖσιν ἐχθροῖς εὖ βεβηκόσιν ποτὲ
> ψυχῆς ἀφειδήσαντε προὐστήτην φόνου.
> τούτω φιλεῖν χρή, τώδε χρὴ πάντας σέβειν·
> τώδ' ἔν θ' ἑορταῖς ἔν τε πανδήμῳ πόλει
> τιμᾶν ἅπαντας οὕνεκ' ἀνδρείας χρεών.'
> τοιαῦτά τοι νὼ πᾶς τις ἐξερεῖ βροτῶν,
> ζώσαιν θανούσαιν θ' ὥστε μὴ 'κλιπεῖν κλέος.

Then as to fame on the lips of men, do you not see how much you will add to you and me if you obey me? Which of the citizens or strangers when he sees us will not greet us with praise? 'Look on these sisters, friends, who preserved their father's house, who when their enemies were firmly based took no thought of their lives, but stood forth to avenge murder! All should love them, all should reverence them; all should honour them at feasts and among the assembled citizens for their courage!' Such things will be said of us by all men, so that in life and death our fame will never die.

Electra's framing of the promised *kleos* (particularly its emphasis on being looked upon, greeted, and honoured at feasts and on public occasions even after death) points, as Juffras has brilliantly argued, to the evocation of the statues and cult of Harmodius and Aristogiton.[61]

The allusion is mediated, I would suggest, through the engagement with the same motif in Aeschylus' *Oresteia*. The emphatic placement of ἴδεσθε at the beginning of the τις-speech (S. *El.* 977) further cues the connection, since Orestes uses this very expression at the opening of his speech when he is revealed as a tyrant slayer (*Cho.* 973).[62] This intervening layer both strengthens Electra's rhetoric (since a former slayer of Aegisthus had been styled in the same way that she claims she and her sister will be), but also undercuts it. The awareness of the complications with Orestes' claim in *Choephori* tugs beneath the surface of the image that she paints. Furthermore, the problem of gender in her claim is exacerbated since the stage image of Orestes as tyrant slayer in *Choephori* overshadows any attempt to imagine her and Chrysothemis in such a pose. Meanwhile, the previous female stage figure to take on the statue's pose may well be evoked, dragging further negative associations into the equation. The allusion also draws attention to a crucial difference – Electra is without sword as she makes this claim that they could become tyrant slayers. Some of the audience could well think of the failed attempt of the chorus in *Agamemnon* to fulfil such aspirations when weaponless. The effect of this is that even while Electra tries to persuade Chrysothemis, the experienced theatregoer would know better than to believe what she says. The 'ghosts' of the previous production raised here enable the sword to be an absent presence in this play.[63] The further implication of this is that even while a persuasive case has been made for an axe (rather than sword) being used by Clytemnestra in a fifth-century revival of the *Oresteia*, the engagement with the tyrannicide motif in *Electra* would ensure that the ghost of the sword prop, and its meaning(s), lived on.[64]

II *Ajax*'s battlefield *sphagia*

Aeschylus is not the only tragic playwright to exploit the sword's civic resonance, demonstrating the rich dramatic potential of this strategy as well as drama's role in shaping perceptions of this object's ideological significance.[65] While swords make multiple appearances on the tragic stage after 458 BC, the impact of the sword in Sophocles' *Ajax* (conventionally dated to the 440s) is especially notable for its exploitation of the prop's intersection with its symbolic counterpart in Athenian society.[66] A matrix of contemporary allusions make the play's action powerfully relevant for an Athenian audience. These include: the direct address to Athens (*Aj.* 861); the use of military terms that resonate with the Athenian audience (*Aj.* 565 and 575–6); the evocation of Ajax's hero cult in Athens; and the reference to voting with pebbles (*Aj.* 449) and to jurors (δικασταί, *Aj.* 1136).[67] The sword's dramatic significance should be understood within this framework of Athenian resonance. The prop's prominence in the production is well established in scholarship, yet Sophocles' exploitation of its civic associations has not been appreciated.[68] The recognition of the sword's framing to evoke the Athenian hoplite experience challenges the interpretation of it as a symbol belonging solely to the past and enables fresh insights into the play's impact on the audience.[69] The prop's association with battlefield *sphagia*, and the ideological values attached to this (see Chapter 3), 'zooms' it from the Homeric past into the Athenian present with troubling implications for the audience's sense of civic identity.[70]

Aeschylus had already, in his *Seven Against Thebes* 377–83, established the place of *sphagia* within the battles of the mythological past and had perhaps used the reference to link with the present.[71] In *Ajax*, however, the evocation of the ritual is made far more impactful through the focus on the sword, the key instrument in the battlefield ritual and visually dominant prop in this play.[72] The link between the sword in Athenian society and the prop on stage is reinforced through references within the play to the manufacture of swords.[73] These allusions invite the audience to consider the process of the prop's manufacture, drawing attention to its existence outside the framework of the play and to its contemporary counterparts in Athens.[74]

Moreover, the characterization of the chorus as hoplites and Menelaus' claim of hoplite superiority (over archers) reinforces the framing of *Ajax*'s world, and its weapons, through the lens of fifth-century Athenian warfare.[75] The effect of continuity between past and present expressed through the prop is rendered powerfully uncomfortable within the play by the perversion of the *sphagia* ritual enacted by its hero.[76] First Ajax's slaughter of the livestock in the camp is presented as a form of corrupted *sphagia* ritual and then, even more provocatively, his own suicide is formulated in these terms. While a network of verbal allusions (explored below) establishes this reading, the dramatic power of this imagery comes from the focus on the prop that embodies its symbolic complexities.

The sword, and the bloody slaughter enacted by it, is given noticeable attention in the competing accounts of Ajax's nocturnal rampage.[77] This focus acquires specific meaning from Tecmessa's explicit description of the slaughtered animals as *sphagia*; S. *Aj.* 218–20:[78]

τοιαῦτ᾽ ἂν ἴδοις σκηνῆς ἔνδον
χειροδάικτα σφάγι᾽ αἱμοβαφῆ,
κείνου χρηστήρια τἀνδρός.

Such are the sacrifices, slaughtered by his hand and bathed in blood, that you will see within the hut, sacrifices of that man, ominous of the future.

Tecmessa advises the chorus on what they will see and in the process, instructs the audience on how to view both Ajax's action and his sword.[79] The explicit reference to *sphagia* (*Aj.* 219) is made more emphatic by its framing with the 'weighty' compound epithets, χειροδάικτος and αἱμοβαφής, that vividly evoke the signature characteristics of the battlefield rite (i.e. slaying by hand and blood).[80] This reading is strengthened by the emphasis earlier in the play on these same features (demonstrating Sophocles' intent to frame Ajax's actions to fit the model of battlefield *sphagia* from the outset).[81] The play's setting in a military camp offers contextual support to the evocation of this specific type of ritual. The combined force of this allows subsequent cognates from the verb σφάζω to allude to battlefield *sphagia*.[82] It also impacts on the sword's meaning. When the audience is confronted by the sight of this weapon at *Aj.* 346, they have been primed to view it as an instrument of *sphagia*. The emphasis on looking in Tecmessa's description (*Aj.* 218–19) and the prop's revelation (*Aj.* 346) links the two passages and connects in important ways to the battlefield experience of *sphagia* (see below).

While Ajax's actions are characterized in a way that evokes battlefield *sphagia* (with its multiple sacrificial victims, focus on bloodshed and simple use of a sword to enact the ritual), they also represent a perversion of it.[83] The emphasis on Ajax going out alone and at night, his delusion over his actions, and his torturing of some of the victims, all point to the corruption of the motif.[84] The collective ways in which Ajax's deed is presented as a perverted version of *sphagia* are designed to create a disquieting effect that would be heightened by the *sight* of Ajax with his bloody sword. Looking upon *sphagia* and its sacrificial instrument (i.e. the hoplite's sword) was, through the logic of the ritual, a prerequisite to fighting. The sacrifice mirrors the battlefield killing that will take place, becoming anticipatory: 'It is an act and a wish: "We kill. May we kill."'[85] The sight of its bloodiness prepares the hoplite for the bloodshed on the battlefield. The rite was therefore presented before the army, an intense focus of communal attention.[86] The experience of looking upon Ajax's bloody sword would, through its association with perverted *sphagia*, generate discomfort. This would be further intensified for Athenian audience members as they watched the interaction between Ajax and Eurysaces (*Aj.* 545-83). This scene's problematic interplay with the pre-performance ceremony for Athenian war orphans was established long ago by Goldhill.[87] His reading can be nuanced further, however, by considering the role of *sphagia* in Athenian warfare. Ajax expects his son to brave the sight of blood (*Aj.* 545-7):

αἶρ' αὐτόν, αἶρε δεῦρο· ταρβήσει γὰρ οὔ,
νεοσφαγῆ τοῦτόν γε προσλεύσσων φόνον,
εἴπερ δικαίως ἔστ' ἐμὸς τὰ πατρόθεν.

Lift him up, lift him up here! He will not be frightened to look on this newly spilt blood, if he is truly my son. You must begin now to break him in by his father's harsh rules and make his nature like mine.

Ajax's expression of paternally framed military expectations is formulated to chime with the pre-performance proclamation that emphasized both the bravery of the orphans' fathers and the readiness of the orphans, dressed in full armour, to fight on behalf of the city.[88] Ajax's insistence that his son should be willing to look upon not only bloodshed but specifically sacrificial bloodshed (indicated by the use of νεοσφαγής to modify the noun) intersects uncomfortably with expectations for the war orphans.[89] As hoplites, the city expects them to look on the bloodshed of *sphagia* and battle. Therefore while Ajax's advice to his son presents, as Goldhill argues, the polar opposite to the ideals of fifth-century democracy expressed through the Athenian war orphans, it also unsettles them.[90] If he is holding his bloodied sword as he delivers these lines (as would be appropriate given the earlier textual focus on it), then the dramatic point would be conveyed even more effectively (with the display of the instrument of *sphagia*).[91] The already powerful impact of presenting Ajax's slaughter of the animals as a corruption of *sphagia* is heightened through the further exploitation of this motif in a disturbing appropriation of Athenian civic discourse relating to the hoplite ideal. The more explicit invitation to reflect on the Athenian experience of war, generated by the Chorus' Third stasimon (*Aj.* 1185-1222), is thus anticipated here, demonstrating a sustained dramaturgic interest in framing the play's action, and its weapons, through a contemporary lens.[92]

The image of the bloody sword, familiar from the battlefield as a positive ritual symbol reinforcing the conviction to fight for the city and its ideology, here embodies the perversity of the misguided violence that has been carried out.[93] The corruption of the ritual and the pervasiveness of the 'wrong' kind of bloodshed juxtaposed with the uncomfortable continuity in the visual symbol of the bloody sword highlights the precariousness of hoplite ideology. It points simultaneously to the dangerous elasticity of the symbols through which a citizen's sense of identity was constructed. The renegotiation of an object's symbolic meaning could benefit society reaffirming identity in times of crisis.[94] Yet the examples of Clytemnestra and Ajax address the risks presented by the objects' openness to appropriation. This highlights that theatre, a medium that thrives on the flux of semiotic meaning and generates dramatic effect precisely from the reconstruction of the symbolism attached to objects, offered the ideal space for exploring the anxiety arising from the society's dependence on such forms in the construction of its citizens' identity.[95]

The disquiet generated by the mutability of the sword's symbolism is reinforced by the presentation of this object's failure to perform its usual function of securing divine favour.[96] The chorus' misplaced relief that Ajax has set right his relationship with the divine (*Aj.* 710-13) confirms its former disruption.[97] Ajax's announced intention (in his 'deception' speech) of undertaking rites of purification (*Aj.* 655-6) reassures the chorus that the equilibrium of the divine relationship will be restored.[98] Their words about Ajax 'once more' (αὖ, *Aj.* 711) enacting these rites, however, are steeped in threefold dramatic irony since Ajax will this time be the victim of his sacrifice; far from 'correcting' the previous corrupt *sphagia* his suicide repeats and magnifies it; and his relationship with the gods remains pointedly unrestored.[99] The sword's problematic symbolism as instrument of failed *sphagia* is exacerbated by Ajax's suicide and continues to confront the audience until the play's end.[100]

The sword's prominence in Ajax's death and its framing as an instrument of *sphagia* is marked by the hero's designation of it using the term σφαγεύς (*Aj.* 815) at the very opening of his suicide speech (*Aj.* 815-22):[101]

ὁ μὲν σφαγεὺς ἔστηκεν ᾗ τομώτατος
γένοιτ' ἄν, εἴ τῳ καὶ λογίζεσθαι σχολή,
δῶρον μὲν ἀνδρὸς Ἕκτορος ξένων ἐμοὶ
μάλιστα μισηθέντος, ἐχθίστου θ' ὁρᾶν.
πέπηγε δ' ἐν γῇ πολεμίᾳ τῇ Τρῳάδι,
σιδηροβρῶτι θηγάνῃ νεηκονής·
ἔπηξα δ' αὐτὸν εὖ περιστείλας ἐγώ,
εὐνούστατον τῷδ' ἀνδρὶ διὰ τάχους θανεῖν.

The killer stands where it will be sharpest, if one has time to work it out, a gift of Hector, the acquaintance I most hated, and whose sight I most detested; it stands in the enemy soil of Troy, newly sharpened with a whetstone that cuts away the iron. And I have planted it there with care, so that it may loyally help me to a speedy death.

The term, often translated simply 'slayer', carries ritual nuances (setting up the sword as an instrument of sacrifice).[102] Verbal echoes link this 'sacrifice' to the earlier slaughter – the sword, reported as νεόρραντος (freshly sprinkled, *Aj.* 30) the night before, is described using the same term by Ajax (in anticipation of the impact of his suicide upon it, *Aj.* 828).[103] Beyond establishing the link between the two 'sacrifices', the echo informs the audience expectation over the outcome of the reiterated *sphagia*.[104] Tecmessa's description of the corpse further confirms this connection, *Aj.* 898–9:[105]

> Αἴας ὅδ᾽ ἡμῖν ἀρτίως νεοσφαγὴς
> κεῖται, κρυφαίῳ φασγάνῳ περιπτυχής.

> Here lies our Ajax, newly slaughtered, folded round his hidden sword.[106]

Her use of νεοσφαγής (fresh-slaughtered) recalls the same term being used by Ajax as he claims that his son, Eurysaces, will brave looking upon the 'fresh-slaughtered' bloodshed (*Aj.* 545–7, discussed above). This allusion to the earlier scene sets up the further engagement with the theme of ritual perversion here. It is also offers an important context for Tecmessa's subsequent speech; *Aj.* 915–19:

> οὔτοι θεατός· ἀλλά νιν περιπτυχεῖ
> φάρει καλύψω τῷδε παμπήδην, ἐπεὶ
> οὐδεὶς ἂν ὅστις καὶ φίλος τλαίη βλέπειν
> φυσῶντ᾽ ἄνω πρὸς ῥῖνας ἔκ τε φοινίας
> πληγῆς μελανθὲν αἷμ᾽ ἀπ᾽ οἰκείας σφαγῆς.

> He must not be looked upon! I shall cover him completely with this cloak folded about him, since none that was a friend could bear to look upon him spurting blood upwards to his nostrils, and the black gore from the deadly wound inflicted by self-slaughter.

Tecmessa responds to the chorus' query over where Ajax lies with the forceful injunction that he is not to be looked upon. Her words take on a different dimension when considered in parallel to the earlier scene in which Ajax suggests that his son will not be afraid to look upon bloodshed.[107] Ajax's claim is made disturbing through its engagement with the underlying idea of the hoplite ideal of looking at *sphagia* as a precursor to bloodshed in battle. Tecmessa's comment, by contrast, exploits this idea to different effect, marking the extent of the corruption of *sphagia* here with this prominent denial of a central aspect of this sacrifice (the communal viewing of it).[108] The reinforcement of the ways in which Ajax's death evokes, and perverts, *sphagia* through the rest of her speech intensifies the disquiet caused by this. The graphic emphasis on the blood and its trajectory (*Aj.* 918–19) reflects characteristic features of *sphagia* (offering a verbal equivalent to the iconographic prominence of these same aspects in Fig. 18).[109] The use of the term σφαγή (emphatically placed at the line's end) in her reference to Ajax's 'self-slaughter' (*Aj.* 919) reinforces his suicide as a form of perverted *sphagia*. Its transgressive nature, however, is marked by the pairing of οἰκεία and σφαγή, shifting the focus from the community to the individual and emphasizing the self-destructiveness of the act.[110] The earlier detail of this sacrifice being enacted using a sword belonging to an enemy (*Aj.* 817–18) had already marked the transgression.[111] This *sphagia* and its agent (the sword) cannot be looked upon, in marked contrast to the hoplite experience of the ritual. Sophocles exploits the tension this generates, leading up to the charged moment of Teucer's encounter with the sight (*Aj.* 1003). In the meantime, the audience's awareness of the disjunction between the hoplite experience of *sphagia* and this dramatization invites reflection on the sword's role in representing civic values in society.

The question of what the audience could *see*, and when, in the staging of the suicide is critical to the understanding of this dramatic effect. It is a well-worn subject in scholarship, however the argument about *sphagia* introduces a new significance to the issue of the sword's visibility and the approach taken to iconography (below) offers a fresh contribution to the debate. Within the range of hypotheses for the staging of the suicide, the sword's visibility is envisaged as absolute, partial, or non-existent.[112] A crux to the argument is whether the verbal emphasis on the sword in Ajax's suicide speech draws attention to a prop on stage or compensates for its absence.[113] Those who argue that the words act as a substitute for the visible presence of the prop must explain the deictic pronouns in the passage (which ordinarily would be taken as an indication of gesturing towards the object on stage).[114] On the other hand, those who believe that the suicide took place in front of the audience must account for how this could be managed in practical terms.[115] The reconstruction of the staging presented here draws predominantly on Most.[116] On this account of the staging, the sword is not seen by the audience during the suicide speech but Ajax gestures towards it (as though it is placed just inside the *skene* to one side of the door).[117] Ajax leaps through the opening of the *skene* (at *Aj.* 865) and is understood by the audience to fall on his sword, although they do not see this.[118] The dummy representing

Ajax impaled on his sword is revealed on stage, already covered by Tecmessa's veil, at *Aj.* 925.[119] The covered corpse remains on stage and is uncovered only on Teucer's command, revealing the sword, at *Aj.* 1003.[120] At the end of the play, the body of Ajax is probably carried off.[121] The fate of the sword, however, is unclear. It might remain centre stage sticking out of the ground or it may be removed and taken with Ajax to his burial.[122] Either possibility would have created a powerfully disturbing end to the play: the sword left behind would be a confrontational final stage image embodying the unresolved nature of its corrupt violence in the drama, while the removal of the polluted sword (for it to be buried with Ajax) would carry its own worrying implications.[123]

The sword is visually present from *Aj.* 1003 to the end, but what of its absence from view (either because it is off-stage or covered under the veil) from *Aj.* 815 onwards?[124] The verbal attention given to it compensates for this, as noted above, and is made more effective through the dominant visual presence of the sword in the earlier part of the play that forges a strong mental image for the audience to draw upon. A further consideration here, however, is the extent to which the audience's knowledge of the existing iconographic tradition for the suicide of Ajax enables them to imagine exactly how the sword is stuck in the ground, what it looks like impaling Ajax's body, and the graphic bloodiness of the wound it inflicts.[125] Finglass, noting the prominence of the sword on vases depicting the suicide, imagines Sophocles looking at one of them and contemplating his ability to outdo their powerful effect: 'Sophocles, in his different medium, could achieve just as moving a picture by the mere force of his words, without the need for showing the sword standing ready to kill.'[126] The playwright's words, however, perhaps take their force precisely from the conjured images of the iconographic tradition.[127]

While the focus on how the sword has been positioned carries dramatic meaning within the scene, it also highlights a convention of the iconographic tradition.[128] Four Attic vessels, all dated earlier than Sophocles' play, evidence this convention in their depictions of Ajax's suicide.[129] Amongst these examples the Exekias painter's amphora, dated to 540 BC, is particularly notable since it shows the earth piled up around the sword in a manner that resonates closely with the description in Sophocles' play.[130] Further echoes between the play and vase composition can be seen in the isolation of the hero and on his careful concentration on the task at hand, conveyed on the vase through his furrowed brow.[131] While the Exekias vase is the most explicit in showing the piled earth, there is a hint of the equivalent motif in the Brygos cup's tondo and the uprightness of the sword in the other images implies it.[132] The striking focus in the text on the sword standing ready and being fixed in the earth (*Aj.* 815, 819 and 821) should be understood in the context of this iconographic tradition. If the focus is taken as a deliberate cue to the audience, then this would signal Sophocles' intention not only to compete with the alternative artistic medium, but, more importantly, to exploit it, allowing it to become a substitute for the stage image. If we accept a reconstruction of the scene in which the sword is not visible, then a significant aspect to Sophocles' dramaturgic strategy here would be to invite the audience to imagine the sword in the ground through calling on their experience of encountering this image before.[133]

The same strategy may motivate Tecmessa's explicit commentary on her intention to cover Ajax with her veil (*Aj.* 915–16). It is possible to identify independent dramatic motivations for this gesture, in its likely allusion to *Iliad* 22, its symbolic meaning within the imagery of the play and the pathos it adds to Teucer's arrival.[134] Yet the detail also has the impact of evoking the established iconographic motif of Tecmessa covering Ajax's impaled corpse.[135] Representative of this schema is the tondo image of the Brygos cup now in the Getty collection, Fig. 19.

It is not only the covering of the corpse, or the placement of the sword (fixed in the ground), that chimes with the words of the play, but also the bloodiness of the wound. This is described in graphic terms in the play.[136] The image is just as emphatic in highlighting the blood: 'Blood flows from the entrance wound, in added red painted on the black background beneath the body, as well as from the exit-wound, running in streaks of dilute glaze down across the middle.'[137] The similarities have led scholars to connect the vase to Sophocles' play, although the earlier date of the painted image has forestalled further discussion of the significance of this relationship.[138] The resistance to pushing the implications further is characteristic of the privileging of literature over iconography.[139] Yet, the closeness between the iconographic representations and details in Sophocles' play demand consideration. The acknowledgement of the iconographic tradition's importance to the play brings rich rewards in understanding its dramaturgic design and the statement it makes about the sword as a *tangible* object relating to the Athenian civic experience.

The correspondences between the images and the play suggest that even if Sophocles had not looked upon these particular vessels (which happen to have survived), he was aware of the iconographic tradition they represent and exploited it in his drama.[140] It is worth noting the distinction between claiming that Sophocles' conceptualization of the tragic scenario was influenced by the iconography and that he evoked it in performance to dramatic effect; I am suggesting both.[141] The verbal descriptions of the sword planted in the ground and Tecmessa veiling the body can be understood to have been designed to

Fig. 19 Brygos cup (Getty 86.AE.286): interior. Digital image courtesy of the Getty's Open Content Program.

evoke familiar imagery, represented for us in the surviving examples of the Exekias amphora and Brygos cup. This would strengthen the dramatic power of the moment through enabling it, though not on stage, to be imagined vividly by the audience.[142] If the body is concealed when it is first brought onto stage (which would create greater dramatic tension leading up to the moment of its unveiling at *Aj.* 1003), then the audience look upon the veiled form.[143] The textual cues discussed above inform how they might visualize the impaled body, as seen in artistic representations, in their minds. Not only does this enable the drama to be effective even while the body is covered, it also sets up an expectation over what the corpse looks like. This acts as preparation for the actual sight of the body, at its unveiling (*Aj.* 1003). The iconographic tradition includes the schema of both Ajax falling forward on his sword and, as in the example of the Brygos cup (Fig. 19), of him lying face up. The text of Sophocles' play remains open to either possibility, although I think it slightly more likely that the dummy was on its back (which would be dramatically more effective).[144] In this case, for some audience members (picturing the iconographic schema of the Brygos cup) the revelation confirms, and makes concretely visual, what they had imagined, while for others (thinking of Ajax as falling face forward) the image in their mind's eye acts as 'false preparation' creating shock at the revelation.[145]

The transition from the image of the impaled corpse in the mind's eye to the sight of it makes for a powerful progression especially given Tecmessa's earlier claim at *Aj.* 917 that no friend could bear to look on him. The language of her comment is telling in its use of the verb τλάω implying both the endurance required to look and the suffering implicated in doing so. This moment reverberates, as noted above, with the earlier comment that Eurysaces should not shy away from looking upon blood and the intersection of that claim with the Athenian hoplite ideal; in fact, Ajax's slaughter, framed as *sphagia*, must be looked upon. The experience is softened, however, for the audience by allowing them first to imagine what the corpse looks like (through the evoked iconography) before seeing the image realized on stage.[146] The 'phasing' of the audience's encounter, through the dramaturgic exploitation of iconography, invites reflection on the battlefield experience of looking directly upon bloodshed and the understanding of the sword's role in *sphagia*.[147] The sword and blood are the only element of this corrupt *sphagia* that assert visual continuity with the battlefield rite. It is the sight of the prop that intensifies the audience's 're-enactment' of looking, even while the corrupt elements to the rite's dramatization disrupt it.[148] The effect of the comparison is to highlight the horror of Ajax's actions but the sword simultaneously asserts continuity, prompting questions about battlefield violence and its legitimization. The role of the communal viewing of *sphagia* and the sword's symbolism in shaping hoplite identity is problematized by the prop's handling in *Ajax* which disrupts both.[149]

Moreover, the significance of the prop's progression from an object present but hidden (visually imagined in the mind's eye) to one that is visible on stage is taken further through Teucer's deliberation over how to extract Ajax's corpse from the sword (*Aj.* 1024–5). This reinstates the object's tangibility, it is a physical presence to be negotiated. However, importantly, in this passage and in Teucer's later instruction to Eurysaces about helping to lift the body (*Aj.* 1409–11), there is no suggestion of the sword being touched; it is tangible and yet untouchable. This is in marked contrast to the logical battlefield response to looking upon *sphagia*, the sight affirms the hoplite's conviction over the rightness in engaging in battle and, therefore, prompts the taking up of weapons. The importance of the tangibility of the sword as a symbol of civic identity in another respect is underlined by the citizen's commitment, vocalized in the Harmodius drinking song, to take up the sword against tyranny.[150] The aversion to touching the sword further evidences the powerful agency of this prop and heightens the disquieting effect of this play's intersection with the Athenian experience.[151] The strategy of exploiting the iconographic tradition, to allow the imagined sight of the sword before its visible presence, enables this question of tangibility to be set into emphatic relief. The careful progression of the sword's ontological status in this part of the play, from imagined, to seen, and finally to (in)tangibly present destabilizes this symbol of civic identity and invites scrutiny of its place within Athenian society.[152]

The consideration of whether Sophocles' conceptualization of Ajax's suicide as a battlefield *sphagia* was indebted to an existing tradition offers further definition to the effect of its dramaturgy. Iconographic evidence has been used to suggest that the presentation of Ajax's deed as an act of Hector may have predated Sophocles' play; it is possible that iconography may also hint towards the earlier existence of the *sphagia* motif.[153] The fragments from an early fifth-century red-figure cup by Onesimos offer crucial evidence.[154] One of the fragments shows a woman moving purposefully towards the right, the lower part of an ankle-length pleated *chiton* and a left leg extended back with the heel of the barefoot raised from the ground are visible.[155] Lying on the ground behind the woman's foot is a ram (identified by its curly horns). The ram is on its back and its head is turned back under itself with the throat cut.[156] In front of the woman's foot on the ground there is a large right foot (its big toe points towards her shin) and the toes of the left foot can be glimpsed at the fragment's edge. It has been convincingly argued that this fragment is part of an image (from the cup's exterior) that depicted

Tecmessa rushing towards the corpse of Ajax.¹⁵⁷ The image presents several points of correspondence with Sophocles' play. The covering of the corpse by Tecmessa, which Williams and Sparkes suggest the cup depicted, offers an obvious parallel.¹⁵⁸ The rendering of Tecmessa's heel raised in motion together with the placement of the image running around the exterior of the cup creates a dynamic urgency to the scene that is also significant. It mirrors the effect produced in *Ajax* by the extraordinary staging of the search for the hero.¹⁵⁹ Thirdly the slaughtered ram, confirmed by the other animal on the exterior as one of the animals slaughtered by Ajax in his madness, is striking.¹⁶⁰ The juxtaposition of the ram with the corpse of Ajax in the image invites a comparison that is reinforced by the composition's parallel positioning of the bodies (on their backs). The pairing between Ajax's death and the slaughter of the herds is, as discussed above, prominent in Sophocles' design. Even more significantly, the motif of the slaughter of the animals (and by extension the death of Ajax) as a form of *sphagia* in the play is also conveyed in this iconographic representation through the ram's pulled back head and slit throat (resonating with the iconography for battlefield *sphagia*, Fig. 18).

The parallels between this composition and Sophocles' play are suggestive, raising the possibility that the conceptualization of the suicide as *sphagia* predated his production.¹⁶¹ Nevertheless, the *effect* of Sophocles' framing of the myth on stage would be quite different from this image, not least because of the stage presence of the sword. The tangible object, the prop manipulated by the actor and later seen sticking out through the dummy, placed squarely in front of the audience would have a powerful impact on them.¹⁶² This materiality and its intersection with the civic experience (through the audience's awareness of this as the same object brandished by the tyrannicides in the Agora sculpture, carried on the battlefield and displayed at the Great Panathenaea and Dionysia) is what makes the enacting of the perverted *sphagia* in this play so effective and affective.¹⁶³ The observation that '*Sphazein* and its compounds, the verb for killing in the sacrificial act, occur more frequently in *Ajax* than in any other Sophoclean play' reflects the playwright's serious intention to engage with this element of Athenian experience in this drama, but it is the prop that makes this engagement so powerful.¹⁶⁴

One of the major implications of this analysis is to suggest that the sword in *Ajax* should not be seen as belonging solely to the heroic past.¹⁶⁵ The prop instead problematizes the audience's relationship to its own battlefield violence and its divine legitimization through the *sphagia* ritual. This is effected through the sword's presentation as a perpetrator of perverted *sphagia* and fatally destructive violence. The impact of this is heightened by the sword's juxtaposition with, and handling by, Ajax, one of the Athenian eponymous heroes whose statue stood in the Agora.¹⁶⁶

Brook reflects on how witnessing the corrupt and conflated rituals associated with the hero through the play would make it difficult for the audience to envisage a burial ritual that was not also corrupt, casting a shadow across the play's ending.[167] The sword, as a uniquely confrontational and problematic symbol of that corruption, reinforces this. There is no resolution to the tense interplay between Ajax's sword and the ideological significance of the object for an Athenian audience. The treatment of this prop complicates the Athenian audience's feelings towards Ajax and their own hoplite sword. If the pre-performance ceremonies 'highlight the contemporary values against which Ajax's depiction and indeed the whole tragedy resounds', then the sword (and not just the exchange between father and son) presents a focal point for the reflection on these values.[168] Sophocles, it can be argued then, takes an object that was already prominent in the myth's iconography but manipulates its distinctive meaning for Athenian audience members in his dramatization.[169] Sophocles' daring in exploiting the connotations of the sword's role in the *sphagia* ritual was already implicitly recognized within antiquity by the nickname given to one of the actors specializing in the role of Ajax. The actor Timotheus of Zacynthos was known as σφαγεύς ('slayer', the term applied to the sword at *Aj.* 815), in recognition of his virtuosity in performing the suicide scene.[170] The choice of sobriquet highlights the status of the sword as a focal prop that could stand for the experience of the entire play.[171] Even more importantly, it points to the impact not only of the scene's staging but also of Sophocles' dramaturgic strategy of linking this agency-endowed prop with the hoplite experience of *sphagia*.[172] The dramatic force of this prop for the Athenian audience member, who viewed it against the backdrop of contemporary allusions within the play, lay in its ability to problematize the symbolic associations of the 'sword of democracy' and the approval of its violence expressed in the *sphagia* ritual. A major part of the suicide scene's power is rendered by its problematization of the sword's symbolism in relation to *sphagia* – the object is shown enacting the wrong kind of violence, failing to secure divine favour, and disrupting the communal gaze. The hoplite ideals of looking upon blood and taking up weapons are scrutinized. The destabilizing of the sword's civic symbolism unsettles the sense of identity that rests upon it, inviting reflection on that identity. Yet even this powerful manipulation of the prop's meaning did not stand beyond the reach of comic reframing; in the next chapter the 'redrawing' of the sword on the comic stage and later tragedy is examined and the mutability of this civic symbol (reflected and effected by drama) is further demonstrated. The complexities of theatre's role in shaping citizen identity are explored in greater detail through the close examination of the intergeneric interplay situated in the handling of the sword.

5

Swords Redrawn on Stage

I The comic redrawing of swords

The dramaturgic manipulation of the sword in the *Oresteia* and *Ajax* establishes its powerful status as a point of intersection between theatre and society (an intermediary with the potential to generate confrontational dramatic effects). Both productions also highlight its association with graphically violent slaughter on the tragic stage.[1] While the moment of impact itself may not have been seen, it is carefully prepared for, described, and most importantly, represented indexically through the presentation of the bloody sword beside the corpse(s).[2] The symbolic associations for the prop that this implies is encapsulated and further confirmed by the appearance of the personification of Death on stage in 438 BC, explicitly carrying a sword in Euripides' *Alcestis* (74–6).[3] The sight of the sword juxtaposed with corpses and carried by Death himself establishes an expectation in the audience over the outcome of the prop's presence.[4] The sword could therefore be exploited to create an atmosphere of imminent violence on the tragic stage.[5] Its powerful status as both a point of intersection between the tragic stage and society and as a symbol for the violent bloodshed associated with the genre made it the perfect target for comedy, providing an eloquent means through which the rival genre could express its relationship to tragedy and contemporary society.[6] The comic treatment of this prop affects the impact that its tragic manipulation had on perceptions of the object's symbolism within Athenian society. At the same time, comedy stakes its own claim on contributing to civic discourse by influencing views of the sword.

The surviving iconographic evidence for the performance of tragedy, limited though it is, supports the idea of the centrality of this prop to perceptions of the genre.[7] Vase paintings also offer insights into the framing of this prop on the comic stage. The notion of the sword as a particularly 'tragic' prop, which does not belong to the world of comedy, is attested by the fourth-century 'Choregoi' vase, Fig. 20.[8] This bell-krater shows Aegisthus (to the left, in front of the doors) presented as a

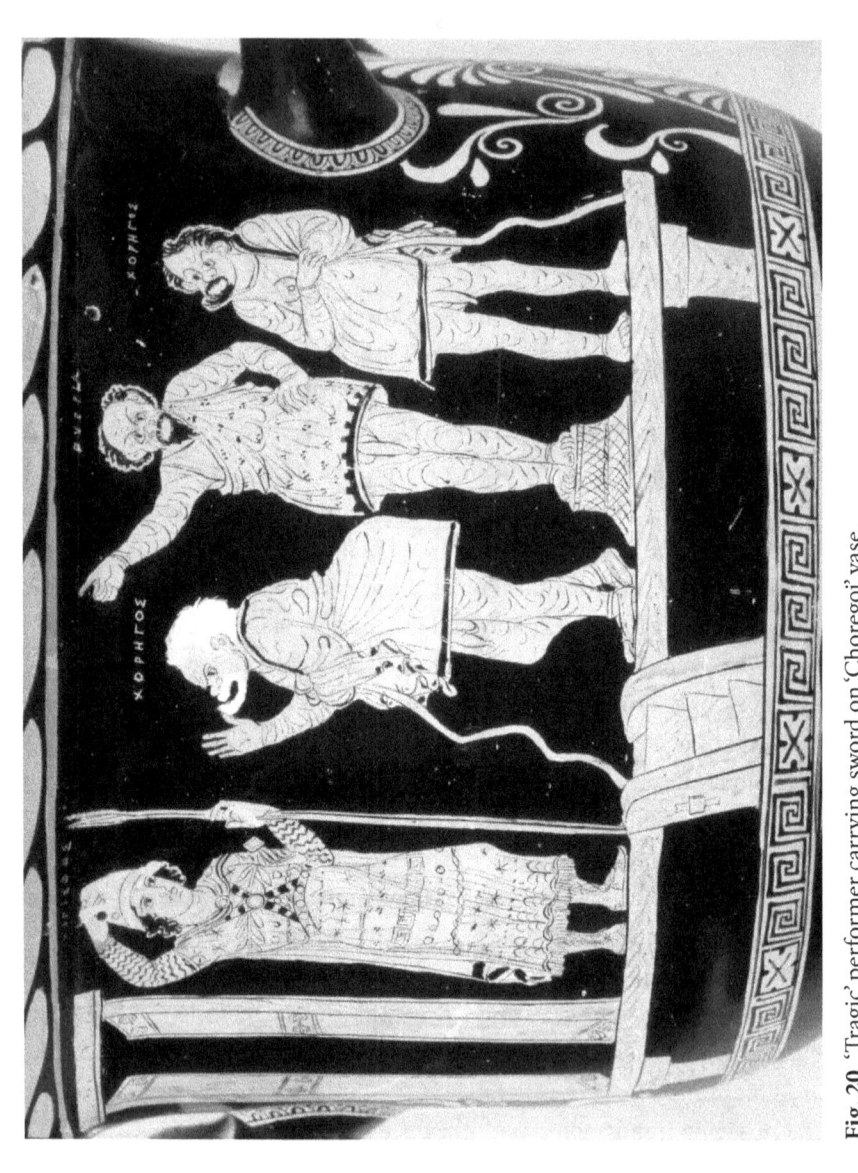

Fig. 20 'Tragic' performer carrying sword on 'Choregoi' vase.

parody of a tragic character. The sword that he carries (its hilt visible at his left side), along with the two spears is one of the indicators that marks this character as 'tragic'.[9]

The tragic sword's association with violence is evoked even more strikingly on the Apulian bell-krater attributed to the 'Reckoning Painter' and dated to the second quarter of the fourth century BC.[10] The performance it depicts is still sometimes categorized as a 'phlyax' drama, despite arguments for such an independent theatrical tradition having been called into question long ago.[11] The decisive evidence of the 'Telephus' parody vase, discussed below, suggests that the 'Reckoning Painter' image may also be linked to Attic drama.[12] The costumes, including masks, make it clear that this is a comic scene though arrestingly, two men are shown waving swords in the air, either side of a female character (on her knees) whom they each grab. The scene's violence is initially shocking, but the characters' costumes and comic bodies soon negate any anxiety generated by the sight of the swords.[13] This image highlights the important role of the *visual* to the deflation of the sword on the comic stage – even before the prop's symbolism has been undercut through *verbal* manipulation, the comic world's aesthetic detracts from the imminent violence the sword is understood to hold on the tragic stage and in the real world.[14]

The same effect, and more, is revealed in the better-known example of the fourth-century Apulian bell-krater by the Schiller painter, dated to *c.* 370 BC, which has been convincingly linked to the parody of Euripides' *Telephus* in Aristophanes' *Thesmophoriazusae* (689–761).[15] The comic framing is shown to rely on props as well as costumes and masks in this vase.[16] The Kinsman, disguised as a woman, clasps a dagger in one hand and a wineskin wearing booties in the other; the mother of the 'baby' rushes up from the left with a 'giant drinking cup'.[17] The composition demonstrates precisely the ways in which heightened tragic moments generated from the use of the sword could be deflated by their transposition onto the comic stage.[18] The framing of the prop, juxtaposed as it is with comic masks, a demonstrably 'fake' baby, and over-sized wine cup (which confirm that it is alcohol and not blood that is at risk of being spilt) detracts from its tragic power. The 'comic' props (wineskin and drinking cup) counterbalance the impact of the dagger – it has the central position in the composition and yet the comic body and comic prop flanking it reassure the viewer. Directly above the dagger is a mirror (the blade points to it, drawing the eye upwards), which can be taken as an indexical element in the composition, evoking the earlier cross-dressing scene in the play.[19] The effect is to bring to mind the humour of that episode and to reinforce the comic framing of this one. The dagger's immersion in the comic context neuters its tragic effect.

It is significant that the tragic sword is allowed to keep its form in this parody (since while it is described in the play as a 'dagger', this is simply a diminished sword).[20] The similarity in form of the parodic substitute to the original prop is highlighted by considering the difference of approach taken with the wineskin. The alarming prospect of seeing an enactment of the baby being threatened with the blade is dispersed through the use of a comic substitute that makes only a minimal, and farcical, attempt to imitate the object being represented.[21] The sword by contrast is allowed to retain the core of its tragic form, even if it is literally diminished in the process of being transposed onto the comic stage.[22] This 'shrinking' of the tragic in physical terms eloquently reflects the broader strategy of bringing down the grandeur of the rival genre through parody. The 'shrinking' is not so drastic here, however, as it is in the case of the Aeschylean voting urns in *Wasps* (on which see Chapter 2) and it is, above all, the comic world surrounding the blade that renders its threat negligible.[23] This is important since the power is being removed from a prop that tragic dramaturgy had linked to its contemporary counterpart in society. It is not just the sword's tragic status that is challenged, but also its ideological symbolism. The treatment of the tragic sword in this parody, and in the depiction of it on this vase, hints towards the strategies that Aristophanes deploys in handling the perception of the hoplite armour that he presents on stage (see below).

A greater appreciation of Aristophanes' negotiation of the tragic sword and the implications of this for the Athenian audience can be gained from the examination of two further examples of its presence on the comic stage. *Acharnians*, performed in 425 BC and our earliest fully extant play by Aristophanes, also includes a parody of the hostage scene from *Telephus*. In this iteration, the comic protagonist Dicaeopolis takes a charcoal basket and threatens to 'kill' it if the Chorus of Acharnians do not allow him to speak (*Ach*. 325–51).[24] This parody (which predates the other by fourteen years) is significant since it offers an explicit reference to the prop as a sword (ξίφος, 342). Moreover, the association of the prop with tragedy is reinforced through the language used to describe its anticipated action; the threat of the sword is emphasized by a series of verbs linked to violent slaughter on the tragic stage (esp. 327 ἀποσφάζω, 331 διαφθείρω, 335 ἀποκτείνω, 336 ἀπόλλυμι). The use of 'trigger' words, associated with the prop's symbolic status in tragedy, heighten the stakes especially if the sword on stage maintains its tragic form (as it may well have in this parody).[25] It demonstrates the absolute confidence that the comic world, visually surrounding the sword on stage (particularly through the bodies of the chorus and, of course, the substitute prop for hostage) combined with the undercutting of the tragic words with comic puns, is enough to diffuse the tragic sword's effect.[26]

The self-consciousness of this engagement, and awareness of the different 'rules' for this prop in the two genres, is highlighted by Dicaeopolis' reflection on the episode after he has agreed to put the sword down (347–51):[27]

ἐμέλλετ' ἄρ' ἅπαντες ἀνασείειν βοήν,
　　ὀλίγου τ' ἀπέθανον ἄνθρακες Παρνάσιοι,
　　καὶ ταῦτα διὰ τὴν ἀτοπίαν τῶν δημοτῶν.
　　ὑπὸ τοῦ δέους δὲ τῆς μαρίλης μοι συχνὴν
　　　　ὁ λάρκος ἐπετίλησεν ὥσπερ σηπία.

So you were all getting ready to shake your shouts at me, and some Parnasian coals were very nearly killed, and all because of their fellow demesmen's eccentricity. And in its fear this basket has dirtied me with a load of coal dust, like a squid.

His claim that the coals were 'very nearly killed' (348), generates humour through being false in two respects. The coals as inanimate objects were never at risk, although part of the fun of this substitute prop in the parody, highlighted by this speech too, is that it is endowed with human attributes (which simultaneously points to the over-attachment of the Acharnians to their deme's produce).[28] The idea that the coals were 'very nearly killed' would be appropriate in tragedy, a genre which accommodated death and thrived on near misses, but its incongruity here only serves to highlight that the sword would never have been used in such a violent way within the genre of comedy.[29] Dicaeopolis, in playing along with the dramatic logic of the parody and emphasizing its near-tragic consequences, underlines this generic difference while also setting up the joke that reinforces it.[30] We are told (350–1) that the basket, in its fear, has 'voided excrement' (in the form of a load of coal dust) on Dicaeopolis, just like a cuttlefish [ejecting its ink].[31] This deceptively simple joke presents a complex nexus of images including one implied by the paratragic context. In tragedy, the sword can impose a fatal wound that is described in graphic terms as spurting blood.[32] Within the comic frame, the sword's impact produces a different kind of release with the blood being substituted through engagement in characteristic scatological humour.[33] The careful choice of vocabulary ('τιλάω is not merely "shit" but more precisely "have a loose diarrhoeic discharge"') modifies this common Aristophanic motif to allow the comparison to ink as well as to blood to be made.[34] The cuttlefish imagery reinforces the idea of the spurting blood-like liquid as well as the context of danger.[35] The simile also self-consciously matches the elaborate graphicness of tragic descriptions for blood. The pretension, however, is undercut by the slapstick visual humour of the stage image in front of the audience – Dicaeopolis covered in black coal dust. This 'reality' creates a safe distance from all three figurative images (diarrhoea, ink, and (implied) blood).[36] The parody undermines the imminent violence implied by the tragic sword through the visual juxtaposition of it with explicitly comic props and through the comic reinterpretation of its impact (mess, not death).[37] As a statement about tragedy, this sequence takes on fresh meaning after Dicaeopolis' visit to Euripides' house (393–479).[38] It has been argued that one of the intended effects of Dicaeopolis' visit is to highlight Euripides' over-reliance on props in his tragedies.[39] From this perspective, the hostage parody prepares the audience for this challenge to tragedy's dramaturgy by highlighting the props' vulnerability to comic undercutting.

The engagement with the sword in this comedy, however, is not only significant for the stance it presents towards tragedy.[40] It also has implications for the audience's perception of this object's status in society. It is significant that later in the same comedy, Lamachus appears in full panoply (*Ach.* 572). The direct identification between this comic character and the real-life military commander (he represents) asserts the relationship between the armour on stage and its counterparts in contemporary Athens.[41] Moreover, the shield prop seems to have been designed to evoke the piece of armour that Lamachus used on the battlefield.[42] The audience are invited therefore to identify the weapons making up Lamachus' armour on stage as the same objects that a hoplite might use in war. The contemporary setting of comedy means that the effect of this is perhaps not as startling as it would be in tragedy.[43] Yet, the prominent awareness of these props' social lives makes their treatment on the comic stage significantly loaded since it offers a direct opportunity to impact on views of the object outside the theatre. To this end, it is important to recognize that the comic setting is itself disarming – Lamachus' appearance in full panoply, including a sword, at 572, would look as incongruous as Aegisthus on the Choregoi vase (Fig. 20) or as the sword in the Telephus hostage scene.[44] Aristophanes, however, goes much further than mere visual juxtaposition in his comic strategy to deflate the power of these symbols and to derive humour from them. The armour is systematically ridiculed, piece by piece, by Dicaeopolis from its helmet crests (575, 584–9) to its apotropaic shield device (580–3) and its sword (591–2).[45] A range of strategies is used to subvert the grandeur of the armour, including its disempowerment through the expression of faux fear and its debasement by its misappropriation (as vomit stick and bowl).[46] These strategies suggest that the props are not comic substitutes but are real pieces of armour (or at least look like them) since the joke lies in the re-contextualizing and repurposing of familiar objects from the battlefield. Crowning this insulting appropriation of the pieces of armour is the suggestion made by Dicaeopolis for how Lamachus could use the sword to prove his strength (590–2):

ΛΑΜΑΧΟΣ
οἴμ᾽ ὡς τεθνήξεις.

ΔΙΚΑΙΟΠΟΛΙΣ
μηδαμῶς, ὦ Λάμαχε·
οὐ γὰρ κατ᾽ ἰσχύν ἐστιν· εἰ δ᾽ ἰσχυρὸς εἶ,
τί μ᾽ οὐκ ἀπεψώλησας; εὔοπλος γὰρ εἶ.

Lamachus
Oh! Now you're doomed!

Dicaeopolis
Not at all, Lamachus! It's not a matter of strength – though if you're really strong, why not peel back my foreskin? You're well enough equipped!

Lamachus reacts to Dicaeopolis' insult over the provenance of his helmet crests (589) by threatening to kill him (590), using an expression of despair (οἴμοι) and verb (θνήσκω) germane to tragedy.[47] The threat is diffused through the comic obscenity, and absurdity, of Dicaeopolis' response and the attention it draws to a prominent, and iconic, part of the comic costume (its phallus). The joke operates on two levels, referring either to the possibility of Lamachus circumcising Dicaeopolis with his sword or sexually arousing him with his phallus.[48] Though the first reading of the joke can be taken as an 'abject surrender' by Dicaeopolis, importantly the spectre of violence lurking in this suggestion fades with the realization that the proposed action would affect a self-consciously artificial, and comic, part of the costume.[49] The phallus in this respect plays the equivalent role of the charcoal basket in dispelling audience anxiety over proposed violence and diminishing the symbolic status of the sword. The first reading of the joke pits the sword against the phallus in a neat encapsulation of the contest between comedy and tragedy pervading this play.[50] The alternative reading of the comment as a sexual proposition goes even further in undermining the sword. The double entendre of εὔοπλος (592, well-equipped) equates Lamachus' sword to his comic phallus.[51] The sword, which had been allowed to enter the comic frame in its battlefield form, here becomes transformed, being in effect substituted by the phallus through this joke.[52] Even more significantly, this forms part of a network of references to this comic attribute in this 'very phallocentric play'.[53] The phallus is aligned, particularly at the end of the play, with peace and the pleasures this brings (in explicit contrast to war and its pain, see, for example, 1216–17).[54] The substitution of the sword for the phallus in this scene, therefore, marks more than the contestation of its status as a tragic prop, the episode also enacts Dicaeopolis' wish for peace by disarming, even if only metaphorically, warmongers such as Lamachus.[55]

The choice to represent Lamachus' sword as simultaneously belonging to the world of tragedy and to the contemporary battlefield is telling. Aristophanes acknowledges tragedy's strategic linking of its violence to the audience's experience and seeks to undermine the sword's symbolic power both on the tragic stage and on the battlefield. The continuity implied visually by the prop, between the tragic parody earlier in the play and Lamachus' appearance, is therefore vital. The connection between the scenes is further reinforced through the verbal echo between 350 and 581. The same phrase ὑπὸ τοῦ δέους is used by Dicaeopolis to explain the basket's response to the sword and his own feigned reaction to the shield. The parallel invites the consideration of the tragic weapon (the parodied sword) and Lamachus' weapons as equivalent. This is further reinforced by the ways in which Lamachus comes to represent tragedy (in general) within the comedy.[56] Moreover, the language of violence used in the hostage scene works well with this doubling, belonging as much to the world of tragedy as it does to the description of real events in the Peloponnesian war.[57] The comic undermining of the sword prop in *Acharnians* is thus concerned with debunking the fear of the violence this object embodies both on the tragic stage and in society. This blending of the tragic and civic in the comic presentation confirms the perception of tragedy's intersection with, and relevance to, the real-life symbolic objects of society. It suggests that the deflation of one type of sword could stand for the other (and vice versa). Aristophanes applies the same treatment to both, reducing them through the tools of his trade (scatological humour, absurdity, and obscenity). The targeting of the grandeur of tragic effect and the seriousness of war in society in this way generates humour and perhaps even some relief.[58] The sword's ability to embody the suffering of war in art outside the theatre, exemplified by the white-ground *lekythos* discussed in Chapter 3 (Fig. 17), suggests that its comic disempowerment went beyond concerns with generic discourse or lampooning of an individual (or class of individual).[59] The comedy offers an antidote to the sword's symbolism in the context of loss.[60] In the realm of comedy, it is not a fatal weapon – it is the opportunity for a joke; in this sense, the genre is not as 'honest' with the audience as Aristophanes implies.[61] How far the laughter, and the strategy it represents, carried beyond the experience of the play is difficult to establish.[62] Beneath the humour, Aristophanes' treatment of the prop points to the complex nexus of associations established for this symbolic object through the intersection between its dramatic (tragic and comic) handling and the civic experience. This in turn points to the complexity, and significance, of theatre's relationship with the citizen's sense of identity. The examination of prop's intergeneric handling invites the comparison of each genre's 'tensions and ambiguities' in relation to civic ideology.[63] At the same time, comedy's renegotiation of the object's meaning highlights a key aspect of such symbols within society and simultaneously dispels and affirms the anxiety that this characteristic could generate.[64]

The generic and ideological implications of comedy's exploitation of the sword's symbolic status in society can be elucidated further through *Wasps*, staged in 422 BC. It is again a paratragic context that invites engagement with the symbolic associations of this prop. In the run-up to a debate with his son, the comic hero, Philocleon, calls for a sword and claims that he intends to fall on it if he loses (Ar. *Wasps* 522–3):[65]

> καὶ ξίφος γέ μοι δότε·
> ἢν γὰρ ἡττηθῶ λέγων σου, περιπεσοῦμαι τῷ ξίφει.
>
> And give me a sword. If I lose the debate to you, I'm going to fall on it!

The allusion to this prop, which is not yet on stage, provides a means of imposing (or attempting to impose) a tragic frame on the comic action.[66] It is not only the prop that is tragic but also Philocleon's reaction to the situation. The humour is created in the juxtaposition of the 'reality' of the comic playworld in which Philocleon's claims will never take place and the apparent sincerity with which he aspires to reframe the action as tragic (construing the debate as a matter of life and death).[67] The reference operates at further levels, however, since rather than simply evoking the general tragic associations of the sword, the phrase also makes a more precise allusion.[68] The reference to falling on a sword, as Biles and Olson recognize, evokes images of Ajax's violent death.[69] The stage image of the sword sticking out of the dummy in Sophocles' *Ajax* would, for those who had seen that production approximately twenty years earlier, hover behind Philocleon's words here.[70] The image though is soon banished through Bdelycleon's question in response to Philocleon's pronounced intention, as he asks what his father will do if he loses the debate (524).[71] By ignoring the threat made by Philocleon, Bdelycleon further dissipates the possibility of it being fulfilled. Philocleon's reply (525) confirms the reassertion of the comic frame through its pun about wine and jury pay.[72] Without the prop on stage in any case, the imminence of the threat is in the first place minimized (and therefore easier to demolish).[73] Once the prop is brought onto stage it is counterbalanced (just as the sword prop on the vase paintings were) by a comic prop, Bdelycleon's basket (κίστη).⁷⁴ His command for it to be brought out (529) mirrors Philocleon's request for a prop, as each equip themselves before the *agon*.⁷⁵ While the sword is associated with tragedy, Bdelycleon's prop sets him up as a representative of comedy, initially through its association with food and then, at the revelation of its contents (writing equipment), through its evocation of the playwright's craft.⁷⁶ Bdelycleon's prop is immediately put to use (538) whereas, in another exploitation of the comic potential to the phallic associations of ξίφος – Philocleon's 'sword', it is implied, has become floppy (714).⁷⁷ In this contest between the props, comedy wins.

From this perspective, the treatment of the sword presents a further example of Aristophanes exploiting its association with tragedy to be able to assert comedy's superiority. Yet here, too, there is more at the stake through the simultaneous engagement with the sword's meaning in society. The context for Philocleon's paratragic outburst invites his demand for a sword to be read through the model of the tyrannicides.⁷⁸ *Wasps* displays an intense engagement with the motif of conspiracies to overthrow the democracy which culminates, in the lines before Philocleon's request for a sword, in a series of full-blown accusations of tyranny.⁷⁹ The chorus levels this charge at Bdelycleon at 417, 464–5, and again at 487; he defends himself by objecting at some length to the bandying around of the term (488–99). Xanthias adds a memorably 'off-colour' example to corroborate Bdelycleon's claim that accusations of tyranny are rife (500–2).⁸⁰ This 'repeated and absurd' charge along with the vivid and humorous refutation of it could not be missed in performance and acts as 'false preparation' for Philocleon's demand for the sword.⁸¹ His initial demand at 522, 'give me a sword', leaves open the possibility that he intends to take up the stance of a tyrannicide. It is only his qualifying statement in the following line that determines that Ajax, or a similar tragic hero, is the image being evoked here. The explicit reference, later in the play, to the Harmodius drinking song, at 1225, seems to suggest that the tyrannicide was on Aristophanes' mind. Moreover, Xanthias' apparently gratuitous example of the charges of tyranny infiltrating the world of sex workers (500–2) in fact presents the opportunity to mention Hippias (the tyrant who survived the tyrannicides' plot).⁸² The raising of the possibility evokes associations with the sword, and its ideological meaning; the undermining of this prop therefore impacts not only on views of its grandeur in tragedy but also the sword's symbolic status in society. The two strands are difficult to separate here since tragedy exploited the sword's association with the tyrant slayers; offering Aristophanes the opportunity to reflect on both the nature of that tragic engagement and its intersection with society.⁸³ The absurdity of the claim about tyranny gains greater significance in this respect, since it is not only a comment upon a topical concern, or rather over-used political weapon, but also perhaps contests the status of democracy's 'foundational' myth and questions the aggrandizing of that myth through its retrojection into the tragic past.⁸⁴

The presentation of Philocleon stopping short of adopting the stance of a tyrannicide here may reveal more about Aristophanes' technique in general. When the motif is evoked in *Lysistrata* (630–5, discussed in Chapter 3), it is far more explicit and in the political circumstances, its debunking is more shocking.⁸⁵ It is also part of a sustained engagement with weapons in that play that presents the gesture as one of a series of disempowering subversions of pieces of armour.⁸⁶ The motif in *Wasps* is framed in a way that connects it with Cleon, through the assumption that the repeated accusations of tyranny reflect one of his political strategies and later through his imagined choice of song at the symposium being none other than the one about Harmodius (1225).⁸⁷ Philocleon's near adoption of the pose reflects Cleon's influence on the behaviour of his followers. The comic hero's failure to come good on the assumed trajectory of his demand for a sword, however, highlights the ineffectiveness of this group (ridiculing Cleon's apparent power). Moreover, the redirection of the intended use of the prop to evoke *Ajax* highlights the harm that association with Cleon might inflict. The comparison between the engagement with the motif in *Wasps* and *Lysistrata* is instructive as it highlights the different ways in which the tyrannicides could be exploited within comedy as well as demonstrating the ways in which a shift in the historical context might affect perceptions of their swords' status. The negotiation of the motif is not solely driven by a concern for its manipulation in tragedy. The sword, along with the voting urns and pebbles in the dog trial scene (on which see Chapter 2), are used to explore civic identity within this comedy.

Furthermore, it is possible that these lines also play out the intersection between comedy and contemporary experience without the filter of tragedy interposing. The humour to Philocleon's claim may be far darker, even than the evocation of the tragic hero Ajax implies. If, as Plutarch reports, the Athenian military commander Paches had killed himself in court at the outcome of his *euthyna* (trial of accountability after holding office) in 427 BC, then Philocleon's words and the prop, once it appears, would take on a profoundly unsettling dimension.⁸⁸ The evidence is problematic, and skepticism over its credibility remains, yet if Paches had killed himself in the court, then the play's sustained engagement with this institution would offer contextual support to the evocation of this recent event.⁸⁹ Moreover, Aristophanes demonstrates in *Frogs* his willingness to make this type of close-to-the-bone joke about deaths occurring in strikingly similar circumstances.[90] The event marked an aberration – the sword being used not on the battlefield but in an Athenian court, not against an enemy but to inflict a fatal wound on an Athenian. Its evocation in the comedy is at once alarming and reassuring. The initial allusion to the event must have created a frisson in the theatre audience, but this would soon be dissipated by the incongruity of the sword in a comic context, the knowledge that in the comic world it would not kill anyone, and its further debunking through the phallic humour at 714–15. The reference to Paches would therefore offer another opportunity for comedy to assert its function of rewriting the object's symbolism to offer temporary relief from its usual implications. This appropriation of tragedy's strategy and comic rewriting of the prop's symbolism, however, has a destabilizing effect on the object's affirmation of civic identity.

While this is far from exhaustive as a study of the sword on the comic stage, the selected examples offer insight into the range of strategies adopted by Aristophanes in his treatment of this prop. The 'rewriting' of the sword's symbolism in comedy through its subjection to the comic context, to phallic and scatological humour, to ridiculous repurposing, and its immersion into a world in which it is incapable of perpetrating violence, has implications for the object's status in tragedy and society. The sword afforded a particularly rich opportunity for comedy to engage in a dialectic with its rival genre and the world outside the theatre. The treatment of this prop by Aristophanes confirms his understanding of tragedy's exploitation of its civic symbolism and reveals his implicit censure of this strategy. He demonstrates that he can go further than tragedy in exploring the intersection by bringing Lamachus onto the stage and juxtaposing his sword with the paratragic one. This functions as a statement of comedy's superior suitability to pursue such a strategy and implies criticism of tragic trespass in co-opting contemporary objects into its dramatic frame.[91] A comment about the difference in the function of the two genres can also be understood from Aristophanes' transformation of the strategy's purpose. The comic playwright undermines, rather than reinforces, the horror associated with the sword in tragedy and real life. The figurative substitution of the sword with the phallus in *Acharnians* and *Wasps* invites positive associations with the festival context and its parades, celebrating this aspect of the civic experience in lieu of the battlefield and alluding to this alternative symbol of Athenian power.[92] What was the impact of this on the audience? While there might be benefit to diffusing anxiety, it is possible that the comic treatment of the sword also had a destabilizing effect on how an Athenian citizen thought about its civic symbolism. Reducing the brandished swords of

Harmodius and Aristogiton (in the case of *Wasps*), or hoplites, to phallic symbols created a counter-discourse.[93] This alternative interpretation of the object's meaning minimized its ideological status as a weapon of democracy, privileging instead a comic perspective on male identity (defined through the phallus).[94] This also had the potential to impact on tragedy's subsequent exploitation of the prop's symbolism. The performance memory of the tragic sword's treatment on the comic stage, which *inter alia* exposed and contested tragedy's strategy in appropriating such objects, could influence the audience's response. The 'redrawing' of the sword's symbolism was a dynamic process in operation between (and within) dramatic genres that simultaneously drew upon and shaped the object's civic meaning. The juxtaposition in this chapter between the discussion of the tragic sword within comedy and its subsequent manipulation in tragedy is intended to reflect that dynamic. The 'redrawing' of the sword in the final tragedy considered here implies a response to both its tragic past and its handling on the comic stage.[95]

II Swords redrawn again in *Phoenician Women*

The sword's heightened ideological significance in the final decade of the fifth century is reflected by the intense engagement with this prop on the tragic stage. Two Euripidean tragedies dated to consecutive years in this decade, *Phoenician Women* (409 BC) and *Orestes* (408 BC), reveal a notable focus on the sword.[96] The address of topical concerns in these plays both explains and shapes the exploitation of this prop.[97] The heated debate on tyranny in *Phoenician Women* frames this focal prop in an arrestingly contemporary way, allowing it to intersect with the recent introduction of the oath of ideological allegiance instituted on the suggestion of Demophantus in 410/409 BC after the fall of the oligarchy.[98] The oath as an unprecedented act would have made this 'a significant and highly memorable moment in late-fifth century Athens.'[99] This, together with the probable swearing of the oath just before the Dionysia (or even in the theatre itself), primed the audience to make the connection between the prop and the tyrannicides' swords.[100] Euripides exploited this to mark his tragedy out from previous dramatic treatments of the myth, highlighting the topicality of its action through this means and ensuring its impact on the audience. The manipulation of this civic symbol, particularly at a time of crisis, interrogates notions of Athenian identity (and problematizes its ideals).[101]

The sword represents a complex nexus of ideas within the tragedy; Euripides interweaves the prop's symbolism within the framework of the myth with its meaning in fifth-century Athens so that the dramatic action's outcome gains topical resonance. Through the framing of the prop, the curse of Oedipus (which determines the violence perpetrated by the sword in the play) is made to resonate with the oath of Demophantus and its call to action. This dramaturgical strategy allows Euripides to invite the Athenian audience to reflect upon the implications of the ideological position that had just, through communal participation in the oath, been acknowledged (and performed) as central to civic identity. The play's conspicuous network of references to the sword evidences Euripides' sustained interest in defining, and redefining, its symbolism within the dramatic action.[102] It embodies violence, as we might expect, but more particularly it is framed as an instrument of fate fulfilling both the oracle of Apollo and the curse of Oedipus.[103] Jocasta relates the oracle's warning to Laius that if he had a child he would be killed and his whole household would wade through blood (*Phoen.* 20). Through the action of the play, it is the sword that inflicts this bloodshed on members of the family, above all, on Polynices and Eteocles, but also on Jocasta and Menoeceus; and it is further associated with the threat of violence to Oedipus and Haemon.[104] The sword as the means through which Oedipus' curse is accomplished is vividly, and explicitly, encapsulated in Antigone's response to her father's query about how his sons had died (*Phoen.* 1555–9):[105]

ΑΝΤΙΓΟΝΗ
οὐκ ἐπ' ὀνείδεσιν οὐδ' ἐπιχάρμασιν,
ἀλλ' ὀδύναισι λέγω· σὸς ἀλάστωρ
ξίφεσιν βρίθων
καὶ πυρὶ καὶ σχετλίαισι μάχαις ἐπὶ παῖδας ἔβα σούς,
ὦ πάτερ, ὤμοι.

Antigone
Not to reproach you nor to rejoice at your misfortune but in grief I tell you: the avenging spirit you sent forth, with its cargo of swords and fire and cruel battle, went against your sons, alas, dear father!

The idea of the sword's agency and its association with the fulfilment of the curse is set up earlier in the play. The dramatic focus on the sword, and tension associated with it, is established in the prologue (*Phoen.* 66–8) with the detail that the brothers would divide their inheritance with whetted iron. Jocasta refers to it again in her curse at the end of her 'highly charged operatic monody' (350–5).[106] She aligns the sword with strife and Oedipus, acknowledging that either might be blamed for her suffering. The words are made emphatic by her heightened emotion and the mode of their delivery. It is also significant that Polynices' sword has been prominently displayed and manipulated on stage before this (261-9) and that soon after her curse, he will refer again to that stage action (361-4). This has the effect of anchoring her words in a concrete stage reality. The sword becomes a visual embodiment of the danger posed by the curse. At the same time, the repeated references to the curse throughout the play reinforce the sense of inevitable momentum towards the swords' fatal use by its end. Her words are, therefore, part of a network of references that create a sense of determinism for the prop leading it to its fulfilment in the brothers' duel.[107] The careful manipulation of the verbal references to the curse complemented by the tension created through the focus on the dangerous potential of the visually present swords demonstrates Euripides' exploitation of the prop and its prominent contribution to the effect of the tragedy.

This dramatic effect, generated from the prop's mythological framework, is reinforced in the scene of Jocasta's attempted mediation between the brothers (*Phoen*. 261-637). The tension associated with the sword is heightened and gains contemporary impact through the evocation of the tyrannicides. The negotiation of the prop's symbolism begins with its first appearance, brandished by Polynices as he enters the city (*Phoen*. 261-77):

τὰ μὲν πυλωρῶν κλῇθρά μ' εἰσεδέξατο
δι' εὐπετείας τειχέων ἔσω μολεῖν.
ὃ καὶ δέδοικα μή με δικτύων ἔσω
λαβόντες οὐκ ἐκφρῶσ' ἀναίμακτον χρόα.
ὧν οὕνεκ' ὄμμα πανταχῇ διοιστέον
κἀκεῖσε καὶ τὸ δεῦρο, μὴ δόλος τις ᾖ.
ὡπλισμένος δὲ χεῖρα τῷδε φασγάνῳ
τὰ πίστ' ἐμαυτῷ τοῦ θράσους παρέξομαι.
ὠή, τίς οὗτος; ἢ κτύπον φοβούμεθα;
ἅπαντα γὰρ τολμῶσι δεινὰ φαίνεται,
ὅταν δι' ἐχθρᾶς ποὺς ἀμείβηται χθονός.
πέποιθα μέντοι μητρὶ κοὐ πέποιθ' ἅμα,
ἥτις μ' ἔπεισε δεῦρ' ὑπόσπονδον μολεῖν.
ἀλλ' ἐγγὺς ἀλκή (βώμιοι γὰρ ἐσχάραι
πέλας πάρεισι) κοὐκ ἔρημα δώματα·
φέρ' ἐς σκοτεινὰς περιβολὰς μεθῶ ξίφος
τάσδ' ἔρωμαι, τίνες ἐφεστᾶσιν δόμοις.

The gatekeepers' bolts have allowed me to pass easily inside the walls. And so I am afraid that having taken me within their net they will not let me go again without a wound. For this reason I must turn my eyes this way and that for fear of trickery. **With this sword in my hands** I shall give myself the confidence to venture on. Ah, who is that? Or am I starting at a mere noise? Everything seems frightful to bold men when their feet tread on their enemy territory. Still, I trust my mother – and at the same time mistrust her. She persuaded me to come here under a truce. But help is at hand (for an altar stands nearby) and the house is not without inhabitants: come, let me put my sword into the dark of its encasement and ask these women standing near the house who they are.

Polynices' explicit statement of his fear and his movement, turning his head this way and that (as the embedded stage direction (265–6) reveals), creates tension over imminent violence. The unsheathed sword held ready for action and, we can presume, turned in the direction of the noise at 269, contributes to the sense of foreboding.[108] This reading of the sword's meaning is reinforced again by Polynices as he tells his mother (*Phoen.* 361–4):

οὕτω δ' ἐτάρβησ' ἐς φόβον τ' ἀφικόμην
μή τις δόλος με πρὸς κασιγνήτου κτάνῃ,
ὥστε ξιφήρη χεῖρ' ἔχων δι' ἄστεως
κυκλῶν πρόσωπον ἦλθον.

But I'm terribly afraid that my brother will kill me by some trick, and so I have come through the city sword in hand and constantly looking around me.

By the association of the sword with mortal danger, tension is created before the appearance of Eteocles. The affectiveness of this staging depends on the audience's experience. Polynices' words and the sight of his sword could resonate with the audience in a profound way, perhaps evoking real-life images of violence. At the same time, the association of the prop with the stage memories of corpses would create a sense of anticipation from its presence; the prop's inevitable trajectory towards violence is reinforced at the end of the brothers' exchange. In the meantime, however, Eteocles' criticism of his brother at 515–17 projects a new meaning onto Polynices' sword. Rather than an instrument of self-defence, it is implicitly labelled an 'enemy's sword', highlighting Polynices' role in bringing danger to the city and associating this with the prop. The hostile dimension to his prop is further highlighted at the collapse of the mediation with its accompanying threat of drawing swords (*Phoen.* 592–7):

ΕΤΕΟΚΛΗΣ
τῶν μακρῶν δ' ἀπαλλαγεῖσα νουθετημάτων μ' ἔα.
καὶ σὺ τῶνδ' ἔξω κομίζου τειχέων, ἢ κατθανῇ.

ΠΟΛΥΝΕΙΚΗΣ
πρὸς τίνος; τίς ὧδ' ἄτρωτος ὅστις εἰς ἡμᾶς ξίφος
φόνιον ἐμβαλὼν τὸν αὐτὸν οὐκ ἀποίσεται μόρον;

ΕΤΕΟΚΛΗΣ
ἐγγύς, οὐ πρόσω, βέβηκεν· ἐς χέρας λεύσσεις ἐμάς;

ΠΟΛΥΝΕΙΚΗΣ
εἰσορῶ· δειλὸν δ' ὁ πλοῦτος καὶ φιλόψυχον κακόν.

Eteocles: And you take yourself outside the walls – or you're a dead man
Polynices: And who's going to kill me? Who is so invulnerable that he can thrust his murderous sword at me and not receive the death he would inflict?
Eteocles: He's standing nearby, not far off. Are you looking at my hands?
Polynices: I'm looking. But Mr. Wealth's a cowardly warrior, afraid to lose his life.

The tension created by the prop's earlier brandishing on stage culminates in this intense exchange that seems close to descending into physical violence.[109] It seems likely from Eteocles' taunt at 596 that he had drawn his sword and Polynices' subsequent claim (that soon his sword would no longer hesitate to be bloodied, 625) suggests that he wields his too. The props, visually mirroring each other on the stage, are given equal symbolic meaning as bloody instruments of reciprocal death.[110] This association with blood enables the prop to intersect with another prominent network of imagery in the play, setting the fraternal hostility (and associated symbolism of the sword) within a wider framework of violence.[111] The stage presence of the props while these words of menace are spoken by each brother is important dramaturgically. The audience experience the imminent violence and unrelenting hostility marked through the drawn swords.[112] They also see the prop and, through the explicit verbal cues, understand its destined end.[113] The acknowledgement of the sword's agency, implied by Jocasta (350–5), reinforces this. While there are extensive references to the spear in the play, therefore, it is the sword that, through its powerful stage presence before the messenger speech and revelation of the corpses, has the more significant role in creating tense anticipation over the inevitable deaths of the brothers.[114]

This battle over the sword's meaning and display of imminent violence gains particular significance and resonance for Athenian audience members through this scene's prominent concern with the theme of tyranny.[115] In the *agon*, Polynices introduces the term in his criticism of Eteocles' actions, accusing him of breaking his oath to the gods and holding onto power (τυραννίς) for himself

(*Phoen.* 481–3). Eteocles' response to this charge, emphatically placed as the first in his speech, takes an unexpected form (*Phoen.* 504–8):

ἄστρων ἂν ἔλθοιμ' αἰθέρος πρὸς ἀντολὰς
καὶ γῆς ἔνερθε, δυνατὸς ὢν δρᾶσαι τάδε,
τὴν θεῶν μεγίστην ὥστ' ἔχειν Τυραννίδα.
τοῦτ' οὖν τὸ χρηστόν, μῆτερ, οὐχὶ βούλομαι
ἄλλῳ παρεῖναι μᾶλλον ἢ σῴζειν ἐμοί·

> I would go to where heaven's constellations rise, go beneath the earth, if it lay in my power, in order to possess Tyranny, greatest of the gods. Hence, mother, I do not want to yield this good to another: I want to keep it myself.

In this startling line of defence, Eteocles justifies his actions through the glorification of tyranny which he not only personifies but also sets at the head of the pantheon. In a further shocking statement, he offers a focalized description of autocratic power as χρηστός (good).[116] This formulation must have sounded oxymoronic to Athenian ears.[117] In fact, since Athenian citizens had just sworn an oath to act against anyone who aimed to become a tyrant in Athens, the impact of these words could well have been visceral.[118] This effect is further heightened by the ending to Eteocles' speech in which he proclaims boldly that he will keep hold of tyranny even in the face of warfare (*Phoen.* 521–5):[119]

πρὸς ταῦτ' ἴτω μὲν πῦρ, ἴτω δὲ φάσγανα,
ζεύγνυσθε δ' ἵππους, πεδία πίμπλαθ' ἁρμάτων,
ὡς οὐ παρήσω τῷδ' ἐμὴν τυραννίδα.
εἴπερ γὰρ ἀδικεῖν χρή, τυραννίδος πέρι
κάλλιστον ἀδικεῖν, τἄλλα δ' εὐσεβεῖν χρεών.

> Since this is so, let fire come, let swords advance, yoke your horses, fill the plains with chariots! For I shall never surrender my tyranny to him. If one must commit injustice, it is best to do so for the sake of tyranny, being god-fearing in all else.

The violent action taken against Eteocles to take his tyranny from him, though exaggerated in form, can be read through the lens of the Athenian call to action against would-be tyrants. The emphatically placed individual mention of swords (at the end of line 521), though part of a collective description for war, is important since for the Athenian audience member, already thinking of the oath and the act of the tyrannicides, it asserts the symbolic meaning of the sword as a tool against tyranny in this play. The explicit blasphemy of Eteocles' words here, and in his earlier suggestion that tyranny is the greatest of the gods (*Phoen.* 506), confirms the negative alignment of his views.[120] The audience is not being asked to adjust their perspective to a playworld in which tyranny is represented as desirable and divinely supported. Instead, Jocasta's speech confirms that an Athenian perspective on tyranny is retrojected into the mythological setting as she questions her son's choice to honour tyranny excessively and highlights the suffering that he will bring to the city by choosing it (*Phoen.* 549–50 and 559–67). The provocative engagement with this motif is designed to evoke the Athenian experience; a strategy which is evident elsewhere in the play.[121] Eteocles' brazen words about tyranny, and the bringing of swords against it, cue the imaging of Polynices with his sword, which has been prominently displayed on stage, as a would-be tyrant killer. This is further supported by his alignment with democratic values, made conspicuously explicit in his earlier claim, to his mother, that the greatest hardship of exile is the loss of παρρησία ('freedom of speech', *Phoen.* 391).[122] Euripides, thus, invests the familiar myth of the seven against Thebes with a fresh topicality and in the process, complicates views of the sword and Athenian tyrant slaying.[123]

The delay between the oath's approval and its institution in Athens would have allowed Euripides to take it into account when composing *Phoenician Women*.[124] His treatment of the sword in the play problematizes this civic effort to reframe Athenian identity and offer a positive assertion of democracy's resistance to overthrow.[125] The ending of the *agon* with swords drawn underlines this. The sense of imminent violence expressed by that stage action makes real the implications of the Demophantus oath and highlights the probability of retaliation to any action against tyranny; reminding the audience perhaps that the tyrant slayers had themselves been killed.[126] Polynices' words, seemingly intended as a warning to Eteocles, in fact resonate beyond the frame of the play (*Phoen.* 594–5):

ΠΟΛΥΝΕΙΚΗΣ
πρὸς τίνος; τίς ὧδ' ἄτρωτος ὅστις εἰς ἡμᾶς ξίφος
φόνιον ἐμβαλὼν τὸν αὐτὸν οὐκ ἀποίσεται μόρον;

Polynices: And who's going to kill me? Who is so invulnerable that he can thrust his murderous sword at me and not receive the death he would inflict?

Moreover, the image of swords drawn had earlier been established in iconography as the antithesis to the democratic way to resolve matters.[127] This is exemplified through the early fifth-century Brygos cup that shows on one of its sides, the quarrel over arms of Achilles; Fig. 12 (upper side).[128] The sense of imminent violence is conveyed through the way in which the warriors have to be restrained by those around them. The better preserved of the two warriors, shown at the top left of the image (Ajax), is shown with his sword being held back by one figure, while another grasps its scabbard.[129] This scene is set in contrast to the orderly voting depicted on the other side of the cup. Together the two scenes offer the viewer alternative approaches to resolving the issue, the more peaceful of the two functioning as a celebration of Athenian democratic processes.[130] The neat division between the two approaches, however, is blurred by the Euripidean scene that shows swords drawn after evoking the democratic symbolism of that weapon. Polynices' nervy entry into the city is worth further consideration in this respect. Part of the power of its effect is in the unexpected sight of the sword being drawn within the urban space (highlighted by his explicitly marked action of putting it away when he encounters the group of Phoenician women (276–7)). The same incongruity of weapons within Athens is exploited to comic effect in *Lysistrata* through the protagonist's ridiculing of armed men shopping at the market (555–64).[131] The tragic scene, however, through the focus on the weapon and emphasis on the potential ambush, creates a battlefield of the city. The oath, it could be argued, envisaged the same, by inviting civic violence in response to the threat to democracy. The prominent honouring of Thrasybulus with a gold crown for his role in the assassination of the oligarch Phrynichus (witnessed by the audience in the theatre before this play) is thus problematized by the play's action.[132]

Euripides explores the implications of the sword as instrument of civic violence further through the subsequent multiplication of suffering in the play; especially through the sword-inflicted deaths of Menoeceus and Jocasta (both, tellingly, additions to the myth).[133] Though Menoeceus' patriotism is praised by the chorus (*Phoen.* 1054–9), his self-slaughter for the city is significantly undercut by its near trivialization within the play's scheme. This effect is achieved through only the briefest of attention being given to this heroic deed at the beginning of the messenger speech (1090–2). There is no pathos to the messenger's account of the young man's death, the description is blandly factual and vivid only in its detail about the sword.[134] Menoeceus' sacrifice is simply a precursor to the battle, meriting not even its own sentence.[135] When the opportunity for pathos arises, with Creon lamenting his son as he brings the corpse onto stage (*Phoen.* 1307–21), here again the focus soon shifts away from Menoeceus; first by the news that Jocasta has left for the battlefield (1322) and then by the arrival of the messenger (1332). Menoeceus' death is presented as merely collateral and the glory it wins in compensation is minimal.[136] The death of Jocasta, by contrast, as a victim of events, inflicting her wound not through the force of an ineluctable curse or through patriotism but through grief, gains much greater emphasis.[137] The detail that she killed herself using the sword belonging to one of her sons is particularly effective, since it highlights an unanticipated aspect to the prop's determinism.[138] Both Menoeceus' and Jocasta's deaths draw attention, in different ways, to the multiplication of violence arising from Polynices' taking up of arms. The triumphant aspect to the sword of the would-be tyrant killer is eclipsed by the suffering that this play presents.[139] The intermeshing of the symbolism of the tyrant slayers' swords within the complex of imagery associated with the brothers' duel reinvents the myth for 409 BC and challenges the audience to reflect on their identity in the aftermath of recent violence and their sworn promise to perpetrate further bloodshed if necessary.[140]

The significant emphasis given to swords in the myth's reframing is reinforced by the comparison that Euripides invites between his play and Aeschylus' *Seven Against Thebes*.[141] Amongst the plays' shared motifs is Oedipus' curse as a dominating force in the action.[142] In Aeschylus' tragedy, the chorus describe Oedipus' prediction that wielding iron his sons would one day divide his property (*Sept.* 727–33 and 785–90).[143] The form of the weapon, however, is far less explicit than in Euripides' play.[144] In the later tragedy, it is essential that the sword is given prominence as the fatal weapon since it allows for the effective intersection of the myth with contemporary ideological concerns (as well as the powerful stage image of counter-balanced drawn swords). *Phoenician Women* is markedly different from *Seven Against Thebes* in this respect, yet at the same time Euripides owes a debt to Aeschylus' *Oresteia* for the provocative theatrical appropriation of this symbol of civic identity.[145] The extent of the suffering caused by the curse and fatal weapon is deliberately expanded in Euripides' version. This is highlighted through the emphasis on the three deaths and three corpses on stage, which outdoes the Aeschylean focus on the double death.[146] The purpose of this is not simply to compete with the earlier playwright but to stress the critical nature of the situation in 409 BC.[147]

The traces of engagement with Sophocles' *Ajax* point to a similar intention. In the text of the play that survives, Euripides twice makes direct reference to battlefield *sphagia* (*Phoen.* 173–4 and 1110).[148] The first of these references sets the sacrifices in a negative light, allowing them to 'presage' the Argive defeat and introducing the 'sinister' imagery of the bloodthirsty earth.[149] It also offers a backdrop for the later hints towards Menoeceus' sacrifice as a kind of *sphagia* for the Theban side. This is suggested through the use of σφάζω and its cognates to describe the act of killing (913, 933, 964, 1010).[150] Moreover, the emphasis on the blood of the slaughter and its fall to the ground reinforces the characterization of this killing as a form of *sphagia*.[151] The messenger's description of this sacrifice as a precursor to battle and the detail of the sword being plunged into the throat (1090–2) leaves no doubt as to the deliberate rapport between his death and battlefield *sphagia*.[152] The description of the action as a self-slaughter (1010 and 1316) highlights the perversity of this so-called *sphagia* and reveals Euripides' adoption of one of Sophocles' strategies for marking the transgressive nature and horror of Ajax's suicide (see Chapter 4). The exploitation of the symbolic status of battlefield *sphagia* in both tragedies and presentation of a near travesty of it within the dramatic action must have been unsettling for the Athenian audience. Euripides reinforces this effect by denying a sense of ritual restoration. Creon's desire for burial rites, which would enact this restoration, remains unfulfilled as his quest for Jocasta (to tend to Menoeceus' corpse) proves futile.[153] Despite the nobility of Menoeceus' action (1314), we will not see him receiving the care that is eventually promised to Ajax nor will his corpse be allowed to dominate the action (as Ajax's does in the final part of the Sophoclean tragedy). The evocation of *Ajax*, therefore, highlights the grimness of the world of *Phoenician Women* in which Menoeceus shows himself to be a model citizen, giving his life for the city, only to be sidelined. This corroborates Euripides' interest in using past productions to define his play's statement about the city's contemporary situation. He profits from Sophocles' dramaturgic strategy (exploiting the sword's symbolic importance in *sphagia*), while also outdoing it by presenting the sword's role in ritual perversion as a community-approved action taken by a patriotic citizen and by layering this association of the sword on top of the symbolism evoked from engagement with the tyrannicide motif; his dramatic statement and the urgency with which it confronts notions of identity is emphatic.

The performance proximity of *Lysistrata* in 411 BC and its shared, and explicit, engagement with the motif of tyranny and the tyrant slayers is also worth considering. Euripides' treatment of swords in *Phoenician Women* reveals the way in which the tragic status of the prop could continue to be exploited, despite its comic deflation (explored above). Moreover, it demonstrates an example of a tragic playwright reclaiming one of the prop's interfaces with society from comedy. In *Lysistrata*, Aristophanes exploits the cultural status of the tyrannicides as role models, exploring the implications of this to produce a ridiculously incongruous onstage travesty of the familiar statue (as discussed in Chapter 3). Euripides returns to the motif and invests it with ethical complexity, exposing its tragic ramifications within his play. His choice to engage with the symbolism of the tyrannicides' swords seems likely to have been motivated, as suggested above, by the introduction of Demophantus' oath. A corollary of this, however, is that Euripides' tragedy offers a response to Aristophanes' *Lysistrata*. The difference in treatment highlights the change in political circumstances but also makes a statement about generic definition; moreover, it demonstrates Euripides' artistry in being able to make the comic serious again.[154] At the same time, while the ridiculing of the aspiration to be like Harmodius in *Lysistrata* may have asserted a marginally destabilizing influence on society, the grim implications of Polynices taking up his sword seem far more disquieting.

The cultural impact of the tragedy in the theatrical sphere was marked by responses to it in comedy. A surviving fragment of Aristophanes' *Phoenician Women* (fr. 570), which is assumed to have offered an extended parody of Euripides' play, reveals that the presentation of the single combat was targeted in particular.[155] The fragment is quoted by Athenaeus in a passage discussing hoplite fighting.[156] The comic over-emphasis on the framing of the contest as a one-to-one combat resulting in two deaths does not detract from the potential of this parody to remind the audience of the messenger's description of the fatal blows and the powerful way in which the play manipulated the sword to create the sense of inevitability to this ending.[157] The parody by Strattis, in a comedy of the same name, further corroborates the impact of the swords in Euripides' play.[158] Amongst the surviving eight fragments, fr. 47 and fr. 48 are of particular interest as they record lines spoken by Jocasta and intended to offer compressed comic parodies of two of her speeches in the Euripidean mediation scene.[159] It seems plausible, then, that the scene's debate between the brothers and drawn swords featured in the comedy. Even if the swords in this scene were subjected to the strategies employed by Aristophanes in the parodies discussed above, the evocation of the original is significant. It demonstrates the impression made by that specific scene and reinforces the original effect even while parodying it.

The play's influence can be detected outside theatre.[160] The impact of its tense action is even reported to have left its mark on those entering battle. Diodorus Siculus, the first-century BC Greek historian, records the following about the Athenian general Thrasybulus on the eve of the Battle of Arginusae (13.97.6–7):[161]

τῶν δ' Ἀθηναίων ὁ στρατηγὸς Θρασύβουλος, ὃς ἦν ἐπὶ τῆς ἡγεμονίας ἐκείνην τὴν ἡμέραν, εἶδε κατὰ τὴν νύκτα τοιαύτην ὄψιν· ἔδοξεν Ἀθήνησι τοῦ θεάτρου πλήθοντος αὐτός τε καὶ τῶν ἄλλων στρατηγῶν ἓξ ὑποκρίνεσθαι τραγῳδίαν Εὐριπίδου Φοινίσσας· τῶν δ' ἀντιπάλων ὑποκρινομένων τὰς Ἱκέτιδας δόξαι τὴν Καδμείαν νίκην αὐτοῖς περιγενέσθαι, καὶ πάντας ἀποθανεῖν μιμουμένους τὰ πράγματα τῶν ἐπὶ τὰς Θήβας στρατευσάντων. ἀκούσας δ' ὁ μάντις ταῦτα διεσάφει τοὺς ἑπτὰ τῶν στρατηγῶν ἀναιρεθήσεσθαι.

And in the case of the Athenians Thrasybulus their general, who held the supreme command on that day, saw in the night the following vision. He dreamed that he was in Athens and the theatre was crowded, and that he and six of the other generals were playing the *Phoenician Women* of Euripides, while their competitors were performing the *Suppliants*; and that it resulted in a 'Cadmean victory' for them and they all died, just as did those who waged the campaign against Thebes. When the seer heard this, he disclosed that seven of the generals would be slain.

Thrasybulus' vision of the generals performing in *Phoenician Women* is paradoxical. It offers concrete details of the theatrical experience (crowded and the verb for acting is used ὑποκρίνομαι). Yet the characters supposedly represented by the generals (the warriors of the seven against Thebes) remain offstage in the play (with the exception of Polynices).[162] How can we account for this play suggesting itself to Thrasybulus? Its recent performance, just a few years before the battle of Arginusae in 406 BC, might offer one explanation, although the other play mentioned in the passage dates to the 420s.[163] Far more compelling is the consideration of the one warrior who appears onstage in the play. The fraught use of Polynices' sword onstage offers a powerful symbol of the tension over imminent violence that pervades the play. The impact of this effect betrays itself in Thrasybulus' anxiety dream the night before battle. The anxiety appears misplaced since the seer's interpretation of the dream seems, in the event of the battle itself, to be wrong. It would turn out to be unexpectedly correct, however, for the six generals who were put to death by the Athenians after the battle.[164] The play's interest in problematizing the implications of democratic ideals, therefore, makes it a fitting choice and there is a dramatic irony to Thrasybulus being unaware of this. While the general could not have been conscious of the play's aptness in this respect, this could certainly have proved a decisive factor in Diodorus' choice to include this detail in his narrative. In his account of the generals' trial and execution, Diodorus is sympathetic to their fate and is critical of the Athenian demos for its treatment of them (13.101–3). It seems likely therefore that the historian would have welcomed the allusion's prompt to reflect on the problems of the democratic ideal.

The impact of *Phoenician Women* is in part the result of the powerful symbolism of its sword prop – as the embodiment of violence and yet also, an instrument for pursuing a 'just' cause. The object's power in performance is testimony to Euripides' skills as a playwright, redrawing its tragic force (after its treatment in comedy); it also highlights the potency of this symbol of civic identity. Its treatment in this drama both enriched and problematized its role in shaping the citizen, leaving behind an uncomfortable ambiguity to an object which was a critical part of both Athens' constructed past and present. The power of theatre to mediate its relationship with society through its objects, the complex richness of this negotiation (through the axis of theatre history and in response to political preoccupations) and its significance for civic identity has been set out through the consideration of the sword. In the final chapter, the conclusions of this sustained investigation are tested against, and further developed by, the example of the mask.

6

The Mask in Hand

This chapter explores the mask as a symbol of theatre's significance to civic identity. The City Dionysia's role in displaying Athenian ideology and scrutinizing it through its dramas is well established.[1] Moreover, theatre's importance to the city is underscored by its funding as a *leitourgia* ('public service').[2] Athenian pride in meting out justice and defending its democracy was matched by civic investment in theatre.[3] Citizen participation in dramatic choruses, and the rules against the inclusion of disfranchised citizens and non-citizens (*xenoi*) at the Dionysia, reinforced the perception of theatre as an expression of Athenian identity.[4] The citizen's right to perform in the chorus could be equated with his right to vote, to speak in the assembly, and to seek justice.[5] This points to this activity's significance to the construction of citizen identity.[6] The third-century travel writer Herakleides Kritikos acknowledges this when he describes 'sincere' Athenians as keen pupils of the arts and constant theatregoers.[7] The desire to learn the arts as well as watch them performed is presented as a civic ideal.[8] The acknowledgement of this ideal can be found already in the fifth century, through the military exemption available to men performing in the chorus.[9] Through this law, the society both authorized and validated its citizens' participation in this activity, demonstrating the civic value attached to it.[10]

From the chorus member's perspective, choral training and performance represented an enactment of his citizenship, as the exercise of a citizen right and contribution to society.[11] The *proagon*, which took place a few days before the production, offered the opportunity to display this formally as the unmasked citizen was presented as a cast member before his peers (reinforcing the social significance of his engagement in this activity).[12] At the same time as expressing civic identity, choral participation may have shaped it.[13] Choral performance's potential in this respect is closely examined in Plato's *Laws*.[14] The philosopher's exploration of this concept may have been prompted by a related phenomenon within Athenian society.[15] The collective experience of choral performance invited reflection upon the citizens' role within society.[16] Furthermore, *theatre* performance invited questions about identity, scrutinizing its stability and exposing its construction.[17] This impacted upon the view of the 'self' within society.[18] The citizen's adoption of another's identity, and especially his playing of the 'other', when performing in a dramatic chorus prompted such questions.[19] This set this type of chorus apart within Athenian society and allowed it to become associated with the exploration of citizen identity.[20] Moreover, the use of masks afforded the dramatic chorus a distinctive means of representing the experience. The mask as a semiotic shorthand, and an object which existed both on and off stage, allowed for reflection upon the citizen's experience of performing in the theatre.[21] The iconographic treatment of the mask (explored below) engages with the facets of theatrical discourse that can be related to citizen identity: the celebration of theatre as an Athenian enterprise, its collective nature, the power of transformation and the experience of spectatorship. The simultaneous tension in the object's handling (in both art and theatre) reveals the anxieties it aroused and confirms the perceived high stakes of its symbolism. The mask carried meaning for the identity of all citizens, whether they were spectators or performers in the theatre festivals.[22]

The mask's operation as a symbol that both celebrates aspects of citizen identity and confronts latent anxieties about it is consistent with the *modus operandi* of voting equipment and sword (explored in the previous chapters). It is also comparable to voting equipment as a prop that reinforces its association with Athens through its 'anachronistic' effect within the world of tragedy.[23] However, the mask stands apart through the distinctive insights it offers into the theatre/society dialectic. While the previous chapters acknowledge this dialectic, the mask puts it into sharp relief as an object that becomes symbolically meaningful for society because of its existence in the theatre. Symptomatic of this difference is the mapping of the mask's 'social' life (section I) through the consideration of theatrical iconography. This closing case study also highlights a fresh complexity to the relationship between the object, its symbolism, and genre. The mask, through distinctive characteristics to its appearance, asserts the boundaries between dramatic genres.[24] Yet the iconographic record demonstrates that, as a symbol, it invites reflection on theatre's relationship to civic identity irrespective of genre. Furthermore, the pattern of this prop's 'stage life' (traced through satyr drama, comedy, and then tragedy) offers a valuable contribution to the study through disrupting any nascent assumptions about tragedy's primacy.[25] Finally theatre's interplay with iconography, explored briefly in the previous chapters, is here offered greater consideration. The close integration between the mask's 'social' and 'theatrical' life thus offers rewards alongside its challenges.[26]

I Society

The existence of the mask as a cultural entity outside the bounds of the theatre festival is well-established in scholarship.[27] Its 'social life' is strikingly evidenced by an Attic red-figure *chous*, dated to *c.* 420 BC, that shows two boys playing with a theatre mask.[28] The casual informality of the interaction, with the boys treating the mask as a plaything, demonstrates the presence of these objects in the fabric of everyday life.[29] The more formal aspects to the mask's 'social life', however, reveal the object's elevated significance and its symbolic status in relation to Athenian identity.[30] The dedication of theatre masks at the sanctuary of Dionysus after their use in performance is indicative of this.[31] One of the effects of the masks being displayed was to remind the viewer of the individual play which had been performed.[32] The mask also functioned, however, as an index sign for the performance context of the theatre festival.[33] In the case of the City Dionysia, the productions contributed to the display of Athenian wealth and power to the outside world.[34] The dedicated masks, as reminders of that festival, therefore symbolized the role of theatre in shaping external perceptions of Athens. This publicly displayed object, subjected to the communal gaze, prompted reflection on theatre performance as a civic activity which moulded and reaffirmed Athenian identity.[35]

The mask's status as a symbol of this is corroborated by its treatment in vase paintings that commemorate and celebrate the cultural institution of Athenian theatre. The Attic red-figure *pelike*, painted by the Phiale Painter and dated to *c.* 430 BC, which shows two chorus-men preparing to perform (Fig. 21), offers a compelling example of this.[36] One performer is already fully dressed in costume, while the other is yet to put on his mask – it lies on the ground in front of him. The image evokes the process of staging a performance, the experience of the performer and spectator, and the production itself. The transformative power of the mask is demonstrated through the contrast between the masked chorus member already 'in character' and the one who is still dressing.[37] The performer who is yet to put on his mask gazes down at it, reflecting, it seems, on its transformative power. This invites the viewer to share that contemplation and prompts reflection on his own identity.[38] The choice of mask, the female 'other', further cues this by highlighting the exploration of citizen identity that could be effected through theatrical transformation.[39] This vase found its way to Italy carrying with it the association of Athens with theatre and the mask as a symbol of its significance within that society.[40] The migration of theatre-related vases extended their role in projecting Athenian identity.[41] The mask's status as a symbol

Fig. 21 Chorus men preparing for tragic performance on Phiale Painter's *pelike*. *c.* 440–430 BC. Photograph. 2020 Museum of Fine Arts, Boston. Boston, Museum of Fine Arts 98.883. Reproduced with kind permission of the Museum.

for the theatrical experience (both from the point of view of the performer and spectator) is confirmed by its prominence in these compositions and is reinforced by the wider audience for them.

An extraordinary example of this phenomenon is the Attic red-figure *chous*, dated to *c.* 400 BC and found in Phanagoria, on the Taman peninsula of the Black Sea (Fig. 22).[42] This important vase for the study of comedy has only recently regained the attention it deserves.[43] Within the tiny frame of its image field, no fewer than five theatre masks are depicted along with five figures, two of whom are marked unmistakably as comic performers through the padding and phallus of that genre's costume.[44] The performers are placed in the centre of the composition under the jug's beak; one performer sits and looks straight ahead at the mask that the other performer holds out towards him.[45] The juxtaposition between the seated performer and the mask that faces him is arresting. The directness of the performer's gaze line and the offered mask's proximity creates a confrontational dimension – the performer and the mask stare at each other.[46] The effect of the mask's agency is reinforced through its headband – decorated with added gold, this sets it apart from the other masks and puts it on a par with the performers instead.[47] The mirroring between the gold headband worn by the seated performer and the mask confronting him captures the unsettling blending of self and other inherent to the experience of performing.[48] The contrast between the facial features of the mask and the performer lays emphasis on the mask as 'other'. This celebrates the transformational power of theatrical performance while highlighting its ability to contest the security of identity.

Further reflection on the disquieting aspect to performance is invited through the mask (held in the seated performer's right hand) which is shown fully frontal and staring out from the composition to confront the *chous*' viewer.[49] Frontality in vase painting, and the reciprocal gaze it produces, places the identity of the viewer under scrutiny, as Frontisi-Ducroux's important study has demonstrated.[50] The seated performer, confronted with a mask, is shown subjected to this scrutiny and the vase's viewer shares the experience through the frontal mask. The composition is thus designed to reflect on performance's interrogation of identity (extending it from those performing to the audience).[51]

The disquiet that this generates is balanced, however, by the reassurance offered through the image's recognition of the collective element to theatre. This is conveyed through an important variation on the perhaps near-contemporary convention (see below) of the performer or playwright contemplating a mask.[52] On the *chous*, it is a fellow performer who holds out the mask and creates the face-to-face juxtaposition between mask and performer. This emphasizes the

Fig. 22 Comic performer confronted with mask 'backstage'. Attic red-figure chous, dated to c. 400 BC and found in Phanagoria. The State Hermitage Museum, Taman collection, ΦA 1869.47. Photograph Jeffrey Rusten and reproduced with his kind permission.

nature of theatre as a collective enterprise since either a negotiation is taking place between the performers or one is assisting the other.[53] This extends the symbolism of the mask so that it stands for the collective element to the participation of Athenian citizens in theatre performances which is integral to the activity's significance for the formation of identity.[54] The masks on the *chous* also form part of its celebration of the display involved in comic performance and the Athenian *techne* this implies (projecting civic pride).[55] The discovery of this vessel at such a great distance from Athens demonstrates the wide reach of this image's conceptualization of the mask's symbolic significance. Moreover, it establishes that the treatment of the comic mask did not differ from satyr drama or tragedy in this respect – depictions of masks from all three genres were similarly designed to invite reflection on performance's impact on the citizen's sense of identity.

The parallels in themes raised by the handling of masks in the Phanagoria *chous*' composition and the earlier representation of a satyr mask preserved on a fragment of red-figure *chous* or *oenochoe* are striking. The fragment, dated to c. 440–420 BC, and found in the excavation of the southwest area of the Athenian Agora, shows an *aulos* player and performer from the satyr chorus holding a satyr mask in his right hand (Fig. 23).[56] The details preserved on this fragment hint towards the composition's setting either in rehearsal or perhaps after the performance. The musician's *auloi* are shown carried in his left hand, a detail also included for one of the musicians in the Phanagoria composition; more remarkable, however, is the depiction of his *phorbeia* (headstrap for the *auloi*) with the intricate detail of its two holes for the pipes.[57] The *phorbeia* is shown around the musician's neck, implying either a break from sustained playing in rehearsal or the end of a performance. The performer playing the member of the satyr chorus is still in costume (wearing the distinctive shorts of the genre), but has taken his mask off in an equivalent gesture to the musician's removal of his *phorbeia*.[58] The mask, held in his hand, is turned to face him. While we cannot determine the mask's significance from the performer's facial expression (since the fragment breaks off at the top of his torso), other elements to the composition imply its symbolic status. The expression of the musician gazing across to the performer but also down towards the mask reveals that it is the object of concern and perhaps even anxiety. The hands of the performer reinforce the focus on the mask and place it as an object of contention. The right hand holding the mask, grasps it firmly from beneath with fingers curling round to below its ear (as though to keep control of it, implying its dynamism). The performer gestures

Fig. 23 Performer holding satyr mask. Fragment of Attic red-figure *chous* or *oenochoe*, dated to *c*. 440–420 BC, found in Athenian Agora P32870, reproduced with kind permission of the American School of Classical Studies, Athens: Agora Excavations.

with his left hand held out, fingers spread in support of his point (the subject of which seems to be the mask, as the musician's gaze implies).

Meanwhile, the mask itself asserts it presence, and agency, through its lifelike features, with its eyelids offering an intensity to its gaze towards the performer. The slight curve to its mouth and playfully pointed ears hint towards mischief which animates the image but also, framed by the musician's anxious gaze, lends it a disturbing quality. An equivalent dynamic to the composition of the later Phanagoria *chous* is created, by pointing to the disquieting aspects to performance through the agency of the mask, while offering reassurance through the presentation of performance as a collaborative affair (conveyed through the performer's and musician's shared focus on the mask). Whether the image depicts a moment in rehearsal or after the show, it evokes the experience of performance and presents the mask as a symbol for the citizen's participation in that experience. These parallels between the images are significant for pointing to the continuity of the mask's iconographic function as such a symbol even across genres. The findspot and date of the fragment are also revealing, pointing towards the impact of this type of iconography on Athenian views of themselves (since this vase was made in Athens and stayed there). It also highlights that in the same period as the tragic mask is shown separate from the performer to reflect on the nature of performance (see the Boston *pelike* discussed above, Fig. 21), the same phenomenon can be seen represented in response to satyr drama.[59] The dating of the fragment to perhaps as early as 440 BC highlights that the motif of contemplating the theatre mask was already well established by the time of the Phanagoria *chous* (Fig. 22), the Pronomos vase and the performer's grave relief (Fig. 24).

The connection between the mask as a symbol of participation in performance and interlocutor with Athenian identity is established most explicitly by the Pronomos vase.[60] This well-known Attic red-figure krater, dating to *c.* 400 BC and found in Ruvo, Italy, presents an entire cast holding their masks after the performance of a tragic tetralogy.[61] The composition's multiplication of the 'performer holding mask' motif suggests its status as a convention by this date and highlights the vase's intense engagement with questions raised by performance.[62] The painter exploits the power of depicting the gaze between mask and performer as part of this strategy. One of the chorus members, to the left of the figure costumed as a 'king', is shown staring straight into the eyes of his satyr mask.[63] His casual stance, leaning with his elbow on the shoulder of his fellow performer, diminishes the sense of confrontation implied by the comic *chous* (Fig. 22) and satyr rehearsal fragment (Fig. 23). Meanwhile, the depiction of the other choreut, equally relaxed (with hand on hip), sharing in the gaze towards the mask offers reassurance through underlining the collective element to performance. Again a frontally facing mask, this time in another part of the composition (held by the chorus member below 'Heracles'), invites the connection between the performer's experience and the audience's. The reflection on identity (invited through the masks' treatment, and the composition's gaze lines) is reinforced through the inscription of the chorus members' names. The names of the performers gazing upon the mask are: Euagon (the figure holding the mask) and Dorotheos.[64] Together these names would resonate with an Athenian viewer's experience of the competition. Dorotheos was a very familiar Athenian name and could represent any citizen, while Euagon (a name unattested in Athens in this period) would function to express the aspiration (success in the competition) felt by that citizen in performing.[65] Beyond these two figures, the use of five other common Athenian names in the inscriptions for chorus members anchors it to that city's experience.[66] Athenian self-image (expressed through a specific collective experience) as well as projected identity (shaping other's perceptions), are at stake in this composition.[67]

The potential of the theatre mask to define an individual citizen's identity by the end of the fifth century is evidenced through the grave *stele* depicting a performer or playwright, now in the collection of the Piraeus archaeological museum (Fig. 24).[68] This grave *stele* shows a young beardless man holding a female mask in his right hand.[69] The long-haired mask is turned to face the young man who holds it. It has been argued that the *stele* commemorates a professional tragic actor, a chorus member, or a tragedian.[70] The *stele*, which can be dated on stylistic grounds to the final decade of the fifth century, may therefore be our earliest example of the iconographic convention that depicts the playwright contemplating his art by looking at a mask.[71] This motif is exemplified in the well-known Menander relief that shows the fourth-century comic playwright looking at a mask held in his hand (while two other masks rest on a table behind it).[72] If, however, the grave *stele* celebrates the life of a performer, then it can be viewed as a further iteration of the motif that we have been exploring (and should be understood as sharing in its iconographic syntax).[73] Produced within the same time frame as the *chous* and the Pronomos vase, this image confirms tragic masks functioning symbolically in an equivalent way to the comic and satyr mask.[74] Moreover it demonstrates that the motif crossed the boundaries of media – appearing not only in vase painting but also in plastic art, perhaps hinting towards a greater pervasiveness than the limited number of surviving examples would suggest.[75] The thematization of the act of viewing on *stelai* creates the necessary context for the mask to retain the symbolic function explored in vase painting.[76]

Fig. 24 Fragment of grave *stele* showing a performer or playwright contemplating mask. Photograph, Gösta Hellner © DAI Athens (D-DAI-ATH-Salamis 13), reproduced with kind permission.

The medium also creates new meaning for the mask, highlighting the ontological paradoxes of identity created in theatre performance and reinforcing the questions it poses about the citizen's identity.[77]

One of the functions of such a relief is to celebrate the individual by situating his identity within the framework of the society's ideals.[78] This is demonstrated by the hoplite *stele* (Fig. 16) discussed in Chapter 3. The mask's presence on this *stele* evokes the experience of theatre and civic pride in participation in this cultural activity. Slater argues that the deceased must have been a professional actor despite the rarity of grave *stelai* marking professions.[79] It is possible, however, to read this motif as operating in the same way as the image of the hoplite or athlete on grave *stelai*, representing not a profession but an activity characterizing the *arete* of the male citizen. The *stele* reveals how this individual, or his kin, framed his identity as a citizen through his participation in, most likely choral, performance.[80] This iconography demonstrates the value attached to theatre festivals by Athenian society and the mask's status as a symbol for performance's role in shaping civic identity. The choice to depict a female mask, that is the 'other', is important here.[81] It highlights perceptions of theatre as a powerfully transformative experience (a celebrated *techne*) marked by the gender contrast between the mask and performer.[82] At the same time, the alignment between tragic theatre and the female, with its attendant implications for the assertion of male civic identity, is in operation here.[83] A parallel might be drawn with the function of gender in defining the male citizen in iconography of the Stieglitz cup and in the *Oresteia* (see Chapters 1 and 2). This demonstrates the ways in which the cultural discourse on citizen identity could cut across these symbolic objects despite the differences between their 'social' lives. This brief review of the mask's life as an object in society has shown that its display in the sanctuary after performance and treatment in iconography allowed it to assert the role of the theatrical experience in affirming Athenian identity.[84] Its handling as a prop in performance further defines and problematizes this object's 'civic' status.

II Theatre

The mask's existence as an object outside the performance is brought to the audience's attention by Aristophanes through his reference to the mask maker in *Knights* 232.[85] This passing allusion to the social life of masks, however, should be viewed against the backdrop of the more explicit engagement with this idea in earlier plays. The handling of masks as props on stage highlights the powerful agency of these objects, inviting reflection on their status and symbolism outside the performance.[86] A superb example of this is preserved in Aeschylus' satyr drama, *Theoroi* or *Isthmiastae* (*The Sacred Delegation* or *At the Isthmian Games*) produced before 456 BC.[87] Amongst the surviving fragments, known from a papyrus dug up in Oxyrhynchus and published in 1941, are the following lines:[88]

ἄκουε δὴ πᾶς· σῖγα δ'ειθελειδ . [.].
    ἄθρησον, εἰ. [..] .. [
εἴδωλον εἶναι τοῦδ'ἐμῇ μορφῇ πλέον
τὸ Δαιδάλου μ[ί]μημα· φωνῆς δεῖ μόνον.
    ταδ[..] . ει ..
    ὁρα . [.] . (.) ρ[
    χώρει μάλα.
—εὐκταῖα κόσμον ταῦτ[α τῷ θεῷ φέρω
    καλλίγραπτον εὐχάν.
—τῇ μητρὶ τῇμῇ πράγματ'ἂν παρασχέθοι·
    ἰδοῦσα γάρ νιν ἂν σαφῶς
    τρέποιτ' ἂν αἰάζοιτό θ', ὡς
    δοκοῦσ'ἔμ' εἶναι, τὸν ἐξ
    ἐθρέψεν· οὕτως ἐμφερὴς ὅδ'ἐστίν.
εἶα δή, σκοπεῖτε δῶμα ποντίου σεισίχθο[νος
κἀπιπασσάλευ' ἕκαστος τῆς κ[α]λῆς μορφῆς. [
ἄγγελον, κήρυκ'[ἄ]ναυδον,
ἐμπόρων κωλύτορ[α,
ὅ[σ] γ'ἐπισχήσει κελεύθου τοὺς ξένο[υς] φο[β - υ -.
χαῖρ', ἄναξ. χαῖρ', ὦ Πόσειδον, ἐπίτροπο[σ θ']
    ὑφ[ίστασο.

Now listen, everyone, and … […] in silence!
Look and see whether [you] th[ink] at [all]
that Daedalus' models are a closer image of my form
than this is. All it needs is a voice!
[*Remains of two lines, including* this *and* see]
Come on now!
[*A single voice*]
I bring these votives to the god to adorn his house –
fine paintings to fulfil a vow!
[*The full chorus*]
It would cause my mother some problems!
If she saw it, I'm quite sure
she'd turn about and cry out in horror, because

she'd think it was me, the child
that she brought up! That's how like me it is!
Ho there! Set your eyes on the house of the sea god, the earthshaker,
and each of you nail up there [an image] of their fair form
as a messenger, a voiceless herald, a restrainer of
travellers,
which will make visito[rs] halt in their path [by the]
fea[rsome look in its eyes].
Hail, lord! Hail, Poseidon, [and] unde[rtake to be our]
guardian!

The satyr leader instructs the chorus to nail the 'images' of themselves on the temple of Poseidon (as dedications).[89] It is likely that these 'images' were represented by masks.[90] The scene therefore presents the masked performers, costumed as satyrs, contemplating masks identical to those that they are wearing. The visual playfulness and profoundly metatheatrical content of this scene creates an arresting effect.[91] The handling of masks onstage invites reflection on the performer's process of transformation backstage, and since it is (significantly) the chorus prompting this, it is specifically the citizen's experience of performing that is evoked. The stage image of a chorus member looking upon his mask intersects in a thought-provoking manner with the iconographic schema of such contemplation.[92] Once the artistic convention was established, playwrights could exploit this dimension to the stage image (see below). *Theoroi*, as a precedent, invites subsequent scrutiny of the experience of performance to be viewed through the perspective of the chorus and its citizen performers.

The stage action proposed by the satyr chorus invites further self-reflection through its allusion to the dedication of masks at the sanctuary of Dionysus.[93] The importation of this social practice into the theatrical frame has a dramatic justification. The play's scenario is assumed to be that the satyrs have escaped training with Dionysus and arrived at the Isthmian games instead.[94] Poseidon has appropriated Dionysus' place as leader of the satyrs. The dedication of masks at Poseidon's temple (rather than at the sanctuary of Dionysus) expresses this. The change of recipient allows for some distancing so that the actual practice of dedication is not replicated and ridiculed on stage.[95] Even as a travesty of the practice, however, the scene invites the audience to think about the mask's place in society and the meaning of its post-performance display to those who viewed it. The satyrs' explicit consideration of responses to the sight of their dedicated masks highlights the role of the communal gaze to identity's construction and intensifies the audience's process of self-reflection.[96] The scene's impact extended beyond this production. Its visually arresting presentation, striking metatheatrical dimension, and intersection with Athenian experience created a performance memory powerful enough to reverberate down to Euripides' *Bacchae*.[97] In the meantime, however, the motif's metatheatrical potential was exploited on the comic stage by Cratinus who developed it further by applying it to tragic masks and making it a part of the theatrical discourse between playwrights.

In the late 420s, Cratinus produced a comedy, *Seriphioi*, that played with the myth of Perseus and engaged in tragic parody.[98] One of the central pieces of evidence for the metatheatrical aspect to the drama, preserved thanks to its unusual vocabulary, is fr. 218:[99]

αἶρε δεῦρο τοὺς βρικέλους

Bring the tragic masks here

The implication of the fragment is that this comedy's stage action involved the handling of masks as props. The staging's effect is the same in general terms as *Theoroi*, yet the dramatic situation is importantly different and alters the prop's symbolism.[100] The masks are handled, not in anticipation of their dedication but for their use in performance (a paratragic 'play within a play').[101] This emphasizes the metatheatrical dimension to the masks' symbolism above all. The effect of the visual juxtaposition between masked performer and mask he holds is also markedly different. Cratinus' staging produces a pronounced contrast between the performer's comic mask and the tragic mask he holds. It is not clear whether the tragic masks were put on by the comic characters during the play.[102] The handling of the masks in juxtaposition to the comic performer, however, would be enough to hint towards the absurdity of the proposed performance. The potential visual effect of this can be inferred from the 'Sant' Agata Antigone' Apulian bell-krater, dated to *c.* 370 BC. Its depiction of an unknown comedy's tragic parody includes a comic male character dressed in a *peplos* and carrying a tragic female mask.[103] The mask prop in Cratinus' production is emphatically 'other' (tragic) and should be a powerful symbol of theatre's transformative experience, yet the comic framing disempowers it (cf. the tragic sword in Chapter 5). The comedy offers reassurance over tragedy's interrogation of identity by undermining the tragic mask's symbolic status. However, the Phanagoria *chous* (Fig. 22) demonstrates that in this same period, the comic mask could be presented as unsettlingly powerful in this same respect. It seems then that a part of this stage action may be concerned with claiming comedy as the superior, or safer(?), genre through which to explore identity. The iconographic tradition demonstrates masks from all three genres shared a symbolic status and function in expressing theatre's exploration of identity. The mask's stage life however enables an appreciation of the dynamics, and negotiations, at play in this joint ownership.

Comic rivalry may also have been a factor in the formulation and interpretation of the scene. It has been argued that Cratinus here offers a response to the costume-borrowing scene in Aristophanes' *Acharnians* 406–80.[104] If so, then he goes further than his younger rival Aristophanes by presenting tragic masks (rather than the clothing and accessories borrowed by Dicaeopolis). The further impact of this is to allow the mask to take its place within the theatrical discourse opened by the self-conscious play with costume in *Acharnians* and later continued in the cross-dressing scene in *Women at the Thesmophoria*.[105] Aristophanes acknowledges the *Seriphioi* scene's participation in this discourse through an intertextual nod towards it in the *Women at the Thesmophoria* scene.[106] The place of the mask, and the *Seriphioi* scene, within this network of scenes has implications for the interpretation of the prop's handling in *Bachhae* (discussed below). The scene's interplay with the mask's social life is not as pronounced as *Theoroi* yet it invites a glimpse of the mask as an object which exists offstage after the performance waiting to engage the performer and audience in the theatrical experience. The self-conscious incongruity between performer and mask can be viewed as a comically extreme expression of the function of 'playing the other'. Even while undermining the exploitation of the tragic mask as a symbol for theatre's exploration of identity, *Seriphioi* simultaneously draws attention to it. Meanwhile the scene asserts comedy's right to reflect on theatre and the construction of identity.

Tragedy's awareness of the mask's potential in this respect and its capability in exploiting it, despite comedy's handling of the prop, is demonstrated by Euripides' *Bacchae*.[107] The theatrical self-consciousness of this play, probably produced in 405 BC, has long been recognized in scholarship.[108] The Agave scene, however, has still more to offer to our understanding of the play's self-awareness and significance for its audience. By taking the mask's theatrical and social life into account, the full extent of this scene's allusion to previous plays can be appreciated and its engagement in the discourse on theatre and citizen identity is revealed.[109] The appearance of Agave on stage holding the head of Pentheus carries its own significance within the play's symbolic design as the realization of Dionysus' victory prefigured through his earlier costume change.[110] Pentheus' appearance on stage disguised as a maenad (*Bacch.* 913) signifies both Dionysus' mastery over him as well as the king's imminent death.[111] This cross-dressing scene also, however, forms a prominent moment in the 'play within a play' directed by Dionysus.[112] The same actor, who has exited as Pentheus (dressed in maenad disguise to spy on the women), returns, approximately 189 lines later, as Agave. He is probably in the same costume but is now wearing Agave's mask while holding Pentheus' mask in his hand.[113] In the world of the play the mask held by the actor represents Pentheus' severed head, but the verbal cue from Cadmus (1277) as well as the self-consciousness of the cross-dressing scene, allows it to be simultaneously perceived as a theatre mask by the audience.[114] The use of full 'helmet' masks in ancient Greek theatre established the metonymy between head and mask offering symbolic logic to this staging.[115]

The already striking stage image of a mask being handled by a masked actor is enhanced by the visual similarity between the masks. The juxtaposition presents the realization of a comparison cued in the mind's eye of the audience before Pentheus goes to the mountain, 925–7:[116]

ΠΕΝΘΕΥΣ
τί φαίνομαι δῆτ'; οὐχὶ τὴν Ἰνοῦς στάσιν
ἢ τὴν Ἀγαυῆς ἑστάναι, μητρός γ' ἐμῆς;

ΔΙΟΝΥΣΟΣ
αὐτὰς ἐκείνας εἰσορᾶν δοκῶ σ' ὁρῶν.

Pentheus What do I look like? Do I not have the carriage of Ino or my mother Agave?
Dionysus When I look at you I think I see their very image.

Dionysus' reply invites a general visual equation between the disguised Pentheus and his mother or aunt.[117] There is much to be gained dramatically if Pentheus bears resemblance to his mother. It would make Agave's appearance, alive and well, looking like Pentheus when he had left the stage to go to his death, more painful for the audience. The text confirms details of the visual similarity. Pentheus is promised long hair by Dionysus before he goes into the house (831). When he appears cross-dressed on stage, his hair is arranged in a snood (928–9) that he later removes, as the messenger tells us, when begging his mother to recognize him (1115–6). With the snood removed, Pentheus' long hair must have flowed down from his decapitated head (mask). It matches Agave's hair that as a maenad would be hanging loose (as the first messenger confirms 695: καὶ πρῶτα μὲν καθεῖσαν εἰς ὤμους κόμας). The possible visual effect of this similarity is captured by the image of Agave holding Pentheus' head, preserved on a papyrus fragment found in Egypt (Fig. 25).[118] Even in this crude drawing, the arresting

140 *Theatre Props and Civic Identity in Athens*

Fig. 25 Agave holding Pentheus' head depicted on papyrus fragment. Courtesy of the Penn Museum.

effect of the similar features (wide eyes, brows, straight nose, curly hair) between Agave and the head that she carries can be felt. Moreover, the choice to present Pentheus' mask frontally in the image responds to the scene's engagement in the discourse of theatre and identity.

The stage image of Agave carrying a mask that was visually similar to her own presents a reworking of the motif found in Aeschylus' *Theoroi*. The self-consciousness of this interperformative allusion is marked through the verbal emphasis on looking at the mask and the similarity of the proposed stage action. Agave, after calling the people of Thebes to look at the head (1203) ends her speech by suggesting that it should be nailed to the house (*Bacch*. 1212–15):

> Πενθεύς τ' ἐμὸς παῖς ποῦ 'στιν; αἱρέσθω λαβὼν
> πηκτῶν πρὸς οἴκους κλιμάκων προσαμβάσεις,
> ὡς πασσαλεύσῃ κρᾶτα τριγλύφοις τόδε
> λέοντος ὃν πάρειμι θηράσασ' ἐγώ.

> And where is my son Pentheus? He should bring a ladder to the house so that he can nail to the triglyphs the head of this lion I caught before coming here.

Seaford notes that 'the Greeks attached to their buildings the heads of victims of sacrifice' and perhaps also hunt; on this reading Agave's proposed stage action reinforces figurative motifs within the play as well as the audience's sense of her delusion.[119] This interpretation misses, however, the potential interperformative allusion and metatheatrical dimension to these lines. The echo of language (the same verb for nailing is used in both *Theoroi* fr. 78a, 18 and *Bacchae* 1214), the emphasis on looking at the prop, the similarity of the envisaged stage action, and the striking presentation of a masked figure on stage carrying a near-identical mask, suggests that this moment in *Bacchae* may have recalled (for some audience members at least) the earlier moment in *Theoroi*.[120] The satyr drama's engagement with the idea of the dedication of masks after performance invites the interpretation of Agave's proposition through the same lens. The suggestion of nailing the mask to the house symbolizes Dionysus' absolute victory since the *skene* building, once a symbol of Pentheus' power (as a palace) is transformed (in the imagination) into his sanctuary. The god has symbolically taken over the palace. On a metatheatrical level, the end of Dionysus' 'play within a play' is signalled by the dedication of the mask.[121] At the same time, the audience may self-consciously reflect on their own practice of dedicating masks after the end of a performance and appreciate the stark contrast between the positive framing of their actions (in comparison to the disturbing travesty of it suggested here).

Moreover, the allusion to this passage of *Theoroi* heightens the emotional impact of Agave's belated recognition of her son (*Bacch.* 1275–84):[122]

ΚΑΔΜΟΣ τίς οὖν ἐν οἴκοις παῖς ἐγένετο σῷ πόσει;
ΑΓΑΥΗ Πενθεύς, ἐμῇ τε καὶ πατρὸς κοινωνίᾳ.
ΚΑΔΜΟΣ τίνος πρόσωπον δῆτ' ἐν ἀγκάλαις ἔχεις;
ΑΓΑΥΗ λέοντος, ὥς γ' ἔφασκον αἱ θηρώμεναι.
ΚΑΔΜΟΣ σκέψαι νυν ὀρθῶς· βραχὺς ὁ μόχθος εἰσιδεῖν.
ΑΓΑΥΗ ἔα, τί λεύσσω; τί φέρομαι τόδ' ἐν χεροῖν;
ΚΑΔΜΟΣ ἄθρησον αὐτὸ καὶ σαφέστερον μάθε.
ΑΓΑΥΗ ὁρῶ μέγιστον ἄλγος ἡ τάλαιν' ἐγώ.
ΚΑΔΜΟΣ μῶν σοι λέοντι φαίνεται προσεικέναι;
ΑΓΑΥΗ οὔκ, ἀλλὰ Πενθέως ἡ τάλαιν' ἔχω κάρα.

Cadmus Well, what son was born in that house to your husband?
Agave Pentheus, his father's son and mine.
Cadmus Whose head do you have in your hands then?
Agave The hunters told me it is a lion's.
Cadmus Look at it properly: the effort of doing so is slight.
Agave Ah, what am I seeing? What is this that I carry in my hands?
Cadmus Look at it, get surer knowledge.
Agave Great woe is what I see, unhappy me!
Cadmus Does it seem like a lion to you?
Agave No: in my misery I hold Pentheus' head!

The exchange intersects in a painfully precise way with the scene from *Theoroi*. The satyrs, in the passage quoted above (p. xx), make the striking claim that their mothers looking (εἶδον) at the masks would cry out in lamentation (αἰάζω), since they would mistake them for (the decapitated heads of) their children. The details correspond to the dramatic action here: Agave, a mother (1275–6), looks at the mask (emphasized at each line 1279–84), and cries out (1280). Euripides transforms the Aeschylean passage – it is no longer a playful speculation about hypothetical responses (emphasized in the satyr play by the repeated ἄν), it is a terrible reality. Here a mother holds the exact visual replica of her son (the mask that had represented him on stage) and yet does not recognize him. When she does, then she responds with horror, just as the allusion to *Theoroi* allows the audience to anticipate she would. Euripides undercuts the satyric scene and transforms it through its newly grim theatrical frame that makes a reality of the playfully envisaged horror.[123] Pentheus' mask operates as a symbol of Dionysus' power in the play but also on this reading demonstrates Euripides' too.[124]

This reframing of the mask's horror has implications for our understanding of the play's interaction with comedy as well. We know that Aristophanes had associated this idea of horror with masks through his use of the term μορμολυκεῖον (Mormo-Goblin) in two of his plays, staged within a decade of *Bacchae*.[125] The first of these references is made in fr. 31 of *Amphiaraus*, a comedy produced at the Lenaea festival in 414 BC.[126] A scholion on Aristophanes' *Peace* 474, explaining the line's reference to Lamachus' 'Mormo', quotes from Aristophanes' *Amphiaraus* (fr. 31):[127]

οὕτως ἔλεγον τὸ ἐκφόβητρον· καὶ τὰ προσωπεῖα τὰ αἰσχρὰ
μορμολύκεια, καὶ τὰ τραγικὰ καὶ τὰ κωμικά. καὶ ἐν Ἀμφιάρεω·
– υ ἀφ᾽ οὗ κωμῳδικὸν μορμολυκεῖον ἔγνων

They call Mormo a bogy and hideous masks both tragic and comic Mormo-goblins, as in *Amphiaraus*:
'since the time I recognized the comic Mormo-Goblin'

The same term is related to masks again in Aristophanes' *Old Age* (probably dating from after 410 BC) in fragment 130, recorded by the second-century AD lexicographer Phrynichus (*Ecloge* 346):[128]

τίς ἂν φράσειε ποῦ ᾽στι τὸ Διονύσιον
ὅπου τὰ μορμολυκεῖα προσκρεμάννυται

Who can tell me where Dionysus' precinct is,
where the Mormo-Goblins are hung on display?

It is not clear from this second reference whether tragic or comic masks are meant.[129] The comic frame, however, would detract from any fear implied by the term even if the masks in question were tragic. In *Bacchae*, the idea of the theatrical mask as an object of horror is taken from the safety of the satyric and comic setting and exploited by Euripides to make the Agave scene powerful on both the dramatic and metatheatrical level.[130] The dramatic strategy may be viewed as the equivalent to the comic reframing of the tragic sword, on which see Chapter 5. *Bacchae*, however, offers an example of the inverse strategy in operation (the comic being set within a tragic frame) and so demonstrates the dialectic nature of props' reformulation between genres.

Euripides engages further in this intergeneric discourse through his presentation of Pentheus' mask as the tragic equivalent of a μορμολυκεῖον (Mormo-Goblin). The transformation of Dionysus' mask through the action of the play is well known.[131] The shift in the perception of Pentheus' mask is equally significant. The chorus describe Pentheus as a ἀγριωπὸν τέρας (wild-faced monster, 542) as they react to his rage and locking up of the priest of Dionysus. The descriptor is undermined soon after its utterance by Dionysus' escape. It finds dramatic fulfilment, however, by the time the audience is faced with Pentheus' mask in the Agave scene.[132] Now the alternative meaning of τέρας (542), as a marvel (something to behold), is particularly apt. The mask was most likely presented as blood spattered, but the more disturbing change is to the audience's perception of its symbolism.[133] It now represents the utter, and pitiable, destruction of Pentheus. Euripides transforms the comic idea of the μορμολυκεῖον as the source of feigned horror by displaying a mask in his tragedy that is truly horrifying in its symbolism. The significance of this assertion of the mask's power may reach beyond the expression of generic interplay, posing a challenge to the claim that the mask 'lost something of its frightening potency' towards the end of the fifth century.[134] This reinstatement of the mask's status by Euripides asserts theatre's seriousness and importance. The simultaneous allusion in the Agave scene to the cultural practice of dedicating masks after performances bolsters the assertion. The comic debunking of the 'bogeyman' masks hanging on the temple of Dionysus in Aristophanes' *Old Age* fr. 130, quoted above, implies an undervaluing of the practice of dedicating masks and its meaning. Euripides contests this comic allusion to the custom, reworking it so that in his play the proposed dedication of a μορμολυκεῖον is as disturbing as it is pathetic. The proposed stage action demands that the audience reflect on the meaning of the masks they hung on the sanctuary of Dionysus. The stage image of the figure with mask in hand cues particular consideration of the relationship of those theatre masks to identity.

The stage image of Agave holding Pentheus' mask evokes consideration of the experience of performing. This is brought into sharp focus by the allusion to the intensely metatheatrical *Theoroi* (discussed above), but is also cued by the 'play within a play' that precedes this scene.[135] *Bacchae*'s interplay with Aristophanes' *Women at the Thesmophoria*, marked particularly in Pentheus' last scene before his death, would have created a horizon of expectation amongst the audience that would prime them to read Pentheus' head as simultaneously a mask.[136] In both plays, male characters are persuaded to disguise themselves as women to spy on an all-female religious festival.[137] An explicit signal to the interperformative allusion strengthens the general parallel between the dramatic scenario. In both plays, concern is expressed over the pleats of the female costume worn by the male character; *Thesmo.* 256:[138]

ΚΗΔΕΣΤΗΣ
ἴθι νυν κατάστειλόν με τὰ περὶ τὼ σκέλει.

Kinsman
Come on, arrange the pleats around my legs.

The stage action is echoed in *Bacch.* 935–8:

ΔΙΟΝΥΣΟΣ
ζῶναί τέ σοι χαλῶσι κοὐχ ἑξῆς πέπλων
στολίδες ὑπὸ σφυροῖσι τείνουσιν σέθεν.

ΠΕΝΘΕΥΣ
κἀμοὶ δοκοῦσι παρά γε δεξιὸν πόδα·
τἀνθένδε δ' ὀρθῶς παρὰ τένοντ' ἔχει πέπλος.

Dionysus And your girdle is slack, and the pleats of your dress hang crooked below the ankle.

Pentheus (looking over his shoulder at his ankles) That seems true of my right foot, though on this side the dress falls properly over the tendon.

It would be appropriate for this verbal attention to be accompanied by the pleats' adjustment, inviting the audience to focus on the costume.[139] This focus and the intervention of another stage character in adjusting the costume reinforces the connection between the scenes. One effect of this is that it anticipates the tragic reframing of the mask in the Agave scene (discussed above), by reformulating the cross-dressing scene's costume to make it grotesque.[140] Another effect is that it invites the audience to reflect on the self-conscious play with costume on stage, activating their awareness of this stage moment's place within a network of such scenes.[141] The Agathon scene is layered with meanings from past productions, namely the Telephus costume-borrowing scene in *Acharnians*.[142] Intervening between the two in stage history was Cratinus' *Seriphioi* (which through its handling of tragic masks interacted with the costume scene in *Acharnians*). Euripides echoes both forms of metatheatrical engagement in the same order as they had chronologically played out in stage history. Dionysus, as god of drama, rather than playwright, offers a 'costume' to Pentheus who is shown dressed up in it. Then after the messenger scene Agave is presented on stage handling a tragic mask that represents Pentheus' head. In other words, Euripides offers a tragic parody of Aristophanes, followed by a tragic parody of Cratinus, presenting two different ways of engaging with the idea of an actor's experience of performing. The first follows the model of *Acharnians* and *Women at the Thesmophoria* by using costume, whereas the Agave scene draws on Cratinus' use of tragic masks as symbols for dramatic role-playing. The stage image of Agave, seen as a performer holding a mask, invites the audience backstage, at the same time as they accept the theatrical illusion of the stage image (seeing it as a representation of Agave holding Pentheus' head). This ability to engage in multiple perspectives characterizes the ancient audience's experience of viewing in the theatre in general but the idea of 'double vision' takes on a special meaning in the viewing experience of this play.[143]

Viewing the stage image of Agave holding the mask through the iconographic tradition unfolds further perspectives on it. When she is emphatically commanded to contemplate the head in her hand by her father Cadmus and confirms that she is looking at it (1279–84, quoted above, p. xx), it seems likely that Agave holds the mask prop turned towards her. In other words, she adopts the pose of the performer depicted on the grave *stele* now in the Piraeus museum (Fig. 24). The dating of the *stele* allows that it might precede *Bacchae* by a few years.[144] The satyr rehearsal fragment (Fig. 23) and Phanagroia *chous* (Fig. 22) in any case offer earlier examples of the offstage performer confronted by his mask and strengthen the suggestion that this iconographic convention was known at the time of *Bacchae*'s production. The intersection with the iconographic tradition (that connected the experience of theatre with Athenian identity) intensifies the audience engagement with the stage image of Agave, and sets their communal gaze within the context of that tradition.[145] The image draws its dramatic power not only from what it signifies within the play (a mother holding the head of her son), but also for the demand it makes of the audience to reflect on the status of theatre outside the moment of performance.

If Agave is viewed as a performer holding a mask, then the 'performer' in this representation would be female. What does this say about the Athenian experience of performing? An understanding of the iconographic conventions for depicting offstage actors offers the necessary interpretative tools to make sense of such an image. The similarity between Agave's face and the mask in her hand, explored above in relation to *Theoroi*, exhibits a phenomenon known from the artistic representations of offstage actors. The effect of 'melting', through which the actor's face, when represented in proximity to the mask of a character he has played, takes on characteristics of that mask, can be clearly seen on the Pronomos vase.[146] The face of the actor who has played the part of Heracles shares characteristics with the mask he holds in his hand. This suggests that the power of the dramatic illusion is such that it becomes difficult to imagine the actor beneath the mask as a separate entity.[147] Such images deliberately invite the viewer to reflect on the power of theatre. In the case of Agave the result of the 'melting' is far more arresting since the performer has taken on female characteristics.[148] This carries significant ramifications. It points to the perception of the power of theatrical performance in a comparable way to the image preserved on the Attic red-figure bell-krater fragment, found in Olbia.[149] This important piece of earlier evidence, dated to 430–420 BC, includes within its composition the feminine adjective κάλη (beautiful) inscribed over two tragic male performers playing female roles.[150] The stage image of Agave similarly invites reflection on the idea of the male performer's exploration of the feminine through the process of participating in tragedy.[151] Viewing the scene through the filter of the artistic convention for representing performers offers an intense significance to the mask prop that is, not coincidentally, a focal point in the stage action. The mask becomes a symbol not only for the experience of performance but also for its contestation of gender, ultimately reaffirming male identity.

Euripides exploits the theatrical life of the mask prop to engage with earlier stage history from both comedy and satyr drama in his tragedy, evoking metatheatrical moments from both to enrich the dramatic power of the scene set before the audience. The extent of *Bacchae*'s interperformative allusions in this respect has not yet been recognized; the Agave scene plays on the viewer's memory not only of Aristophanes, but his comic rival Cratinus, and even Aeschylean satyr drama.[152] The scene holds internal power within the play at the same time as presenting a rich contribution to the discourse about theatre that had been embedded in performances across the decades of the fifth century. The simultaneous interplay with the iconographic tradition, and its reflection on the nature of theatre, reinforces the suggestion (raised in relation to Sophocles' *Ajax*) that tragedy gained meaning from, and consciously exploited, the visual language of art.[153] *Bacchae* presents a particularly striking example of this interplay between theatre and iconography since it engages with art that represents theatre. This generates a far more complex metatheatrical statement from the mask – not only does it comment on theatre's reflection on theatre, but also the ways in which other arts respond to theatre. At the same time, the mask's status in society, its 'social life', pushes the manipulation of this prop in the play beyond the narrowly metatheatrical, inviting the audience to consider the place of theatre in their civic experience and identity.

Conclusion
Evaluating Objects

The theatrical handling of objects with civic resonance for an Athenian audience member created powerful drama and impacted on perceptions of citizen identity. The three case studies display the range of dramatic effects that could be generated from the exploitation of such objects' symbolic meaning. This dramaturgic strategy drew attention to the object's meaning within society and also exerted influence over it, allowing the plays to enter into civic discourse on the citizen's sense of identity. This engagement with the discourse was made more profound by theatre's exploration of two central aspects to the symbolic objects' *modus operandi* within society. The communal gaze that reinforces the object's status, constructing its cohesive property, is mirrored in the theatre. The self-consciousness of the process is highlighted through the verbal emphasis on looking, when these props become the dramatic focus.[1] The dramatic action can corroborate the gaze's power in this respect but it can also problematize it, drawing attention to the precarity of the social cohesion generated from these objects. The demonstration of the objects' openness to symbolic renegotiation is similarly double edged. On the one hand, it offers recognition of an essential quality to these objects – their semiotic mutability allowed them to remain a dynamic force in the construction of identity.[2] At times of civic crisis the renegotiation of their symbolism could be an effective means of reaffirming collective identity. The *Oresteia*'s presentation of the shift to the sword's meaning across the trilogy displays both the dangers of symbolic appropriation and the positive reassurance that it could be reversed. The *Phoenician Women*, by contrast, exploits the mutability of the object's meaning to problematize it within the drama and invites reflection on the framing of its symbolism within society at democracy's restoration. Comedy too plays its part in this as its reframing of these symbols reflects on their dynamic place in the construction of identity while contesting tragedy's affirmation of their meaning.[3] Collectively the theatrical treatments of these objects both destabilize and affirm their symbolism within society. The nature of theatrical performance and its programming at

Athens made it the ideal medium through which to explore such objects' meanings and the *modus operandi* of their symbolism.[4] This secured theatre a prominent place in the cultural discourse on civic identity.

The intergeneric approach, motivated by exploring theatre's engagement with the discourse on civic identity through these objects, contributes to the understanding of theatrical genre's operation and self-definition. Comedy's relationship with society, and self-perception of its function within it, can be delineated through its handling of these props. The strategies for disempowering the tragic sword revealed both the desire to assert dominance over the effects of that genre, while also articulating comedy's possessiveness over the role of commenting on society through engagement with the contemporary (Chapter 5). This draws attention to one of the important generic implications of this study – that tragedy, comedy, and satyr drama could comment 'directly' on society through negotiating the meaning of these objects. The exploitation of the frisson this could generate within the theatrical frame, displayed in Aeschylus' handling of the voting urns and pebbles in the *Oresteia*, demands the nuancing of claims about tragic distance (as a characteristic defining the genre in contrast to comedy). There are generic implications also to the recognition that the substitution of an ideologically significant civic object on stage (and the statement made by this) is not comedy's strategy exclusively, as the examples of Electra's *hydria* in Euripides' *Electra* and the chorus of elders' staves in *Agamemnon* have shown (Chapter 2). The dialectic nature of props' reformulation between genres is demonstrated further by *Bacchae* in its striking renegotiation of the mask's meaning (in response to both satyr drama and comedy, Chapter 6). The dissolution of generic difference is underlined by considering the mask as a symbol of civic identity – while the iconographic tradition differentiates them through portraying features characteristic to each genre, the masks share the same symbolic function in these compositions.

The interdisciplinary engagement with iconographic evidence has also prompted the call to a re-evaluation of the relationship between theatre and art. The explicit comparison in *Lysistrata* (630–5) between the image presented by the figures on stage and the public statues of the tyrant slayers implicitly acknowledges the place of art in the theatre audience's process of viewing theatre in general.[5] The comparison of the 'framing' of the object in iconography and on stage proves revealing, offering insight into the operation of civic discourse in both art forms and prompting the acknowledgment that both played a role in shaping it.[6] The iconographic tradition for representing voting carries implications for the perception of the political stance of the *Oresteia*, for example, and demonstrates that gender played a part in the discourse of defining the male citizen through his participation in the vote even before this trilogy. Moreover, the analysis of drama's 'framing' of objects conceptualizes the performance of a play as a series of 'stage images' some of which shared a meaningful relationship with images (or artistic conventions) from the iconographic tradition.[7] This claim brings with it a welcome challenge to the lingering philological bias informing the assumption that only vase paintings produced in response to stage productions are relevant.[8] The playwright's engagement with the iconographic tradition is highlighted above all in the analysis of the stage image of Agave carrying Pentheus' head in Euripides' *Bacchae* (Chapter 6); although it is also identified as potentially in operation in Aeschylus' *Oresteia* and Sophocles' *Ajax* (Chapters 2 and 4). Moreover, this approach invites a fresh perspective on the iconography that relates directly to the theatre (the value of which has been well-established in scholarship over the past few decades).[9] The engagement with iconography in this study is intended to allow the important tradition of artistic representation in the visual landscape of life beyond the theatre to begin to take its rightful place in our assessment of how theatre created meaning in fifth-century Athens.[10]

The object-oriented approach to identity adopted here has rich potential to shed light in further areas. The power dynamics between the objects' symbolic status could be examined as a means of investigating the relationship between different dimensions of citizenship.[11] The citizen's phenomenological experience of the objects could be fruitfully considered.[12] Much might be gained from the application of this study's approach to explore identities of other members of the Athenian demographic. The use of the *metic*'s processional cloak in *Eumenides* demonstrates that other objects populating the stage were linked, in their social life, to the identity of other groups in Athenian society.[13] At the same time, the objects in this study could be re-evaluated to assess what these symbols of male citizenship meant to other groups; the handling of the sword by the female figure on the white-ground *lekythos* (discussed in Chapter 3) prompts the consideration of how far the theatre similarly problematized these objects through exploring the perspective of others.[14] Objects offer the equivalent of 'free spaces' in this respect since their symbolism's polyvalent capacity, and the ambiguity over the ownership of their meaning, allows for distinctions in identity to be challenged and blurred.[15] While the sword has been argued to have special significance for the identity of the Athenian male citizen, might it not also have an identity value for the *metic* fighting on behalf of the city?[16]

The findings invite the consideration of what these objects meant in performances hosted by other cities. While this initial study has necessitated the adoption of an Athenocentric approach, it is hoped that this analysis might further the valuable scholarship now being produced on theatre outside Athens.[17] Claims, for example, that Athenian playwrights wrote with a Panhellenic audience in mind should be nuanced by the recognition that Athenian audience members may have nevertheless found that the production resonated in a specific way through the symbolic associations carried by certain objects.[18] A full understanding of the 'export' of Athenian drama depends on the appreciation of the ways in which the meanings of objects in performance were transformed by that relocation. The image on the cover of this book is instructive. On a fourth-century bell-krater fragment produced in southern Italy, a tragic actor is shown holding a sword in his left hand and contemplating a mask held in his right.[19] Both objects carried symbolic associations for the Athenian citizen in the fifth century, but what did they mean in this different time and place? The new performance context created the opportunity for new meanings to emerge.[20] This study is intended to offer a model for the exploration of 'significant' objects in performances in other cities or regions. Thinking beyond the re-performance of plays to their adaptation in Roman culture, it would be rewarding to consider whether theatre played the same role in shaping civic identity through its manipulation of ideologically significant objects.[21]

This approach has allowed for a series of new readings and insights to emerge, such as: the appreciation of the *Oresteia*'s voting as a corrective to the disquieting use of the tyrant-slayer motif, the corrective that Ajax's sword carried 'present' resonance and the identification of his suicide as a form of perverted battlefield *sphagia*, the link between the 'tragic' and 'social' sword in the *Acharnians*, Philocleon's engagement with the tyrant-slayer motif in *Wasps*, the acknowledgment of the importance of Demophantus' oath to the interpretation of *Phoenician Women*, the recognition of the extent of *Bacchae*'s interperformative allusions and the statement made for society through the stage image of Agave with Pentheus' head. Beyond these select specific interpretations, the analysis offers fresh contributions to ongoing debates in the field, furthering discussions of (for example): the type of weapon used by Clytemnestra, the staging of Ajax's suicide and theatre's dependence on art. The broader value of the study can be found, it is hoped, in the potential gains it has demonstrated for the study of citizen identity, performance analysis and the interplay of dramatic genres.

Appendix

Clytemnestra's Sword in the *Oresteia*

The debate over the type of weapon used by the Aeschylean Clytemnestra in the murder of Agamemnon has a long history in scholarship.[1] Since the text nowhere explicitly states whether the weapon used was a sword or axe, arguments have been made for each.[2] Fraenkel in his monumental commentary on Aeschylus' *Agamemnon* made a detailed case in favour of the sword.[3] His analysis relies on three key passages from the trilogy that were already at the end of the nineteenth century established as pivotal for the weapon question.[4] They are:[5]

(i) *Ag.* 1262–3; Cassandra's lines:

> ἐπεύχεται, θήγουσα φωτὶ φάσγανον,
> ἐμῆς ἀγωγῆς ἀντιτείσεσθαι φόνον.

> As she whets a sword for her man, she boasts that the wages of my being brought here will be murder.

(ii) *Ag.* 1525–9; Clytemnestra's lines:

> ἄξια δράσας, ἄξια πάσχων,
> μηδὲν ἐν Ἅιδου μεγαλαυχείτω,
> ξιφοδηλήτῳ
> θανάτῳ τείσας ἅπερ ἔρξεν.

> He is suffering his deserts for an action that deserved them: let him utter no loud boasts in Hades, after making a payment that matched his deed, death by the stroke of the sword.

(iii) *Cho.* 1010–13; Orestes' lines:

ἔδρασεν ἢ οὐκ ἔδρασε; μαρτυρεῖ δέ μοι
φάρος τόδ᾽, ὡς ἔβαψεν Αἰγίσθου ξίφος·
φόνου δὲ κηκὶς ξὺν χρόνῳ ξυμβάλλεται
πολλὰς βαφὰς φθείρουσα τοῦ ποικίλματος.

Did she do it or did she not? This garment is my witness to how it was dyed by Aegisthus' sword; and the stain of blood, joining with the lapse of time, has contributed to ruining many of the dyes in the embroidery.

The position on whether a sword or axe was used relies on the interpretation of these passages as well as two more general allusions to the murder weapon.[6] The passages above place the onus of the argument on those who wish to make a case for the axe.[7] It is therefore unsurprising that Fraenkel's position met with widespread acceptance, until it was challenged in a characteristically spirited manner by Davies who was convinced that Clytemnestra's weapon was an axe. Davies' view was critiqued in turn, however, for its interpretation of both the textual evidence (Sommerstein) and iconography (Prag).[8] Both pieces of criticism offer cogent reasons for rejecting Davies' argument. I do not intend therefore to retread old ground by rehearsing the details of the controversy here but offer a new piece of evidence in favour of the sword.[9]

The significance of two lines from the Chorus' deliberation during Agamemnon's murder (*Ag.* 1350–1) has been overlooked. While the lines appear in Fraenkel's text of the play and receive a generous footnote in the commentary, they are not included in the discussion on Clytemnestra's weapon.[10] The second chorus member to offer an opinion in the choral deliberation says (*Ag.* 1350–1):

ἐμοὶ δ᾽ ὅπως τάχιστά γ᾽ ἐμπεσεῖν δοκεῖ
καὶ πρᾶγμ᾽ ἐλέγχειν σὺν νεορρύτῳ ξίφει.

I think we should burst in straight away, and get proof of the crime when the blood is flowing freshly from the sword.

Or:

And I think we had best rush in at once, and prove the deed while the newly drawn sword is there.[11]

The chorus member imagines, and invites the audience to envisage, either a sword that has just been drawn or one that is flowing with blood (depending on the interpretation of νεόρρυτος).[12] While the weapon supposed here is mere speculation by the chorus member, it is made importantly 'real' by the presentation of the statement as fact – there is not hypothetical, or prophetic, language hindering the projected image.[13] The excitable delivery (marked by the ὅπως τάχιστα followed by the emphatic particle γε) adds further to the impact of the line and its image; its urgency adding to the impression that the sword is drawn right now and the action in response should be immediate. Its occurrence in a heightened moment within the drama, resulting from the unusual formation of the chorus as well as the offstage cries, further strengthens its force.[14] These lines create a strong mental image of the sword as the murder weapon that I suggest then becomes concrete, taking visual form as a prop in front of the audience just twenty lines later at the appearance of Clytemnestra (*Ag.* 1372). This makes for the strongest dramaturgy (the effect of these lines is discussed below) and is also consistent with Aeschylus' technique in making imagery concrete in this trilogy.[15] Far from being concerned, as critics were long ago, over how the chorus member could know which type of weapon had been used, we should acknowledge Aeschylus' deliberate inclusion of this reference in preparation for its appearance.[16] The consideration of these lines therefore sheds fresh light on the weapon debate (presenting a further obstacle to advocates of the axe), but also more importantly allows further appreciation of the dramatic effect of the prop once it is on stage.[17]

The question of whether the murder weapon (whether sword or axe) appeared on stage with Clytemnestra has also proved divisive, depending (as it does) on different understandings of Aeschylus' dramaturgy.[18] I follow Garvie, Prag, Sommerstein, and Raeburn and Thomas in proposing that when Clytemnestra is revealed on the *ekkyklema* after the murder, she holds a sword in her hand.[19] This, as Sommerstein points out, enhances the dramatic impact of her boast about Agamemnon's corpse as (*Ag.* 1405–6):[20]

τῆσδε δεξιᾶς χερὸς ἔργον, δικαίας τέκτονος.

the work of this right hand of mine, an artificer of justice.

The deictic pronoun draws attention to her hand and perhaps implies a gesture here, emphasizing both her hand and the sword.[21] Furthermore, Clytemnestra's use of the 'very rare' adjective ξιφοδήλητος (by the stroke of a sword) to describe the death of Agamemnon (*Ag.* 1528, quoted above) takes on a new force if a bloodied sword is visually present before the audience.[22] It is debated whether the description refers to Agamemnon's death or Iphigenia's, although there is nothing to stop different members of the audience interpreting it as one or the other.[23] For those in the audience who assumed that it referred to

Iphigenia, her death is brought vividly into the frame through this prop (supplying an image that is notably omitted (*Ag.* 248) from the otherwise powerfully graphic description of her sacrifice in the *parodos*).[24] As a reference to Agamemnon's murder, it reinforces the significance of the prop in making real the action of Clytemnestra.

This sense of immediacy had already been created, as discussed above, in advance of Clytemnestra's appearance with the prop, through the chorus member's description of the sword as 'freshly-flowing' (*Ag.* 1351). This reference is revealed to be anticipatory as the mental image is realized on stage. The use of the *ekkyklema* together with the systematic detailing of the deed by Clytemnestra (*Ag.* 1372–94) enhances the sense of tangibility further.[25] Her description of the act may have been accompanied by gestures with the sword, as has been suggested, for example, for line 1384, 'the actor can very effectively mime the blows to the rhythm of these punchy words'.[26] Whether the action was mimed or not, the presence of the sword would enrich the words enabling the visualization of the murder at the same time as confronting the chorus and audience with the irrefutable evidence of its bloodiness and Clytemnestra's boldness. Fresh attention is drawn to the prop, as well as to Clytemnestra's audacity in wielding it, with every reference to Agamemnon being struck (alluded to an insistent six times in the scene).[27] The impact of this would have been made greater by the shock of her appropriation of the male's role in the iconographic tradition.[28] The chorus member's comment about going into the palace to apprehend the act (*Ag.* 1350–1) is deliberately vague about the murderer; allowing the audience to imagine Aegisthus being caught with his sword freshly flowing. This would exploit the device termed by Taplin as 'false preparation' with its double function of creating tension in anticipation of seeing Aegisthus and surprise when Clytemnestra is revealed with sword in hand.[29]

Further arguments for the importance of the sword in the scene can be made by considering this prop's place within the trilogy.[30] Fraenkel, in suggesting that the sword is played down in the scene to allow heightened focus on the entangling robe, overlooked the significance of this prop to the *Agamemnon*'s ending and within the trilogy.[31] Sommerstein, in his challenge of Fraenkel's denial of the sword's prominence, acknowledges the meaningfulness of its presence to the ending of the play.[32] He argues that Aegisthus appears on stage unarmed in deliberate contrast to Clytemnestra who has his sword; thus highlighting the gender inversion between them.[33] Its significance reverberates beyond the *Agamemnon* as subsequent references to the murder of Agamemnon conjure up the stage image of Clytemnestra standing with her sword. This would certainly be the case when Orestes explicitly mentions the sword at *Cho*. 1010–11 (quoted above) while drawing attention to the blood stains it caused.[34] At the same time, verbal echoes link Clytemnestra's sword and Orestes' and contribute to the 'mirroring' of the two acts of bloodshed. The reappearance in *Choephori* of the adjective ξιφοδήλητος (by the stroke of a sword) prompts this association.[35] The rarity of the adjective and its appearance in the context of the murders (after the event at *Ag*. 1528 and in anticipation of it at *Cho*. 729) suggests its deliberate deployment to this end.[36] Another element to the verbal framing offers further potential support to this connection.[37] Above all, however, it is the visual mirroring between the murder tableaus, and the sword held in the hand of first Clytemnestra and then Orestes, that forges the association between the two deeds.[38]

The prop thus plays a part in the structural design of the trilogy, contributing to the mirroring effect between actions and showing itself prominently at the end of the *Agamemnon* and beginning of *Eumenides* as a problem to be resolved.[39] While within the world of the *Oresteia*, the swords are understood to be distinct from one another (one belonging to Aegisthus, the other to Orestes), it would have been dramatically effective to use the same prop across the plays, allowing it to be reimagined as belonging to Orestes to reinforce the mirror effect. The audience could be encouraged to note this by the αὖτε in line 980. In the context it refers to the cloth but could be extended to apply not only to the murder, but also to the murder weapon (they are seeing the sword for a second time).[40] This would complicate Orestes' utterance (*Cho*. 1010–11) about the bloodstains caused by Aegisthus' sword but such complexity is in keeping with the ethically challenging nature of the trilogy.[41] The prop could then be described as 'haunted' by its previous appearance in the trilogy creating an intra-performative allusion.[42] The connection between the two swords takes on particular force for the Athenian audience through the comparison that emerges between the engagement with the tyrannicide motif evoked by this prop in *Agamemnon* and then *Choephori* (see further Chapter 4). Clytemnestra's appearance with a sword thus makes most sense of the text and importantly makes for a powerful dramatic moment in the *Agamemnon* that ripples, by design, across the rest of the trilogy.

Notes

Introduction

1 Connor (1994) 41 and Ober (1994) 102 on citizenship and civic ideology.
2 The discourse is complex through its reliance on flexible 'democratic knowledge', Ober (1994) 103–4. The instability of props' meanings on stage mirrors this. Theatre's contribution is made complex through the intergeneric contestation of the prop's meaning.
3 The study of Athenian citizenship has a long history reaching back to the nineteenth century, though intellectual and historical factors fostered important changes to the approaches taken in the last decades of the twentieth century see Scafuro (1994). Representative of this sea change are: Hall (1989), Manville (1990), Boegehold and Scafuro (1994), and Zeitlin (1996). Vlassopoulos (2007) 33 and Blok (2017) 30–6 for recent overviews of the field.
4 Defining citizenship narrowly through legal status or participation in political bodies is associated with the 'old paradigm', although Scafuro (1994) 2–4 challenges an overly strict adherence to this characterization of earlier scholarship. See also Blok (2017) 31–2.
5 The experience of citizens beyond the institutions (such as the law court and Assembly) see Schmitt-Pantel (1990), Manville (1994), Cartledge (2000), Phillips (2003), and further bibliography in Blok (2017) 32 n. 91. Manville (1990) 13 on 'intangible qualities'. For the influence of performance studies, and its notion of 'scripts', on the analysis of Athenian culture see Goldhill and Osborne (1999) and on citizenship see Farenga (2006) and Duplouy (2018).
6 On the issue of the social and political (*oikos* and *polis*) see Manville (1990) 23–6, Scafuro (1994) 6–9 and Patterson (1994). Vlassopoulos (2007) on blurring. Azoulay (2014) 703–4 on ways of categorizing different types of 'political' engagement; Blok (2017) 47–99 on religious and political; Dmitriev (2018) on the importance of kinship and family to the Athenian concept of citizenship.
7 Performance studies: Farenga (2006) and Duplouy (2018); sociology (above all Bourdieu's *habitus*): Duplouy (2018); structuralist theory: Loraux (1981b), Hall (1989) and Zeitlin (1996) (on this strand to scholarship on citizenship see Blok (2017) 34); anthropology: Manville (1990) and Gehrke (2009); political science: Vlassopoulos (2007). This list is far from exhaustive, see also Scafuro (1994) 1.

8 See above all Woodward (2007) on material culture and identity. In this introduction, I draw on scholarship from a range of disciplines that address times, places, and cultures beyond ancient Athens. It is not my intention to make claims of universality, rather the analyses of these studies can offer a helpful way of thinking through the ancient material. Two studies in Classics that acknowledge the importance of material culture to identity are: Morgan (2009) who explores the expression of ethnic identity through material culture in early archaic Greece and Kosmin (2015) who highlights the significance of the citizen's phenomenological experience of democracy.
9 It is notable that an object-oriented approach was absent amongst the papers delivered at the 'Citizenship in Classical Antiquity: Current Perspectives and Challenges' conference (University College, London, July 2019).
10 Plutarch *Solon* 21.4.
11 Thuc. 1.6. Knowledge of this past fashion survived within social memory in fifth-century Athens as the Thucydidean passage makes clear and Aristophanes' *Knights* 1321–31 confirms. On the expression of identity through dress see Lee (2015).
12 The tree, planted within civic space, can be argued to be part of the city's material culture (the trend towards blurring distinctions between natural and cultural geographies, see Head (2010), invites this reading).
13 Hdt. 8.55.
14 Further confirmed through the inclusion of the olive wreath amongst the recognition tokens in Euripides' *Ion* on which see Mueller (2016a) 71.
15 I use the terms 'citizenship' and 'civic identity' interchangeably; even while Isin and Wood (1999), esp. 19–20, assert the theoretical distinctions between 'citizenship' and 'identity' (critical to the agenda of their study), they also acknowledge affinities between the concepts. The objects discussed in this study impact on Athenian citizens' notion of themselves (i.e. their identity as citizens); this is captured by the term civic identity. The focus is on male citizens since, though I recognize the importance of Blok's work in highlighting the ways in which women could perform their citizenship (Blok (2017)), it has been necessary to restrict this initial study on the relationship between objects and citizenship to the dominant cultural categorization (an examination of objects' influence on female notions of their citizenship would make an excellent subject of future study though, see further the Conclusion).
16 See Azoulay (2017).
17 'Ideologization', Raaflaub (2003) 63 and 83; Hall (2006) 114 on visual codes; expressing the democracy's values through adopting the tyrannicides' pose see Azoulay (2017) 44.
18 On architecture's role in this respect see Patronos (2002).

19 Mueller (2016a) 70–108 offers a persuasive and nuanced analysis of the dynamics at play.
20 On 'intangible qualities' see Manville (1990) 13. I do not deny the value of defining citizenship through a constitutional and institutional lens (in fact this underpins my own approach in parts), but recognize that the concept runs beyond this. Manville's categorization of citizenship as an institution, a concept and an ethic is instructive (Manville (1990) 4). The concern of this study is with the idealized concept of the citizen rather than the blurring of the reality on the ground (on which see Vlassopoulos (2007) 34–8).
21 The settings represent the combination between 'la politique' ('politics' as institutionalized decision making) and 'le politique' ('the political' as interactions sustaining the civic community) that Azoulay (2014) esp. 703–4 argues to be central to the understanding of the Athenian political experience.
22 The symbolism of each is established in detail in Chapters 1, 3 and 6 respectively.
23 I take 'institutional' to apply not only to the Assembly and law court, but also to the army and the city's festivals. For theatre as an 'institution' see Cartledge (1997). See Manville (1990) 20 on military service and attendance at state festivals as manifestations of a citizen's active role in the *politeia*; see also Goldhill (1986) 63–4.
24 Manville (1990) 22 on the public reinforcement of the citizen's military duty to defend the polis and Frost (1994) 52–3 on the way in which fighting forged a sense of citizenship (even before Kleisthenes' reforms). Goldhill (1989), Hall (1989), Zeitlin (1996), Duncan (2006) and Zumbrunnen (2012) on theatre performance and civic identity. Macdowell (1978) 40, Scafuro (1994) 2, and Lanni (2012) 119 on law court.
25 Thuc. 2.37–9; justice (37), drama (38), and land fighting (39) with Manville (1990) 13–16. The reference to drama is implicit, 'competitions and sacrifices' as a means of relaxing from toil (2.38), but the description clearly fits; drama's place in civic experience is also implied by Aristophanes *Ach.* 9–12 (on this play's reflection on Athenian identity see Whitehorne (2005)). While the speech is problematic as a record of the words spoken by Pericles, it can be understood to offer a reflection of the perceived ideal characteristics of citizens (see above all the seminal work of Loraux (1981a) on its ideological function). On the speech's emphasis on the collective values of Athens see Bosworth (2000) esp. 6. On the issue of Thucydides' speeches see further Chapter 1 n.1.
26 Schmitt-Pantel (1990) on the importance of collective activities to the formation of Athenian identity (and Azoulay (2014) 690 on the role of the 'Paris school' in emphasizing collective ritual's importance to citizenship). Pritchard (2012) 202 on hoplite fighting as a 'regular experience'.
27 Stansbury-O'Donnell's analysis of the impact of spectatorship's depiction in Archaic vase painting on the viewer's sense of identity (Stansbury-O'Donnell (2006)) can be

fruitfully applied to the interpretation of the communal gaze's importance to these objects' impact on citizen identity; see Chapter 1 n. 36.
28 More nuanced than considering, for example, solely an activity explicitly concerned with citizen identity (such as his registration, on which see Manville (1990) 8).
29 In the case of swords, this experience ranged from passing the tyrannicides' statue in the Agora to the ideologically heightened encounter of the civic space in festivals and finally to the battlefield. Intangible qualities see Manville (1990) 13.
30 On the role of cultural memory to the formation of collective identity see Assmann and Czaplicka (1995) and Gehrke (2009) on importance of past to construction of identity. On the role of artefacts to the construction of a collective sense of the past see Radley (1990). The active engagement in such retrojection is exemplified through the representation of voting pebbles in images belonging to the mythological past (see Chapter 1).
31 This characteristic connects in a profound way to the flexible character of 'democratic knowledge', on which see Ober (1994) 103–4, mirroring it in form and function.
32 The approach pushes beyond the purely semiotic by recognizing these symbols as material objects that could be handled by individuals in society; on the important shift to reassert the significance of objects' materiality see Jones and Boivin (2010) 336–7.
33 Both because the engagement is multisensory and active (cf. viewing the iconography, the visibility of which is in any case problematic on which see Marconi (2009) esp. 157 n. 3 for bibliography). For parallel claims about the construction of modern citizenship see the useful overview of scholarship offered by Ricke (2017) 178–81, esp. the reference to Trnka, Dureau, and Park (2013) on sensory considerations. While asserting the greater valence of voting, I acknowledge the importance of architecture to the formation of polis identity, see Patronos (2002).
34 On the sense of embodiment see Telò and Mueller (2018b) 1; on agency see Patronos (2002) 18 with Jones and Boivin (2010). Not every citizen will have experienced a personal haptic experience of the objects explored, yet for those who had, the object's power to shape identity was enhanced.
35 The approach of Turner et al. (1994), applying self-categorization theory to articulate the relationship between personal and social identity, has informed my adoption of a model that recognizes the dialectic between the individual and collective identity and sees the distinction between them as a question of shift in perspective (rather than an absolute).
36 Both the sensory and materialist turn in Classics might contribute much to the study of objects' impact on the citizen's sense of identity. Kosmin (2015) demonstrates this potential in his exemplary discussion of ostracism through a phenomenological approach. Telò and Mueller (2018a) has shown the capacity of new materialisms to

unlock the experience of objects on stage. The further pursuit of this approach, however, would be ill-advised in a study intended to *establish* the place of objects in framing civic identity and theatre's role in contributing to civic discourse through them (the thick description and theoretical engagement required to do justice to such an approach risked obfuscating an already complex argument). Nevertheless this would make a very promising area of future study.

37 It did this in other ways too, see, above all, Loraux (1981b) and (1985), Hall (1989), Zeitlin (1996), Duncan (2006), and Zumbrunnen (2012); and Carter (2010) 50 n. 12 for further bibliography on the related subject of tragedy and politics.

38 The concept of the prop's 'social life' is indebted to the work of Arjun Appadurai (1986). For theatre studies' adoption of this approach see Harris and Korda (2002*b*), a study to which my work is also indebted. I follow their definition of props as all moveable physical objects on stage since the semantic range of the ancient Greek terminology for prop, σκευή, suggests an appropriately broad conceptual category, see Wyles (2007) 7 n. 1.

39 The first seeds for scholarship on the 'social' life of the prop were sown, as Harris and Korda (2002) 12–13 note, in the early twentieth century by Walter Benjamin, see Benjamin (1928); the idea, however, is already present in the fifth century BC. The concept of the 'theatrical' or 'dramatic life' (i.e. its history on stage) is informed by the work of Sofer (2003).

40 Euripides' presentation (Ar. *Acharnians* 393–489) surrounded by costumes and props from past tragic performances (see Olson (2002) *ad loc.* (*contra* the suggestion made by Macleod (1974) that the costumes are in fact represented by scripts)). On this scene see Muecke (1982), Foley (1988), Wyles (2007) 123–35, and Compton-Engle (2015) 90–1.

41 Reference to the mask-maker (σκευοποιός, also meaning 'prop-maker' see Aristotle *Poetics* 1450b20 (Ch. 6)) in *Knights* 232 and to the stage-crane handler (μηχανοποιός) in *Peace* 174, *Daedalus* fr. 192 and *Gerytades* fr. 160 (see also Strattis' *Atlantos* fr. 4 and *Phoenissae* fr. 46 with Miles (2009) 135–7 and 187–90). The intrusion of craftsmen and mechanics into the theatrical event, on which see Harris and Korda (2002) 6–7 and 11–12, highlights the life of these objects beyond the performance as something manufactured and requiring handling before and after the production. On the significance of props' production to the interpretation of ancient drama see Hall (2018).

42 It is widely accepted that Aeschylus intended to allude to the clothing worn by *metics* (non-citizen, immigrant, residents) at the Panathenaea festival in Athens through the (likely) use of dark red/purple costuming for the Erinyes; see n. 47 below.

43 Two exceptions are the excellent discussions offered by Mueller (2016a) 134–54 (on the Athenian resonance of Ajax's shield) and Duncan (2018) on the effect of the mask's social life on its theatrical impact. Tellingly, however, these appear in studies

concerned with props (rather than as a section of a study on the relationship between theatre and society). For studies of the interface between Athenian theatre and society see, above all, Sommerstein et al. (1993), MacDowell (1995), Green (1996), Pelling (1997), Goldhill and Osborne (1999), McGlew (2002), Hall (2006), Carter (2011), and Zumbrunnen (2012).

44 This trend has a long history; already in the late nineteenth century Sir Richard Jebb (1888) *ad loc.* was noting the effectiveness for an Athenian audience of the evocation of the ephebic oath prompted by Sophocles' *Antigone* 671.

45 This develops further the recognition that certain passages of tragic drama carried specific resonances for Athenian audience members, see Carter (2010) 53. Throughout the study, the use of 'on stage' and 'onto the stage' are used to indicate the positioning of an object within the playing space (irrespective of whether that might be on an elevated platform or in the orchestra).

46 On Euripides' propensity for putting ordinary objects on stage see Revermann (2013) 45. The 'anachronistic' presence of writing tablets in the tragic world, see Easterling (1985) 4–5, heightened the awareness of this object's 'social life' in Athens (I am grateful to Edith Hall for this point). Costumes too, even in tragedy, could resonate with the present as Heracles' breastplate on the Pronomos vase (Naples, Museo Archeologico Nazionale 81673, H 3240) demonstrates see Wyles (2011) 22–4. On possible exceptions to mythological setting for tragedy see Bowie (1997).

47 The seminal articles in making this case are Headlam (1906) and Goheen (1955). Despite the textual difficulties affecting the line in which this costuming is mentioned, *Eumenides* 1027, Headlam's understanding of the scene has found general acceptance see Taplin (1977) 412–13, Sommerstein (1989) *ad loc.* and Podlecki (1989) *ad loc.* Essential here is the recognition of audience reception in the creation of specific meaning on which see Hesk (2007) 79 and Revermann (2013) 41. Awareness of the potential 'Athenian' meaning to props is confirmed by Ar. *Peace* 45–8. While some dramas may have been composed with a wider audience in mind, see Taplin (1993b) 537–8, the culturally constructed symbolism of certain objects could nevertheless generate specific meaning for an Athenian audience, see the Conclusion.

48 I am indebted to Mueller's formulation of props as 'sites for cultural negotiation', Mueller (2016a) 5.

49 Other objects could be argued to meet with these criteria, this selection of props, however, seemed the most fruitful for the reasons set out in section I.

50 The case studies do not present an exhaustive survey of every stage appearance of the prop but discuss significant examples.

51 On identity in *Ion* see Loraux (1981b) 197–253, Lape (2010) 95–146 and Mueller (2016a) 70–108.

52 So far as we know (based on extant drama).
53 The date of *Theoroi* is unknown, see Chapter 6 n. 87, and so the date range offered here, and in the book's title, takes the *Oresteia* as a secure starting point.
54 Hesk (2007) 81–2.
55 The assumed difference in each genre's relationship with society, see above all Taplin (1986), underpins this trend. Poe (2000) provides a helpful discussion of how comedy's interaction with props differs from tragedy.
56 Even if some objects are 'transformed' in the process of being appropriated from one play to the next, it is still possible to trace this as a significant moment in the object's trajectory. This offers a new approach to considering satyr drama's 'political' engagement (previously attempted through the hunt for topical references in language, see Taplin (1986) 167).
57 On the importance of understanding ancient plays as part of a matrix of dramatic performances and on the meanings generated from the dialectic between tragedy and comedy, see, for example, Farmer (2016) and Nelson (2016). On costume and the body across genres see Reinke (2019).
58 On this characteristic of a community's symbols see Patronos (2002) 16.
59 Ober (1994) 103–4 on this characteristic of 'democratic knowledge'.
60 Taking its lead from the exemplary work of Sofer (2003) and Mueller (2016a).
61 See the Conclusion on this study's approach to iconography.
62 I am grateful to Edith Hall for pointing this out to me, see further Hall (2006) 110.
63 Recent examples of such studies in Classics include Mueller (2016a) and Telò and Mueller (2018b) on tragedy; and Swift (2017) on Roman society. These studies respond to an earlier broader trend marked by the materialist turn beginning in the 1980s see Harris and Korda (2002) 15 and the excellent theoretical overview in Telò and Mueller (2018b) 1–11. The advantages of such an approach for the investigation of the theatre–society interface has been well-established outside Classics, see above all Harris and Korda (2002) and Sofer (2003).
64 The exploration of the 'social' lives of theatre objects, for example, pushes beyond the limits of the pre-ceremonies at the Dionysia, explored in Goldhill's influential article (Goldhill (1987)), to investigate the impact of ideology encoded in objects outside the frame of the theatre festival. The impact of the ground-breaking work by Edith Hall and Froma Zeitlin on this discussion will be clear; as will the influence of scholars such as Eric Csapo, Helene, Foley, Richard Green, Toph Marshall, Oliver Taplin and Peter Wilson. Moreover, I acknowledge the important gains made by scholarship on performance, and particularly props, which has emerged in the last decade or so: Revermann (2006), Chaston (2010), Hughes (2012), Rosenbloom and Davidson (2012), Harrison and Liapis (2013), Milanezi and Guen (2013), Marshall (2014), Compton-Engle (2015), Mueller (2016a), Coppola, Barone and Salvadori (2016), and Telò and Mueller (2018a).

Chapter 1

1. This is evidenced by multiple sources; above all in Thucydides' account of two ideologically laden speeches: the Athenian embassy addressing the Spartans at 1.77 (where the purpose of aggrandizing Athens is made explicit at 1.72.1) and Pericles' Funeral Oration at 2.37. Whether Thucydides records the actual words used by the Athenian embassy and by Pericles or relies on his own sense of what ought to have been said (see Hornblower (1997) n. on 1.73, p. 117, cf. principle set out at 1.22.1 with Hornblower (1997) *ad loc.* (for a brief summary of viewpoints), Yunis (1996) 61–3 (arguing they are purely Thucydidean) and Garrity (1998) defending the notion of the original speaker's words being recorded), both passages remain a valuable reflection of Athenian identity's construct. Related to the importance of law courts to cultural identity is their role as a locus for communication between the masses and the elite (in a context in which the masses had the power to judge the elite), see Ober (1989) 145. The close relationship between judicial engagement and governance (illustrated by the laws of γραφή παρανόμων and ἀτιμία underpins the importance of law courts to civic identity. Aristotle's later identification of the right to participate in judicial functions as a defining characteristic of the citizen of a democracy (*Pol.* 1275a22–23) is indicative of its earlier status.
2. Text and translation Henderson (1998).
3. Dover (1968) *ad loc.* While our surviving manuscript for *Clouds* represents the revised version of the play, I assume that this joke was part of the original production in 423 BC (the opposite assumption would not, in any case, substantially affect the argument here). On revisions to *Clouds* see Revermann (2006) 326–32.
4. Olson (1998) *ad loc.* notes that Aristophanes presents jurying as an 'Athenian obsession' in his early plays. *Wasps*, of course, offers the most elaborately developed exploitation of this; see Chapter 2.
5. Text and translation Henderson (1998).
6. Text and translation Henderson (2000).
7. Dunbar (1995) *ad loc.* offers the translation 'non-jurors' and implies the prominence of this characteristic activity: 'Hearing that the men come from Athens immediately raises the alarming possibility that they may be among the many jurors to be found there.'
8. It suits the pair's rhetorical purpose to emphasize an alternative badge of cultural identity for Athens (the city of beautiful triremes) which as Dunbar (1995) *ad loc.* points out would have had particular resonance in 414 after the magnificent fleet (Thuc. 6.30–2) had set out to Sicily in 415 BC. Yet the identity formed around law courts is presented as irrepressible here; the idea of inescapable involvement in the courts is raised again by the joke at *Birds* 1286–9, on which see Garner (1987) 101 and Dunbar (1995) *ad loc.* Criticism of the system is embodied by the 'odious' figure

of the sycophant and his shameless intention to exploit the allies for personal gain by using the courts, see Dunbar (1995) n. 1410-69, pp. 673-4.

9 Olson (1998) n. 503-5, p. 180 includes this joke in *Knights* as an example of Aristophanes' presentation of the law courts as an Athenian obsession. This reference, however, seems markedly different from the subsequent examples: the Athenians are described in positive terms as delighting or rejoicing in their law courts (the verb used is γηθέω) and, as Sommerstein (1981) *ad loc.* notes, the reason for their instructed closure is because it is festival time (cf. the pointed advice of Hermes in *Peace*). There is some disparagement of the law courts in the suggestion, at 1332, that they stank (because of the mussel shells used as ballots) on this see Sommerstein ibid., but overall this joke does not display the same level of critique as the others, though it does demonstrate law courts as an important aspect of Athenian identity.

10 Boegehold (1963) 367 (pebbles/shells) and on synecdoche, Boegehold et al. (1995) xxvii s.v. *Psephos*, with E. *IT* 945 and *Electra* 1263. This is also implied for urns as demonstrated by, for example, Ar. *Birds* 1032 (with Dunbar (1995) *ad loc.* who notes that the urns suggest that the inspector has been sent to set up a legal system on the Athenian model; i.e. the urns stand for the whole process) and they gain further attention at *Birds* 1053. Garner (1987) 46 describes the voting urns as 'vivid symbols of the judicial procedure'.

11 On the connection between voting and democratic ideology see Easterling (1985) 3 and Cammack (2013). On participation in law courts and civic identity see Lanni (2012) 133-4. See also below.

12 The placement of the urns (one closer to the jury and one further away) seems to have determined which was 'guilty' and which 'not guilty'; for a fuller description of the process see Boegehold (1963) 367 and Boegehold et al. (1995) 23-30.

13 The narrowness of their necks to prevent spilling limited the voter's view of the number of ballots (Bothmer (1974) 15) and their third handle allowed their contents to be easily poured out (facilitating the count).

14 Bronze Greek *hydria*, *c.* 460 BC, J. Paul Getty Museum 73.AC.12. Boegehold (1963) 369 sets the emergence of this form of voting to the late 460s.

15 This *hydria*'s similarity to one in the collection of the Metropolitan Museum, New York 26.50 (the inscription upon which identifies it as a prize offered at the games for Hera at her sanctuary in Argos) suggests that it too served as a prize, see Bothmer (1974) 15. Another bronze *hydria* in the collection of Metropolitan Museum, New York 1999.460 confirms that in the same period such prizes were offered at games in Athens (the inscription on that vessel identifies it as a prize at the competition in honour of the Dioscuri).

16 *Ath. Pol.* 68.3. Bronze would be robust for sustained use and would symbolically convey the value attached to justice but Ar. *Birds* 1053 implies the use of terracotta.

17 Boegehold (1963) 366-7.

18 For ease of reference I refer to 'pebbles' in the remainder of the discussion, while acknowledging that either a pebble or shell could be used.
19 MacDowell (1978) 40 notes that the juror becomes a symbol of Athens; put another way, to be Athenian is to be a juror.
20 So, for example, the statute of the East Locrians, which defines terms for establishing their colony at Naupactus, and is dated on that basis to c. 460 BC (see Tod (1946) 33), specifies as its ninth condition that anyone who tries to subvert the terms agreed in the statute should be put on trial and judged by ballots being cast into an urn (*GHI*^{2} 24, 45–6). The commitment of this community to ensuring access to justice is demonstrated by the statute's seventh condition that agrees the fast-tracking of colonists from Naupactus in trials (*GHI*^{2}24, 32–6). It is important that Eastern Locris is understood to have had an oligarchic government in this period (*OCD* s.v. Locris). On Athenian democracy set in the context of other Greek democracies see Hesk (2017) 2–3.
21 Kosmin's important discussion of ostracism highlights the fruitfulness of an approach that considers the citizen's *experience* of Athenian democratic institutions, see Kosmin (2015).
22 To be eligible they needed to be in possession of full citizen rights, *Ath. Pol.* 63.3 with MacDowell (1978) 34.
23 MacDowell (1978) 34 and 40, and (1995) 51; Ostwald (1986) 68 and 160.
24 The pebble's familiar use as a counter, equivalent to an 'abacus bead', in arithmetic, see Boegehold (1963) 370–1, reinforced this symbolism. On the allusion to this function of pebbles in Ar. *Wasps* 656 see Chapter 2.
25 Schwartzberg (2010) 455–6 and 458.
26 Schwartzberg (2010) 459, and also risked the impact of 'domination' on decision making see Hesk (2017) 5.
27 Dem. 24. 149–51 and 20.118 (for deciding based on his 'best judgement' (γνώμῃ τῇ δικαιοτάτῃ); the juror's duty to protect the city's constitution is explicitly articulated in the first Demosthenic speech against Aristogeiton ([Dem.] 25.11), see Ostwald (1986) 158–60.
28 The comic presentation of the number of trials in Athens is discussed above. While hearings did not take place on certain days (such as on festival days and days with Assembly meetings, see MacDowell (1978) 34), the apparent financial reliance of some citizens on jury pay (reflected in *Wasps* 291–311) implies the frequency of court cases. See further Manville (1990) 18 and his reference to Hansen (1979).
29 On the power of 'doing' rather than witnessing in the shaping of identity, see the Introduction.
30 Importantly both institutions gave the *demos* (i.e. Athenian citizens including the non-elite), the opportunity to exercise its power; on this function of the Boule see Manville (1990) 194–7 and Pritchard (2004) 224–5.
31 Rhodes (1981) 125.

32 Schwartzeberg (2010) 456–7 and on range of use of εἰσαγγελία and its procedure see Rhodes (1979).
33 'cumbersome' Rhodes (1981) 128; he accepts (p. 126) that this form of vote was used by the Assembly when a quorum had to be reached for decisions to be valid which implies the large numbers involved.
34 In cognitive terms promoting 'system 2' deliberation, as opposed to the snap decisions associated with 'system 1', on these systems and their exploration in ancient texts see Hesk (2017).
35 By comparison juries may have been dominated by the older generation see MacDowell (1978) 34–5 (although this is challenged by Crichton (1991)). A significant portion of the citizen population (below the age of thirty) would have been excluded from jury service see Hansen (1995) 187. On participation in the Assembly and Boule see Manville (1990) 18.
36 Viewing's impact on the formation of identity is helpfully modelled by Stansbury-O'Donnell (2006) 52–88, see esp. 71–2. While he analyses Archaic vase paintings, his model can be fruitfully applied to the experience of the communal gaze at public occasions in Athens. In his model, the collective focus (of internal and external viewers) on the vase painting's 'narrative nucleus' confirms its status as an idealized representation. The viewer's identity is constructed (by himself and his peers) in relation to the ideal expressed by the image's central focus. The focus of the citizen peer group on the procedure for voting allows the urns, which represent the democratic ideal, to exert an equivalent effect to an image's 'narrative nucleus'.
37 Exemplifying the principle outlined by Boegehold (1963) 366: 'The vote is fundamental to democratic government, because the individuals who make up the demos rule only when they can register their decisions effectively.' On the dynamic between the individual and collective in the formation of the sense of civic identity, see Introduction, p. 4.
38 The origin of this practice of voting is a thorny issue (Boegehold (1963)) and I do not mean to imply the law courts' precedence in a literal sense, since they represented the distilled power of older institutions (Ostwald (1986) 70). Voting by ballot, however, was associated with the courts primarily, and so its symbolism within that setting informed the interpretation of its use elsewhere; Busolt (1920) 454–5 made a related argument long ago for the impact of the terminology of voting. The fourth-century view of the power of the *dikasteria* as the backbone of Athenian democracy (Ostwald (1986) 70) reflects this.
39 Andocides *On the Mysteries* 97.
40 See Introduction, p. 2, and Patronos (2002).
41 The trial took place in the Assembly 'convened in a judicial mode', see Gish (2012) 172 and 174; the urns and pebbles embody this experiential crossover for citizens. On its notoriety see Gish (2012) 162.

42 Xen. *Hell.* 1.7.9–10. Text and translation (slightly adapted) from Brownson (1918). My emphasis.
43 On the issue of the legality of Callixeinus' proposal and Xenophon's role in representing it as illegal, see Pownall (2000) 502–4. On the trial as a model of Athenian democratic deliberation, see Gish (2012).
44 Neither the well-known concern over Xenophon's bias (on which see Kelly (1996) 157–8 in general and Pownall (2000) and Gish (2012) (arguing against bias) on the account of this trial in particular), nor the thorny issue of the discrepancy between Diodorus' and Xenophon's account of the trial (on which see Asmonti (2006) 1–2) affects the usefulness of this passage as evidence of late-fifth century views on the centrality of the objects in this process.
45 Xen. *Hell.* 1.7.34. Two of the Arginusae generals prudently did not return to Athens, Xen. *Hell.* 1.7.1. The recognition that *hydriai* could be used as urns for ashes, Bothmer (1974) 15, offers another resonance although it is not explicitly marked in the text.
46 On the emotional charge of symbols relating to identity see Patronos (2002) 16.
47 For the establishment of a sense of Athenian citizenship by *c.* 500 BC see Manville (1990).
48 Williams (1980) 142 identifies eight 'certain examples': Douris, Vienna 3695; Douris, Paris *Cab. Méd.* 537 and 598 (fragments); Douris, Vatican Astarita 133 (fragments); Douris, Vatican Astarita 132 (fragments); Makron, Athens Acropolis collection 315 (fragments); Brygos, London E69 (1843, 1103.11); Brygos, now Getty 86. AE. 286 (formerly Bareiss); and Leiden Rijksmuseum PC75. Spivey (1994) 51 includes further examples cf. Lissarrague and Schnapp (2007) 26.
49 See Williams (1980), Spivey (1994) 41–7, and Boegehold et al. (1995) 131 for details of further distinctions between their iconographic schema. Spivey (1994) prefers 'iconographic formulae' (39) and the 'consonance of presentation' (48) to schema.
50 Spivey (1994) 51.
51 Spivey (1994) 50. Athena also plays an important role here. On the agency of identity-shaping objects see the Introduction, p. 4, with Patronos (2002) 18.
52 Suggested as a prototype for the cups by Spivey (1994) 49. This alternative format for the iconographic schema has further implications since it freed the two exterior images from the interpretative impact of the tondo image (on which see Catoni (2015) 22–8; the viewer was not prompted to consider the voting image in relation to Ajax's suicide (e.g. as in the Brygos cup (Ch. 4, Fig. 19) but was free to interpret it in relation to his own experience.
53 Neer (2002) 144 on ambiguity.
54 Attic red-figure kylix, from Vulci, attributed to the Painter of Louvre 265, *c.* 475–470 BC, Leiden Rijksmuseum PC 75. Illustrated in *LIMC* II Aias 112. On the

importance of the tondo images in this series of cups as a 'key' to the direction of their narrative see Catoni (2015) 22–8.
55 Musée des Beaux-Arts, Dijon, CA 1301. Beazley (1963) 829 no. 37. On dating see Neer (2002) 138 and 142.
56 Neer (2002) 136.
57 Schmidt (1967) 80 notes the issue of preservation. Up until Neer's publication (Neer (2002) 138–42), the cup had not gained the attention it deserved (see Oakley (2003) 510); Beazley (1963) 829 no. 37 and Schmidt (1967) provide only brief descriptions. Neer (2002) 138–42 offers a more detailed discussion but seems to be working from photographs provided by the museum (implied by certain details being overlooked). The description offered here is based on first-hand examination of the vase.
58 Neer (2002) 138 misses this object from his description.
59 Beazley suggest that they have a supervisory role labelling them 'superintendants', Beazley (1963) 829 no. 37. Schmidt (1967) 80 goes further by considering whether they are simply observing or adjudicating, and reflecting on whether they are holding ballots to hand over to the electorate or to cast them as votes themselves; the proportions are problematic (see below). Most recently Lissarrague and Schnapp (2007) 28 refer to the urns as being under the control of these seated magistrates. Boegehold (1963) 367–8 notes the necessity of such supervision in the fifth-century system of voting.
60 Schmidt (1967) 80 and Neer (2002) 139. I am grateful to Lucy Jackson for pointing out that the viewer may see only one end of the ballot (shell) held long ways in the hand of the figure standing to the right of the urn. The shape of the object held by the damaged figure (if a ballot) adds further support to the view that the seated figures hold ballot shells.
61 Damage to the cup prevents greater clarity on this point.
62 Neer (2002) 138 by contrast interprets this gesture as indicating surprise.
63 The beardlessness is taken as a point of great significance by Neer (2002) 138 and 140–1. I return to it later in the discussion. While there is damage to the surface of the vase in precisely the area showing the bending voter's face, there is enough of a clean-shaven chin line surviving to suggest that he may well have been depicted without a beard.
64 Traces of very short paint strokes along the jawline, consistent with the strokes used in the depiction of beards elsewhere on the vase indicate this; there are not many since the angle of the figure's body limits the extent of the jawline that is visible.
65 On ways of wearing the *himation* see Lee (2015) 113–16.
66 The certainty of Neer's description is misleading: 'Directly behind this jar, and partially obscured by it, is a bearded adult: he bends forward and drops a *psēphos* into the container'; Neer (2002) 138.

67 The man standing over the urn is bending forward, but even so he is still notably shorter than the man beside him (who is also stooped).
68 Beazley identifies the seated figures only as superintendants, Beazley (1963) 829 no. 37. The figure standing behind the tall man seems, from the curve of his spine, to be involved in this issue as well (rather than 'standing quietly off to one side' as Neer (2002) 138 suggests). This mirrors the support and involvement of the secondary figure (standing behind the seated figure) in the other discussion of an issue on Side B.
69 It can be presumed (though this part of the cup is damaged) that he holds the stave which he is shown leaning upon in his other hand.
70 The distinction is made by Beazley (see above). Neer (2002) 139 argues that the figures on this vase represent equality, but does not note the significance of this gesture to his argument.
71 The positioning of the right-hand figure's stave in this pair indicates that this other figure is likely to have been turned towards his companion in conversation since his right hand resting on the stave would be consistent with him turning to the right.
72 Neer (2002) 138 identifies the vote on Side B as more agitated. Schmidt (1967) 80 goes much further in suggesting that the two sides of the vase depict different phases of the voting processes: Side A showing voting with ballots, Side B the drawing of lots to determine the pairings for the *agon* (debate). Schmidt's argument, however, depends on conjecture over a damaged portion of the vase (the left-hand voting urn of Side B, from which she argues the beardless man may be drawing a lot) and is perhaps also prompted by the broader context for her discussion of this vase (her consideration of the use of lots to determine pairs in choruses for Dionysus).
73 A strictly Doric style would have a pin on each shoulder; on different styles of female dress (and combinations of Ionic and Doric elements) in fifth-century iconography see Barker (1922). He identifies female Doric dress as more typically depicted on temple sculptures, with Ionic being more prominent in vase painting. This adds to the intrigue of the style of dress depicted here. On the *peplos* see Lee (2015) 100–6.
74 See the helpful discussion of hairstyles in Lee (2015) 72.
75 I am grateful to Anna Dugdale for pointing this out. If it is an indication of status then this presents a challenge to the interpretation of this figure as a slave on which see n. 79 below.
76 As noted by the curator, Catherine Gras in her description of the cup (published in proceedings available in the museum archive). The Attic red-figure *skyphos*, dated to 430–420 BC, now in the Ashmolean, AN1934.339 offers a helpful parallel since it represents a female character similarly clothed and in the same pose as the seated figure here and so provides potential insight to the damaged part of the composition (I am grateful to Anna Dugdale for drawing this to my attention).

77 Brooke (1962) 22 on the formation of pleats on the Ionic *chiton* and Lee (2015) 106–10 on the *chiton* in general.
78 Female: see, for example, Eos (whose *chiton* is also patterned with dots along its border) on the interior of the Attic red-figure cup by the Douris painter and now in the Louvre (G115), dated to *c.* 490–480 BC; male: see the *erastes* on the interior of the Attic red-figure cup by the Briseis painter, Louvre G278) dated to *c.* 480 BC.
79 This supports Catherine Gras' reading of the image as two women (see above, n. 76). She concludes that this must be a female slave and her mistress. Both Beazley (1963) 829 no. 37 and Neer (2002) 138 leave the sex of this seated figure undetermined. The Attic red-figure kylix in the collection of the Walters Art Museum (48.90), dated to *c.* 450 BC and attributed to the Stieglitz painter, depicts a similarly clothed figure (in pleated long *chiton*, with dots at its border and with a *himation* wrapped round) on its tondo. The *sakkos* hanging to the right of the figure invites her identification as female. Further support for this reading of the image on the tondo of the Stieglitz cup in Dijon is offered by the Attic red-figure *skyphos* (Ashmolean, AN1934.339) that shows a similarly dressed female in the same pose, see above n. 76.
80 The placement of the images (exterior/interior) neatly corresponds to the ideological ideal of male/female domains (see Cohen (1989)).
81 Schmidt (1967) and see also, for example, Osborne (2008) 6.9, p. 222.
82 It is not clear whether the images depict voting in the law court or the Assembly (in the circumstances discussed above); the setting, however, does not impact on the analysis here since the ideological significance of the action in either location was equated (see above). A case might be made for the depiction of ostracism, with the 'ballots' on the cup representing *ostraca* (pottery sherds); if so, the symbolic equivalence between that procedure and voting with ballots, on which see Rhodes (1981) 129, secures the relevance of the evidence. On the procedure see Hansen (1995) 34; the use of urns in the process is suggested by Missiou (2010) 48 though Kosmin (2015) 123 and 135 describes the sherds as cast into a circular enclosure (undermining the case for the depiction of ostracism on this cup).
83 The debates taking place alongside this action arise from it, rather than offering a competing subject; thematically they are linked since deliberation is another signature activity of the democracy.
84 This interpretation applies the model set out by Stansbury-O'Donnell (2006) esp. 71–2. The gaze lines of internal viewers in both exterior images draw attention to the urns (although Side A is more emphatic).
85 Side B's composition is cluttered compared to Side A, with nine figures squeezed into its frame (cf. seven on Side A) and displays greater division between its units (i.e. three vignettes delineated by the positioning and gaze of its figures: the two seated figures to the far left conversing, the central four figures engaged in a dispute, and

the three figures concerned with the right-hand urn). On the indications of agitation see Neer (2002) 138 and 140–41.
86 On the violence see Spivey (1994) 50.
87 Neer (2002) 138–42 reflects on its ambivalent elements; his claim of the complexity generated by 'inconsistencies' (between the images and reality) is based in part on a misunderstanding of fifth-century voting (p. 139), but other aspects of the composition do appear to be designed to challenge the viewer.
88 Stansbury-O'Donnell (2006) 52–88 on spectatorship in vase painting and the impact of sympotic viewing of cups to the construction of social identity in Archaic Athens. The frontality of the short figure on Side B also prompts this (see Frontisi-Ducroux (1995) on this effect of frontality).
89 Boegehold (1963) 367–8 on concern with corruption. Whether these seated figures should be viewed as superintendants (Beazley (1963) 829 no. 37) or jurors, Neer (2002) 139, and see also Schmidt (1967) 80), is debated, although their status as fellow citizens is a safe assumption. A further indication of corruption may be indicated by the apparent infiltration of an under-age voter (the beardless figure), as argued by Neer (2002) 138 and 140–1; although if the vote represented here is at the Assembly and not the law court (see p. 173 n. 82), this would lower the minimum age to be eligible to vote (to 18, see Blok (2017) 206).
90 On the democratization of competence see Schwartzberg (2010) 455–6.
91 The assertion of such influence may be wishful thinking on the part of the painter.
92 Neer reads the cup as a glorification of *isonomia* (Neer (2002) 139–40 and 149). On this term see further Chapter 3, p. 57.
93 The description of the cup above highlights aspects of the images which assert and breakdown superiority.
94 On this effect in Athenian voting see Schwartzberg (2010) 460–1.
95 For this interpretation of the short bearded figure and the dispute see above p. 27.
96 This adjustment would correspond to the contemporaneous shift in the understanding of *isonomia*, see Rosivach (1988) 50. The concern over influence is explored on stage soon after the production of this cup in *Eumenides* (implied by Athena's instruction to the jurors to judge with their honest opinion, *Eum.* 674–5, and reinforced by the references to their oath *Eum.* 483–4, 489, 679–80 and 708–10). Decades later, *Wasps* demonstrates both the acknowledgement of influence (Philocleon boasts about attempts to affect his vote, 548–58) and offers a parodic articulation of the potential for interference (*Wasps* 990–2). The power dynamic to Bdelycleon's interference, see Konstan (1995) 25–6, reinforces its significance. On both plays see Chapter 2.
97 Neer (2002) 138: 'The interior is fragmentary and depicts a woman approaching a seated figure – the sex is uncertain due to breakage – who is clad in a long chiton and himation. But it is the exterior that is of real interest: it shows two sets of

jurymen, or *dikastai*, in the act of casting their votes.' Yet the choice of representation in the tondo has been argued to be 'key' to understanding the narrative context for a cup's images, Catoni (2015) 22–8.
98 Catoni (2015) 22–8 makes the argument for the significance of the tondo images in these cups functioning as 'keys' to their intended narrative direction, but does not consider the gender implications of the choice of interior representations.
99 Interior myth identified by Davies (1973).
100 A further example is offered by the Brygos cup in the British Museum, E69 that shows a man leading a woman in its tondo (discussed briefly by Catoni (2015) 25).
101 On the equivalence between the casting of the ballots and the female's gesture as significant actions in the images, see p. 28. The damage to the cup makes the presence of an object on the interior conjectural. The assertion that female activity could be understood as 'performing' citizenship, Blok (2017), might be fruitfully explored in relation to this cup; the composition would nevertheless still mark the contrast between the construct of male and female citizenship. Pericles' citizenship law in 451/0 BC, on which see Boegehold (1994) and Blok (2009), may have altered the perception of the interior image's function within the composition.
102 The relationship between this cup and the trilogy is explored further in Chapter 2.
103 See Hesk (2017) 13 on this function of theatre.
104 The action's ideological significance is emphasized in the narrative through Miltiades' framing of it as even more important than the tyrannicides' celebrated action, see Taylor (1991) 18–19 and Chapter 3. On Marathon's importance to Athenian self-definition see Gehrke (2009) and Markantonatos (2013a) 69–70.
105 The language is metaphorical (the polemarch does not literally have a ballot); the adoption of the terminology of the pebble-ballot form of assessing opinions reflecting the powerful impression made by this practice see Busolt (1920) 454–5. While the precise dating of Herodotus' work is debated, on which see Dewald and Marincola (2006) 2–3, the conventional date of his birth sets his adulthood within the period of the Stieglitz cup (and the symbolic status of voting within cultural discourse it implies).
106 See Introduction, p. 3, for the relationship between collective activity and civic identity.
107 This concept is explored further in the analysis of *Eumenides* in Chapter 2.

Chapter 2

1 On 'stage life' see Sofer (2003).
2 In marked contrast to vase painting see Chapter 1, p. 33.
3 Goldhill (1986) esp. 78 and Cartledge (1997) on this social function of theatre.

4 Almost two hundred years ago, Hermann (1820) put forward the theory that Aeschylus' *Danaid* trilogy (dated to earlier than the *Oresteia* see Bowen (2013) 21) ended with a trial. The supposed defendants in this trial have been debated, on which see Robertson (1924). The hypothesized ending, however, owes much to the *Oresteia*'s model and to later sources on the myth (see Bowen (2013) 30 and Johansen and Whittle (1980) 49). I follow Johansen and Whittle (1980) 53 in doubting the inclusion of a trial (*pace* Farenga (2006) 384). Further potential forerunners have been proposed based on the series of cups discussed in Chapter 1: Williams (1980) 142 and Spivey (1994) 40 and 50-1.
5 On general significance see, for example, Calder (1958) 154.
6 For legacy: Bakewell (2013) highlights the theatricality associated with the voting but does not consider subsequent productions and Garner (1987) 109-23 does not consider the props.
7 Athena emphasizes the setting (*Eum.* 685-90).
8 Bakewell (2013) 150 on Athena voting.
9 Athena has explained that a tie will result in acquittal (*Eum.* 741) - Sommerstein (2009a) 449 notes that this was the regular rule in Athens citing *Ath. Pol.* 69.1.
10 On textual issues (affecting understanding of staging) see Taplin (1977) 395-401 and Bakewell (2013) 149 n. 2.
11 I accept the case made by Sommerstein (1989a) 222-4 on the number of jurors. See also Bakewell (2013) 150 n. 5 and Fletcher (2014) 67-8.
12 *Wasps* 94-6 may imply that jurors in Athenian courts held their pebbles for a length of time before voting (favouring the first suggestion), although the usual concerns with comic exaggeration apply. The alternative gains support from Athena's instruction to the jurors to take up (αἴρειν, 709) their ballots.
13 Musée des Beaux-Arts, Dijon, CA 1301. Revermann (2013) 45 argues for theatre props having regular dimensions. Sommerstein (1989a) 566-84n, p.185 proposes that the urns may have borne 'distinctive marks' to indicate which was for condemnation and which for acquittal, though in the fifth-century law courts the distinction seems to have depended on positioning alone, on which see Boegehold et al. (1995) 28.
14 Both materials were used for *hydriai* see Bothmer (1974) 15.
15 See Sommerstein (1989a) 566-84n, p.185 and Bakewell (2013) 150 and 154.
16 The casting of the vote towards urns on the ground has the advantage of engaging meaningfully with the trilogy's network of imagery, offering a positive symbolic substitute for blood cast on the ground (on this motif see Lebeck (1971) 84).
17 Taplin (1977) 391 suggests that benches and urns are brought on but does not specify when; Sommerstein (1989a), p. 185 envisages their arrival between the end of the choral song and Athena's entry. The blocking suggested here allows for the

symbolic reversal of fatal movements towards the *skene* earlier in the trilogy, see Bakewell (2013) 154.
18 They are the focus for an even longer period than Sommerstein (1989a), p.185 acknowledges.
19 Text and transl. of these passages from Sommerstein (2009a).
20 I follow Bakewell (2013) in envisaging the Chorus on one side, Apollo and Orestes on the other, and Athena in the middle. The jurors may have gazed towards the urns reinforcing this effect.
21 Bakewell (2013).
22 Bothmer (1974) 15 on the sheen and Shirazi (2018) 102–7 on the light-emitting quality of bronze in antiquity. This sheen would be further enhanced through the torch procession at the end of the play, on the symbolism of which see Taplin (1977) 415. On the progression of imagery in the trilogy see Lebeck (1971) and on the beacon see Weiss (2018) 176–84. The imagery in *Ag.* 390–3 refers to bronze adulterated with lead (Sommerstein (2009a) 47 n. 84). The urns would also present a positive incarnation of the metalwork formerly sullied by Clytemnestra's disingenuous pledge of fidelity (Holm (2012) interprets her words, *Ag.* 611–12, as referring to the fabrication of bronze vessels). Bakewell (2013) 155 suggests the urns are associated with death (through earlier allusions in the trilogy).
23 The jurors on stage are verbally equated to their contemporary counterparts through the use of the term δικασταί (483, 684, 743), though their masks and costumes would have mediated the extent to which they were felt to mirror 'real life' jurors. On tragic costume indicating the past see Wyles (2011) 86–7. On 'distancing' masks see Calame (1995) 114 and Monaghan (2008) *contra* Wiles (2007) 42. Bakewell (2013) 151–2 notes audience familiarity with the legal process on stage but does not explore the theatrical implications of this.
24 On semiotics in Greek theatre see Revermann (2006) 36–45 and Wyles (2011) 46–60. While Easterling (1985) 2–3 argues that language is used to 'naturalise' the process of voting into the heroic world, she does not consider the visual impact of these 'anachronistic' voting objects.
25 Billings (2018) 49 acknowledges the importance of this for props in general, noting that this makes them 'ontologically fraught'.
26 Sommerstein (1989a) 17 notes the general similarities between Orestes' trial and an ordinary court in Athens; reinforced, for example, by the reference to jurors as δικασταί (483, 684, 743) and by Athena's echo of the oath used in law courts (674–5 with Sommerstein (2009a) 441 n. 144). For the equivalent effect in Aristophanic 'Assembly' scenes, see Rhodes (2004) esp. 224.
27 On this point see Bakewell (2013) 151–2 with n. 18. The denotation of jurors as δικασταί (483, 684, 743) is indicative of this strategy. Athena's specification that she will select 'the best among my citizens' to serve as jurors (*Eum.* 487) seems designed

to appeal to aristocrats (interpreting it as a reference to the elite members of the Areopagus) and to the ordinary citizen (understanding it as an acknowledgment of the honour associated with serving in the jury, paralleling the analogous democratization of the *kalokagathia* concept on which see Ober (1989) 250–60), see MacLeod (1982) 127.

28 Sourvinou-Inwood's concept of 'zooming' and 'distancing', despite criticism (see, for example, Foley (1995)), remains helpful as an analytical tool; Sourvinou-Inwood (1989) and (2003) with Goldhill (2000) 44, n. 49.
29 Revermann (2013) 40 on 'presence' of props cf. words.
30 On the use of benches in law courts see Ar. *Wasps* 90 and in theatre of Dionysus see Csapo (2007) 103–8 and Lech (2009a). On the comparison of the two experiences see Hall (2006) 359.
31 Sommerstein (1989a) p. 186 suggests that the theatre audience may be the intended target for the reference to the public (στρατός) at line 566 and supports this proposition by noting that Athena addresses the Athenian people directly in three instances (572, 683, 707–8). Note, however, Taplin's reservations over accepting this (or any other 'direct' audience address in tragedy); Taplin (1986) 166. More recently, Villacèque (2007) has made the case for the existence of such addresses in tragedy in general (*contra* Bain (1975) and Taplin (1986)), and see judicious comments of Carter (2010) 62–3 on these lines in *Eumenides*.
32 See the Introduction on the importance of communal viewing and collective acts to identity.
33 For the already extensive scholarship on this passage in the mid-twentieth century, see Fraenkel (1950) *ad loc.* The divine vote prefigures the one taken in *Eumenides* but with significant differences, see Raeburn and Thomas (2011) *ad loc.* and Bakewell (2013) 156–9. It is significant that there is not a semantic distinction between the voting pebbles and urns used on the divine plane cf. the court in Athens (in contrast to Homeric epic in which gods use their own words to signify objects, on which see Minchin (2011)). On the cultural biography of objects see Appadurai (1986).
34 Spivey (1994) 40 on ennobling fifth-century voting. See the Introduction, pp. 2–3, on the role of the past in forging the symbols of a society's collective identity.
35 On the place of communal focus and collective activity in the formation of social identity see the Introduction.
36 On the difficulties of offering precise dates for vase paintings, see Burn (2010) 22. On conflict and order on the cups see Spivey (1994) 50. Neer (2002) 145–6 overlooks the implications of the relative chronologies of these artistic responses.
37 Spivey (1994) 49.
38 The suggestion that Aeschylus alludes to art can be supported by the compelling case for the equivalent phenomenon in Aeschylus' *Myrmidons* see Giuliani (2013) 195–207. Visual prompts in Aeschylus' staging of the court scene may have further

cued this: Athena's presentation in her aegis (*Eum.* 404), raising her arm to declare the victor (Bakewell (2013) 153 n. 22 on *Eum*.752 with Williams (1980) 138 and Spivey (1994) 44 on the cups). The potential dramatic exploitation of iconography is explored further in Chapters 4 and 6.

39 *Eum.* 483–4, 489, 674–5 (implied by allusion), 679–80 and 708–10.
40 Sommerstein (2009a) 441 n. 144.
41 Attic red-figured cup attributed to the Stieglitz Painter, Musée des Beaux-Arts, Dijon, CA 1301.
42 The cups show the vote taking place through the open placement of ballots in a pile in front of Athena; I follow Boegehold (1963) 370 in resisting the assumption that these vases reflect contemporary practice or an accurate depiction of past practice. See Boegehold et al. (1995) 23–30 for a description of Athenian court procedure between 460–*c*. 410 BC.
43 She undertakes the supervisory role enacted by human figures on the Stieglitz cup, allowing Aeschylus to avoid the negative power dynamics implied by that composition (on which see Chapter 1).
44 *Ath. Pol.* 25.1–2, Plut. *Cim.* 15.2–3 and Plut. *Per.* 9.5 with Ostwald (1986) 47–50, Rihll (1995), Lewis (1997), esp. 358–9, and Samons (1999) 225–7.
45 On Aeschylus' innovation, Sommerstein (1989a) 5.
46 This line of enquiry was already well established in the late nineteenth century, see Campbell (1880) 428. A helpful overview of the shifting politics attributed to Aeschylus in scholarship is offered by Bowie (1993) 10–11. Further treatments include: Macleod (1982), Sommerstein (1989a) 31–2, Marr (1993), Griffith (1995), Samons (1999) (on the link to the Alcmeonids), and Goldhill (2000).
47 Neer (2002) 142–6 is the exception: although his interest lies in the potential of Aeschylus' *Eumenides* to illuminate his discussion of the vase paintings.
48 Spivey (1994) 51. In this case legitimizing the 'novel' role of the law courts, established only a few years earlier; on the stage presentation relating to the law court experience (though nominally representing the Areopagus), see above p. 39.
49 Neer (2002) 144 identifies ambiguity, pondering whether the vases celebrate the 'epic style of voting at the expense of the new democratic courts; or do they heroize contemporary life?'. Despite the controversial aspects of Neer's work in general, see Smith (2005), his analysis remains valuable. The argument that *Eumenides* adopted a reconciliatory stance has a long history; an early example of this view is offered by Smertenko (1932) 233. See more recently Sommerstein (1989a) p. 218, Marr (1993) and Hesk (1997) 85. This adds another dimension to the analysis of the trilogy's 'horizontal relationships' (between the elite and other communities) presented by Griffith (1995).
50 Resonating with Athena's ideals of stability expressed in her charter speech for the Areopagus court, especially 693–5, on the possible political implications of them see

Sommerstein (1989a) *ad loc.* This invites the modification of Meier's claim (Meier (1990) 89) that Aeschylus evolved 'new concepts' to articulate and bring into equilibrium the experience of rapid political change.

51 The considerable volume of scholarship on gender in the *Oresteia* owes a debt to the seminal articles by Winnington-Ingram (1948) and Zeitlin (1978). Since the Stieglitz cup is unique, it would be unsafe to make the claim of a direct response to its iconography specifically. It seems reasonable, however, to assume that both the Stieglitz cup and trilogy are responding to wider patterns of Athenian ideological thinking. This corroborates Goldhill's linking of the bias inscribed into Athenian civic ideology with the *Oresteia*'s gender discourse (Goldhill (1986) 59). On iconography's role in shaping the conceptualization of civic life see Lissarrague and Schnapp (2007) esp. 50.

52 The presentation of the objects as belonging to both the Areopagus and the popular court, on which see above p. 39, is essential to this effect. On the possibility that the law-court voting system was historically adopted from the Areopagus see Rhodes (1981) 129.

53 Sommerstein does not accept Jacoby's suggestion (Jacoby (1954) 24) that the trial was Aeschylus' invention, but does concede that the tragedian made the following 'major innovations', making: the trial of Orestes the first to be held in the court; the Erinyes prosecutors (instead of Clytemnestra's kin); and the jury consist of Athenian citizens rather than Olympian gods; Sommerstein (1989a) 4–5. The last of these is the most important to the argument presented here. On the earlier tradition's influence on audience expectation see Bakewell (2013) 150 n. 3. On the cultural impact of drama's *embodiment* of narrative, see Taplin (2016).

54 Sommerstein (1989a) n. 1028, pp. 281–2. While the overlap between everyday life and the theatrical presentation of the *metic* robes would be mediated by the Erinyes' masks (Sommerstein (1989a) 10), the urns and pebbles would have offered a direct visual analogue to those used in the law courts. They also gain greater force as objects with which the citizen interacted.

55 Taplin (1986) 171.

56 Csapo (2002) on this rise in 'realism'; the application of his argument for the ideological basis for the critique of performance 'realism' (esp. 145–6) to this example suggests that the voting procedure was perceived as elevated enough to be a palatable dramatic subject.

57 On Athenian involvement in their allies' legal affairs: Thuc. 1. 77. 1 and [Xen.] *Ath. Pol.* 1.16 with MacDowell (1978) 224–8 and Rhodes (1985) 39. Goldhill (2000) 45 argues that the pre-performance display of tribute was introduced shortly after the *Oresteia*, but views it as part of a long process of Athenian imperialism. It may not seem unreasonable to include allies amongst those with whom this staging might resonate, although it is far from clear when Athenian control over aspects of their

allies' judiciary were imposed. The decree regulating Athenian relations with Erythrae (*IG* i², 10), however, offers an example of Athens dictating punishments (if not hearing the cases) in an ally's judicial system and has been dated to Ephialtes' reforms (i.e. just before the *Oresteia*) see Meiggs (2008) 61–4. The dating of this aspect of Athenian control of their allies is linked to the notoriously thorny issue of the Athenian empire's growth on which see Rhodes (1985) *passim*, Meiggs (2008) and for the revisionist late dating of strict imperialism see Mattingly (1996) with Liddel (2010).

58 West (2006) 38.
59 Patronos (2002) 13–14 notes that references to the collective cultural memory intensify in times of political crisis and shifting power relations. The place of the voting equipment in the cultural past is asserted along with its status as a positive symbol of Athenian ideology in response to the Areopagus reforms.
60 On the deliberateness of this silence and general reluctance to depict civic machinery in vase painting see Neer (2002) 136 and Lissarrague and Schnapp (2007) 25.
61 This engagement in the discourse through props is in addition to the other means through which drama might express attitudes about laws and their administration on which see Garner (1987) 105–25.
62 The date of *Inachus* is unknown. I work from the assumption that it was produced after the *Oresteia*, though I acknowledge that since Sophocles is said to have first competed against Aeschylus in 468 BC (*TGrF* 4 T 36–7), it is possible that *Inachus* predates the *Oresteia*.
63 Text: Radt TrGF4 fr. 288, p. 265 and translation Lloyd-Jones (1996).
64 Text: Radt TrGF4 fr. 295, p. 267.
65 Calder (1958) 155 argued this eloquently long ago when positing a trial as part of the dramatic action.
66 Calder (1958) 154–5 and on satyr play issue 148 and 155 n. 58.
67 Lloyd-Jones (1996) 113 and 116–17.
68 On *Eumenides* see above.
69 The reference to the *kemos* reveals that two voting urns must have been used, on which see Boegehold et al. (1995) 28–9. It is unclear whether the *kemos* was used in the *Eumenides*, although as Boegehold (1963) 368 notes the outcome of the vote is not known at *Eum.* 734–51 (which might suggest its use?). While the jurors in *Inachus* are described as 'bean-throwing' and beans were used to elect public officers by lot in Athens (see *LSJ* s.v. κύαμος), it seems fair to take this as a poetic means to indicate the use of voting counters such as the pebbles used in the *Oresteia*; cf. the use of the term πάλος (lot) in *Eum.* 742 to designate voting pebbles for metrical convenience see Sommerstein (1989a) *ad loc.*
70 The new setting does not prevent the play from inviting reflection on Athenian civic identity; for this principle see Hesk (2007) 81–2.

71 On this concept see Wyles (2019b).
72 Bakola argues this for the trial in *Plutoi* (which she dates to the Lenaea of 429 BC) and suggests that *Eumenides* (which she sets closer to 424 BC based on Aristophanes' response to it in *Knights* 529f) may have been a reworking of that earlier engagement, see Bakola (2010) 49, 135–8, 174–7, and 208–13; and Bakola (2013). See also, with greater caution about Cratinus' *Eumenides*, Farmer (2016) 92–3.
73 For Hagnon's trial in *Plutoi* the only clue to staging is *PCG* 4 fr. 171.66-7 which instructs the summoned witnesses to stand 'here'. On the limitations of what survives of Cratinus' *Eumenides* see Bakola (2010) 176.
74 *PCG* 3.2 fr. 101, p. 78. Henderson (2008) 161 suggests that *Farmers* may have been produced at the Dionysia in 424 BC, the Lenaea 423 BC, or the Dionysia in 422 BC.
75 Fr. 110 further indicates the play's ideological engagement see Henderson (2003) 174.
76 On the relationship between these two comedies see Biles and Olson (2015) xxix–xxxii (on the *agon* scene see xxx). A fragment of Cratinus' *Pytine* seems to imply the possible use of voting props in that comedy's *agon*, fr. 207 K-A: ἀπὸ ποτέρου τὸν καῦνον ἀριθμήσεις; ('From which one will you tally up the lots?'); see Biles and Olson (2015) xxx, n.10, this is their translation. The identification of καῦνον with κλῆρον is made in Schol. VΓ on Ar. *Peace* 1081, see Kassel-Austin (1983), *PCG* 4, p. 228. On the relationship between Aristophanes and Cratinus see Ruffell (2002).
77 Wyles (2020).
78 Σ Ar. *Frogs* and *Life of Aeschylus* 12 inform us of fifth-century revivals of Aeschylus' plays, on which see Biles (2006–7). Hammond (1984) 379 n. 19 and 386 supports the case for a revival of the *Oresteia* in the 420s. I argue this point further in Wyles (2020).
79 *Wasps* 855. Ladling cups is the standard translation for this term. The scholia on this passage, however, in fact offer the following possibilities: (a) ladles, (b) small cups (*kotyliskoi*), or (c) wine pitchers (*oinochoai*); Σ Ar. *Wasps* 855a–c for which see Boegehold et al. (1995), 216 Test. 270. Sommerstein (1983) *ad loc.* makes a persuasive case for ladling cups by noting that they would have been already present on stage beside the soup pot mentioned at 811–12; Biles and Olson (2015) *ad loc.* reach the same conclusion.
80 On comedy's interest in food see Compton-Engle (1999) 326 and Wilkins (2001); on its use of 'homely' things see Poe (2000) 285 and diminishing status of props in paratragedy see Revermann (2013) 37.
81 On terms for voting urns see Boegehold et al. (1995) 210. On vessels used to gather water from wells and public fountains see Lynch (2011) 151–2.

82 On jury numbers see MacDowell (1995) 151. For the assumed use of a pebble: Biles and Olson (2015) 987n. suggest that a 'small domestic item' may have been used instead of a pebble, but the text remains open to either possibility. MacDowell (1971) 987n assumes that a pebble is used for the voting (the earlier reference to Philocleon's piles of pebbles in the house (*Wasps* 109–10) supports this). On the thematic significance of Philocleon's dissociation from the collective aspect of the jury system see Konstan (1995) 25.
83 καδίσκος is the diminutive of κάδος (water jar) but its use in Lycurgus' *Against Leocrates* 149 does not seem to have a diminishing effect. The full context, however, is unclear since Lycurgus is likely to be quoting from earlier poetry, on which see Boegehold (1980). On the bathetic force of this diminutive elsewhere in *Wasps* see Biles and Olson (2015) 321n.
84 Text and translation Henderson (1998).
85 This is the diminutive of ἀρυτήρ (ladle): *LSJ* s.v. ἀρύστιχος.
86 See Revermann (2013) 37 on comic parody's diminishing of props' status and see further Chapter 5.
87 This offers an entertaining variation on the prop-accumulating scenes in *Acharnians* and *Knights* on which see Nelson (2016) 62. Biles and Olson (2015) 805–25n (pp. 331–2) suggest that the interest and humour of this sequence in *Wasps* is in the first instance visual.
88 For voting urns as a focal point in trials see Garner (1987) 46 and 98. This is emphasized earlier in *Wasps* 321 when in Philocleon's song he uses voting urns to stand for (through the figure of synecdoche) the law court, see Biles and Olson (2015) *ad loc.*
89 I have argued elsewhere that this part of the scene alludes to *Eumenides*' voting scene through a series of verbal prompts especially *Wasps* 993 cf. *Eumenides* 744) and *Wasps* 997 cf. *Eumenides* 845–6 and 879–80; see Wyles (2020). This focus is particularly marked since comic props are more often brought onto stage only to be ignored, on which see Poe (2000) 286 and Revermann (2013) 37–8.
90 On *deixis* in fifth-century drama see Jacobson (2011). Text: Biles and Olson (2015).
91 Bakewell makes a persuasive case for its significance; Bakewell (2013), esp. 150–1.
92 By contrast the *hydria*'s shape offered greater concealment of the votes see Bothmer (1974) 15.
93 The scene's satirical enactment of jurors' prejudice and irresponsibility, Konstan (1995) 25, contributes to this. The *kemos*' use demonstrates that secrecy in the voting procedure was a live concern see Boegehold et al. (1995) 27–9.
94 On legal terminology and procedure see, for example, Biles and Olson (2015) 891–2n, 894–7n, 922–3n, 950–1n, 958–9n, 962n, 977n, 979n, and MacDowell (1971) esp. 976–7n. For further aspects of the scene that conform to 'audience expectations of juridical practice' see Marshall (2014) 141. For the semiotic equivalence of the voting pebble see n. 82 above.

95 For other ways in which Aeschylean grandeur is perhaps undermined in *Wasps* see Wyles (forthcoming). On Aristophanes' approach to tragic theatre in general in *Wasps* see Farmer (2016) 117–54, Telò (2016) 27–121, and Wright (2013).
96 This comic assertion takes on a further self-reflective dimension given that trials could be perceived as equivalent to a comic performance on which see Hall (2006) 387. See also Chapter 5 on comedy's appropriation of this role through its treatment of swords.
97 See above all: Slater (2002) 98–9, Jedrkiewicz (2006) 63, Telò (2010) 283–7, and Farmer (2016) 133.
98 On the *Acharnians*' scene: Compton-Engle (2015) 88–94, Wyles (2007) 125–35, Muecke (1982), and MacLeod (1974).
99 On comedy's use of 'homely' things see Poe (2000) 285.
100 Creating a further, overlooked, dimension to the 'combining' of the *oikos* and *polis* in this play (on which see Hutchinson (2011) 62–7).
101 On diminishing props' status in paratragedy see Revermann (2013) 37.
102 For a related marking of generic territory in *Thesmophoriazusae* see Zeitlin (1981) esp. 305–6.
103 See further Chapter 5.
104 Hammond recognizes its use to comment on *Choephori*, Hammond (1984) 378–80. Euripides' manipulation of the urn may also comment on Sophocles' *Electra* which also creates rich symbolic meaning through the exploitation of an equivalent prop within its dramatic action (on which see Segal (1980) 134–7, Mueller (2016) 111–33, and Billings (2018)). The uncertainty of dating and inability to establish which play was performed first (Finglass (2007) 1–4), however, limits such analysis. I follow Hammond (1984) 386–7 in assuming Sophocles' play was the later of the two (based on his view that the play shows signs of being composed in response to Euripides').
105 Cropp and Fick (1985) 23 propose 422–417 BC on the basis of metrical resolutions. Cropp remains of this view, Cropp (2013) 31–3, though see Roisman and Luschnig (2011) 28–32 who argue for a date shortly after 415 BC.
106 Hammond (1984) and Marshall (1996) 96 on Euripides' *Electra* and Wyles (2020).
107 The embedded 'stage directions' concerning the urn and the stage focus on this prop were noted long ago by Hammond (1984) 373.
108 On characters' comments 'refreshing' focus on props (or costumes), see Wyles (2007) 187 and (2011) 51–2.
109 Hammond (1984) 380–1. Roisman and Lushnig (2011) 241–3 offer a very brief overview of 'Electra's pots' in *Choephori*, Sophocles' *Electra*, and Euripides' *Electra*; on the self-consciousness of its transformation in Euripides' play see Miles (2013) 193–4.

110 On τεῦχος as a pivotal symbolic term in *Eumenides* see Bakewell (2013) 155.
111 Hammond (1984) 380–1.
112 Mueller (2016) 116 describes its 'secular transformation' as 'iconoclasm'. The Euripidean prop is itself similarly targeted in Plato Comicus' *Skeuai* (fr. 142 K-A) see Miles (2013). Aristophanes engages with a similar technique in *Wasps* 656 when he alludes to the pebble's function as a mathematical aid (on this function see Boegehold (1963) 370–1), juxtaposing this everyday function of the object with its symbolically elevated one of representing a citizen's vote (established at *Wasps* 109–10). It is telling, however, that the pebble retains its judicial symbolism in the mock trial scene.
113 This is given further emphasis through the revelation that Electra does not need to carry out the duty of fetching water (*El.* 64–6); this 'performance' of her role as dutiful wife (*El.* 67–76) heightens the self-consciousness of the object's symbolism.
114 On the progressive transformation of negative images to positive in *Eumenides* see Lebeck (1971) 131–3. This seminal work on the trilogy's chains of imagery can be fruitfully applied to the shifting meanings of props.
115 Bakewell (2013) 155.
116 Ar. *Birds* 1032 with Dunbar (1995) *ad loc.*
117 Ar. *Birds* 1053; implying the use of terracotta in this instance.
118 Konstan (1998) on its ideological engagement.
119 *PCG* 7, Test. ii, p. 409.
120 *PCG* 7, fr. 33, p. 410. Translation adapted from Boegehold et al. (1995) 219.
121 On the wordplay see Garner (1987) 46.
122 See Chapter 1.
123 Aristophanes (*Frogs* 33, 190–2, and 693–6) refers to the battle and the decision afterwards to give additional rights to slaves who had fought in it, rather than to the trial.
124 On this function of comedy's rewriting of objects' symbolism see Chapter 5.
125 Hall (2006). For examples of explicit references to tragic figures see Antiphon 1.77 and Andoc. 1. 129, with Garner (1987) 100. Garner's discussion of law and drama (Garner (1987) 95–130) focuses more on the congruity of administrative and institutional procedure of theatrical presentations and law, as well as offering commentary on laws emerging from tragedies.
126 Hall's important discussion mentions voting urns in passing, Hall (2006) 386.
127 Xen. *Hell.* 1.7.9–10.
128 On the theatre's influence on law courts see Hall (2006) 353–92; the principle could be extended to include the Assembly (when it engaged in the law court's style of voting, on which see Chapter 1).
129 Hall (2006) 353–92.

130 They were also used in the selection process for theatre judges; see Pickard-Cambridge (1988) 95–8 and Garner (1987) 97–8 (though he is incorrect to suggest that different vessels were used in law courts). For the evidence on the selection of judges and their voting process see Csapo and Slater (1995) no. 113, p. 161 (Isocrates *Trapeziticus* 33–4) and no. 122, p. 163 (Lysias *On the Wound by Premeditation* 3).

Chapter 3

1 As has been well established in scholarship, see especially Rosivach (1988), McGlew (1993) and Raaflaub (2003); I follow them in treating tyranny as an ideological symbol. This is not the place to engage with the debate over the nuances of tyranny's use in the slogans 'polis tyrannos' and 'demos tyrannos' (on which see Raaflaub (2003) 77–82) since the sword focuses attention primarily on tyranny as expression of concern over usurpers (see Henderson (2003) 155 on this concept).
2 Self-definition and 'civic duty' see Raaflaub (2003) 70–2.
3 Rosivach (1988) 44–5, Raaflaub (2003) 70, Henderson (2003) 156; for Assembly see Ar. *Thesm.* 338–9.
4 Rosivach (1988) 45–6; for Dionysia see Ar. *Birds* 1072–4 with Wilson (2009). Tyrannicide honours at Panathenaea see Shear (2012).
5 See Goldhill (1987). For festivals as opportunities to articulate and legitimate civic ideology see Pritchard (2004) 224.
6 On the statue group, see below. 'Ideologization', Raaflaub (2003) 63 and 83.
7 On the essential part played by the 'military outlook' in the Athenian sense of citizenship see Goldhill (1986) 63–4 with Pritchard (2004) 209–10 on the numbers of citizens involved.
8 Manville (1990) 22.
9 The story of the tyrannicides Harmodius and Aristogiton is related in Hdt. 5.55–7, Thuc. 6.53–9, and [Aristotle] *Ath. Pol.* 17.3–19.1; Thucydides account is valuable in confirming the popular tradition that it seeks to correct. The drinking songs, recorded by Athenaeus 15.695a–b (= *PMG* 893–6) and discussed below, are important evidence for the ideological significance attached to the pair's actions. For the story's status as a 'foundation myth' see Ludwig (2002) 159–60, Henderson (2003) 174, Shear (2007) 152 and Teegarden (2014) 32.
10 See Raaflaub (2003) esp. 64, 72 and 83.
11 This is worth emphasizing since it has been overlooked for reasons explained below.
12 For the group's 'superb isolation' Azoulay (2017) 36; also Raaflaub (2003) 63–4. On unusualness of honour see Dem. 20.70. The sculpture replaced one by Antenor

which Xerxes had stolen; for the ideological implications of both actions see Hall (1989) 67–8.
13 Azoulay (2017) 40–2.
14 For a detailed description of the poses see Azoulay (2017) 40–2. Keesling (2003) 173 accepts that the figures corresponded 'in pose and general appearance' to the Roman marble copy in Naples (National Archaeological Museum, Naples, 6009 and 6010). The Museo dei Gessi's copy (Fig. 13), however, leaves less to the imagination when it comes to the swords' prominence in the composition (cf. the hilts in the Naples copy). Further confirmation of the pose is offered by the tyrannicides' representation on the reverse of a set of Athenian silver coins, dated to 84–83 BC and celebrating Sulla's own tyrant deposition, see Heijnen (2018) 88–9.
15 The dynamic of the action would result in the raising of the scabbard.
16 The fifth-century iconographic evidence for the tyranncides clusters around two periods: 470–450 BC and *c.* 400 BC. The first group includes: an Attic black-figure white-ground *lekythos* (Vienna, Kunsthistorisches Museum 3644); an Attic red-figure *stamnos* (Würzburg, Martin von Wagner Museum 515); fragments of a red-figure *skyphos* (Rome, Museo Nazionale Etrusco di Villa Giulia 50321) and (uncertain) Attic red-figure *skyphos* fragment in Agrigento, Museo Archeologico Regionale 206391. In the later set: two red-figure *oenochoai*: Boston, MFA 98.936 and Rome, Museo Nazionale Etrusco di Villa Giulia 44.205; and amphorae with tyrannicides as shield emblem: British Museum, London, B 605; Roemer-und Pelizaeus-Museum, Hildesheim, 1253, 1254; Archaeological Museum, Cyrene, no inventory number. All representations in the first set include at least one sword, as do those of the second group that I have been able to check (BM and MFA holdings). The set of red-figure *choes* (jugs) produced at the end of the fifth century, discussed by Azoulay (2017) 80–3, also include swords in their iconography: Boston, MFA 98.936, Rome, Museo Nazionale Etrusco di Villa Giulia inv. 44255, and Ferrara, Museo Nazionale di Spina, no. 6406; as do several fifth-century *staters* from Cyzicus (see, for example, Boston MFA 04.1343 with Azoulay (2017) 188–9). See also Neer (2002) 168–82.
17 For further discussion of the significance to this reconfiguration of the tyrannicide statue's iconography see Neer (2002) 177–81.
18 Athenaeus 15.695a–b (= *PMG* 893–6). For a discussion of these songs see Lambin (1992) 273–82 and on the debate over the number of songs preserved in Athenaeus' account see esp. 275 – I follow him in accepting four.
19 Athenaeus 15.695a (= *PMG* 893). My translation. 'Political equality' can also be rendered 'equality under the law' for the term see Ostwald (1969) 96–136 and Rosivach (1988) 47–52.
20 Athenaeus (our source for the songs) was writing centuries later although Lambin (1992) 309 suggests that his source was written in the period 375–275 BC. Raaflaub

(2003) 65–6 accepts that the songs express sentiments close to the events but notes that the Aristophanic references to them (see below) suggests familiarity beyond the elite. On the shift in *isonomia*'s meaning see Rosivach (1988) 50. This mirrors the statue's appropriation of aristocratic topoi on behalf of the city, see Neer (2002) 170–1.

21 The singer invites his audience to assess him against the tyrannicides, constructing an identity for himself through the juxtaposition (the effect is equivalent to 'transposition' on which see Stansbury O'Donnell (2006) 72 and below on *Lysistrata*'s more explicit exploration of this).

22 On the evocative, rather than literal, nature of certain lyrics see the important argument of Bowie (1986) 16 on Archilochus fr. 4.

23 Lambin (1979) and (1992) 273–82 is mistaken to deny the primary meaning of ξίφος; the textual evidence is more complex and the iconographic evidence more significant than his analysis acknowledges.

24 Further reinforced through Theseus' depiction in the style of the tyrannicides, see further Chapter 4 p. 75.

25 Alluded to in: Ar. *Ach.* 980 and 1093; *Wasps* 1225; *Lys.* 630–3; and *Storks* fr. 444 K–A (quoted by scholium on Ar. *Wasps* 1238a), perhaps produced in the 390s (on which see Henderson (2008) 323) which demonstrates the longevity of the song's cultural prominence. I owe these references to Crawford and Whitehead (1983) 151 and Lambin (1992) 458 n. 35.

26 Henderson (1987) 148.

27 Text and translation Henderson (2000).

28 Although Aristogiton is the older of the pair, he would still make a striking visual contrast to the comic old men. The more explicit use of comic imitation, with the effect of undercutting grandeur, in Ar. *Wasps* 1168–73 lends further support to this suggestion.

29 The stripping that takes place at 615 is a standard precursor to choral dancing, Compton-Engle (2015) 53, but here carries the further benefit of evoking the iconographic schema for the tyrannicides. Aristogiton is shown with a *chlamys* draped over his arm in the Naples copy of the statue group as well as the black-figure white-ground *lekythos* dated to *c.* 470 BC (Vienna, Kunsthistorisches Museum 3644), the late fifth-century BC Attic *oenochoe* (Boston MFA 98.936) and the fifth-century BC *stater* from Cyzicus, Boston MFA 04.1343.

30 Henderson (1987) n. 633–5. On the contrast between the ideal and comic body see Foley (2000) with Compton-Engle (2015) 26. The further dimension to the fun here is that the tyrannicides' poses were associated with the schema for commemorating athletic victory (Keesling (2003) 174) – this presents another ideal beyond the old men's attainment.

31 A further aspect to the comic framing is the possible double entendre to line 632 see Henderson (1987) n. 630–1 with Lambin (1979). On the debunking of the sword through its phallic substitution, see further Chapter 5.

32 Henderson (1987), p. 151; see also Henderson (2003) 173 on popular paranoia over tyranny reflected in this play.
33 Azoulay (2017) 44.
34 See Henderson (1987), p. 151, on accusations of tyranny as evidence of patriotism. Raaflaub (2003) 72: 'Leaders and citizens defined their civic virtues and identities, their democracy and their liberty in opposition to tyranny, past and potential.'
35 Stansbury O'Donnell (2006) 72 explores this process of 'transposition' through which the viewer places himself next to the represented ideal visually and conceptually, so that the gaze of the group marks the ideal and the viewer as equivalent on some level and constructs a social identity for the viewer based on his embodying some aspect of that ideal.
36 McGlew (2012) esp. 91–2 and 99, and Azoulay (2017) 6. For the reflection of this political focus on history in comedy see Henderson (2003) esp. 174–5.
37 Thuc. 6.53.3 and 6.60.1 with Henderson (2003) 169. Ober (1994) on Thucydides' programmatic use of this example, at 1.20, as part of his agenda to criticize Athenian democracy by highlighting the unreliability of 'democratic knowledge'.
38 Meyer (2008) 13 notes the unusualness of this in Thucydides' work.
39 McGlew (2012) for an overview of the interpretations.
40 Azoulay (2017) 15 on historians and philosophers setting their narratives in deliberate distinction to popular belief. This accounts for the details of the assassination in Thucydides' account (he describes the tyrannicides as carrying daggers, τὰ ἐγχειρίδια, 6.57.1 and 6.58.2) being at odds with the iconographic and poetic evidence discussed above; I take this as another example of Thucydides' attempt to correct popular tradition.
41 McGlew (2012) 92. I accept the compelling case made by Shear (2007) 153–7 (*contra* MacDowell (1962) 136) for the swearing of the oath just before the Dionysia (on the day after the Proagon); if the oath were sworn as part of the pre-performance rituals in the theatre itself, as argued by Wilson (2009), 24, then this would make an even more forceful impact on the response to the festival's plays. For an alternative view on when the oath was sworn see Teegarden (2014) 36–7.
42 Andocides *On the Mysteries* 97 (text and transl. Loeb; slightly adapted).
43 The opening reference is implicit but no less forceful for that (see Ahl (1984) 178–9 for this effect in ancient literature).
44 As argued by Shear (2007) 152. Teegarden (2014) 32 also assumes the swearer would take the tyrannicides' actions as his model.
45 The suggestion of its dominance is reinforced through the physical proximity of the inscribed oath to the tyrant slayers' statue, on which see Shear (2007) 152. On the significance of the reference to the 'vote' in this oath see Chapter 1.
46 McGlew (2012) 97–8 claims that the oath's promise is theoretical, noting that Athenians 'did not start running around identifying fellow citizens as tyrants and

summarily executing them' (98); *contra* Shear (2007) 152: 'The good Athenian is required not only to model himself on Harmodius and Aristogeiton, the Tyrannicides and the "founders", as it were, of the democracy, but also actually to become them by performing exactly the same deed.' See Wilson (2009) on the relationship between the oath and the crowning of Thrasybulus. Teegarden (2014) 37–53 makes a case for the impact of the oath on the Athenian mobilization against the Thirty Tyrants.

47 For this location of the oath swearing, Shear (2007) 158. If the oath were sworn in the theatre (Wilson (2009) 24), then the juxtaposition with the parade of war orphans would lay emphasis on the sword's use on behalf of democracy. For an alternative suggestion for how it was organized, advocating a 'decentralized' model, see Teegarden (2014) 36–7.

48 See, for example, Goldhill (1986) 63–4 and 144–5, Manville (1990) 20–2, and Pritchard (2004) 209–10.

49 Manville (1990) 9–10 and Pritchard (2012) 202. Christ (2001) on the tension between the ideology of participation and reality (which confirms, nevertheless, the ideal). Pritchard (2012) 202 notes that the introduction of military pay for hoplites in the 450s resulted in fighting as a hoplite becoming a regular experience of increasingly large numbers of poor Athenians.

50 Pritchard (2012) 204 on the public funeral as an expression of the ideological democratization of war. Goldhill (1986) 145 on communal event. Morris (1994) 74 on this event as an opportunity to create an alternative, civic, symbolic system for honouring the dead (cf. former elite trends).

51 Thuc. 2.43, see Chapter 1 n. 1 on the issue of its reliability, with Goldhill (1986) 64 and, on the public endorsement of this value, Manville (1994) 22. This can be understood to resonate particularly with hoplite fighting since earlier in the same speech, Pericles emphasizes Athenian ability in land battles, see Thuc. 2.39. The hoplite was the 'normative citizen soldier in the democracy's popular culture' Pritchard (2012) 208.

52 Raaflaub (2003) 64–5 (quotation from p. 65); he compares their association with Achilles and Diomedes in one of the drinking songs (*PMG* 894) to the heroization of the Persian war dead in Simonides' Plataea elegy.

53 Taylor (1991) 18–19.

54 Text and translation Henderson (1998).

55 Translated by Sommerstein (1981) as 'crossed swords with'. While line 772 undercuts the claim through its comic wordplay and trivializing of Marathon's legacy, it does not dismiss it and by highlighting the commemoration of the event draws further attention to its significant place within cultural memory.

56 As noted in Pericles' Funeral Oration, Thuc. 2.36 (see Chapter 1, n. 1 on the issue of its 'accuracy'); see also Xanthaki-Karamanou (2013) 213–14 on Thucydides' use of

the motif more generally. The idea is also raised by Bdelycleon in *Wasps* (for example, 678–9 and 684–5).

57 The reading of Demos' response as being shaped by his experience of Cleon's exploitation of his tenuous family connection to Harmodius (Sommerstein (1981) *ad loc.*) seems rather convoluted. Olson and Biles (2015) 1226n. offer a more persuasive interpretation, taking this passage in *Knights* as exemplifying the use of the motif in recognition of a truly noble deed (in contrast to its implied appropriation for self-promotion by Cleon at *Wasps* 1226). On Marathon's role in defining Athenian identity in drama see Papadodima (2013) and more generally, see Gehrke (2009) 85–92.

58 On Demos as personification of Athenian demos see Carter (2010) 57.

59 McGlew (2012) 91–2 suggests that they 'lay never far below the surface in the Athenians' collective political thinking', with Shear (2012) who argues that their cult was celebrated at this festival. For the Panathenaea's role in reinforcing Athenian values in general see Phillips (2003) esp. 202.

60 Amphorae with tyrannicides as shield emblem: British Museum 1866,0415.246; Roemer- und Pelizaeus-Museum, Hildesheim, 1253, 1254; Archaeological Museum, Cyrene, no inventory number. Associated with the Panathenaea of 402 BC, Shear (2012) 110. Though produced late in the fifth century I accept these amphorae as evidence of a pre-existing cultural concept, discussed above, that linked the tyrannicides' deeds with the defence of Athens.

61 McGlew (2012) 99.

62 It is possible to see the swords and sheaths on the amphora in the British Museum (1866,0415.246). Shear (2012) 110 notes that it is the statues, rather than the deed, that is represented on these amphorae and so it is fair to assume that the ancient viewer familiar with the statue pair from the Agora, would assume the detail of the swords in the miniature. Teegarden (2014) 45 suggests that the vases characterized the overthrow of the Thirty as an act of tyrannicide.

63 Shear (2012) esp. 117–18.

64 Parker (2008) 146 with inscriptional evidence: *IG* I³ 34, 41–2; *IG* I³ 71, 56–8; and for same requirement made of colonists: *IG* I³ 46. 15–17.

65 Athenian power is demonstrated through the imposition of penalties for erring in this requirement see *IG* I³ 34, 41–3. The connection of the two ideas is raised in Pericles' Funeral Oration (Th. 2.35–46), the ideological function of which has been well established (see above all the seminal work of Loraux (1981a)).

66 It could still hold meaning, for example, for the sector of society identified by van Wees (2004) 55–7 as 'working-class hoplites' who may not have owned a 'full' panoply (possessing only the requisite spear and shield). For the numbers of citizen hoplites, and the estimate of the involvement of approximately 30 per cent of Athenian adult males, Pritchard (2004) 209 n. 8.

67 A full panoply included shield, helmet, breast plate, greaves, sword and spear, Crowley (2012) 31.
68 The closely connected notions of fighting and ideology are brought out with superb clarity in Lysias' later funeral oration (Lys. 2.17–19). This speech can be taken to reflect well-established patterns in cultural thought. Also relevant here is Athens' self-presentation at the outbreak of the Peloponnesian war as the 'greatest and freest city', see Raaflaub (2003) 80.
69 The Erythrae decree, *IG* I³ 14, conventionally dated to the mid-fifth century but argued by Moroo (2014) to date to late 435/4 BC, includes a clause which seems to threaten death to anyone aiming at restoring tyranny (line 32, with Malouchou (2014) 93 on the possibility of reading the accusative form). If the decree were set up in the Acropolis, as suggested by Moroo (2014) 106, then this public display of the principle reinforced its place within Athenian ideology.
70 For the Panathenaea's role in reinforcing Athenian values see Phillips (2003) esp. 202. Participating at festivals promoted a heightened awareness of identity, as a performance of citizenship (see Blok (2017) 202–5), prompting reflection on the values shaping it.
71 On this effect of viewing see Chapter 1 n. 36.
72 On this ceremony see Isocrates *On the Peace* 8.82 and Aeschines *Against Ctesiphon* 3.154 with Goldhill (1987), with counter-arguments of Carter (2007) 40–3, and further comments in Goldhill (2000) 46. Goldhill (2000) 47 dates the introduction of the tribute ceremony to 'shortly after the *Oresteia*' to coincide with the transfer of the Delian league treasury from Delos to Athens; the war-orphan ceremony may have been introduced at the same time. It should be noted that while conventionally the treasury's relocation is dated to 454 BC, this is based only on the first tribute list, *IG* I³ 259, see further Rhodes (2013) 213.
73 Demonstrated by Isocrates' appropriation of the motif to demonstrate the cost of war (*On the Peace* 8.82 with Goldhill (1987) 63).
74 Goldhill (1987) 61–2 and 68.
75 As noted by Crowley (2012) 104, in his argument that the hoplite represented the ideal man for Athenians.
76 Text and translation Adams (1919), lightly adapted and my emphasis.
77 The two superlatives used of the proclamation are indicative of this agenda.
78 I follow Carey (2003) 216 in this deictic reading of the pronoun (rather than the adverbial usage (*LSJ* s.v. ὅδε IV 1.b.) rendered in Adams (1919)).
79 Goldhill (1987) 64 mentions this reciprocity in passing.
80 The *kata-* prefix implies that the war orphans were 'fully armed' and therefore presented in a complete set of armour (with the sword included).
81 Wilson (2009) 26 suggests, based on Ar. *Birds* 1074–5 and the interpretation of Demophantus' oath as updating older practice, that this was well-established as one of the pre-performance ceremonies.

82 The presence of 'outsiders' draws attention to the tension between the 'emic' and 'etic' construction of the community's identity (on which see Patronos (2002) 8), and so heightens the citizen's self-consciousness over the significance of the identity-forming ceremonies taking place.
83 For the sword's role in hoplite fighting see Lazenby (1994), 96–7, Hanson (2002) 26, Everson (2004), 163–4 and Crowley (2012) 56–7.
84 On which see n. 4 in the Introduction.
85 On the heroizing characteristic of nudity in Greek art see Osborne (1997). The tyrannicides' statue displays the equivalent effect.
86 Moore (1997) 190 supports the suggestion that the vase represented an Amazonomachy though notes that the remaining fragment cannot offer evidence of this.
87 On the relationship between the symposium, vase paintings, and the formation of Athenian sociopolitical identity see Neer (2002) *passim*. On the assertion of elitism amongst hoplites see van Wees (2004) 57–60. On the elite appropriation of civic iconography see Morris (1994) 74 and 81–2 (however I do not agree that this appropriation must be perceived as subversive). A related phenomenon can be detected from the inclusion of a *oenochoe* depicting the tyrannicides in Dexileos' elite cenotaph, *c*. 394 BC, see Neer (2002) 176–7.
88 A similar motif can be found, for example, on the Attic white-ground *lekythos*, now in Boston and dated by the museum to *c*. 440 BC (Museum of Fine Arts, Boston 97.375); Oakley (2004) 29 with Fig. 9.
89 Goldhill (1986) 144–5 on the difference between the mentality of Homeric hero (in pursuit of individual glory) cf. the fifth-century hoplite fighting for his city.
90 On ideologization see Chapter 3 n. 6.
91 It is dated by the Piraeus museum to *c*. 420 BC. Arrington, however, dates it to *c*. 410 BC on the basis of inscriptional evidence, see Arrington (2015) 221–2 and further below. Another example is offered by the late fifth-century Attic tombstone for Sosias and Kephisodoros, now in the Staatliche Museen, Berlin 1708, that depicts two armed hoplites; discussed briefly (and illustrated) in van Wees and Viggiano (2013), 62–3 with Figs 2–3, see also Osborne (1998) 37.
92 As Arrington (2015) 222 notes.
93 Goette (2009) 199 overlooks the sword.
94 On the composition see further Squire (2018) 530.
95 This corresponds to the shift identified by Osborne (1998) 39 to *stelai* demonstrating the assertion of collaborative virtues.
96 As implied by the names from the *stele* appearing on casualty lists: *IG* I³ 1190, 42 for Lykeas and *IG* I³ 1191, 250 for Chairedemos; the connection is made by Goette (2009) 199 and Arrington (2015) 222. The identification of Lykeas on the *stele* with the Lykeas mentioned in the casualty list is made more compelling by the rarity of

97 In addition to the *chiton* that he wears (in contrast to Chairedemos), he also carries a spear, shield (given prominence by the way in which Lykeas grasps its inner strap) and sword (its scabbard strap is visible running across his body).

98 Goette (2009) 199 uses this as an example to further his argument that trierarchs wanted to be depicted in grave reliefs as armed warriors. Arrington (2015) 223 by contrast argues that this choice of representation indicates a strategy of 'middling' (by playing down wealth).

99 This is the case whatever the motivation for the choice of iconography. Osborne (1998) 37 argues that the late fifth-century grave *stele* for Sosias and Kephisodoros (Berlin 1708) communicates apprehension rather than pride over the hoplite role (and he takes this as representative); this reading however does not sit well with the example discussed here.

100 Goette (2009) 202 with Morris (1994) 74 and 81–2 on elite appropriation, in *stele* imagery, of polis iconography. Morris' argues that this expresses the assertion of superior status by the elite, but acknowledges (pp. 73–4) that distinct social groups might interpret artefacts differently. In this case, the *stele* could be viewed by the non-elite citizen as an expression of civic ideals (cf. Morris' argument about white-ground *lekythoi*, p. 80).

101 Oakley (2009) 208 (on domination) and 210 (on 'arming-departure scene').

102 *ARV*² 1241, 6; Oakley (2009) Figs 55 and 56, pp. 514–15. Formerly in the Hirschmann collection, it was sold by Sotheby's in 1993 (Sotheby's (1993) 116). The powerful combination of the downward-facing gaze and sword at the moment of a warrior's departure re-emerges on a slightly later white-ground *lekythos* by the Quadrate painter, *c.* 440–430 BC, Antikensammlung, Staatliche Museen zu Berlin, Inv. 30219,47; Oakley (2004) 72 (Figs 42–4) and 74. On this vase a female figure gazes down at the sheathed sword that she holds in front of her, ready to pass to a male figure (her husband?). Oakley notes the use of gaze to indicate the sadness of the event; Oakley (2004) 74. The focus on the sword reinforces the invitation to consider its significance for those left behind. A further example of this same motif is offered by the red-figure fragment of a bell-krater by the Phiale Painter dated to *c.* 430 BC (Athenian Agora P18364, Moore (1997) 191 with Pl. 43). A variation of the scene, with a woman handing a helmet to a man wearing only his sword, can be found on a white-ground *lekythos* attributed to the Achilles Painter and in the collection of the British Museum D51 BM 1891,0806.85, dated 460–430 BC; discussed briefly by Lewis (2002) 161 and Fig. 4.23 (though her interest is in the scene's goose as a symbol of domestic harmony) and Oakley (2004) 61 with Fig. 36, p. 63. On the canonical form of hoplite-departure scenes in earlier Attic red-figure pottery see Lewis (2002) 39–40.

103 Oakley (2009) 210.
104 Sguaitamatti (1982) 84.
105 For anger as a female Athenian reaction to news of their husbands' deaths on the battlefield see Hdt. 5.87 (with the usual provisos).
106 Oakley (2009).
107 On the personal in white-ground *lekythoi* see Morris (1994) 82.
108 The immediacy of this, however, is mediated through the distance between the reality and this idealized representation of the grave, on which see Morris (1994) esp. 80.
109 Cf. Stieglitz cup discussed in Chapter 1.
110 Highlighting the principle of non-uniformitarianism on which see Morris (1994) 73–4.
111 McGlew (2012) 91–2.
112 I accept the scepticism of Jameson (2014) 107 over the assumed significance of the way the animal fell; *contra* Flower and Marincola (2002) 184 (note on Hdt 9.41.4). On the purpose being both propitiatory as well as divinatory see Parker (2011) 159 and Jameson (2014) 112. For an example of multiple victims being slaughtered in the rite see Hdt. 9.61–2 on the Battle of Plataea.
113 Plutarch specifies that the seer carries out the rite at the Battle of Plataea, Plut. *Arist.* 18, as noted by Flower and Marincola (2002) 61.2n; yet, as Jameson recognizes in his discussion of the cup (Jameson (2014) 123), while the sacrificer may be a seer, he is also presented through his armour as a member of the fighting force; hence my term 'hoplite-seer'.
114 Jameson (2014) 103, 108, and 125, and Parker (2011) 159 and 162, on the stripped back nature of the rite and focus on the action and blood. See Jameson (2014) 115 Fig. 6.1 and 122–3 on this cup and on another fifth-century Athenian representation of *sphagia*: Fragment of a red-figure calyx-krater, formerly in the Bareiss Collection, now in the J. Paul Getty Museum, Malibu (86.AE.213), *c.* 430 BC (illustrated in Parker (2011) 163 Fig. 5). This second example is equally graphic in showing the sword plunged into the neck of the sacrificial victim, demonstrating that, even sixty to seventy years after the earlier cup (Fig. 18) was painted, the artistic perception of the focal point of *sphagia* remained consistent.
115 On communal focus see Parker (2011) 162–3 and for spectatorship's impact on identity see Stansbury-O'Donnell (2006) 52–88.
116 Jameson (2014) 123.
117 Text Wilson (2015); my translation.
118 *LSJ* s.v. καλός II.2. On Marathon's importance see Gehrke (2009) 85–92 and the summary (and further bibliography) offered by Markantonatos (2013a) 69–70. The sequential logic of the actions is reinforced by ἐνθαῦτα (thereupon).

119 Further evidenced in Herodotus' account of the Battle of Plataea (Hdt. 9.61–2) and Thucydides in his description of the first battle in Syracuse (Thuc. 6.69) with Hornblower (2008) *ad loc.* on the paradigmatic nature of Thucydides' reference to details such as the pre-battle sacrifice.

120 Parker (2011) 162–3. A scholion on Thuc. 6.69 notes that the *sphagia* was carried out in front of the army, see Smith (1913) *ad loc.* On the significance of this to *Ajax* see Chapter 4.

121 On the parallel between the sacrifice and battlefield killing see Burkert (1983) 66, Parker (2011) 159, and Jameson (2014) 126. While Crowley (2012) 31 suggests that not every hoplite would own a sword, the understanding of its symbolism did not depend on literally possessing this object; van Wees (2004) 48, in any case, asserts that 'most' soldiers carried a sword.

122 While the *sphagia* rite was practised by other Greeks, the interpretation of its meaning depended on the set of symbolic associations attached by each city to the sword (see Patronos (2002) 17 on the community-specific associations of meaning and value embedded in symbols).

123 On the centrality of the city's relationship with the divine to Athenian citizenship see Blok (2017) 47–99.

124 Goldhill (1986) 63–4 and Manville (1990) 20 and 22 on fighting and citizen identity, Pritchard (2004) 209–10 on the importance of the hoplite army to enacting the Cleisthenic ideal of 'mixing up' citizens. See also Christ (2001).

125 Neer (2002) for the importance of sympotic vase painting to Athenian identity.

126 Its placement also implies the significance of this iconography within the cup's scheme see Catoni (2015).

Chapter 4

1 Pritchard (2018) highlights the ways in which comedy and tragedy use the figure of the hoplite. Revermann (2006) 36–45 and (2013) 14 on symbolic coding from society informing audience interpretation of theatre.

2 The Gnathia bell-krater fragment of the tragic actor, illustrated on this book's cover, (Würzburg H4600 (L832)) indicates the closeness, in semiotic terms, between signifier (i.e. prop) and referent (sword). The similarity of the sword across the representations can be observed by comparing the Gnathia fragment with the tyrannicides' stamnos (Würzburg, Martin von Wagner Museum 515; Fig. 14) and the fragments showing *sphagia* (Cleveland Museum of Art 1926.242; Fig. 18).

3 See Raaflaub (2003) 66 and Azoulay (2017) 189–94 (and his dismissal of Carpenter's objections (Carpenter (1997) 178)); the phenomenon is striking since it applies to Theseus alone. There are some exceptions (with different weapons used in some of

Theseus' exploits see Azoulay (2017) 192–4). On the tyrannicides and the sword see Chapter 3.
4 Theseus as mythological prototype for tyrannicides see Hall (1989) 58 and 68.
5 This builds on Rosivach (1988) 46; he acknowledges drama's role in shaping views on tyranny but does not explore the ways in which this was achieved. This discussion also develops the analysis of tyranny's place in the trilogy beyond Seaford (2003) 100–2 by considering the visual together with the verbal.
6 On *metic* cloaks see Introduction, p. 5 and Chapter 2, p. 43.
7 This has been overlooked in part through being obscured by the debate over whether Clytemnestra used a sword or axe, on which see the Appendix.
8 Raaflaub (2003) 70–2, quotation on 71.
9 On the contemporary resonance for the audience of tragedy's references to tyranny see Hesk (2007) 78.
10 Seaford (2003) 100.
11 See Appendix on Clytemnestra's use of the sword.
12 On the sword's presence on stage see n. 15 below.
13 See Hall (1989) 208–9, Seaford (2003) 101 and, briefly, West (2006) 38.
14 The chorus' reference to Orestes freeing the city (*Cho.* 1046) reinforces his rhetorical claim. On the negative connotations of τύραννος in fifth-century Athens see Raaflaub (2003).
15 For this staging I follow Sommerstein (2009a) 373. The sword is confirmed as the murder weapon by the explicit reference to it at *Eum.* 42, its use in the killing is anticipated at *Cho.* 576, 584 and (obliquely) 729, and the mirroring between the tableaus in *Agamemnon* and *Choephori* suggests its present on stage after the murder (see the Appendix). Moreover, dramatic logic implies that Orestes has it with him when he exits from the murder tableau scene at the end of *Choephori*. When the audience next hear of him, through the Pythia's description, he is sitting with olive branch and sword at Delphi's navel stone, *Eum.* 40–5. In *Choephori*, Orestes draws attention to the suppliant branch he is carrying in preparation for his journey to Delphi (*Cho.* 1034–9). The presence of the sword alongside the branch in *Choephori* would be dramatically coherent, allowing for the presence of both at Delphi, and has the advantage of underlining the sword's problematic symbolism before its appearance in *Eumenides*. It is understandable that Orestes would prefer to emphasize the branch (as a symbol of salvation), rather than the sword; it represents a form of euphemism advocated by the chorus too (*Cho.* 1044–7). Taplin's influential premise of significant stage action being marked in the text (Taplin (1978) 16–19) should not be taken as 'proof' against the presence of unmarked props (see Altena (1999–2000)). Mueller (2016a) 60 makes an eloquent case against the requirement of textual confirmation for staging. In any case, the textual cues at *Cho.* 576 and 584 ensure that the sword, if not visually present, would be evoked in the audience's

imagination here. The symbolic associations at stake, and the impact of this on the audience, remain the same whether the prop's appearance is delayed until *Eumenides* or not (though the balance of evidence suggests that it was present in the murder tableau).

16 Juffras makes an effective argument for Electra's use of the same verb (Sophocles' *Electra* 975) forming one of the cues for evoking the tyrannicide statues in that play, Juffras (1991) 100–3.

17 For the statue group see Chapter 3. The allusion would be unmistakeable in performance if Orestes adopted the iconic pose of Harmodius (with the sword held above his head) that became recognizable as the 'visual signature' not only of the tyrant slayer but the statue pair, see Azoulay (2017) 41–2. Aeschylus had lived through this historical event, as Hall (1996) 4 notes, as well as the setting up of Critius' and Nesiotes' bronze portrait group of the pair in 477 BC.

18 See Garvie (1986) 316 on Orestes' initial mood.

19 Demonstrated by Harmodius' 'youthful ardour' and Aristogiton's 'controlled stance', Azoulay (2017) 41.

20 The statue pair's symbolism is in reality ambivalent, see Neer (2002) 175 and Azoulay (2017) 10, but the ideal they represent overlooks this.

21 Garvie (1986) 317 on reversal.

22 For disharmony as a key aspect of the *Oresteia's* atmosphere see Zeitlin (1965) 499–500.

23 Already hinted towards on the visual level, before being substantiated on the verbal level, by the suppliant branch carried in Orestes' left hand; on branch see Sommerstein (2009a) 337.

24 On the related evocation in *Phoenician Women* of the negative consequences for the tyrannicides see Chapter 5 n. 126.

25 Wilson (2009) 26–7.

26 On this ideal see Chapter 3.

27 See Chapter 1, n. 36 on this function of gaze. Orestes evokes a communal gaze (*Cho.* 973), yet the sword's symbolism cannot allow the positive construction of identity through this.

28 On the celebration of Athenian institutions, see West (2006) 38–9; on patriarchy see the seminal article, Zeitlin (1978); on Argive alliance see Sommerstein (1989a) 30.

29 See, for example, *Eum.* 899.

30 For the revelation of Orestes sitting, sword in hand, on the *ekkyklema* in *Eumenides* see Sommerstein (1989a) 93.

31 Azoulay (2017) 44.

32 Furthermore, the allusion to the Argive alliance in his speech, *Eum.* 762–77, implies that his sword from now on will be used in Athens' defence (demonstrating its assimilation of Athenian values). On *Eumenides'* allusions to the alliance see Sommerstein (1989a) 30.

33 On reforms see Chapter 2.
34 [Aristotle] *Ath. Pol.* 25.4 and Diodorus 11.77.6.
35 This is implied, if the lines directly before (*Ag.* 1362-3) are taken to suggest that the chorus should 'risk life and limb by rushing indoors' (Raeburn and Thomas (2011) *ad loc.*).
36 Sommerstein (2009a) 201. See Medda (2001) for full discussion of issues.
37 Raeburn and Thomas (2011) 238-9 offer a different reading of the attribution of lines, based on the *OCT*, but also assume that the chorus are without swords and raise sticks as they deliver 1652.
38 On both issues see the Appendix.
39 See Medda (2001) 43-5 and Sommerstein (1989b) 301 n. 17. Sommerstein argues their feebleness in response to the murder would be incomprehensible if they were armed and, (2009a) 201 n. 341, he reasons that since they were too old to fight at Troy ten years before this, they certainly do not wear swords. Neither argument is conclusive and since the text is not explicit on this issue, it leaves open the possibility of the chorus carrying swords in performance. The chorus' feebleness of response, for example, could be argued to be heightened if they were carrying swords and far from being 'incomprehensible', it would demonstrate the dangers of deliberation (the reason for not taking action is not their lack of weapons but rather their failure to be able to decide how best to proceed) which connects to the issue of polyphony (on which see Fletcher (2014)). Even the exchange between the chorus and Aegisthus could be argued to be more effective, in showing their powerlessness, if the chorus carry swords that they do not use (leaving Clytemnestra as the only one on stage to have actually used a sword). While I consider the impact of the chorus carrying staffs rather than swords in the analysis above, I acknowledge that the alternative (that they carry swords) is also a possibility with its own dramatic merit (see Wyles (2014) 40, for example).
40 There are difficulties with this line and debate over this term although Sommerstein (2009a) and Raeburn and Thomas (2011) 61 accept the reading given here; see the *apparatus criticus* (Raeburn and Thomas (2011) 61) for details of manuscript variants and emendations.
41 This builds further on the analysis of Raeburn and Thomas (2011) 238-9 that acknowledges the use of this term to both gird the chorus to fight and attempt to meet the threat issued by their opponents.
42 On this concept, see Wyles (2011) 71-3.
43 I owe this observation in part to Raeburn and Thomas (2011) 239 who note the contrast between the chorus' boldness in raising their staves with *Ag.* 72-82. For this type of semiotic incompetence displayed by characters elsewhere in Aeschylus see Wyles (2011) 71-3. On the treatment of age in these lines (*Ag.* 72-82), see Lebeck (1971) 17-18.

44 Raeburn and Thomas (2011) 238 on this change of metre and its effect.
45 The chorus hint towards this at *Ag.* 1646–8.
46 Established long ago, see Taplin (1977) 358 and (1978) 125–6; see also Garvie (1986) 317. See further the Appendix.
47 This would, as in the case of Orestes (see n. 17 above), be particularly forceful if the strikingly distinctive pose of Harmodius were adopted (on pose's fame see Azoulay (2017) 41–2). On the sense of immediacy see the Appendix, pp. 155–6.
48 On the meanings of this stage action see Taplin (1978) 78–83; and on the way in which it represents Agamemnon as behaving as an 'eastern despot' see Hall (1989) 205–9. Importantly the tyrannicides' monument came to represent Athens' struggle against the Persian King, see Azoulay (2017) 44.
49 For its presentation as the primary motive see Zeitlin (1965) 466 and 490.
50 See above, n. 46, and the Appendix on the mirroring of the tableaus.
51 Hall (1989) 205 on democracy being placed above tyranny in *Eumenides*.
52 On this usurpation see the Appendix.
53 Patterson (1994) on the marriage bond as a potent symbol of political order in Athenian ideology.
54 The stage image and dramatic situation is more complex than this, of course, given that one of the corpses is his mother, but there is at least a moment when Orestes' rhetoric allows the tableau to seem less problematic than it really is.
55 In fact, she takes the place of an Athenian king in *Eumenides* as West (2006) 39 notes. Fletcher (2014) 67 on Athena counterbalancing Clytemnestra.
56 See Appendix on the sword's place within the trilogy's design.
57 The sword is importantly different from the voting urns/pebbles as a prop that is physically present while its symbolism is contested through the trilogy (cf. the positive assertion of the voting urns/pebbles meaning is combined with their first appearance on stage). This difference demonstrates the range in Aeschylus' dramatic technique while also reflecting on the different types of negotiation of civic symbols within society.
58 While our knowledge of the politics in the period is insecure, it seems reasonable to assume unrest and even potentially violence in this setting.
59 Raaflaub (2003) 71–2 notes that the tyrannical framing of the Olympians in *Eumenides* forces the audience to reflect on political tensions troubling their polis at the time; this can be extended by considering the engagement with the theme earlier in the trilogy.
60 Text and translation Lloyd-Jones (1994).
61 Juffras (1991).
62 On this epic convention see de Jong (1987). While the two types of looking are, on the surface, different, Orestes' command collapses this distinction by implying that he should be viewed as a statue.

63 On the 'haunted' stage see Carlson (1994a) and (1994b), and Sofer (2003).
64 Marshall (2001b) on axe in revival.
65 On other aspects of *Ajax*'s debt to Aeschylus' *Agamemnon* see Garner (1990) 50 and *Eumenides* see Murnaghan (2014) 210–14.
66 For the date of *Ajax*, see Garvie (1998) 6–8 and Finglass (2011) 1–11 (both conclude 440s is most likely). For the pervasiveness of references to sword props in tragedy see Dingel (1967) and Wyles (2011) 141.
67 On the effect of the address to Athens (*Aj.* 859-63) and allusion to it at 1222 drawing the audience almost directly into the action see Ringer (1998) 46. On military terms see Mueller (2016a) 142 and 146, and on cult see Henrichs (1993). The framing of the judgement of the arms along the lines of the Athenian legal procedure is also implied by *Aj.* 1241–2. This matrix of references is consistent with the characterization of Sophoclean plays as 'marked by their genesis in the fifth century Athenian *polis*', Goldhill (1987) 70.
68 Cohen (1978), Taplin (1978) 85–8, Segal (1980), Seale (1982) 175 and Mueller (2016a) 15–41.
69 On the sword belonging to past, see Mueller (2016a) 149 and 154; for scholarship on Ajax as hero of past see Garvie (1998) 15 and Murnaghan (2014) 200–1.
70 On the Homeric resonances see Mueller (2016a) 15–30, Weiberg (2018) 68–70 and Wyles (2019a) 60–1. On the wider scholarly concern with the interaction of *Ajax* with the *Iliad*; see, for example, Garner (1990) 51–63. On 'zooming' see Sourvinou-Inwood (1997) and Mueller (2016a) 5 on props' ability to 'catapult' viewers into the present.
71 On the passage's resonance with the Persian war see Flower and Marincola (2002) on Hdt 9.41.4.
72 Present on stage from at least 346, on which see Mueller (2016a) 20 (or perhaps earlier see Taplin (1978) 85 and Segal (1980–1) 127). On the question of how visible it is during the suicide see below. My analysis seeks to further the excellent discussions of Segal (1981) 138–42 and Brook (2018) 50–74 on the play's engagement with multiple rituals (covering between them: sacrificial, funerary, purification, curse, supplication, dedication, scapegoat ritual, and the rite of cathartic madness) by considering battlefield *sphagia* and focusing on the prop.
73 *Aj.* 650–2 (debates over Ajax's intention to deceive (for an overview of scholarly position on this issue see Garvie (1998) 184–6 and Finglass (2011) 328–9) do not affect the claim being made here about the impact of this phrase in his speech that refers to 'quenching' in sword manufacture (see Cohen (1978) 30 and Holm (2012) 487)). See also *Aj.* 1034–5.
74 On this aspect of props' materiality see Harris and Korda (2002b) 16–17 and, applied to Greek tragedy, Hall (2018). We cannot know whether real swords were used on stage or not. Heracles' breastplate on the Pronomos Vase (Naples, Museo

Archeologico Nazionale 81673, H 3240) suggests that real armour could be used in performance, see Wyles (2010) 251–2. Even if 'fake' swords (made of wood, for example) were used in performance, the dramatic illusion would nevertheless demand that the audience thought about them being forged. The familiarity of this part of the metal-working process is indicated by its frequent depiction on fifth-century vase paintings, Acton (2010) 119. If the biographical detail about Sophocles' father being a sword-maker can be trusted (recorded by Ister (*FGrH* 333 F35) but doubted in *Life of Sophocles* 1), then this might add a self-conscious dimension to the reflection; for another way in which this detail might be relevant to *Ajax* see Mueller (2016a) 154.

75 On the Athenian resonance of Ajax addressing the chorus as ἄνδρες ἀσπιστῆρες (shield-bearing men) at *Aj.* 565, see Mueller (2016a) 142. Hoplite superiority is claimed by Menelaus in his exchange with Teucer, *Aj.* 1120–3. Teucer's retort, 1123, envisages a fight in which Menelaus would be 'fully armed' (ὁπλίζω, lit. 'equipped as a hoplite'). The war orphans were described using the same verb (with the intensifying κατά- prefix) in the pre-performance ritual (Aeschines *Against Ctesiphon* 3.154) confirming the contemporary Athenian resonance of this language, see Chapter 3.

76 Brook (2018) 51 and 60 notes that doubling of corrupt sacrifice but does not identify it as battlefield *sphagia* explicitly.

77 *Aj.* 9–10, 29–31, 51–8, 94–5, 147, 229–32, 235–9, 285–7, 295–300, 323–5, as summarized with context in Wyles (2019a) 55–6.

78 Text and translation of *Ajax* are from Lloyd-Jones (1996).

79 There is perhaps an earlier hint towards this reading in the chorus' allusion to Artemis (*Aj.* 172–8), see Brook (2018) 53.

80 Garvie (1998) *ad loc.* on epithets. On these characteristics of battlefield *sphagia* see p. 71. Killing and the blood were not typically emphasized in sacrifices more generally, on which see Jameson (2014) 103. The focus on them points to battlefield *sphagia* being evoked here (rather than the general sacrificial ritual envisaged by Brook (2018) 56). Segal (1981) 139 offers a persuasive analysis for the significance of the evocation of oracular sacrifice, χρηστήρια, *Aj.* 220, noting the irony of the term. However, the focus on blood and the sword elsewhere in the play points to battlefield *sphagia* as the more developed of the two allusions and the more significant to the play overall.

81 *Aj.* 10 (hands that have slaughtered with the sword), *Aj.* 30 (freshly dripping sword), *Aj.* 57 (killing with his own hand), *Aj.* 95 (sword stained (with blood)), *Aj.* 147 (killing with flashing iron). Cohen (1978) 26 long ago acknowledged the association between the sword and the play's 'persistent' imagery of blood and slaughter.

82 Brook (2018) 53 notes that the repeated use of the verb σφάζω and its cognates 'insists that the violence of Ajax's offstage actions be understood as having the qualities of a ritual sacrifice'. The cluster of such terms (*Aj.* 546, 815, [841], 898, 919)

after Tecmessa's reference to *sphagia* at *Aj.* 219, should, I suggest, be seen through the lens of this specific type of sacrifice.

83 Finglass (2011) n. 218-20 suggests that the use of ritual terminology emphasizes the horror of the action and notes the contrast between the ordered killing of sacrifice and Ajax's frenzy. Brook (2018) 54-5 notes that the aftermath of the sacrifice does not follow the ritual motions, such as the division of meat; the lack of consumption, however, fits well with the model of battlefield *sphagia* (see Jameson (2014) 103). At the same time as arguing for the specific evocation of the battlefield *sphagia*, I recognize that other forms of ritual are conflated with it (see Brook (2018) 50-74).

84 Athena highlights these characteristics (*Aj.* 1-133) that are subsequently emphasized elsewhere in the play. A further hint (towards sacrificial perversion) is given at *Aj.* 283-9 with the mention of Ajax cutting out the tip of the tongue from a ram and throwing it down; Garvie (1998) *ad loc.* and Segal (1981) 139. Finglass (2011) n. 2018-20 notes that the location of the slaughter (inside the hut) represents a further transgression of sacrificial norms. Brook (2018) 54 concludes that Ajax's so-called sacrifice of the herds 'must be considered both failed and corrupt'.

85 Jameson (2014) 126.

86 On *sphagia* in front of the army see Thuc. 6.69.2 and Chapter 3, p. 73; Parker (2011) 162-3 for communal attention.

87 Goldhill (1987) 70-1.

88 Aeschines, *Against Ctesiphon* 3.154, discussed in Chapter 3.

89 While the term does not always carry sacrificial associations (so, S. *Tr.* 1130), it certainly can (see E. *Hec.* 894) and the context here invites a reading that exploits the ritual nuances of the term; examples given in *LSJ* s.v. νεοσφαγής. Furthermore the modified noun, φόνος, can be used of sacrifice (*LSJ* s.v. φόνος I. 4) see, for example, A. *Sept.* 44.

90 Goldhill (1987) 70-1.

91 For the bloody sword see *Aj.* 30 and 95.

92 At the stasimon's close, the chorus express a longing to be back in Attica to greet Athens (the city is emphatically placed as the final word of the ode (Garvie (1998) *ad loc.*)). This exploits the feelings of the Athenian audience and invites them to bring their experience of battle into the interpretative frame, see the related view of Ringer (1998) 46. This makes explicit the strategy already implied by the formulation of the complaints about the experience of fighting at Troy (*Aj.* 1199-1210) in general terms so that they could resonate with fifth-century Athenian experience. See also n. 67 on the signposts to Athenian resonance elsewhere in the play.

93 Brook (2018) 62 describing it as a negative symbol of corrupt violence.

94 See Introduction, p. 2.

95 For the awareness of the parallel phenomenon of the mutability of verbal meaning at times of crisis in society see Th. 3.82. For dramatic effect created through negotiation of semiotic meaning see Wyles (2007) 96–101.
96 On the importance of divine relations to civic identity see Blok (2017) 47–99. The presentation of the sword's failure destabilizes confidence in its ability to affirm citizen identity through its function, thus creating a sense of disquiet.
97 See Brook (2018) 54 on its failure in this respect.
98 Garvie (1998) *ad loc.* for this interpretation.
99 The unrestored relationship with the divine is emphasized through the verbal echo between Ajax's prayer in his suicide speech (*Aj.* 824–30) and Tecmessa's despair over the corpse (*Aj.* 920-2). Ajax prays to Zeus to send a messenger to Teucer so that he will be first to lift him (βαστάσῃ, *Aj.* 827), yet when Tecmessa finds him she is left to wonder who will lift him (offering the verbal echo of the same verb: βαστάσει, *Aj.* 920) and immediately asks where Teucer is. This highlights that, at this stage at least, Ajax's prayer goes unanswered. The 'sacrifice' accompanying the prayer has been ineffectual. The lack of divine favour is in marked contrast with Aeschylus' treatment of Ajax's suicide in *Thracian Women* (in which, as we learn from scholia on *Ajax*, the suicide was described in a messenger speech that included the detail that a goddess appeared to help Ajax find his vulnerable spot); see Sommerstein (2009b) 101 and on the differences between the two treatments this implies, see Golder (1992) 350.
100 It is possible that the restoration of the divine relationship is marked by the fulfilment of Ajax's prayer (*Aj.* 824–30) at the play's end, if Teucer's instruction to Eurysaces to help him lift the corpse, *Aj.* 1409–11 is acted upon (as Finglass (2011) 525 suggests); Brook (2018) 65, however, maintains that the action does not actually take place within the bounds of the play.
101 On other elements in the speech reinforcing its ritual framing see Brook (2018) 60; though note her citation of Sicherl (1977) 96 should be treated with caution since his claim about the sharpened sword is supported only through reference to the *Odyssey* and he makes no mention of the placement of the sword being a ritual element. The parallels for the prayer before sacrifice, however, are compelling.
102 Garvie (1998) *ad loc.* (with his references to Stanford (1963) *ad loc.* and Segal (1981) 139 with 439 n. 106), Finglass (2011) *ad loc.* (with his note that it is first attested in Mycenaean, citing Weilhartner (2005) 137), and Brook (2018) 60.
103 The connection is further reinforced, as Brook (2018) 62 notes by the word's case and placement. Segal (1981) 139 recognizes that Ajax's suicide 'answers' the perverted sacrifice of the beasts.
104 Brook (2018) 51 and 62–3 notes the impact on audience expectation for the failure of the ritual and, although she does not link the two acts as perverted iterations of

battlefield *sphagia*, she is explicit in her acknowledgement of the important continuity offered by the sword; my analysis makes more of this continuity.
105 Brook (2018) 60 takes this and *Aj.* 919 to confirm the ritual nature of the death, also including *Aj.* 841 (but since this section of the text is taken to be an interpolation (see Garvie (1998) *ad loc.*), I exclude it from my discussion).
106 The translation here is from Garvie (1998).
107 This motif of looking upon the *sphagia* is set up, programmatically, through Athena's injunction to Odysseus in the opening scene of the play but the development of its particular meaning for Athenian audience members, through Ajax's interaction with Eurysaces, heightens its dramatic effect here. On vision in *Ajax* see the classic discussion of Seale (1982) 144–80.
108 The simplicity of the sacrifice, on which see Jameson (2014) 103 and 108, makes the omission of this key feature all the more marked.
109 Fig. 18 shows the blood, in added red trickling down from the wound. It is also relevant that the sword is shown plunged through the neck of the ram (as can be seen in the image reproduced by van Wees (2004) pl. XI), suggesting that this sacrifice involved an act of being pierced by the sword cf. Ajax's fate.
110 On this formulation of *sphagia* see Jameson (2014) 126. Segal (1981) 139 on the notion of this as a 'private ritual'.
111 It would presumably be unthinkable to enact a battlefield sacrifice with an enemy sword since it represents a fundamental inversion of the symbolism of the act (reformulating it to an alarming 'The enemy kills, may they kill'). In the same respect the curse on the army accompanying this sacrifice (*Aj.* 839–42, though it is likely an interpolation on which see Finglass (2011) *ad loc.*) presents a shocking inversion of the act's usual intention.
112 The major views in the debate are helpfully summarized by Finglass (2011) 376–9 and see now the entire volume dedicated to this issue, including some minor revisions to established views, edited by Most and Ozbek (2015). Weiberg (2018) assumes its stage presence without discussion of the issues implied.
113 Garvie (1998) 203 and (2015) 33.
114 For this issue and other arguments for and against its visibility see Most (2015) 291–2, n. 7 and Martinelli (2015) 214–19. For the denial of the deictic pronouns at 828 and 834 implying a visible sword see Finglass (2011) 377 and (2015), but note Martinelli's challenge of this. On *deixis* in fifth-century drama in general, see Jacobson (2011).
115 Garvie (1998) 203, in maintaining a visible suicide, for example, had to accept the possible use of a sword with a retractable blade (supporting this with the evidence of their existence later in antiquity). The circularity of Finglass' argument against such props existing in fifth-century BC theatre (Finglass (2011) 377) and the absence of compelling proof against their use allow the possibility to remain open.

Garvie, however, now thinks that the suicide being visible raises too many practical difficulties of staging, Garvie (2015) 33–4.

116 Most (2015). I find this reconstruction persuasive, although I do not agree with every suggestion. Quibbles with specific aspects of interpretations are inevitable in this debate, see for example Finglass (2011) 376–7 with Martinelli (2015) 213.

117 It does not seem necessary to me, for the sword to be actually set up offstage (suggested by Most (2015) 291). It can be imagined there, when it is in fact already embedded in the dummy out of sight behind the *skene* as Finglass (2011) 376 suggests.

118 Most (2015) 292 with Taplin's useful observation about the sun's impact on how much could be seen through the *skene*'s door, Taplin (1987) 325. Note, however, that Garvie (1998) 204 suggests that reimagining what the doorway represents would be 'impossibly confusing' for the audience.

119 I follow Finglass (2011) 376 in assuming that the corpse is brought onto stage after it has been covered, though note the problem presented by the embedded sword highlighted by Martinelli (2015) 213–14 and therefore accept the use of the *ekkyklema* (Most (2015) 293). Although some scholars maintain the *ekkyklema*'s strict use for displaying the interior of a dwelling only (thus Garvie (1998) 204 and Finglass (2011) 378–9), the state of our knowledge makes certainty of such a convention impossible.

120 Most (2015) 294.

121 Finglass (2011) 525 and Most (2015) 295; doubted by Brook (2018) 65.

122 The former suggestion is put forward by Mauduit (2015) 71–2 with Fig. 29, p. 344. Despite her critique of the suggestion that the sword is pulled out of the corpse before the end, its removal could be implied by *Aj.* 577 and *Aj.* 1407–8.

123 On disquiet of pollution see Brook (2018) 71.

124 Depending on when it is covered, it is either absent from view from 815–1003 continuously or it is glimpsed at 915 before being covered over (as envisaged by Most (2015) 293).

125 For an overview of Ajax's suicide in art see Finglass (2011) 28–30 and Catoni (2015) 15–22; both rely on *LIMC* I Aias I (Touchefeu).

126 Finglass (2015) 209.

127 Golder (1992) makes an important case for the likely influence of the visual language of art on playwrights and their productions (although his analysis of the implications of this for *Ajax* differs from mine). Giuliani (2013) 197–205 also offers a significant argument for the likely impact of vase painting on Aeschylus' bold staging of Achilles wrapped up and silent in his *Myrmidons* (see esp. 204–5 on the impact of transposing this motif from vase to stage). My analysis builds on Giuliani's suggestion by extending it to Sophocles and by introducing the concept of the contribution made by the 'conjured image' of vase paintings in performance.

128 Finglass (2011) 375 suggests that the description of this action shows Ajax, in the aftermath of his world collapsing, managing to 'impose order' on this task.
129 Black-figure Attic amphora attributed to Exekias, dated to c. 540 BC, Musée Boulogne-sur-Mer 558; red-figure *askos*, dated to 490–480 BC; Attic red-figure *lekythos*, Alkimachos Painter, dated to c. 460 BC, Basel Antikenmuseum BS1442; and tondo of Brygos painter cup, c. 490 BC Getty museum, 86.AE.286.
130 As acknowledged by Finglass (2015) 193 who notes the close correspondence between the piled earth in the image and its description in the play (*Aj.* 821).
131 Finglass (2011) 40 interprets the furrows as an indication of anxiety and takes it as a point of difference between the vase and the play. The sureness of Ajax's grasp on the hilt with his right hand and careful patting down of the earth with his left, however, indicate his controlled approach to the task (and within this contextual framing, the lines on his brow more readily suggest concentration). On Ajax's isolation on the vase see Mackay (2002) 67–8 who notes the striking emptiness of the scene as well as the impact of the conventional human bystanders being substituted with inanimate objects; on isolation in the play see Finglass (2011) esp. 40 and 375.
132 Williams (1980) 140 notes the little mound around the sword and suggests, on the reading that Ajax is represented lying on a pebbly shore, that it should be understood to consist of 'something like sand'; see also Catoni (2015) 20 on this detail. The representation of the mound around the sword in iconography from further afield implies that it was widely known as a convention; see, for example, the metope of the Temple of Hera at Foce de Sele from the mid-sixth century (Paestum, Museo Archeologico Nazionale); Catoni (2015) 335, Fig. 10.
133 Such a strategy is evidenced for fifth-century dramatists through explicit references to artworks in the corpus, on which see Golder (1992) esp. 327–8 (I do not accept all the elements of his discussion but acknowledge the importance of its central point about theatre's relationship (and debt) to the visual arts) and Hall (2006) 99–141; esp. 116–18 (while she argues that *Eumenides* 48–51 may allude to a previous theatrical sight, she also acknowledges the possibility of iconography being evoked here). Importantly it seems unlikely that the audience saw the sword stuck in the ground in the earlier drama about Ajax's suicide (Aeschylus' *Thracian Women*) since the suicide was reported in a messenger speech (see n. 99) and so, presumably, even if the corpse was brought onto stage, it would have already been extricated from the sword.
134 On this action recalling Andromache see Finglass (2009). On its symbolism see Segal (1980) 127–9. On the pathos added to Teucer's arrival as well as the effectiveness of his unveiling of the corpse see Most (2015) 293–4, n. 13. It is, as Most notes, no longer assumed that the veiling serves a practical purpose in the

staging (i.e. to allow the substitution of the dummy or extra; on previous views maintaining this see Finglass (2011) 377).

135 Davies (1973) 65 notes that the visual evidence points to the existence of this motif in a tradition predating Sophocles' play. He discusses the example of the Brygos cup (Getty 86. AE. 286) and Etruscan scarab (c. 500–475 BC, Boston MFA 21.1199, illustrated Catoni (2015) 333 Fig. 6) arguing that their striking similarities point to a common source for both. The fragments of the Onesimos *kylix*, Louvre c. 11335, offer a further possible example of the motif (see below), although Catoni (2015) 20 n. 27 does not accept this. Even so, the similarity between the Brygos cup and gem is remarkable and hints towards a strong iconographic tradition of which we have only a partial view through the chances of survival. Golder (1992) 358 acknowledges that there must have been other vessels painted with the image on the Brygos cup (to establish Sophocles' knowledge of it); although he then suggests that the audience would not have been familiar with this image but would carry the image of the suicide from Archaic art in their visual memory. I cannot agree with this last point, since the examples of Archaic art are almost exclusively Corinthian, whereas the Brygos cup is one of only a very few fifth-century Attic pieces with this design and hints, as suggested, towards an established motif. It seems far likelier therefore that the audience were familiar with the iconography (a conclusion that arguing in favour of Sophocles' knowledge of it already logically implies).

136 See esp. *Aj.* 828, 898 and 918–19. The freshness of the slaughter is emphasized by the use of the νεο- prefix in the language describing Ajax's suicide, see νεόρραντος (*Aj.* 828) and νεοσφαγής (*Aj.* 898). The effect is further reinforced at *Aj.* 898 by the inclusion of the otiose adverb ἀρτίως (on which see Finglass (2011) *ad loc.*).

137 Davies (1973) 61.

138 Catoni (2015) 21–2 helpfully identifies, and offers some critique of, this tendency.

139 Scholars would be happy to consider the influence of Sophocles on this iconography (if only the vessels were dated later) as has been noted for the Exekias amphora (Finglass (2015) 193) and Brygos cup (Catoni (2015) 61).

140 The resistance to considering the question of this iconography's influence on Sophocles may be attributed to concern over how much can be said about its familiarity (given the limited number of surviving representations of it); on this however see n. 135 above. While acknowledging the need for caution, the similarities are so compelling that it seems fair to work on the basis that Sophocles assumes his audience's familiarity with such images. The similarities are as striking as those that led Giuliani (2013) 197–205 to identify Aeschylus' borrowing of a motif from vase painting in his *Myrmidons*; there too, an innovation in vase painting led to dramatic innovation.

141 Taplin's acknowledgement of the 'tragic potential' of the Brygos cup image seems to hint towards the first of these two claims; Taplin (1978) note on plate 11 (with comments on this in Catoni (2015) 62). Golder (1992) 357–8 asserts the influence of the Brygos cup image on Sophocles but does not believe that the audience were familiar with it (see n. 135 above for my rebuttal about audience familiarity).
142 Finglass (2011) 376 and 405 on backstage. This offers a further dimension to Revermann's claim of the power of props imagined in the mind of audience members, Revermann (2013) 49.
143 Finglass (2011) 376.
144 The detail in Tecmessa's speech about the sight of blood 'up to his nostrils' (*Aj.* 918) perhaps hints towards him being face up (so that she could see this detail clearly), although a case could be made for the inverse (based on gravity's effect). Further support for the argument that he is face up may be found in *Aj.* 1004 (on which see Finglass (2011) *ad loc.*) as Golder (1992) 356 notes. It would be dramatically more effective to show him face up as then Teucer could address him to his face (presumably represented on the dummy with the mask that the actor had worn), rather than the back of his head. I do not think it is necessary to consider the practical concern of which way he would have leapt (or worry about the audience being 'satisfied' on this point) *pace* Most (2015) 293 n. 11; this risks engaging with issues unprompted by the dramatist (see Knight's classic critique of this trend in Shakespearean studies, Knight (1933)).
145 Golder (1992) 358 notes the power of such a dramatic twist. On false preparation see p. 156.
146 This mirrors the play's construction (as a process of revelation) on which see Seale (1982) 174.
147 Reflection on the hoplite experience is reinforced by the allusion to hoplite fighting at *Aj.* 1120–3 on which see n. 75.
148 I do not assume that every hoplite could witness the details of *sphagia* – the realities of what a hoplite could actually see, when 'looking' at *sphagia*, is not as important as the experience of communal focus on the sight (and the understanding of what there was to see).
149 On communal gaze and the construction of identity see Chapter 1 n. 36.
150 See Chapter 3.
151 On its agency see Mueller (2016a) 15–41 and Weiberg (2018) 69.
152 Further highlighting the precarious nature of such symbols in times of crisis (an effect that is further exploited in comedy, see Chapter 5).
153 The sword as a possession of Hector is emphasized at *Aj.* 659–63, 817–20 and 1027; for the idea that it represents Hector see the excellent analysis of Mueller (2016a) 15–30. Davies (1973) 66 suggests that the scabbard seen hanging up in the background of the Brygos cup image alludes to the gift exchange in *Iliad* 7. On this

reading the scabbard would, in Catoni's terms, become a 'pointer-object' for this other narrative, Catoni (2015) 28; see further, on this notion, Mackay (2002) esp. 55–62 on 'indexical elements' in black-figure vase painting which, she argues, serve an equivalent function to 'significant objects' in Homeric epic (her conclusion that such elements heighten the emotional impact of the scene would seem to apply here, if it is indeed understood as Hector's scabbard).

154 Louvre C 11335, dated to *c.* 500–480 BC.
155 Williams (1980) pl. 33.1 and 137 for further details.
156 For this reading of the ram see Sparkes (1985) 38 n. 72 with his details about John Boardman's correction to Williams' view (he had seen it as the rear and tail of a sheep, Williams (1980) 137).
157 Williams (1980) 137–8 and Sparkes (1985) 28 with 38 n. 72.
158 Williams (1980) 137–8 and Sparkes (1985) 28, but Catoni (2015) 20 n. 27 is uncertain (since so little of Tecmessa is preserved on the fragment).
159 Garvie (1998) 195–6 on the unusualness of this staging.
160 The second fragment in the Louvre, C11335, Williams (1980) Pl. 33. 2, shows what has been described as a bull on its back (see Williams (1980) 137). One of the cup's handles (also in the collection of the Louvre) has an animal's leg and hoof depicted on it according to Williams in correspondence with Sparkes, see Sparkes (1985) 38 n. 72.
161 It is difficult to develop this claim further since the inclusion of the slaughtered beasts motif is unique to this cup, see Williams (1980) 138 and Sparkes (1985) 28.
162 I am not suggesting that the prop used on stage by Ajax was quickly stuck through a dummy backstage during the performance. It seems more likely that two identical prop swords were used – one manipulated on stage by Ajax, and the other already in place in the dummy; it only needed to be perceived to be the same object by the audience.
163 On affectiveness of props see Telò and Mueller (2018b).
164 Segal (1981) 139.
165 Mueller (2016a) 149 highlights the idea of the sword representing the past. I agree with the suggestions in her superb analysis for the ways in which it evokes the past but think that it also has the potential to point to the future (i.e. the Athenian present).
166 Hdt 5.66 with Golder (1992) 349 and Murnaghan (2014) 206. Segal (1981) 142 notes that references to Athens at 859–63 and 1222 highlights Ajax's special connection to the city. This is further complicated by the network of references within the play that assimilate the hero and his weapon summarized in Wyles (2019a) 56 and 58; on the symbolic importance of this within the play see Segal (1980) 127–9.
167 Brook (2018) 74.

168 Goldhill (1987) 71.
169 Sophocles in this respect can be argued to be as bold in his interaction with iconography as Prag considers Aeschylus to have been, see Prag (1991) 243. While the battlefield *sphagia* ritual was not exclusive to the Athenians and references to it within the play could therefore resonate with non-Athenian Greeks within the audience, the specifically Athenian references elsewhere in the play (see above, n. 67) suggest that it was intended to confront and affect this target audience above all. His strategy is comparable to Euripides' in *Phoenician Women*, see Chapter 5.
170 864a in Christodoulou (1977); I owe this reference to Mueller (2016a) 30.
171 On prop as symbol for play see Seale (1982) 175 and Wyles (2013) 181–2. While the number of props in *Ajax* has been argued to diffuse their intended effect (Marshall (2012) 193), the evidence just cited suggests that the sword stood apart from the other props in performance.
172 This scene itself was noted for its innovative staging and perceived intention to shock: 815 in Falkner (2002) 355; I owe this reference to Mueller (2016a) 17. On the sword's agency see Mueller (2016a) 15-41 and Taplin (1978) 86.

Chapter 5

1 Forged through graphic description; as Sommerstein (2010) 30 notes, there were 'virtually no limits to the intensity of the horrors described'.
2 As a semiotic sign the sword and corpse are an 'index' for the violent offstage act; on this terminology see Elam (2002) esp. 18–20 and (applied to black-figure vase painting) Mackay (2002). Sommerstein (2010) 30 and 33–4 notes the ways in which violence is prominent even while the fatal blow is not enacted on stage.
3 The pro-satyric status of *Alcestis* does not affect this claim to the 'tragic' impact of the sight of Death with his sword at the play's opening (although it seems possible that the play's engagement with 'comic' elements accounts for the prop's disempowerment by its end (Heracles wrestles Death (Eur. *Alc.* 1140-2) without concern for the sword). On *Alcestis* as a tetralogy compressed into one play see Slater (2005); on its prosatyric status see Slater (2013) 1–14 and Markantonatos (2013b) 92 for further bibliography.
4 Wyles (2011), 69–76 on the sense of 'inevitability' created by pieces of costume.
5 Sommerstein (2010) highlights that although showing the act of killing is taboo and the striking of a blow is only exceptionally displayed, other types of violence are nevertheless presented visually in tragedy. I build on that observation by acknowledging the sword's role in creating an atmosphere of imminent violence that contributes to the dramatic effect (identified by Sommerstein (2010) 34–5 and 38–40), when tragedy seems to come close to showing killing or the striking of

blows. The exception to the rule is Prometheus' pinioning in [Aeschylus] *Prometheus Bound* (discussed Sommerstein (2010) 40–1). The example, sometimes cited, of the apparent shooting of arrows at Niobe's children in Sophocles' fragmentary *Niobe* (fr. 441a Lloyd-Jones) is dismissed by Sommerstein (2010) 35, since Artemis and Apollo are shooting into the house (i.e. the moment of impact is offstage).

6 On props as the site of intergeneric negotiation see Miles (2013); for the sword as symbol of tragedy and its violence see Revermann (2013) 35–6.

7 Important evidence here includes: the fifth-century Maenad vase (Stat. Mus. Berlin 3223, Wyles (2011) Fig. 3), the fourth-century 'Choregoi' vase (formerly J. Paul Getty Museum 96.AE.29, discussed here) and the Gnathia fragment of a tragic actor (Würzburg H4600, the cover image to this book; Revermann (2013) 35–6 acknowledges the symbolic significance of the sword in this composition). Given the limited number of vase paintings relating directly to theatrical performance, it is notable that swords should be present on a significant proportion; on the paucity of evidence, see Taplin (1986).

8 Tarentine red-figure bell-krater, 390–380 BC, formerly J. Paul Getty Museum 96.AE.29.

9 I follow Taplin (1993a), 55–66 in viewing this vase as related to fifth-century Attic performance and in accepting that it offers a deliberate contrast between comedy and tragedy; on the juxtaposition, see Sells (2019) 83–4. Gilula's important critique of Taplin's interpretation (Gilula (1995)) does not affect my argument about the meaning of the sword on the vase (while Gilula questions whether Aegisthus can be taken as a defender of the tragic genre, she accepts, 8–9, that Aegisthus may be presented here as part of a 'tragic burlesque' or that the scene may represent a comic mishap of the actor dressing in tragic costume in error (10), in either case the sword functions as an indicator of genre).

10 Ruvo 901, Trendall (1959) no. 54, p. 32 and Trendall and Cambitoglou (1978) no. 46, p. 70, with pl. 24, 3–4.

11 Trendall for categorization; Webster (1948), for example, produced one of the seminal arguments that such vases depicted Attic drama (Csapo (1986) and (2010a) 52–8 and Taplin (1993b) further confirms Webster's position), though see Herring (2018) 79 for its continued use.

12 Würzburg, Martin von Wagner Museum H5697.

13 The Apulian red-figure bell-krater, *c.* 380–370 BC (Staatliche Museen, Berlin 3045), discussed by Sells (2019) 69–71, offers a further example of this effect.

14 The pathos evoked by the sword on the Attic white-ground *lekythos* (Fig. 17) discussed in Chapter 3 relies on exactly that sense of the sword's violence. On the importance of the visual in comedy, see Poe (2000).

15 Würzburg, Martin von Wagner Museum H5697. For the link see Csapo (1986) with Taplin (1993a) 55–63, Csapo (2010a) 53–8 and Sells (2019) 57–8.

16 The Kinsman's costume operates in a more complex way though, through its 'conflated indices of genre', see Sells (2019) 59–60.
17 The image shows affinities to a sword's representation, although the blade is shorter. In Ar. *Thesmo.* 694 the prop is called a μάχαιρα, for which *LSJ* offer translations ranging from large knife to short sword and dagger. Sells (2019) 58 describes it as a 'sword', but Csapo calls the prop on the vase a 'knife' (Csapo (1986) 381; 'dagger' (or even 'short sword') seems more appropriate to the way in which it is clasped). Revermann (2013) 37 offers an attractive reading of the sword being diminished in status (by becoming a domestic knife) while increased in size, yet this overlooks the significance of the similarity in form between this so-called enlarged knife and short sword; importantly the use of the μάχαιρα on the Greek battlefield is attested (Hdt 7.225.3 records that they were used by the Spartans as they took their last stand at Thermopylae). For the container as a giant drinking cup see Csapo (2010a) 57.
18 Sells (2019) 53–88 emphasizes the value of such vases to our understanding of how parody operated on the comic stage (see esp. 55); his discussion offers a helpful backdrop to my consideration on how the sword is treated in such parodies.
19 Ar. *Thesmo.* 213–65. 'Indexical' see Mackay (2002). Csapo (1986) 384–7 suggests that it evokes the earlier scene (he originally assumed that it was on stage during the hostage parody, though subsequently revised this view Csapo (2010a) 57). Sells (2019) 60 accepts that it refers to the earlier scene while also indicating the relationship between the two figures (as a symbol of gender).
20 See n. 17 above on this weapon and the range of translations for the word μάχαιρα. The same reasoning set out here applies for the swords on the 'Reckoning Painter' vase (discussed above), if they too are taken to represent 'daggers' rather than swords.
21 If, as some suggest, the hostage scene in Euripides' play took place offstage and was described in a messenger speech, see Sommerstein (1980) 326n and Muecke (1982) 20 with Handley and Rea (1957) 36–7, then the parody threatens to 'realize' on stage a sight that had only taken place in the mind's eye of the audience. The wineskin substitute for baby Orestes evokes the scene described in the tragedy, while at the same time dispersing its power. Alternatively, if the scene had been presented on stage in the tragedy, as Collard et al. (1997) 25 suggest, then the parody operates through an interperformative allusion and the wineskin literally takes the place of the original baby (prop?).
22 Significant given the suggestion, Poe (2000) 285, that comedy in general presents 'homely' objects. The reduced form offers a neat expression of the comic genre's penchant for diminutives; the number of examples drawn from Aristophanes in Petersen (1910) is indicative of this.
23 Not only is the anxiety over violence negated but it is even replaced by an eager anticipation of the possible comic outcome of wine squirting everywhere if the Kinsman does indeed pierce the 'baby'.

24 The comic situation is closer to the original in this respect, since in Euripides' play the threat to Orestes' life was made by Telephus in a bid for the Achaians to listen to him, see Olson (2002) 331–2n.
25 A case might be made for the substitution creating comic dissonance between its description and its appearance. The dynamics of the scene and the comic relief in knowing that in fact no violence can come from the sword in this setting, however, weigh in favour of a sword prop being used. Olson (2002) 331–2n assumes a sword (cf. Sommerstein (1980) 345n kitchen knife).
26 For the comic undercutting of tragic 'trigger' words see, for example, φιλανθρακέα appearing *para prosdokian* for φιλάνθρωπον ('humane') in 336 (Olson (2002) *ad loc.*).
27 Text and translation of *Acharnians* from Henderson (1998) unless otherwise stated.
28 On charcoal being produced in Acharnae see Sommerstein (1980) 348n. On the basket's personification, see Olson (2002) 340, and on the related use of the diminutive to create a sense of endearment see Petersen (1910) 240. On stereotypes of Acharnians, see Whitehorne (2005) 37 and Kellogg (2013) 113-48.
29 Sommerstein (2010) 33 (on lack of killing in comedy) and 35 (on near misses in tragedy). Aristotle, *Poetics* 1453b35–1454a (Ch. 14) on the dramatic impact of different types of near misses in tragedy.
30 This fits within the framework of the comedy's interest in playing off 'one style of dramaturgy against another', Foley (1988) 40.
31 *LSJ* s.v. ἐντιλάω offers this rather more graphic translation (cf. Henderson's 'dirtied' above).
32 The spurt of Agamemnon's blood memorably a source of pleasure for Clytemnestra (*Ag.* 1389–90) and Ajax's warm spurting blood upon which both Tecmessa and Teucer comment (*Aj.* 918–9 and 1411–13).
33 For a parallel use of scatological humour to dispel the threat of tragedy in Ar. *Peace* 149–53 see Farmer (2016) 120–1.
34 Olson (2002) *ad loc.* on the verb and on this motif.
35 Since as Olson (2002) notes, 350–1n, cuttlefish release ink to confuse enemy when under threat.
36 On 'reality' of comic stage see Zeitlin (1981) 306.
37 Poe (2000) 279 notes the distancing created by discontinuity here too.
38 For the sword as a symbol of tragedy on the comic stage, see Revermann (2006), 40.
39 Suggested especially by lines 464 and 470, see Muecke (1982) 22 with Zuckerberg (2014) 94–5.
40 On self-definition through tragedy in this play see Foley (1988) esp. 43.
41 While it is known that Lamachus was elected general soon after this comedy, it is debated whether he was already a general in 426/5 BC. The crux of the matter rests on the interpretation of two lines in the play: 593 (in which Lamachus refers to

himself as general) and 1073 (in which he is commanded by generals to set out to protect the pass). Sommerstein (1980), pp. 184–5 assumes that Lamachus is not yet general and takes 593 as anticipatory. Olson (2002) 569–71n, p. 222 assumes, based on 593, that Lamachus was a general in 426/5 BC. I use 'commander' here to indicate that, whether he was already elected or not, he was a prominent military figure.

42 Olson (2002) 572–4n.
43 For evidence of this effect in tragedy see Wyles (2010) 251–2.
44 Henderson (1998) 125 assumes that he wears a full panoply. The multiple items of armour mocked in the scene implies it.
45 The sword is not explicitly mentioned but would be included if his costume is intended to represent the idealized image of the hoplite (seen in the iconographic schema reviewed in Chapter 3). Both Sommerstein (1980) 592n and Olson (2002) 590n assume its presence.
46 While feathers were used to induce vomit, see Olson (2002) 585–6n, the misappropriation here comes from the use of *helmet* feathers (the stuff of war) for such a purpose.
47 Olson (2002) *ad loc.* takes the οἴμοι to be an expression of angry exasperation citing comic parallels, its tragic resonance, however, may carry through given Lamachus' elevated paratragic speech earlier in the exchange.
48 Sommerstein (1980) *ad loc.* offers a helpfully detailed note (cf. briefer note in Olson (2002) *ad loc.*)
49 Sommerstein (1980) *ad loc.*
50 See Foley (1988). On the phallus' association with the comic genre, see Green (2007) 103.
51 Olson (2002) *ad loc.* offers parallel of *Wasps* 27. This is further reinforced implicitly by the double entendre associated with the sword itself, on which see Lambin (1979) esp. 548.
52 *Peace* 141 debunks naval equipment through an equivalent strategy.
53 Compton-Engle (2015) 42 identifies the following references: 158, 161, 237–79, 591–2, 785–7, 1058–66, 1149, and 1216–17.
54 Foley (1988) 39. There may be an even more profound statement about the difference between tragedy and comedy made through the opposition here between sword and phallus as symbols of killing and sex, since Sommerstein (2010) 36–7 acknowledges that each subject had an equivalent status in the respective genres (as subjects 'incessantly' talked about but never simulated onstage).
55 The idea of Lamachus benefiting from the war is raised explicitly soon after his arrival on stage see *Ach.* 597.
56 Foley (1988) 39.
57 Olson (2002) 326–7n notes that ἀποσφάζω is associated with execution, citing Hdt. 4.62.3, 84.2; Th. 3.32.1, Th. 7.86.2. Particularly telling amongst these parallels is Th.

3.32.1 in which the cruel treatment of fellow Greeks by the Spartan commander Alcidas in 427 BC is reported.
58 Poe (2000) 287 on the absurd denaturing seriousness in Aristophanes.
59 On Aristophanes' treatment of Lamachus see Storey (1998) esp. 110.
60 The pathos of the scene on the *lekythos* is evoked in part through its representation of the woman holding a sword. This raises the significant question of whether women were in the audience of this Aristophanic play and how the sword's treatment might have affected them if they were present. Views on the inclusion of women in the audience remain divided, the ambiguity of the evidence allowing for the characterization of the occasion as primarily political (and a male domain, Goldhill (1994)) or religious (and open to the inclusion of women, Henderson (1991)). I find Henderson's interpretation of the evidence slightly more persuasive. If women were present then the comic subversion (through the phallus joke, for example) might resonate rather differently with them, although the function of such jokes could be argued to be the same irrespective of gender. My analysis focuses on the Athenian male audience member although I acknowledge the approach's potential to illuminate views of other groups within society (see the Conclusion).
61 On Aristophanes' assertion of comedy's honesty (in contrast to tragedy) in *Acharnians*, see Foley (1988) 44.
62 The double entendre generated by the sword in the Harmodius drinking song (established by Lambin (1979)) offers a possible trace of this type of humour (and its function of reassurance) in the world outside theatre.
63 Goldhill (1986) 78.
64 See further the Conclusion. Aristophanes dispels anxiety by generating humour from the symbols' transformation, yet the process destabilizes the symbolic status of the objects (confirming the rationale of the concern).
65 Text and translation of *Wasps* from Henderson (1998) unless otherwise stated. I have retained Philocleon's name in the translation (rather than adopting Henderson's 'Lovecleon') for ease of reference.
66 As Revermann (2006), 40 notes: the 'mere mention' of the sword in this passage 'helps to turn the comic 'hero' Philocleon into a paratragic one'; see also Revermann (2013) 36. There are divergent views on whether the sword is brought onto stage, although Biles and Olson (2015) *ad loc.* see no reason to assume that it is not, pointing to the further reference at 714 and suggesting that he 'waves it ineffectively' at 756–7.
67 On comedy's 'rule' of not showing killing on stage, see n. 29 above.
68 So that this becomes 'parodic' in Silk's terms, Silk (1993) 479 (rather than simply 'paratragic').
69 Biles and Olson (2015) *ad loc*. See also Nelson (2016) 164.

70 On *Ajax*'s date see Finglass (2011) 1-11. On the stage image, see Chapter 4.
71 More precisely he asks him to state the penalty he will set if he disregards the verdict, see Sommerstein (1983) *ad loc.*; a question that operates on the assumption that he will still be alive.
72 Since both wordplay and wine belong to the comic domain. On the pun, see Sommerstein (1983) *ad loc.*
73 The sword may be brought out to him but is not yet on stage as he utters the threat. The power that the visual presence of a prop, as a reminder of the outcome its symbolism may 'determine', can generate is well illustrated by the chorus' girdles in Aeschylus' *Suppliant Women*, on which see Wyles (2011) 71-4.
74 Sometimes translated as 'writing case' (see, for example, Henderson (1998)) but Biles and Olson (2015) 529n note that it is a covered basket, citing the parallel of *Ach*. 1098, and emphasize that its contents are a mystery (until 538).
75 The parallel between the commands, which is not supported through a verbal echo, could have been underlined by a stage gesture.
76 For sword as symbol of tragedy see Revermann (2006) 40. On the ways in which Bdelycleon is styled as a comic playwright and director, see Olson (1996) 144 and Farmer (2016) 133. The basket's initial alignment with comedy comes through the performance memory of *Ach*. 1098; there the prop is similarly commanded to be brought onto stage and it is explicitly associated with food (through 1086 on which see Sommerstein (1980) *ad loc.*). The prop in *Wasps*, however, subsequently becomes even more profoundly linked to comedy once the image of Bdelycleon as comic playwright has been established through the revelation of the note-taking equipment it contains. In a later Aristophanic comedy, the same object is understood to have the capacity to hold snakes (*Amphiaraus*, fr. 28) demonstrating the mutability of the prop's function (and meaning).
77 Dicaeopolis is alarmed by a numbness creeping over his hand that affects his ability to hold his sword and leaves him 'weak' (*Wasps* 713-15); it does not take much to extend the meaning here to allow for the proposed interpretation. μαλθακός, which Biles and Olson (2015) *ad loc.* translate as 'weak' on the basis of the context, literally (as they note) means 'soft'; furthermore *LSJ* s.v. II.b points to its application within a sexual context. If, as Biles and Olson suggest, the lines were 'accompanied by a dramatic show of trying and failing to hold the weapon upright in front of him', then this gesture would lend further support to the joke.
78 The explicitness of the references to tyranny which precede this threat to take up a sword make the association with the tyrannicides in the minds of the audience an inevitability since, as Raaflaub (2003) 71 notes, Athenian society was primed to make the connection even at the slightest hint.
79 On this motif see Biles and Olson (2015) 343-5n, Henderson (1987) p. 151 and (2003) 164-5.

80 Biles and Olson (2015) *ad loc.* See also Henderson (2003) 163.
81 Biles and Olson (2015) 488–507n for absurdity. On false preparation see p. 156.
82 The joke relies on the pun made possible by his 'horsey' name, see Sommerstein (1983) *ad loc.* On the tyrannicides' deed, see Chapter 3.
83 On the *Oresteia*'s engagement with this motif, see Chapter 4. This may present another respect in which *Wasps* alludes to the *Oresteia*; for the comedy's interplay with Aeschylus' trilogy see Wyles (2020).
84 On the 'foundational' status of the tyrannicides' act, see Chapter 3. This would correspond to Lysistrata's elite contestation of the myth, on which see Henderson (2003) 175.
85 Henderson (1987) xv–xxv on the political situation in Athens at the time of the play's performance in 411 BC. He argues for its production at the Lenaea, i.e. before the coup (xvi) but acknowledges that the play emphasizes civic strife (xxiii). In this context, the playful undercutting of the tyrannicides' status as role models seems risky. On the play's engagement with the theme of tyranny, see Henderson (2003) 173–4.
86 The passages are: the travesty of the oath over the shield (*Lys.* 183–90), Lysistrata's ridicule of men shopping in their armour (*Lys.* 555–60), and the appropriation of Athena's sacred helmet to imitate pregnancy (*Lys.* 742–52). This might be fruitfully compared to the sustained engagement in *Acharnians*.
87 Henderson (1987), p. 151 on the association of this 'smear-word' with Cleon in Aristophanes.
88 Plutarch *Arist.* 26.3 and *Nic.* 6.1. Paches was held to account through this trial for his apparent misconduct during his command in Mytilene.
89 Sommerstein (1983) *ad loc.* and Biles and Olson (2015) *ad loc.* acknowledge the possibility of this. Roberts (2017) 107 n. 16 offers a helpful summary of the problems with the evidence and the resulting scepticism in scholarship. Plutarch *Arist.* 26.3 is the more detailed of the two descriptions and though it does not specify a sword, this seems the most likely means by which Paches killed himself in the court. The publicness of trials, on which see Lanni (2012), would ensure widespread knowledge of the event (if it took place).
90 *Frogs*' jokes about the fate of the generals who returned to Athens after the battle of Arginusae, on which see Chapter 1, pp. 14–15, offer a strong parallel since humour is derived from the recent death of high-profile military figures not on the battlefield but as a result of the processes of Athenian democracy (and particularly its commitment to accountability).
91 For Aristophanes' related criticism of Euripides' closing of tragic distance in *Thesmophoriazusae* see Zeitlin (1981) esp. 305–6.

92 On the prominence of the phallus in the festivities before the performances, see Csapo (2010b) 141. Amongst the terms for the foundation of the Athenian colony at Brea is the requirement that the colonists should send a cow and panoply to the Great Panathenaea and a phallus to the Dionysia (*IG* I³ 46. 15–17, dated to 440–432 BC) indicating the symbolic status of the phallus in these parades. This requirement may have been extended to all tribute-paying members of the Delian league in 425/4 BC (based on *IG* I³ 71, 57–8, although only the cow and panoply for the Great Panathenaea are mentioned explicitly).
93 Implied also by *Lys.* 630–3 discussed in Chapter 3.
94 For phallus as marker of male identity generally on the comic stage, see Foley (2000) 301. Her argument that the comic costume, including phallus, played a role in drawing attention to the constraints (including war) experienced by the citizen performer beneath (Foley (2000) 305–6) reinforces the suggestion made here.
95 The simultaneous (mis-)treatment of the sword on the comic stage should be kept in mind (retrospectively) for the analysis of the *Oresteia* and *Ajax*, since comedy is conventionally understood to have been part of the Dionysia competition since 486 BC (on the evidence of the *Suda* lexicon s.v. Χιωνίδης and *IG* II².2325 on which see Millis and Olson (2012) 156–7; or perhaps even earlier, see Green (2010) 74.
96 On its prominence in both see my brief discussion of the topic, Wyles (2014). On the rationale for dating *Phoenician Women* to 409 BC, see Craik (1988) 40.
97 Hesk (2007) 81–2 on *Orestes*.
98 On the oath, see Chapter 3. On the importance of tyranny in this play, see Seaford (2003) 107–11.
99 Teegarden (2014) 35.
100 Shear (2007) 153–7 argues that the oath was sworn on the day after the Proagon and notes that this would have made the Dionysia in 409 BC a particularly charged affair. Her consideration (156–7) of the impact of this on our understanding of *Philoctetes* offers a precedent for the approach I take here. Wilson (2009) 24 for oath in theatre. The connection, given the cues in the text, would be unavoidable, see n. 78 above.
101 On other responses to the crisis see Wilson (2009) 18–19. For a parallel crisis to views on Athenian citizenship following democracy's suppression see Bakewell (1999).
102 *Phoen.* 68 (iron, most likely sword), 267, 276, 331–2, 350, 363, 515–17, 521, 594–7, 625, 1091, 1404–24, 1455–9, 1556–8, 1577–9, 1677. While the textual difficulties with the play, and suspicion over portions of the received text, are notorious (for a summary see Craik (1988) 49–52), the emphasis on the sword is nevertheless clear.
103 References to the curse of Oedipus occur at: *Phoen.* 68, 334, 473–80, 624, 764–5, 876–7, 1051–4, 1354–5, 1425–6, 1556–8, 1611.

104 Polynices and Eteocles (1404–24 and 1556–8), Jocasta (1455–9 and 1577–9) and Menoeceus (1091); Oedipus' would-be suicidal sword (331–2) and Antigone swears by the sword to reinforce her threat to murder Haemon on their wedding night (1677).
105 Text and translation of *Phoenician Women* from Kovacs (2002), unless otherwise stated.
106 Craik (1988), p. 187.
107 See Wyles (2011), 69–76 on the sense of inevitability that may be created through props.
108 Altena (1999–2000) 317 explores the possibility that Polynices is wearing armour. While I agree that the text remains open to this, Polynices' entrance seems to imply that the sword is his only defence; this staging would heighten the sense of danger.
109 While the audience must know from convention that this would not happen, on which see Sommerstein (2010), the dramatic effect of the scene is created by exactly the anticipation over whether it might.
110 Polynices sets this up through 594–5 and its relationship to 625. While 594–5 is presented as a generalized statement, it is clearly meant to apply to Eteocles; cf. Teucer's response to Menelaus' 'fable' (*Aj.* 1142–6, on which see Garvie (1998) *ad loc.*) which soon becomes personal (*Aj.* 1150–8). Altena (1999–2000) 314 suggests that Eteocles carries a sceptre, though such an interpretation does not account for 596 and misses the powerful onstage realization of the battlefield doubling later reported in the messenger speech.
111 On the prominence of blood in the play, see Craik (1988) 45. In the choral ode directly after this passage, the imagery of blood and iron is extended back further into the mythological past through the account of the 'steely-hearted slaughter' of Cadmus' sown men bloodying the earth (670–5), setting the threatened violence between the brothers within this wider mythological frame and pushing the history of bloodshed back further than Apollo's warning to Laius. This had also been a significant theme in Aeschylus' dramatization of the myth, see Thalmann (1978) 50–1, the context for Euripides' production however imbue the motif with a different resonance.
112 On the violence of such staging, see Medda (2001) 44–5.
113 Further details in the brothers' heated exchange support this effect; so, for example, Polynices' wish to know where Eteocles will be stationed so that he can be posted opposite to kill him (*Phoen.* 621–2) enables the audience to envisage the circumstances of the sword's fatal use. The fulfilment of the anticipated use of the prop is made clear by the detailed description of the swords in the messenger speech reporting the brothers' death (*Phoen.* 1404–24).
114 *Phoen.* 434, 513, 694, 728, 754–6, 779–80, 825–7, 860, 1080–2, 1086, 1094, 1097, 1192, 1242–7, 1297, 1325–6, 1382–403. The references to the spear before the

messenger speech could be taken as 'false preparation', since the sword will prove the fatal weapon; it is not entirely 'false', however, as wounds are inflicted with spears in the duel. Polynices' sword may have still been embedded in Eteocles' corpse (1421) when it is brought onto stage; Eteocles' sword, cast on the ground after dealing the fatal wound, *Phoen.* 1417, is likely to have been used by Jocasta (as suggested by Craik (1988) 1456n) and may have been shown still plunged into the neck of her corpse when it is brought onto stage.

115 No fewer than five references to it are clustered in eighty lines of the scene: *Phoen.* 481–3, 504–6, 521–5, 549–50, 560–1. Eteocles evokes the negative connotations of the term τύραννος which for Athenians, fresh from swearing the Demophantus oath would encourage the understanding of the term as a reference to dangerously undemocratic autocracy. The significance of this play to our understanding of Athenian views on tyranny has been widely acknowledged, see, for example, Rosivach (1988) 46, Raaflaub (2003) 79 and Seaford (2003) 107–11.

116 This is set in marked contrast to Menoeceus' later use of the term in a far more patriotic sentiment, *Phoen.* 1015–18. The parallels between Eteocles' justification and the sentiments of the Athenian speech in the Melian dialogue (recorded by Thucydides 5.84–111), however, makes his speech unsettling in a different respect; Seaford (2003) 110 and Dillon (2004) 62–3. While the critical issues with accepting the authenticity of the speeches in Thucydides are well known, the Melian dialogue's status as a vehicle through which Thucydides' conveys his perception of Athenian imperialism ensure its value nevertheless.

117 The sophistic resonances of the speech, on which see Papadopoulou (2008) 61–2, may go some way to mediating its impact although its sentiment must still have been shocking (especially in the context of Athens regaining its democratic footing).

118 The wording of the oath is recorded in Andocides *On the Mysteries* 97, see Chapter 3, pp. 59–60 above. On this effect of Greek tragedy, see Telò and Mueller (2018b) 9.

119 I have altered the translation here, adding in 'let fire come' (521) and replacing 'kingship' (523) with 'tyranny' to reflect the term's repetition in the Greek.

120 See Raaflaub (2014) 79.

121 Especially notable is Teiresias' reference to Athens (*Phoen.* 852–7) see Craik (1988) *ad loc.* and pp. 44–5 (on Athenian resonances within the play).

122 On the deliberate Athenian resonance, see Papadopoulou (2008) 59. On the importance of this term to Athenian civic pride, see Craik (1988) *ad loc.* Further support may be offered for the motif by the description of the combat in which Polynices plunges his sword into Eteocles' liver (*Phoen.* 1421), i.e. the same wound as the tyrant-slayer Aristogiton is shown inflicting on the fifth-century *stamnos* (now in Würzburg), Fig. 14. The question of whether Polynices is characterized as sympathetic or a schemer, which Altena (1999–2000) 317–18 astutely raises

prompted by Polynices' reference to his weeping at 366, is relevant here. If he is presented as sympathetic then this reinforces the alignment and Athenian identification. If he seems a schemer then it creates a further undercurrent to the appropriation of the tyrannicide motif.

123 This layering to the sword's meaning mirrors the play's multiple perspectives on the action of war (on which see Papadopoulou (2008) 39–43) – both form part of the same strategy.

124 The decree was passed at the first prytany, i.e. the beginning of the Athenian official year, of 410/9 BC, see Shear (2007) 149.

125 On this function of the oath see Shear (2007). On Euripides' criticism of the political situation in this play see Lamari (2012) and in the near-contemporary *Orestes* see Rosenbloom (2012) 405–31.

126 Thuc. 6.57.4 informs us that Harmodius was slain on the spot and that Aristogiton was 'not gently handled' after being captured. [Arist.] *Ath. Pol.* 18.4–6 offers the further details of Harmodius being killed by a spearman and Aristogiton, after being tortured, provoking Hippias into killing him.

127 On this schema and its relationship to democratic identity, see Chapter 1.

128 Demonstrated also on the Attic red-figured *kylix* attributed to Brygos painter, c. 490–480 BC, British Museum 1843,1103.11 (side B, showing conflict, can be seen at the bottom edge of Fig. 2).

129 For the identification of the figures see Catoni (2015) 22–3.

130 See discussion in Chapter 1.

131 It is significant that, as Henderson (1987) notes 565–6n, the Proboulos in the scene does not deny that such disturbances exist.

132 *IG* I^3 102 with Wilson (2009). Euripides even seems to make a self-conscious reference to this (perhaps new) practice later in the play (*Phoen.* 852–7).

133 Though note the character of a mediating mother featured in Stesichorus' poem, see Papadopoulou (2008) 29–30. On Menoeceus as a new creation see Papadopoulou (2008) 31. On innovation in Euripides' version compared to Aeschylus' see Torrance (2007) 114.

134 There is perhaps a hint of pathos to the detail of the sword being black-bound for this interpretation see Craik (1988) 1091n.

135 It is relayed in a temporal clause. In the context of the speech, Menoeceus' death has become irrelevant as Craik (1988) 1090–2n notes.

136 It highlights, as Papadopoulou (2008) 67 puts it, 'the gap between the idealistic worldview of characters like Menoeceus and the grim reality of the people who generate the crisis'.

137 Through the descriptions of it by the messenger (*Phoen.* 1455–9) and Antigone (1577–9), and through the repeated references to the three corpses: 1481–4, 1502–3, 1524–9, 1552, 1616–18, and 1635.

138 Determinism, i.e. the trajectory determined through the brothers' heated exchange (see above). The audience has been prepared for the possibility that she may kill herself (*Phoen.* 1280–4), but not that she will do so with the sword belonging to one of her sons.
139 Craik (1988) 44 on the relevance (to Athens) of the play's emphasis on suffering.
140 On this function of myth see Papadopoulou (2008) 27.
141 Euripides engages directly with Aeschylus' *Seven Against Thebes* (through dramatic criticism of it) at 724f, which implicitly invites the audience to think of the difference in their treatment of the curse and armour in their respective dramatizations of the myth; while *Seven Against Thebes* famously focuses on shields, Euripides shifts the attention to the swords alluded to by the curse. On Euripides' parody and 'dramatic criticism' of Aeschylus, see Bond (1974) esp. 3, 12 and Papadopoulou (2008) 39, and on Euripides' treatment of this myth (cf. Aeschylus), see McDermott (1991) 129–30 and Torrance (2007) 112–14. On the curse in Aeschylus' play, see Thalmann (1978) 17–20.
142 Blood mixed with the earth (*Sept.* 938–40) is an example of another of the shared motifs that Euripides develops further (on this motif in *Phoenician Women* see Craik (1988) 173–4n).
143 This curse could also have been known to the audience through Stesichorus' *Thebaid*; on the curse in different treatments of the myth see Mastronarde (1994), 23–4. On the play and myth in general, see Papadopoulou (2008) 27–48.
144 The report of their deaths refers to the iron (as a generic term for weapon) 817, 880–5, 888–90, 911–14, 941–3, but spears are specified at 961–2 and 992. Aeschylus may, however, have alluded to the detail of the sword in the curse in his *Oedipus*, see Hutchinson (1985) xxiv and xxix; Papadopoulou (2008) 36–7 assumes a sword.
145 See Chapter 4.
146 References to three corpses in *Phoen.* 1481–4, 1502–3, 1524–9, 1552, 1616–18, and 1635, cf. double death in, for example, *Sept.* 849–51; on the effect of which see Thalmann (1978) 101–2.
147 Zeitlin (1994) 178.
148 It may be that these are alternative descriptions rather than two references. On this textual issue, see Craik (1988) 50. Even if Antigone's scene looking out from the tower is deemed suspect and lines 173–4 are excised, this would not be fatal to the main argument being put forward here.
149 Craik (1988) 172n.
150 On the parallel use of this verb to set up the association between Ajax's killing of the herds and himself with *sphagia* in *Ajax*, see Chapter 4, p. 85 above.
151 See, for example, *Phoen.* 933; on these characteristics of battlefield *sphagia*, see Chapter 3, p. 71.

152 The sacrificial action of plunging the sword through the victim's neck is graphically depicted in the fragments of Attic red-figure *kylix*, *c*. 490–480 BC, Cleveland Museum of Art, Dudley P. Allen Fund 1926.242, see Chapter 3, pp. 71–2.
153 *Phoen.* 1317–21.
154 Euripides creates a similar effect in *Bacchae* through his treatment of cross-dressing (cf. *Thesmophoriasuzae*), see Wyles (2011) 99–100 and the mask prop, see Chapter 6.
155 Assumed parody see Henderson (2008) 373.
156 Athenaeus 4.154E. Henderson (2008) 373 interprets the passage as referring to the old-fashioned style of the duel exemplified in *Phoenician Women* but as Papadopoulou (2008) 43 notes, while the duel seems to aspire to Homeric grandeur, Euripides undercuts this through fifth-century resonances.
157 For the parodic tone created by the over-emphasis see Miles (2009) 280.
158 On this play, see Miles (2009) 183–202; on the question of its precedence over Aristophanes' parody, see 186 and 279.
159 See Miles (2009) 190–4.
160 For traces in Plato's work, for example, see Dillon (2004) and Papadopoulou (2008) 54–5. Craik (1988) 934n identifies an echo of line 934 in Plato's phrase 'ancient wrath' (*Phaedrus* 244d); the similarity of context reinforces the intertext (Plato's discussion of the oracular art cf. Tiresias' prophesying).
161 Text and translation Oldfather (1950). The chronological gap between the event and Diodorus' account is problematic, yet the dream's details are so specific that it seems unlikely to have been purely fictitious.
162 Cartledge (1997) 11 for this interpretation.
163 I follow Cartledge (1997) 11 in assuming that Euripides' *Suppliants* is meant here. On its dating see Collard (1975) esp. 10.
164 On this trial see Chapter 1.

Chapter 6

1 See, above all, Goldhill (1987) and Winkler and Zeitlin (1990). The focus of this chapter is on the impact of the Dionysia's focus on citizen participation in its choruses. The Lenaea festival presents a different prospect both since it reflected introspectively on civic identity (see Aristophanes' *Acharnians* 497–508) and through its laxer rules on choral participation, see MacDowell (1989) 68 and Jackson (2019) 32–3.
2 Putting the funding of a chorus on a par with the fitting out of a trireme see MacDowell (1989) 70. On the *choregia* see Wilson (2000).
3 Not only in the literal sense of the wealthy citizens who funded the chorus, but also metaphorically, placing the citizens as stakeholders in the theatrical

enterprise. Whitehorne (2005) 35 on its role in the self-construction of Athenian identity.

4 On this rule see Plutarch *Phocion* 30, Pseudo-Andocides, *Against Alcibiades* 20–1, and Demosthenes *Against Meidias* 58–61 (Csapo and Slater (1994) 351 and 358) with MacDowell (1989). Jackson (2019) 29–30 scrutinizes the 'dogma' that only citizens could perform in the chorus, but presents a compelling reason to accept the law's applicability to dramatic choruses and acknowledges that it reflects the festivals' ideology (if not practice, on which see 32–3 and 49). The display of this ideal, and its protection, at the Dionysia (MacDowell (1989) 74–7), the most ideologically charged festival, is likely to have influenced perceptions of citizen participation in other dramatic choruses. For the people's participation in the chorus as an Athenian characteristic see Old Oligarch *Constitution of the Athenians* 14. For theatre's association with Athenian identity outside Athens, see Thuc. 2.41 with Taplin (1993b) 539. Blok (2017) 187 on participation as a touchstone of being a citizen. Wilson (2000) 77 suggests that the opportunity was open to adult male citizens of any age (cf. Winkler (1990) ephebes and Foley (2003) 5 citizens under the age of thirty). The absence of theatre from the world of epic, see Hall (2006) 110, would reinforce the citizen's association of this experience with their Athenian present.

5 While accepting non-citizens' *informal* political participation (Vlassopoulos (2007)), due weight must still be given to the formal distinctions between citizens and non-citizens in Athens, see Manville (1990) 8–13.

6 The professionalization of acting makes the equivalent claim for actors more problematic (although Duncan (2006) 25 suggests that for most of the fifth-century, the audience would imagine actors to be ordinary citizens of the democracy); on actors see Easterling and Hall (2002). This discussion errs on the side of caution by focusing on participation in the chorus. Choregic art in any case commemorated the performance through reference to the chorus, on which see Csapo (2010c).

7 Herakleides Kritikos *On Greek Cities* 1.4 = [Dicaerarch.] Περὶ τῶν ἐν τῇ Ἑλλάδι πόλεων 1.4, *FHG* II 59 (p. 255): Οἱ δὲ εἰλικρινεῖς Ἀθηναῖοι δριμεῖς τῶν τεχνῶν ἀκροαταὶ καὶ θεαταὶ συνεχεῖς. See also Csapo and Slater (1995) 301. Herakleides' uses of the adjective εἰλικρινής (literally 'pure' or 'unmixed') suggests those who reflect the Athenian ideal most clearly without taint (i.e. those who provide a model for citizen identity).

8 The context, especially the contrast set up with speech writers (mentioned by Herakleides just before this), implies that the term τέχνη refers to the arts of music and dance rather than the art of rhetoric or a trade. For the negative representation of logographers see Hesk (1999) 218.

9 For the law, MacDowell (1989) 70–2 with Dem. 21.15 and 39.16.; Pritchard (2004) 214 on this exemption for dithyrambic chorus and Lech (2009b) 355 n. 33 on its

extension to dramatic choruses. See also Christ (2001) 405. Goldhill (1997) 54 on spectating as performing citizenship.

10 Wilson (2000) 77 with judicious comments of Jackson (2019) 29–30 (confirming, nevertheless, the ideological significance of this law).

11 The recognition of these performances' value to society is evidenced by the law court tactic of mentioning their sponsorship (i.e. *choregia*) to win over the jury see Ober (1989) 231–3. For the ideological emphasis on everyone playing their part within Athenian democracy see Goldhill (1986) 66 and Blok (2017) 207. On choral training see Wilson (2000) 85–94 and Jackson (2019) 40–2).

12 For the *proagon* see Pickard-Cambridge (1988) 67–8 and Csapo and Slater (1995) 109–10; see esp. *Life of Euripides* for the chorus' involvement in the event, Plato *Symposium* 194 on the large audience and the scholion to Aeschines *Against Ktesiphon* 67 for lack of mask. Wilson (2000) 96 on the *proagon* as means of advertising civic identities. This display may have been mirrored by the mask's removal at the end of the tetralogy, see Taplin (2010); if so, then it would frame the mask as representing the experience of both the performance and performing. The citizen's peer group could be informally aware of his participation in the chorus, though the formal framing of the *proagon* lent a different force to this knowledge.

13 This suggestion takes into account some of the important points raised by Winkler's argument about the formative function of training in the tragic chorus (Winkler (1990) with Wilson (2000) 77 on its value) without committing to the claim that it served as a form of military training for ephebes (Lech (2009b) makes a compelling case against this).

14 Prauscello (2014) *passim*.

15 The 'choral performance' at stake in *Laws* is carefully negotiated (and does not represent the tragic chorus outright, see Jackson (2019) 213), Prauscello (2014) 126–8, yet the function of dramatic choruses in Athens may nevertheless have cued this utopic re-conceptualization. It is also significant, to the argument of civic identity, that Plato views tragic choruses as a distinctly Athenian phenomenon see Wiles (2007) 11. For Plato's engagement with the chorus across his works see Jackson (2019) 212–41. On the emphasis in other sources on the chorus' role in civic education see Wilson (2000) 83 and Foley (2003) 4.

16 Calame (1999). On collective activity and identity see Introduction p. 3. The case made here is entirely distinct from the suggestion that the chorus somehow represents the civic community within the drama (for a critique of which see Carter (2010) 64–9).

17 Duncan (2006) 1–24. See also Foley (2000) 305–6.

18 Duncan (2006) 2.

19 Moments of self-awareness in choral performances, on which see Carter (2010) 64, draw attention to this. Choral performers 'playing the other' see Foley (2003) 5–8, and Carter (2010) 66 on sharp differentiation of assumed identity.
20 On the different types of chorus in Athens, and difficulty in distinguishing between them, see Wilson (2000) 6 and Lech (2009b) 350–1. On the dithyramb see Kowalzig and Wilson (2013). See bibliography in Nelson (2016) 39 n. 55 on dithyramb's lack of masks and Green (2007) 102 on the mask as a point of distinction between the types of chorus.
21 For the mask as a potent symbol of the mimetic nature of theatre see Hall (2006) 114. The suggestion that the mask invited reflection on collective identity, Wiles (2007) 283, is consistent with this.
22 Wilson (2000) 76–7 argues that the majority of choreuts would have been drawn from the elite (see the related case made by Pritchard (2004) for the dithyrambic chorus); yet participation in the tragic or comic chorus was, so far as is known, open to adult male Athenian citizens irrespective of rank (Wilson (2000) 77) and Jackson (2019) 35–7 and 49 allows for the possibility of non-elite participation. The ideological construct enabled the ordinary citizen to aspire to perform and to glory in his (as yet unfulfilled) right to participate; a parallel might be found in the non-elite citizens' non-participation in, yet admiration for, athletics see Pritchard (2013). While the disparity between citizens' experience in performing differentiated the mask's resonance, its status as a symbol for the value the city placed on theatre (and citizens' performing) transcended this. The iconographic evidence suggests the mask's role in confronting the audience's sense of identity (see below). For those who had performed in the past, the experience's inculcation of civic values would be reinforced through the memories prompted by spectating (for this concept see Plato's *Laws* 2.657D with Prauscello (2014) 164–6). The effect of this would be heightened by the sense in which participation at the festival could be perceived as a performance of citizenship, Goldhill (1997) 54 and Blok (2017) 202–5.
23 I am grateful to Edith Hall for pointing this out to me, see further Hall (2006) 110.
24 Masks shared the same material (linen) and shape (helmet) (see Hall (2006) 101–2), but the depiction of their features differentiated between genres, see Marshall (1999) 188 and 191.
25 The prop's 'stage life' (explored in section II) considers the mask as an object handled on stage rather than a piece of costume worn by performers.
26 Duncan (2018) 82 acknowledges that the mask's offstage and onstage lives are 'mutually informing' (although his analysis explores tragedy alone).
27 On its independence see Green (1982). Duncan (2018) presents a helpful analysis of the tragic mask's 'off-stage life'.
28 Attic red-figure *chous* in Eleusis museum showing satyr mask being held by one boy and gazed upon by another, see Green (1994) 79–80 with Fig. 3.16.

29 Halliwell (1993) 196 on the normality of the mask in ancient Greece (cf. its alien status now).
30 For a parallel to the mask's duality as a serious object of ideological significance and a plaything, see Kosmin (2015) 128 on the children's game involving *ostraca*.
31 Green (1982) and (1994) 46. It was well established as a cultural practice by the end of the fifth century as vase paintings depicting this activity evidence; see, for example, the fragment from an Attic red-figure volute krater (Samothrace 65.1041) illustrated in Green (1994) 80. See also Duncan (2018) 85.
32 Further functions of this practice are noted by Green (1994) 79 and Duncan (2018) 85–6.
33 On terminology ('index') see Elam (2002) 18–20.
34 Goldhill (1987) and Wilson (2000) 94.
35 Duncan (2018) 86–7 notes the visibility of their placement and the opportunity this offered to foreign visitors to view the mask.
36 Boston, MFA 98.883. Wiles (2007) 20–5 discusses earlier Attic vases depicting the theatre mask held in the hand; the earliest survives on the fragment of a wine jug dated to 470–460 BC (Athens Agora museum P11810) on which see Moore (1997) 232 with Pl. 67.
37 Wiles (2007) 41 on masks as agents of transformation and Wyles (2011) 63 on this image.
38 I apply the model of Stansbury-O'Donnell (2006) 52–88 to the analysis of images throughout this chapter.
39 Foley (2003) 5–8 on the significance of citizens 'playing the other' in dramatic choruses.
40 The vase's provenance is Cervetri, although it is not known when it came to be there: https://collections.mfa.org/objects/153834 (accessed 17 August 2019).
41 See Taplin (1993b) 536–7 for a related point about Athenian prestige. I avoid the term 'export' since the circumstances of such vases' travel are often unclear. On the importance of the 'outside' perspective to a group's cultural identity see Patronos (2002) 8.
42 The State Hermitage Museum, Taman collection, ΦA 1869.47. For the date see Green (1971) 212.
43 Rusten (2019) with detailed photographs.
44 The vase is only 9.5 cm high, Rusten (2019) 60–3. Rusten makes a convincing case for the figure with the stick representing a third comic actor; despite the lack of visible phallus, the bulk of the figure and his hat suggests his status as comic performer (Rusten (2019) 65 and 72).
45 These performers are most likely actors but I work on the basis that their masks functioned as a symbolic equivalent to a choreut's mask for the citizen viewer; the institutional perspective of drama as a choral performance, see Wilson (2000) 6 and Foley (2003) 3, bolsters such an approach.

46 The line drawing of the vase issued on its first publication in 1874, see Rusten (2019) 60 with Fig. 5.4, misses this by distorting the angle of the mask (so that the performer gazes at its beard) and extending the distance between performer and mask. On the detrimental impact that line drawings, as intermediary images, can exert on the perception of vase paintings see Lissarrague (2010).
47 This mask is the only one with a golden headband; emphasized further by the two performers either side of it also wearing headbands; Rusten (2019) 62.
48 On the awareness of this, and anxiety over it, within antiquity see Duncan (2006) esp. 1–2 and 9.
49 On the power and intensity of the mask's gaze in vase paintings see Wiles (2007) esp. 31–2 and 42 (I am indebted to his discussion although I do not agree with all aspects of it).
50 Frontisi-Ducroux (1995).
51 The Apulian bell-krater from the Long Overfalls group, now in a private collection in Brindisi, also combines a mask in profile with a frontal mask (see Trendall (1988) 154) demonstrating the power of this motif.
52 This is demonstrated, for example, by the Pronomos vase (discussed further below).
53 The entire composition suggests an interest in emphasizing the collective nature of theatre, since it includes a combination of personnel (performers and musicians).
54 See Introduction p. 3.
55 Rusten (2019) 79 on its 'intense, detailed engagement with the variety of comic σκευή (costume, masks, props), evidently for its own sake'. On the proportion of craftsmen in Athens as a distinguishing feature of its democratic identity see Vlassopoulos (2007) 48–9.
56 Athenian Agora excavations P32870, see Camp (1999) 257.
57 Notable since the depiction of the famed piper, Pronomos, on the Pronomos vase (discussed below) does not include his *phorbeia*, see Wilson (2010) 188. Other representations of the *phorbeia*, of which I am aware, show it being worn while the *auloi* are played. On depictions of *auloi* players (and musicians on the Phanagoria *chous*) see Rusten (2019) 70–1.
58 Since the fragment does not include the performer's head this remains conjecture but seems the likeliest composition.
59 The fragment of an Attic red-figure *kylix* dated to *c.* 400 BC (Dresden Staatliche Kunstsammlungen AB 473) and depicting a seated naked figure holding a satyr-mask offers a further example for consideration. It shares some of the characteristics identified here, with the mask gazing intensely perhaps towards a performer, see Sparkes (1988). The image's placement on the cup's interior corroborates the suggestion of performance's significance to Athenian male identity and highlights the mask's role as a symbolic shorthand of this.

60 Attic red-figure krater by Pronomos painter, Naples 81673, H3240. Also relevant is the Peiraeus relief dated to *c.* 400 BC which Csapo (2010c) 94–9 argues is a choregic dedicatory relief to Dionysus; while its engagement with the themes discussed here is not as intense as the Pronomos vase, its presentation of chorus members carrying their masks is significant.

61 Mannack (2010) 5; Burn (2010) 23 notes that the date could fall within a decade either side of 400 BC. On the vase's celebration of a tragic tetralogy see Hall (2010) esp. 165. Almost the entire cast carry masks, though one chorus member does not and another wears his mask.

62 Taplin and Wyles (2010) *passim*.

63 Wiles (2007) 28–33 notes the power of the masks in the composition.

64 I follow Osborne (2010) 152, rather than Mannack (2010) 6 (who inverts the names).

65 Osborne (2010) 150–2 (popularity of name) and 154 (unlikely to reflect a real cast list).

66 Osborne (2010) 150.

67 Osborne (2010) 156–7 on the possibility of the names being designed to sound realistic to an external audience.

68 Although the *stele* was found on Salamis, this was in a repurposed context, see Slater (1985) 340.

69 The head on the left was identified as a mask on the *stele*'s first publication by Tsirivakos (1974).

70 Tsirivakos (1974) and Slater (1985) 341–3. Green (1994) 9 with 175 n. 21 suggests that it may instead commemorate the participation of a young boy in the chorus. The interpretation of the figures carrying masks on the Peiraeus relief as chorus members, Csapo (2010c) 94–9, offers support to the suggestion that this grave relief commemorates participation in the dramatic chorus.

71 For date see Tsirivakos (1974) 92 and Slater (1985) 341.

72 The surviving Roman copies of the Menander relief are perhaps based on an early Hellenistic original, see Green (1994) 83. An earlier example is offered by the marble grave relief (now in Lyme Park, Cheshire) depicting an Athenian comic playwright and dating either to *c.* 380 (so Bieber (1961) 48), or to the third quarter of the fourth century BC (thus Green (1994) 83).

73 Even if the grave *stele* marks the life of a playwright, the debt of its iconography to these earlier images of performers is nevertheless evident.

74 Another striking example, albeit a later one, of a tragic mask displaying this function is offered by the Gnathia fragment of a shaven actor looking at the mask of an old man (see cover image of this book); Tarentine Gnathia bell krater fragment, *c.* 340 BC, Martin von Wagner Museum der Universität Würzburg H4600 (L832).

75 The diversity of scale is striking – from the 9.5 cm high *chous*, to the 75 cm Pronomos calyx-crater and finally the grave relief (the remaining fragment alone is 70.2 cm high, see Slater (1985) 341).
76 Squire (2018) 534 thematization of viewing.
77 This interpretation is based on Squire's formulation of the mirror's symbolic function on *stelai*, Squire (2018) 535. The parallel function of the mask, cf. mirror, is reinforced through its similar placement in an outstretched hand at head height in the composition.
78 Morris (1994) 67 describes memorials to the dead as a 'major arena of self-definition for Athenian citizens'.
79 Slater (1985) 343.
80 The iconography remains ambiguous although the association between choral participation and citizen identity (see above) make it likely that a viewer would perceive this as an allusion to choral performance.
81 Slater (1985) 342 makes the attractive suggestion that the mask points to the tragic playwright's skill in writing female parts (and the same argument could be extended for a performer's skill); the more general reading of what the mask might represent for ideas of theatre may operate alongside this more specific interpretation. The Apulian red-figure bell-krater, dating to *c.* 400–380 BC, and now in the British Museum (1836,0224.175) presents a striking parallel in its depiction of a youth holding out a tragic female mask while Nike crowns him; on masks on Apulian red-figure vases see Trendall (1988).
82 The Boston *pelike* (Fig. 21), discussed above, offers an earlier example of this. The Gnathia fragment, shown on the cover of this book, exploits a similar effect through the contrast in age between performer and his mask.
83 See above all the seminal discussions of Zeitlin (1985) and Loraux (1985).
84 Duncan (2018) 87–8 suggests that the masks' display served as catalysts for ongoing theatrical discourse and definition; they also prompted reflection on civic identity.
85 On props 'introducing' craftspeople as presence in drama see Harris and Korda (2002b) 6–7.
86 Mueller (2016b) 68.
87 *POxy* 2162; *TrGF* 3, fr. 78a and 78c. The date is uncertain. Sommerstein suggests that it must have been late since the setting includes the temple of Poseidon; Sommerstein (2009b) 89. Aeschylus' death offers the *terminus ante quem*.
88 *TrGF* 3, fr 78a. 18–19; text and translation Sommerstein (2009b) 82–7.
89 Sommerstein (2009b) 87.
90 A generic term for image, εἴδωλον is used yet masks seem the likeliest target of the reference. 'The only objects which fit this description are masks'; Green (1994) 45; see also O'Sullivan (2000) 357, Sommerstein (2009b) 83 and Torrance (2013) 278.

232 Notes to pp. 136–138

91 On its metatheatricality see Green (1994) 45-6. The scene's comic representation of visual artifice's power is also striking see O'Sullivan (2000).
92 It seems possible that Aeschylus' play may have contributed to the shaping of this artistic concept, though the state of the evidence only allows for tentative speculation in this respect.
93 Green (1982) and (1994) 46 and 80.
94 Sommerstein (2009b) 82.
95 Religious considerations may inform this decision; see Sommerstein (2010) 30-1.
96 On communal gaze see Chapter 1 n. 36.
97 The reperformance of Aeschylus' plays in the fifth century, on which see Lamari (2015), allows for the possibility that *Bacchae*'s audience profited from a more recent stage memory of this satyr drama.
98 See Bakola (2010) 158-68 and Farmer (2016) 85 on the play. Bakola (2010) 162 on its dating to 423/2 BC.
99 My translation. See Bakola (2010) 159 n.129 on the etymology of βρίκελος (tragic mask).
100 On comedy and satyr drama's interplay in general see Sells (2019) 89-118.
101 Bakola (2010) 160 and Farmer (2016) 85.
102 Bakola (2010) 168 implies the mask's use (by suggesting that the character playing Perseus wears tragic costume in the 'play within a play'). Such a stage action, presenting the mask as a prop and then in use, would provide rich commentary on the status and meaning of the mask but since it remains speculative, I do not explore it further.
103 Sells (2019) 73-5 with images 2.7 a-c; he notes that though the mask is 'now barely perceptible' (75), its depiction is not inconsistent with it being a tragic mask, see also Wiles (2007) 39-40.
104 Bakola (2010) 160-2. On the comic intertextuality between Aristophanes and Cratinus see Ruffell (2002). Bakola's further suggestion, *ibid.*, that Euripides lends the masks from his *Dictys* in this scene would have intriguing implications for the way in which it would collapse the distinction between the theatrical and social life of these objects but it is too speculative to consider further here.
105 On this discourse see Wyles (2007) 96-103.
106 The character asks the tragic playwright Agathon to hand him a breast-band (*Thesm.* 255): αἱρέ νυν στρόφιον creating a parallel to the same imperative, placed in the same position in the line, to ask for an object imbued with metatheatrical resonance in Cratinus' play (fr. 218), see Bakola (2010) 159-60.
107 Marshall (1999) 196 notes that *Bacchae* 'is very conscious of its use of masks'.
108 See, above all, Foley (1980), (1985) 205-58, and Segal (1997) 215-71 and 369-78. The play's date is uncertain since the scholion on Ar. *Frogs* 67 merely informs us that it was produced after Euripides' death at the City Dionysia by his son (see

Seaford (2001) 25). I follow Zuckerberg (2014) 131 and 280 and Hall (2016) 16–17 in dating it to 405 BC; *contra* Chaston (2010) 181, who, arguing that *Frogs* was performed the year after it, dates *Bacchae* to 407/6 BC.
109 With implications for Taplin (1986) 165–6 and 170.
110 Mueller (2016b).
111 Seaford (2001) 222–3 and Wyles (2011) 99–100.
112 Foley (1985), 205-58. The play's equation of Bacchic ritual clothing to theatre costume heightens the dressing scene's self-consciousness see Wyles (2016) 64–5.
113 Ringer (1998) 10. It is generally accepted that Pentheus' mask is used in this scene; see Foley (1980) 130–1, Segal (1997) 248, Seaford (2001) 248 and Nelson (2016) 42. There are three possibilities for how the mask was carried by Agave: on the end of a *thyrsus* (supported by lines 1140–1; favoured by Seidensticker (1978) 303, Foley (1980) 131 and Chaston (2010) 184); held in her hands (supported by line 1277); or on a *thyrsus* initially and then taken into her hands, see Mueller (2016b) 68 n. 29. I favour the second or last possibility, although my analysis would not be seriously affected by insistence on the first.
114 There may be theatrical resonance to Cadmus' use of the term πρόσωπον if this word already denoted masks at this date (it is attested in the following century, see Demosthenes 19. 287, Aristotle *Poetics* 1449a36 with Segal (1997) 248). Even without the verbal cue, I would suggest that it is likely that some audience members would perceive this prop as a mask and head simultaneously.
115 See Chaston (2010), 187, n. 54.
116 Text and translation of *Bacchae* from Kovacs (2003).
117 His response broadens the query's parameters from stance to general appearance. Mueller (2016b) notes that Pentheus becomes the visual double of his mother.
118 Papyrus fragment, Penn Museum, University of Pennsylvania, E16449; the figure was identified as Agave by R.A. Kraft and A. Kuttner who also make the case for this fragment coming from an illustrated papyrus copy of the play: http://ccat.sas.upenn.edu/rak/ppenn/pictures/PPennPictures.html (accessed 16 August 2019).
119 Seaford (2001) 245–6, based on later evidence for this practice.
120 Cadmus insists that Agave should look at the head as he tries to help her to recognize what she has done (1277–85), cf. the multiple references to looking in the extract of *Theoroi* quoted above, p. 135, and Zeitlin (1994) 139 on their 'gaze'.
121 Segal identifies the 'unmasking' as a symbol of the end of the play within the play; Segal (1997) 248. Reflection on the act of dedicating masks develops this idea further.
122 On the mask's emotive role in this moment, irrespective of *Theoroi*, see Duncan (2018) 92.
123 On playfulness of horror in *Theoroi* see O'Sullivan (2000). On the mask's emotive force in that scene see Duncan (2018) 90.

124 Foley (1985) 251–2 on Dionysus' power expressed through Pentheus' mask.
125 I owe these references to Green (1994) 189 n. 165.
126 We know this from Hypothesis IV to Ar. *Birds*, see Henderson (2007) 119–20.
127 Text and translation from Henderson (2007) 124–5. In *Acharnians* too Lamachus' shield device (a gorgon, 574) is called a 'mormo' by Dicaeopolis and elicits a response of mock horror (580–2), on this scene see Chapter 5 pp. 120–4.
128 On dating see Henderson (2008), 173; this is his text and translation.
129 The scholiast, quoted above, acknowledges the term's application to both types of mask, although he may have extrapolated this from the qualifying κωμῳδικός.
130 For the association of the term μορμολυκεῖον with the mask's emotional impact see Duncan (2018) 87.
131 On shift of perceptions of Dionysus' mask, see Foley (1980) 131–3 and (1985) 250–1.
132 Chaston (2010) argues for this descriptor's fulfilment in a different respect.
133 Foley (1985) 251 and Segal (1997) 249. Segal also notes, in the same place, the transformation within the play from Dionysus' smiling mask to Pentheus' blood-flecked one, and see Chaston (2010) 179.
134 Green (1994) 85.
135 As Dunn (2012) 362 notes, the play takes a thematic metatheatrical interest in how mask and costume are endowed with a dramatic persona.
136 The performance memory of the comedy would be fresh in the audience's mind since it was produced in 411 BC, only five or six years before *Bacchae* (on *Bacchae*'s date, see n. 108 above).
137 Muecke (1982) 17–18 on similarity between the scenes. *Bacchae* offers a playful appropriation of Aristophanes' plotline for *Women at the Thesmophoria*: Pentheus takes the part of the Kinsman who in the comedy cross-dresses to infiltrate an all-female festival. Euripides emphasizes the female element to Dionysiac worship (which as Seaford (2001) 166 notes consists both of secret ritual, generally female, and mass participation) once the question of spying has been raised, making a neat parallel to Aristophanes' representation of the Thesmophoria. Zuckerberg (2014) 129–273 on *Bacchae*'s broader engagement with *Women at the Thesmophoria*.
138 Text and translation from Henderson (2000).
139 On Dionysus as *choregos* training Pentheus here see Dunn (2012) 365.
140 Mastery over Aristophanes see Wyles (2016) 66. On grotesque see Seidensticker (1978) 317 and Muecke (1982) 33.
141 The audience's experience of playwrights (tragic and comic) responding to each other's metatheatrical comments, see Zuckerberg (2014) esp. 1–79, supports this suggestion.
142 Muecke (1982) 19.

143 On the ancient audience's ability to enjoy performances on multiple levels see Ringer (1998) 14 and Duncan (2006) 9. On significance of 'doubling' see Seaford (1981) and Segal (1997) 27–31.
144 It may date to 410 BC, see n. 71.
145 That is, as a gaze functioning in the construction of identity.
146 On 'melting' see Pickard-Cambridge (1988) 187 and Green (1994) 44. Pronomos vase: Attic red-figure krater by Pronomos painter, Naples 81673, H3240.
147 Wyles (2010) 233–6.
148 This conceit is further complicated by Pentheus having been disguised as a female within the play.
149 Archaeological Museum of the National Academy of Sciences, Kiev, AM 1097/5219.
150 While significantly the male musicians have the masculine form of the adjective inscribed above them; see discussion of Braund and Hall (2014).
151 Zeitlin offers the seminal exploration of this; Zeitlin (1985) and (1996). An alternative reading would be to see Agave as representing *Tragoidia*, that is the tragic art in general (based on the interpretation of the female figure holding a tragic mask on the Pronomos vase as *Tragoidia* see Hall (2010)). The Pronomos vase was produced after *Bacchae*, but *Tragoidia*'s appearance as a maenad in Dionysus' company in a series of vases earlier in the fifth century, see Green (1997) 85, offers some support.
152 Generic boundaries to studies are in part responsible for this; Duncan (2018) 92, for example, describes the staging as 'unparalleled' (within tragedy). While Sansone (1978) recognized Euripides' engagement with satyr drama in *Bacchae*, he makes the case for general elements rather than specific interperformative allusions. The engagement with *Theoroi* should be seen in the context of other complex responses to Aeschylus within Euripides' work, on which see Torrance (2011). Satyr drama should be acknowledged to play a part in the Dionysian ambiguity generated from *Bacchae*'s blending of the tragic and comic (identified by Seidensticker (1978) 318–19).
153 The case was made by Golder (1992) yet with surprisingly little impact on the field. Estrin (2018) demonstrates another fruitful way in which the consideration of the audience's experience of art can enhance the understanding of drama.

Conclusion

1 Athena's ballot (*Eum.* 734–5 with Bakewell (2013) 150); Orestes' sword (*Cho.* 973) and Ajax's (*Aj.* 545–7 and 915–19); Masks held by the satyr chorus in Aeschylus' *Theoroi* (fr. 78a and 78c) and the mask of Pentheus held by Agave (*Bacch.*1279–84).

2. Cf. Thucydides' analysis of language's mutability during *stasis*, Th. 3.82. This characteristic of the symbols' function also mirrors 'democratic knowledge' on which see Ober (1994) 103–4.
3. The characteristic 'flux', or openness, of Aristophanes' comedy, on which see Poe (2000) 268–70, makes it a particularly effective medium through which to express this.
4. On the impact of Athenian theatre's programming on its potential for semiotic interplay see Wyles (2011) 59–60.
5. See Chapter 3.
6. Dunn (2012) 359–60 on the influence of theatre on society.
7. The significance of drama's relationship to art was asserted long ago by Golder (1992) but the discussion, though often cited, has not produced significant changes in the field. Nor did the outlining of a theoretical basis for such an approach in Don Fowler's seminal article on intertext, Fowler (1997), prompt its pursuit (acknowledging that intertextuality might be identified as a feature of semiotic systems (and not just language) (15), he challenges critics to expand the notion of 'text' (by adopting a Derridan inclusivity) in their analysis of ancient literature (26)). Zeitlin (1994) offers an important discussion, following a different arc.
8. On this issue see Catoni (2015). A refreshing exception to this is Sells (2019) who acknowledges the value of non-theatre-inspired iconography to the study of comedy, see esp. 55.
9. Through its intergeneric approach. Above all the scholarship of: Taplin (1993) and (2007), Green and Handley (1995), and Taplin and Wyles (2010), and further bibliography cited by Catoni (2015).
10. The critical issues with such an analysis pose a challenge, but do not outweigh the value of such an undertaking.
11. This offers a means of responding to the questions posed by Azoulay (2014) 703–4; objects are well placed to address these questions as they symbolize the citizen's experience of 'politics' (institutional) and the 'political' (civic collective experience). The relationship between these symbols, found in these different settings and yet relating to citizen identity poses a challenge to the 'isolationist' approach (on which see Scafuro (1994) 7).
12. Following the exemplary model of Kosmin (2015), see further Introduction n. 36.
13. On the cloak see the Introduction n. 47, also Blok (2017) 271 on the way in which it distinguished *metics* from citizens. Jackson's recognition of *metic* participation in aspects of some dramatic festivals (Jackson (2019) 32–3) intensifies the interest of considering this. Blok's exploration of the ways in which women expressed their citizenship (Blok (2017)) might be fruitfully developed further through this approach.
14. On the importance of this principle see Morris (1994) 73–4.

15 Vlassopoulos (2007) 33 highlights the pitfalls of a structuralist framing of civic identity and adopts an approach that acknowledges the blurring of distinctions in the city's 'free spaces' (such as the Agora); objects offer an equivalent space, encountered by a range of groups within the demographic who have the potential to manipulate their meaning.
16 Van Wees (2004) 241–3, with Thuc. 2.13 and 31, on *metic* participation in fifth-century battles. The mask offers an equally fruitful example since in its public display, as Duncan (2018) 87 notes, it could be viewed by foreign visitors, children, slaves and women.
17 See Csapo (2010a), Bosher (2012), Csapo and Wilson (2015), and Braund, Hall and Wyles (2019).
18 Stewart (2017) 22–30; my analysis goes further in challenging this position since (while I do not deny that playwrights may have also had a Panhellenic audience in mind), I suggest that playwrights deliberately exploited the Athenian significance of objects.
19 Apulian Gnathia bell-krater fragment, *c.* 340 BC, Würzburg H4600 (L832).
20 See Revermann (2006) 36–45 on the importance of the audience's experience of society to their interpretation of theatre.
21 The impact of pantomime's distinct approach to props, see Wyles (2008), would be an important factor here.

Appendix

1 It was being debated at the turn of the twentieth century as Headlam's review of Tucker's edition of *Choephori* elegantly illustrates, Headlam (1902) 352. Fraenkel (1950) vol. 3, 806 summarizes the major views at the time that he was writing; see also Garvie (1986) 289–90, Davies (1987), Sommerstein (1989b), Prag (1991), Marshall (2001b). The most recent commentary of *Agamemnon* simply accepts the sword; Raeburn and Thomas (2011) 213.
2 This issue offers a helpful paradigm for the challenges involved in understanding plays from their scripts alone. It is the performance, and the visual embodiment of the prop present on stage in front of the audience, that gives specific meaning to the ambiguous allusions to the weapon. The openness of the text to reinterpretation under a different director, even within antiquity, is shown by Marshall (2001b) who suggests that a fifth-century revival of the *Oresteia* used an axe (but nevertheless acknowledges that a sword could have been used in the original production).
3 Fraenkel (1950) vol. 3, 806–9.
4 Stated explicitly by Warr (1898) and reiterated by Fraenkel (1950) vol. 3, 806–9; they have remained the central focus of the subsequent controversy.

5 Text and translation of the *Oresteia* from Sommerstein (2009a) unless otherwise stated.
6 They are: Cassandra, contrasting her fate to the nightingale's, Ag. 1149: ἐμοὶ δὲ μίμνει σχισμὸς ἀμφήκει δορί. (while what awaits me is to be cloven by a two-edged weapon) and the Chorus lamenting for Agamemnon's fate; Ag. 1495–6 (and 1519–20) δολίῳ μόρῳ δαμεὶς δάμαρτος> ἐκ χερὸς ἀμφιτόμῳ βελέμνῳ (laid low in treacherous murder by the hand <of your wife> with a two-edged weapon).
7 The only mention of an axe is linked to Clytemnestra defending herself from Orestes in *Choephori* 889 and is therefore irrelevant, on which see Sommerstein (1989b) 301–2.
8 Sommerstein (1989b) and Prag (1991).
9 As will become clear, I find Sommerstein (1989b) compelling and seek only to add to its excellent analysis.
10 Fraenkel (1950) vol. 3 *ad loc.* and Appendix B, 806–9.
11 Fraenkel (1950) vol. 1, p. 173.
12 On the two possibilities see the helpful note of Fraenkel (1950) vol. 3 *ad loc.*
13 Unlike, by comparison, Cassandra's depiction of the murders.
14 On the effect see Raeburn and Thomas (2011) pp. 210–11.
15 For this characteristic see Zeitlin (1965) 488, Lebeck (1971) 81 and 131–3, and Bakewell (2013) 156.
16 Fraenkel dismisses this concern (deeming it an 'insipid objection'), see Fraenkel (1950) vol. 3 *ad loc.* On the effect of this 'preparation' see below.
17 The omission of these lines from the debate, despite their obvious relevance, can perhaps be put down to the early establishment of the 'pivotal' passages (see above).
18 Fraenkel's argument that Aeschylus played down the murder weapon to heighten focus on the robe (Fraenkel (1950) vol. 3, 808–9) misses the importance of the weapon in the staging as Sommerstein, for example, recognizes (Sommerstein (1989b) 300 n. 14). At the root of this is a difference in vision over Aeschylus' dramaturgy.
19 Garvie (1986) 289; Sommerstein (1989b) and (2009a); Prag (1991); and Raeburn and Thomas (2011) 213; *pace* Revermann (2013) 48–9, n. 20. She stands over a bathtub which holds the body of Agamemnon wrapped in a robe see Taplin (1977) 325 and (1978) 125. Although Taplin claims that Clytemnestra does not hold a weapon in her hand (Taplin (1977) 359), he offers no argument to support this assertion. For the principle that props might be present even if not explicitly marked by the text, see Chapter 4 n. 15.
20 Sommerstein (1989b) 300.
21 The phrase 'work of this right hand' incidentally seems to fit more naturally with a sword than an axe – the sword being wielded by the right hand, whereas vase

paintings showing Clytemnestra with an axe often show her grasping it with both hands; on the iconography see Prag (1985).

22 On its rarity see Sommerstein (1989b) 297.

23 Sommerstein (1989b) 296–7 sets out the alternative ways of interpreting it (preferring the reading of it as a reference to the death of Agamemnon). On the importance of acknowledging the multiplicity of views within the audience, see Roselli (2011) 198.

24 As Zeitlin (1965) 489 notes.

25 It should be noted that Taplin does not accept the use of the *ekkyklema* for either the Clytemnestra or Orestes tableau (Taplin (1977) 359). His reluctance to accept its use in *Agamemnon* is based in part on his conviction that this staging should mirror the Orestes tableau, Taplin (1977) 325–6. His concerns over its use in *Choephori*, however, are based on a strict reading of the dramatic convention for this stage machinery that seems unlikely to have been a constraint either at this early date or for Aeschylus (who demonstrates his willingness to challenge convention elsewhere in the trilogy). I follow Sommerstein (2009a), 337, in accepting the use of the *ekkyklema* in *Choephori* and suggest that this mirrors its use in *Agamemnon* (this seems preferable to Taplin's suggestion of mute stage hands carrying in the constituent parts of the tableau).

26 Raeburn and Thomas (2011) *ad loc.* on παίω δέ νιν δίς.

27 *Ag.* 1379, 1384–7, 1405–6, 1430, 1433, 1496=1520; see Sommerstein (1989b) 300 n. 14. The effect of these verbal references is equivalent to spot lighting in theatre, see Wyles (2011) 51–2.

28 Prag (1991) 243 acknowledges Aeschylus' capacity to 'play on his audience's familiarity with a pictorial tradition in order to give an unexpected jolt to a story as he unfolds it'. He notes (246) the impact of allowing the 'unwomanly woman' Clytemnestra to take up the sword instead of the axe.

29 See Taplin (1977) 94. The surprise, however, would be mediated by Cassandra's prophetic description (*Ag.* 1262–3).

30 This broader approach of taking into account the prop's meaning and trajectory within the trilogy has not been adopted by those debating over Clytemnestra's use of it.

31 Fraenkel (1950) vol. 3, 808–9.

32 Sommerstein (1989b) 300 n. 14 challenges this and notes, 301, the sword's role in marking the gender inversion between her and Aegisthus (assuming he is unarmed).

33 Sommerstein (1989b) 298 and 301. *Cho.* 1010–11 is used to support the suggestion that Clytemnestra has Aegisthus' sword (the interpretation of the lines have been disputed as part of the debate, on which see above, over the type of weapon used).

34 The reference is to Aegisthus' sword but can be understood as alluding to the weapon used by Clytemnestra see Sommerstein (1989b) 298.

35 Garvie (1986) *ad loc.* notes how the verbal echo in *Choephori* links the acts of bloodshed but does not push this further by considering props.
36 On the rareness of the adjective and the parallels in context, see Sommerstein (1989b) 297.
37 The second parallel is between the chorus member's description of the νεόρρυτος sword (*Ag.* 1351) at the death of Agamemnon and the Pythia's description of Orestes' sword as νεοσπαδὲς ('newly drawn', *Eum.* 42). An equivalent meaning can be construed for these adjectives (Fraenkel (1950) vol. 3, 637).
38 The staging is a matter of interpretation. I follow Sommerstein (2009a) 363. Taplin (1977) 359 accepts the sword in the hand for Orestes, but not the use of the *ekkyklema* for either tableau (and not the weapon in Clytemnestra's hand, on which see above). For arguments in favour of the stage presence of Orestes' sword after the murder see Chapter 4 n. 15.
39 On structural design, see Sommerstein (1989b) 297. For the revelation of Orestes sitting, sword in hand, on the *ekkyklema* in *Eumenides* see Sommerstein (1989a) 93 (and his refutation of Taplin's suggestion that Orestes enters on foot, Taplin (1977) 364–5; Podlecki (1989) 12–13 and 134 takes a middle line).
40 For the interpretation of it as seeing the robe for a second time see Taplin (1977) 358; though note Garvie (1986) *ad loc.* prefers the reading of it as 'look in turn'.
41 For an analogous effect across playwrights see Wyles (2011) 88–9 on Aegisthus' costume in Sophocles' *Electra*.
42 As opposed to inter-performative on which see Carlson (1994a) and (1994b), Sofer (2003), with Wyles (2011) 88–9.

Bibliography

Acton, P. H. (2010) 'Manufacturing in Classical Athens', PhD thesis, University of Melbourne.
Adams, C. D. (1919) *Aeschines. Speeches*. Loeb Classical Library 106. Cambridge, MA.
Ahl, F. (1984) 'The Art of Safe Criticism in Greece and Rome', *AJPh* 105, 174–208.
Altena, H. (1999–2000) 'Text and Performance: On Significant Actions in Euripides' *Phoenissae*' *ICS* 24/25, 303–23.
Appadurai, A. (1986) 'Introduction: Commodities and the Politics of Value', in A. Appadurai (ed.), *The Social Life of Things: Commodities in Cultural Perspective*. Cambridge, 3–63.
Arrington, N. T. (2015) *Ashes, Images, and Memories: The Presence of the War Dead in Fifth-century Athens*. Oxford.
Asmonti, L. A. (2006) 'The Arginusae Trial, the Changing Role of "Strategoi" and the Relationship Between "Demos" and Military Leadership in Late-Fifth Century Athens', *BICS* 49, 1–21.
Assmann, J. and J. Czaplicka (1995) 'Collective Memory and Cultural Identity', *New German Critique* 65, 125–33.
Azoulay, V. (2014) 'Repolitiser la cité grecque, trente ans après', in V. Azoulay (ed.), *Politique en Grèce ancienne*. Paris, 689–719.
Azoulay, V. (2017 [2014]) (transl. J. Lloyd) *The Tyrant-Slayers of Ancient Athens*. Oxford.
Bain, D. (1975) 'Audience Address in Greek Tragedy', *CQ* 25, 13–25.
Bakewell, G. W. (2013) 'Theatricality and Voting in *Eumenides*', in Harrison and Liapis (eds), 149–59.
Bakola, E. (2010) *Cratinus and the Art of Comedy*. Oxford.
Bakola, E. (2013) 'Crime and Punishment: Cratinus, Aeschylus' *Oresteia*, and the Metaphysics and Politics of Wealth', in E. Bakola, L. Prauscello, and M. Telò (eds), *Greek Comedy and the Discourse of Genres*. Cambridge, 226–55.
Barker, A. W. (1922) 'Domestic Costumes of the Athenian Woman in the Fifth and Fourth Centuries BC', *AJA* 26, 410–25.
Beazley, J. D. (1956) *Attic Black-Figure Vase-Painters*. Oxford.
Beazley, J. D. (1963) *Attic Red-Figure Vase-Painters*. 2nd edition. Oxford.
Benjamin, W. (1928) *Ursprung des Deutschen Trauerspiels*. Berlin.
Bieber, M. (1961) *History of the Greek and Roman Theater*. Princeton.
Biles, Z. P. (2006–2007) 'Aeschylus' Afterlife: Reperformance by Decree in 5th C. Athens?', *ICS* 31-2, 206–42.
Biles, Z. P. and S. D. Olson (2015) *Aristophanes* Wasps. Oxford.

Billings, J. (2018) 'Orestes' Urn in Word and Action', in Telò and Mueller (eds) 49–62.
Bleicken, J. (1986) *Die athenische Demokratie*. Paderborn.
Blok, J. H. (2009) 'Perikles' Citizenship Law: A New Perspective.' *Historia* 58, 141–70.
Blok, J. H. (2017) *Citizenship in Classical Athens*. Cambridge.
Boegehold, A. L. (1963) 'Toward a Study of Athenian Voting Procedure', *Hesperia* 32, 366–74.
Boegehold, A. L. (1985) 'Lykourgos 1.149', *CP* 80, 132–5.
Boegehold, A. L. (1994) 'Perikles' Citizenship Law of 451/0 BC', in Boegehold and Scafuro (eds), 57–66.
Boegehold, A. L. and A. C. Scafuro (eds) (1994) *Athenian Identity and Civic Ideology*. Baltimore.
Boegehold, A. L. et al. (1995) *The Athenian Agora, Results of Excavations conducted by the American School of Classical Studies at Athens 28. The Lawcourts At Athens: Sites, Buildings, Equipment, Procedure and Testimonia*. Princeton, NJ.
Bond, G. W. (1974), 'Euripides' parody of Aeschylus', *Hermathena* 118, 1–14.
Bosher, K. (2012) (ed.), *Theatre Outside Athens: Drama in Greek Sicily and South Italy*. Cambridge.
Bosworth, A. B. (2000) 'The Historical Context of Thucydides' Funeral Oration'. *JHS* 120, 1–16.
Bothmer, D. von. (1974) 'Two Bronze Hydriae in Malibu'. *The J. Paul Getty Museum Journal* 1, 15–22.
Bowen, A. (2013) *Aeschylus: The Suppliants*. Warminster.
Bowie, A. M. (1993) 'Religion and Politics in Aeschylus' *Oresteia*', *CQ* 43, 10–31.
Bowie, A. M. (1997) 'Tragic Filters for History: Euripides' *Supplices* and Sophocles' *Philoctetes*', in C. Pelling (ed.) *Greek Tragedy and the Historian*. Oxford, 39–62.
Bowie, E. (1986) 'Early Greek Elegy, Symposium and Public Festival'. *JHS* 106, 13–35.
Braund, D. and E. Hall (2014) 'Gender, Role and Performer in Athenian Theatre Iconography: A Masked Tragic Chorus with KALOS and KALE Captions from Olbia', *JHS* 134, 1–11.
Braund, D., E. Hall and R. Wyles (2019) (eds) *Ancient Theatre and Performance Culture around the Black Sea*. Cambridge.
Brooke, I. (1962) *Costume in Greek Classical Drama*. London.
Brownson, C. L. (1918) *Xenophon* Hellenica Books 1–4. Vol. 1. Loeb. Cambridge, MA.
Burn, L. (2010) 'The Contexts of the Production and Distribution of Athenian Painted Pottery around 400 BC', in Taplin and Wyles (eds), 15–32.
Burkert, W. (1983) (trans. P. Bing). *Homo Necans: The Anthropology of Ancient Greek Sacrifice and Myth*. Berkeley.
Burtt, O. (1954) *Minor Attic Orators II*. Cambridge, Mass.
Busolt, G. (1920) *Griechische Staatskunde* I. Munich.
Calame, C. (1995) *The Craft of Poetic Speech in Ancient Greece*. Ithaca and London.
Calame, C. (1999) 'Performative Aspects of the Choral Voice in Greek Tragedy', in Goldhill and Osborne (eds), 125–53.

Calder III, W. M. (1958) 'The Dramaturgy of Sophocles', *Inachus*', *GRBS* 1, 137–55.
Cammack, D. L. (2013) 'Rethinking Athenian Democracy', PhD thesis, Harvard.
Camp, J. (1999) 'Excavations in the Athenian Agora', *Hesperia* 68, 255–83.
Campbell, L. (1880) 'Notes on the *Agamemnon* of Aeschylus', *AJPh* 1, 427–39.
Carey, C. (2003) *Aeschines*. Austin.
Carlson, M. (1994*a*), 'The Haunted Stage: Recycling and Reception in the Theatre', *Theatre Survey* 35, 5–18.
Carlson, M. (1994*b*), 'Invisible Presences – Performance Intertextuality', *Theatre Research International* 19, 111–17.
Carpenter, T. H. (1997) 'Harmodius and Apollo in Fifth-century Athens: What's in a Pose?', in J. H. Oakley et al. (eds) *Athenian Potters and Painters*. Oxford, 171–80.
Carter, D. M. (2007), *The Politics of Greek Tragedy*. Exeter.
Carter, D. M. (2010) 'The Demos in Greek Tragedy' *CCJ* 56, 47–94.
Cartledge, P. (1997) '"Deep Plays": Theatre as Process in Greek Civic Life', in Easterling (ed.), 3–35.
Cartledge, P. (2000) 'Greek Political Thought: The Historical Context', in C. Rowe and M. Schofield (eds), *The Cambridge History of Greek and Roman Political Thought*. Cambridge, 7–22.
Catoni, M. L. (2015) 'The Iconographic Tradition of the Suicide of Ajax: Some Questions', in G. W. Most and L. Ozbek (eds), 15–30 with Figs 1–17, 331–40.
Chaston, C. (2010) *Tragic Props and Cognitive Function*. London, Boston.
Christ, M. (2001) 'Conscription of Hoplites in Classical Athens', *CQ* 51, 398–422.
Christodoulou, G. A. (1977) *Ta archaia scholia eis Aianta tou Sophokleous*. Athens.
Cohen, D. (1978) 'The Imagery of Sophocles: A Study of Ajax's Suicide', *G&R* 25, 24–36.
Cohen, D. (1989) 'Seclusion, Separation, and the Status of Women in Classical Athens', *G&R* 36, 3–15.
Collard, C. (1975) *Euripides* Supplices. Groningen.
Collard, C., M. J. Cropp, K. H. Lee (1997) *Euripides Selected Fragmentary Plays I*. Warminster.
Compton-Engle, G. (1999). 'Aristophanes *Peace* 1265–1304: Food, Poetry, and the Comic Genre', *Classical Philology* 94, 324–9.
Compton-Engle, G. (2015) *Costume in the Comedies of Aristophanes*. Cambridge.
Coppola, A., C. Barone and M. Salvadori (eds) *Gli oggetti sulla scena tetrale ateniese*. Padua.
Craik, E. (1988) *Euripides* Phoenician Women. Warminster.
Crawford, M. H. and D. Whitehead (1983) *Archaic and Classical Greece*. Cambridge.
Crichton, A. (1991) '"The Old are in a Second Childhood": Age Reversal and Jury Service in Aristophanes' *Wasps*', *BICS* 38, 59–80.
Cropp, M. J. (2013) (second edition) *Euripides* Electra. Warminster.
Cropp, M. and G. Fick (1985) *Resolutions and Chronology in Euripides*. London.
Crowley, J. (2012) *The Psychology of the Athenian Hoplite: The Culture of Combat in Classical Athens*. Cambridge.

Csapo, E. (1986) 'A Note on the Würzburg Bell-Crater H5697 ('Telephus Travestitus')', *Phoenix* 40, 379–92.
Csapo, E. (2002) 'Kallipides on the Floor-sweepings: The Limits of *Realism* in Classical Acting and Performance Styles', in Easterling and Hall (eds), 127–47.
Csapo, E. (2007), 'The Men Who Built the Theatres', in P. Wilson (ed.), *The Greek Theatre and Festivals*. Oxford, 87–121.
Csapo, E. (2010a) *Actors and Icons in the Ancient Theater*. Chichester.
Csapo, E. (2010b) 'The Production and Performance of Comedy in Antiquity', in G. W. Dobrov (ed.) *Brill's Companion to the Study of Greek Comedy*. Leiden and Boston, 103–42.
Csapo, E. (2010c) 'The Context of Choregic Dedications', in Taplin and Wyles (eds), 79–130.
Csapo. E. and W. J. Slater (1994) *The Context of Ancient Drama*. Ann Arbor.
Csapo. E. and P. Wilson (2015) 'Drama Outside Athens in the Fifth and Fourth Centuries BC', *Trends in Classics* 7, 316–95.
Davies, M. (1987). 'Aeschylus' Clytemnestra: Sword or Axe?', *CQ* 37, 65–75.
Davies, M. I. (1973) 'Ajax and Tekmessa. A Cup by the Brygos Painter in the Bareiss Collection', *AK* 16, 60–70.
de Jong, I. (1987) 'The Voice of Anonymity: Tis-speeches in the *Iliad*', *Eranos* 85, 69–84.
Derks, T. and N. Roymans (eds) (2009), *Ethnic Constructs in Antiquity*. Amsterdam.
Dewald, C. and J. Marincola (2006) 'Introduction', in C. Dewald and J. Marincola (eds) *The Cambridge Companion to Herodotus*. Cambridge, 1–12.
Dillon, J. (2004). 'Euripides and the Philosophy of his Time', *Classics Ireland* 11, 47–73.
Dingel, J. (1967), *Das Requisit in der griechischen Tragödie* (diss.). Tübingen.
Dmitriev, S. (2018) *The Birth of the Athenian Community: From Solon to Cleisthenes*. Abingdon.
Dover, K. (1968) *Aristophanes* Clouds. Oxford.
Dover, K. (1997) *Aristophanes* Frogs. Oxford.
Dunbar, N. (1995) *Aristophanes* Birds. Oxford.
Duncan, A. (2006) *Performance and Identity in the Classical World*. Cambridge.
Duncan, A. C. (2018) 'The Familiar Mask', in Telò and Mueller (eds) 79–95.
Dunn, F. (2012) 'Metatheatre and Crisis in Euripides' *Bacchae* and Sophocles' *Oedipus at Colonus*', in Markantonatos and Zimmerman (eds), 359–76.
Duplouy, A. (2018) 'Citizenship as Performance', in Duplouy and Brock (eds), 249–74.
Duplouy, A. and R. Brock (eds) (2018), *Defining Citizenship in Archaic Greece*. Oxford.
Easterling, P. (1985) 'Anachronism in Greek Tragedy', *JHS* 105, 1–10.
Easterling, P. (1997) *The Cambridge Companion to Greek Tragedy*. Cambridge.
Easterling, P. and E. Hall (eds) (2002) *Greek and Roman Actors*. Cambridge.
Elam, K. (2002) *The Semiotics of Theatre and Drama*. London.
Estrin, S. (2018) 'Memory Incarnate: Material Objects and Private Visions in Classical Athens', in Telò and Mueller (eds) 111–32.

Everson, T. (2004), *Warfare in Ancient Greece: Arms and Armour from the Heroes of Homer to Alexander the Great*. Stroud.
Falkner, T. (2002) 'Scholars versus Actors: Text and Performance in the Greek Tragic Scholia', in P. Easterling and E. Hall (eds) *Greek and Roman Actors*. Cambridge, 342–61.
Farenga, V. (2006) *Citizen and Self in Ancient Greece: Individuals Performing Justice and the Law*. Cambridge.
Farmer, M. C. (2016) *Tragedy on the Comic Stage*. Oxford.
Finglass, P. J. (2007) *Sophocles' Electra*. Cambridge.
Finglass, P. J. (2009) 'Unveiling Tecmessa' *Mnemosyne* 62, 272–82.
Finglass, P. J. (2011) *Sophocles Ajax*. Cambridge.
Finglass, P. J. (2015) 'Second Thoughts on the Sword', in Most and Ozbek (eds), 193–210.
Fletcher, J. (2014) 'Polyphony to Silence: The Jurors of the *Oresteia*', *College Literature* 41, 56–75.
Flower, M. A. and J. Marincola (2002) *Herodotus Histories Book IX*. Cambridge.
Foley, H. (1980) 'The Masque of Dionysus', *TAPhA* 110, 107–33.
Foley, H. (1985) Ritual Irony: Poetry and Sacrifice in Euripides. Ithaca and London.
Foley, H. (1988) 'Tragedy and Politics in Aristophanes' *Acharnians*' *JHS* 108, 33–47.
Foley, H. (1995) 'Tragedy and Democratic Ideology: The Case of Sophocles' *Antigone*', in B. Goff (ed.), *History, Tragedy, Theory: Dialogues in Athenian Drama*. Austin, 131–50.
Foley, H. (2000) 'The Comic Body in Greek Drama and Art', in B. Cohen (ed.) *Not the Classical Ideal*. Leiden, 275–311.
Foley, H. (2003) 'Choral Identity in Greek Tragedy', *CPh* 98, 1–30.
Fowler, D. (1997) 'On the Shoulders of Giants: Intertextuality and Classical Studies', *Materiali E Discussioni per L'analisi Dei Testi Classici* 39, 13–34.
Foxhall, L. and J. Salmon (1998) (eds), *Thinking Men: Masculinity and its Self-Representation in the Classical Tradition*. London and New York.
Fraenkel, E. (1950) *Agamemnon*. Oxford.
Frontisi-Ducroux, F. (1995) *Du Masque au Visage. Aspects de l'identité en Grèce ancienne*. Paris.
Frost, F. J. (1994) 'Aspects of Early Athenian Citizenship', in Boegehold and Scafuro (eds), 45–56.
Gabrielsen, V. (2002) 'The Impact of Armed forces on Government and Politics in Archaic and Classical Greece: A Response to Hans van Wees', in A. Chaniotis and P. Ducrey (eds), *Army and Power in the Ancient World*. Heidelberger althistorische Beiträge und epigraphische Studien 37. Stuttgart, 83–98.
Garner, R. (1987) *Law and Society in Classical Athens*. London.
Garner, R. (1990) *From Homer to Tragedy*. London.
Garrity, T. (1998) 'Thucydides 1.22.1: Content and Form in the Speeches', *AJPh* 119, 361–84.
Garvie, A. F. (1986) *Aeschylus Choephori*. Oxford.
Garvie, A. F. (1998) *Sophocles Ajax*. Warminster.

Garvie, A. F. (2015) 'The Death of Ajax', in G. W. Most and L. Ozbek (eds), 31–46.

Gehrke, H.-J. (2009) 'From Athenian Identity to European Ethnicity – The Cultural Biography of the Myth of Marathon', in Derks and Roymans (eds), 85–100.

Gilula, D. (1995). 'The Choregoi Vase: Comic Yes, but Angels?', *ZPE* 109, 5–10.

Gish, D. (2012) 'Defending *dēmocratia*: Athenian Justice and the Trial of the Arginusae Generals in Xenophon's *Hellenica*', in F. Hobden and C. Tuplin (eds) *Xenophon: Ethical Principles and Historical* Enquiry. Leiden: Brill, 161–212.

Giuliani, L. (2013, translated by J. O'Donnell) *Image and Myth*. Chicago and London.

Godley, A. D. (1922) *Herodotus*. Histories, Volume III: Books 5–7. Cambridge, MA.

Goette, H. R. (2009) 'Images in the Athenian "Demosian Sema"', in O. Palagia (ed.) *Art in Athens During the Peloponnesian War*. Cambridge, 188–206.

Goheen, R. F. (1955) 'Aspects of Dramatic Symbolism: Three Studies in the *Oresteia*', *The American Journal of Philology* 76, 113–37.

Golder, H. (1992) 'Visual Meaning in Greek Drama: Sophocles' *Ajax* and the Art of Dying', in F. Poyatos (1992) (ed.) *Advances in Nonverbal Communication. Sociocultural, Clinical, Esthetic and Literary Perspectives*. Amsterdam and Philadelphia, 323–60.

Goldhill, S. (1986) *Reading Greek Tragedy*. Cambridge.

Goldhill, S. (1987) 'The Great Dionysia and Civic Ideology', *JHS* 107, 58–76; reprinted with corrections in J. J. Winkler and F. Zeitlin (1990) (eds) *Nothing to do with Dionysus?* Princeton.

Goldhill, S. (1994) 'Representing Democracy: Women at the Great Dionysia', in R. Osborne and S. Hornblower (eds), *Ritual, Finance, Politics*. Oxford, 347–70.

Goldhill, S. (1997) 'The Audience of Athenian Tragedy', in Easterling (ed.) 54–68.

Goldhill, S. (2000) 'Civic Ideology and the Problem of Difference: The Politics of Aeschylean Tragedy, Once Again', *JHS* 120, 34–56.

Goldhill, S. and R. Osborne (eds) (1999) *Performance Culture and Athenian Democracy*. Cambridge.

Green, J. R. (1971) 'Choes of the Later Fifth Century', *BSA* 66, 189–221.

Green, J. R. (1982) 'Dedications of Masks', *Revue Archéologique* 2, 237–48.

Green, J. R. (1994) *Theatre in Ancient Greek Society*. London, New York: Routledge.

Green, J. R. (2007) 'Let's Hear it for the Fat Man: Padded Dancers and the Prehistory of Drama', in E. Csapo and M. Miller (eds) *The Origins of Theater in Ancient Greece and Beyond*. Cambridge, 96–107

Green, J. R. (2010) 'The Material Evidence', in G. W. Dobrov (ed.) *Brill's Companion to the Study of Greek Comedy*. Leiden and Boston, 71–102.

Griffith, M. (1995) 'Brilliant Dynasts: Power and Politics in the *Oresteia*', *ClAnt* 14, 62–129.

Hall, E. (1989) *Inventing the Barbarian*. Oxford.

Hall, E. (1996) *Aeschylus*: Persians. Warminster.

Hall, E. (2006) *The Theatrical Cast of Athens*. Oxford.

Hall, E. (2010) 'Tragic Theatre: Demetrios' Rolls and Dionysos' Other Woman', in Taplin and Wyles (eds), 159–80.
Hall, E. (2016) 'Perspectives on The Impact of *Bacchae* in its Original Performance', in D. Stuttard (ed.) *Looking at Bacchae*. London, 11–29.
Hall, E. (2018) 'Matierialisms Old and New', in Telò and Mueller (eds), 203–18.
Halliwell, S. (1987) *The Poetics of Aristotle*. London.
Halliwell, S. (1993) 'The Function and Aesthetics of the Greek Tragic Mask' *Drama* 2, 195–211.
Halliwell, S. (1995) *Aristotle* Poetics. Loeb. Cambridge, Mass.
Hammond, N. G. L. (1984) 'Spectacle and Parody in Euripides', *Electra*' *GRBS* 25, 373–87.
Handley, E. W. and J. Rea (1957) *The Telephus of Euripides, BICS Suppl.* 5. London.
Hansen, M. H. (1979) 'How Often Did the Athenian *dicasteria* Meet?' *GRBS* 20, 243–6.
Hansen, M. H. (1995) *Die Athenische Demokratie im Zeitalter des Demosthenes: Struktur, Prinzipien und Selbstverständnis*. Berlin.
Hanson, V. D. (2002) *Hoplite: The Classical Greek Battle Experience*. London.
Harris, J. G. and N. Korda (2002a) (eds) *Staged Properties in Early Modern English Drama*. Cambridge.
Harris, J. G. and N. Korda (2002b) 'Introduction: Towards a Materialist Account of Stage Properties', in Harris and Korda (eds), 1–31.
Harrison, G. W. M. and V. Liapis (eds) *Performance in Greek and Roman Theatre*. Leiden, 149–59.
Head, L. (2010) 'Cultural Landscapes', in D. Hicks and M. C. Beaudry (eds) *The Oxford Handbook of Material Culture Studies*. Oxford, 427–39.
Headlam, W. (1902) 'Tucker's Choephori of Aeschylus', *The Classical Review* 16, 347–54.
Headlam, W. (1906) 'The Last Scene of the Eumenides', *JHS* 26, 268–77.
Heath, M. (1990) 'Aristophanes and His Rivals', *G&R* 37, 143–58.
Heijnen, S. (2018) 'Athens and the Anchoring of Roman Rule in the First Century BCE (67–17)' *Journal of Ancient History* 6, 80–110.
Henderson, J. (1987) *Aristophanes* Lysistrata. Oxford.
Henderson, J. (1991) 'Women and the Athenian Dramatic Festivals', *TAPhA* 121, 133–47
Henderson, J. (1998) Aristophanes. *Clouds. Wasps. Peace*. Loeb Classical Library. Cambridge, Mass.
Henderson, J. (2000) Aristophanes. *Birds. Lysistrata. Women at the Thesmophoria*. Loeb Classical Library. Cambridge, Mass.
Henderson, J. (2003) 'Demos, demagogue, tyrant in Attic Old Comedy', in Morgan (ed.) 155–79.
Henderson, J. (2008) Aristophanes. *Fragments*. Loeb. Cambridge, Mass.
Henrichs, A. (1980) 'Human Sacrifice in Greek Religion', in J. Rudhardt and O. Reverdin (eds.) *Le sacrifice dans l'antiquité*. Geneva, 195–235.
Henrichs, A. (1993) 'The Tomb of Aias and the Prospect of Hero Cult in Sophokles', *ClAnt* 12, 165–80.
Hermann, J. G. J. (1820) *De Aeschyli Danaidibus dissertatio*. Lipsiae.

Herring, E. (2018) *Patterns in the Production of Apulian Red-figure Pottery*. Cambridge.
Hesk, J. (1999) 'The Rhetoric of Anti-rhetoric in Athenian Oratory', in Osborne and Goldhill (eds), 201–30.
Hesk, J. (2007) 'The Socio-political Dimension of Ancient Tragedy', in M. McDonald and M. Walton (eds), *The Cambridge Companion to Greek and Roman Theatre*. Cambridge, 72–91.
Hesk, J. (2017) 'Greek Thinking, Fast and Slow. Euripides and Thucydides on Deliberation and Decision-making', *Insights* 10 (8), 2–18.
Holm, S. (2012) 'Dyeing Bronze: New Evidence for an Old Reading of "Agamemnon" 612', *CQ* 62, 486–95.
Hornblower, S. (1997) *A Commentary on Thucydides. Volume 1: Books I–III*. Oxford.
Hornblower, S. (2008) *A Commentary on Thucydides. Volume 3*. Oxford.
Hutchinson, G. (1985) *Aeschylus* Seven Against Thebes. Oxford.
Hutchinson, G. (2011) 'House Politics and City Politics in Aristophanes', *CQ* 61, 48–70.
Isin, E. F. and P. K. Wood (1999) *Citizenship and Identity*. London.
Jackson, L. C. M. M. (2019) *The Chorus of Drama in the Fourth Century BCE*. Oxford.
Jacobson, D. J. (2011) 'Show Business: Deixis in Fifth-Century Athenian Drama', PhD thesis, Berkeley.
Jacoby, F. (1954) *Die Fragmente der griechischen Historiker. IIIB Suppl*. Leiden.
Jameson, M. H. (1991) 'Sacrifice Before Battle', in V. D. Hanson (ed.) *Hoplites: The Classical Greek Battle Experience*. London and New York, 197–227.
Jameson, M. H. (2014) *Cults and Rites in Ancient Greece*. Cambridge.
Jebb, R. C. (1888) *Sophocles. The Plays and Fragments*. Part III (Antigone). Cambridge.
Jedrkiewicz, S. (2006) 'Bestie, gesti e logos. Una lettura delle Vespe di Aristofane', *QUCC* 82, 61–91.
Johansen, H. F. and E. W. Whittle (1980) *Aeschylus* The Suppliants. Vol. 1. Copenhagen.
Jones, A. and N. Boivin (2010) 'The Malice of Inanimate Objects: Material Agency', in D. Hicks and M. Beaudry (eds.) *The Oxford Handbook of Material Culture Studies*. Oxford, 333–51.
Juffras, D. (1991) 'Sophocles' *Electra* 973–85 and Tyrannicide' *TAPhA* 121, 99–108.
Kagan, D. and G. F. Viggiano (2013) (eds) *Men of Bronze: Hoplite Warfare in Ancient Greece*. Princeton.
Kassel, R. and C. Austin (eds) (1983) *Poetae Comici Graeci (PCG)*. Vol. 4. Berlin.
Kassel, R. and C. Austin (eds) (1989) *Poetae Comici Graeci (PCG)*. Vol. 7. Berlin.
Keesling, C. M. (2003) *The Votive Statues of the Athenian Acropolis*. Cambridge.
Kellogg, D. L. (2013). *Marathon Fighters and Men of Maple: Ancient Acharnai*. Oxford.
Kelly, D. (1996) 'Oral *Xenophon*', in I. Worthington (ed.) *Voice into Text: Orality and Literacy in Ancient Greece*. Leiden, 149–64.
Kertzer, D. (1988) *Ritual, Politics, and Power*. New Haven, CT.
Knights, L. C. (1933) *How Many Children had Lady Macbeth?* Cambridge.
Konstan, D. (1995) *Greek Comedy and Ideology*. Oxford.

Konstan, D. (1998) 'The Greek Polis and its Negations: Versions of Utopia in Aristophanes' *Birds*', in G. Dobrov (ed.), *The City as Comedy. Society and Representation in Athenian Drama*. Chapel Hill, 3–22.

Kosmin, P. J. (2015) 'A Phenomenology of Democracy: Ostracism as Political Ritual', *ClAnt* 34, 121–62.

Kovacs, D. (2002), *Euripides* Helen, Phoenician Women, Orestes. Loeb, Vol. 5. London and Cambridge, Mass.

Kovacs, D. (2003) Euripides. *Bacchae. Iphigenia at Aulis. Rhesus.* Loeb, Vol. 6. London and Cambridge, Mass.

Kowalzig, B. and P. Wilson (eds) (2013), *Dithyramb in Context*. Oxford.

Lamari, A. A. (2012) 'The Return of the Father: Euripides' *Antiope*, *Hypsipyle*, and *Phoenissae*', in Markantonatos and Zimmerman (eds), 219–39.

Lamari, A. A. (2015) 'Aeschylus and the Beginning of Tragic Reperformances', *TC* 7, 189–206.

Lambin, G. (1979) 'Dans un rameau de myrte', *Revue des Études Grecques* 92, 542–51.

Lambin, G. (1992) *La chanson grecque dans l'antiquité*. Paris.

Lanni, A. (2012) 'Publicity and the Courts of Classical Athens', *Yale Journal of Law & the Humanities*, 24, 119–35.

Lape, S. (2010) *Race and Citizen Identity in the Classical Athenian Democracy*. Cambridge.

Lazenby, J. (1994) 'The Killing Zone', in V. D. Hanson (ed.), *Hoplites: The Classical Greek Battle Experience*. London, 87–109.

Lebeck, A. (1971) *The Oresteia: a Study in Language and Structure*. Cambridge, Mass.

Lech, M. L. (2009a) 'The Shape of the Athenian Theatron in the Fifth Century: Overlooked Evidence.' *GRBS* 49, 223–6.

Lech, M. L. (2009b) 'Marching Choruses? Choral Performance in Athens', *GRBS* 49, 343–61.

Lee, M. M. (2015) *Body, Dress, and Identity in Ancient Greece*. Cambridge.

Le Guen, B. and S. Milanezi (2013) (eds) *L'Appareil Scénique dans les Spectacles de l'Antiquité*. Paris.

Lewis, R. (1997) 'Themistokles and Ephialtes', *CQ* 47, 358–62.

Lewis, S. (2002) *The Athenian Woman. An Iconographic Sourcebook*. London.

Liddel, P. (2010) 'Epigraphy, Legislation, and Power within the Athenian Empire', *BICS* 53, 99–128.

Lissarrague, F. (2010) 'From Flat Page to the Volume of the Pot', in Taplin and Wyles (eds), 33–46.

Lissarrague, F. and A. Schnapp (2007) 'Athènes, la cité, les images', in P. Schmitt-Pantel and F. de Polignac (eds) (2015) *Athènes et le politique: Dans le sillage de Claude Mossé*. Paris, 25–55.

Livingstone, R. (1925) 'The Problem of the *Eumenides* of Aeschylus', *JHS* 45, 120–31.

Lloyd-Jones, H. (1994) Sophocles. *Ajax. Electra. Oedipus Tyrannus.* Loeb. Cambridge, MA.

Lloyd-Jones, H. (1996) *Sophocles Fragments*. Loeb. Cambridge, Mass.
Loraux, N. (1981a) *L'Invention d'Athènes: histoire de l'oraison funèbre dans la 'cité classique'*. Paris.
Loraux, N. (1981b) *Les enfants d'Athéna*. Paris.
Loraux, N. (1985) *Façons tragiques de tuer une femme*. Paris.
Lucas, D. W. (1968) *Aristotle Poetics*. Oxford.
Ludwig, P. (2002) *Eros and Polis: Desire and Community in Greek Political Theory*. Cambridge.
Lynch, K. (2011) *The Symposium in Context*. Princeton, NJ.
MacDowell, D. M. (1962) *Andokides On the Mysteries*. Oxford.
MacDowell, D. M (1971) *Aristophanes Wasps*. Oxford.
MacDowell, D. M (1978) *The Law in Classical Athens*. London.
MacDowell, D. M (1989) 'Athenian Laws about Choruses', in F. Nieto (ed.), *Symposion 1982*. Cologne, 65–77.
MacDowell, D. M (1995) *Aristophanes and Athens*. Oxford.
Mackay, E. A. (2002) 'The Evocation of Emotional Response in Early Greek Poetry and Painting', in I. Worthington and J. M. Foley (2002) *Epea and Grammata: Oral and Written Communication in Ancient Greece*. Leiden, 55–69.
MacLeod, C. W. (1974), 'Euripides' Rags', *ZPE* 15, 221–2.
MacLeod, C. W. (1982) 'Politics and the *Oresteia*', *JHS* 102, 124–44.
Malouchou, G. E. (2014) 'A Second Facsimile of the Erythrai Decree (IG I^3 14)', in Matthaiou and Pitt (eds), 73–96.
Mannack, T. (2010) 'A Description', in Taplin and Wyles (eds), 5–14.
Manville, P. B. (1990) *The Origins of Citizenship in Ancient Athens*. Princeton, NJ.
Manville, P. B. (1994) 'Towards a New Paradigm of Athenian Citizenship', in Boegehold and Scafuro (eds), 21–33.
Marconi, C. (2009) 'The Parthenon Frieze: Degrees of Visibility', *RES: Anthropology and Aesthetics* 55/56, 156–73.
Markantonatos, A. (2013a) 'The Silence of Thucydides: The Battle of Marathon and Athenian Pride', in C. Carey and M. Edwards (eds) *The Importance of the Battle of Marathon to Civilisation*. London. 69–77.
Markantonatos, A. (2013b) *Euripides' Alcestis: Narrative, Myth, and Religion*. Boston.
Markantonatos, A. and B. Zimmerman (2012) (eds) *Crisis on Stage: Tragedy and Comedy in Late Fifth-century Athens*. Berlin.
Marr, J. L. (1993) 'Ephialtes the Moderate?', *G&R*, 40, 11–19.
Marshall, C. W. (1996) 'Literary Awareness in Euripides and His Audience', in I. Worthington (ed.) *Voice into Text: Orality and Literacy in Ancient Greece*. Leiden, 81–98.
Marshall, C. W. (1999) 'Some Fifth-Century Masking Conventions', *G&R* 46, 188–202.
Marshall, C. W. (2001a) 'The Costume of Hecuba's Attendants', *Acta Classica* 44, 127–36.
Marshall, C. W. (2001b) 'The Next Time Agamemnon Died', *The Classical World* 95, 59–63.

Marshall, C. W. (2003) 'Casting the *Oresteia*', *Classical Journal* 98, 257–74
Marshall, C. W. (2012) 'Sophocles *Didaskalos*', in K. Ormand (ed.) *A Companion to Sophocles*. Malden, MA, 187–203.
Marshall, C. W. (2014) 'Dramatic Technique and Athenian Comedy', in M. Revermann (ed.) *The Cambridge Companion to Greek Comedy*. Cambridge: Cambridge University Press, 131–46.
Martinelli, M. C. (2015) 'Aiace e la spada', in G. W. Most and L. Ozbek (eds), 211–22.
Mastronarde, D. (1994), *Euripides* Phoenissae. Cambridge.
Matthaiou, A. P and R. K. Pitt (2014) (eds) *ΑΘΗΝΑΙΩΝ ΕΠΙΣΚΟΠΟΣ: Studies in Honour of Harold B. Mattingly*. Athens.
Mattingly, H. B. (1996) *The Athenian Empire Restored: Epigraphic and Historical Studies*. Ann Arbor.
Mauduit, C. (2015) 'Scénario pour un suicide', in G. W. Most and L. Ozbek (eds), 47–74 with Figs 18–29, 341–44.
May, G. (2012), 'Aristophanes and Euripides: a Palimpsestuous Relationship', PhD thesis, University of Kent.
McDermott, E. A. (1991), 'Double Meaning and Mythic Novelty in Euripides' Plays', *TAPhA* 121, 123–32.
McGlew, J. F. (1993) *Tyranny and Political Culture in Ancient Greece*. Ithaca, NY.
McGlew, J. F. (2002) *Citizens on Stage*. Ann Arbor.
McGlew, J. F. (2012) 'Fighting Tyranny in Fifth-century Athens: Democratic Citizenship and the Oath of Demophantus', *BICS* 55, 91–9.
Medda, E. (2001) 'Testo e scena in Aesch. *Ag.* 1649–54', *Lexis* 19, 33–50.
Meier, C. (1990) *The Greek Discovery of Politics*. London.
Meiggs, R. (2008) 'The Growth of Athenian Imperialism', in P. Low (ed.) *The Athenian Empire*. Edinburgh, 58–80.
Meineck, P. (2017) *Theatrocracy: Greek Drama, Cognition, and the Imperative for Theatre*. London.
Meyer, E. (2008) 'Thucydides on Harmodius and Aristogeiton, Tyranny and History', *CQ* 58, 13–34.
Miles, S. N. (2009) *Strattis, Tragedy, and Comedy*. PhD thesis, University of Nottingham.
Miles, S. N. (2013) 'Accessoires et para-tragédie dans les *Skeuai* de Platon et l'*Électre* d'Euripide', in Le Guen and Milanezi (eds), 182–99.
Miller, M. C. (1997) *Athens and Persians in the Fifth Century* BC: *A Study in Cultural Receptivity*. Cambridge.
Millis, B. W. and S. D. Olson (2012) *Inscriptional Records for the Dramatic Festivals in Athens*. Leiden and Boston.
Minchin, E. (2011) 'The Words of Gods: Divine Discourse in Homer's *Iliad*' in A. Lardinois, J. Blok, and M. G. M. Poel (eds) *Sacred Words: Orality, Literacy and Religion. Orality and Literacy in the Ancient World.* Leiden, 15–36.
Missiou, A. (2010) *Literacy and Democracy in Fifth-century Athens*. Cambridge.

Monaghan, P. (2008) 'Mask, Word, Body and Metaphysics in the Performance of Greek Tragedy', *Didaskalia* 7.1, n.p.

Moore, M. (1997) 'Attic Red-Figured and White-Ground Pottery' *The Athenian Agora*, 30, iii–419.

Morgan, C. (2009) 'Ethnic Expression on the Early Iron Age and Early Archaic Greek Mainland', in Derks and Roymans (eds), 11–36.

Morgan, K. A. (ed.) (2003) *Popular Tyranny*. Austin, TX.

Moroo, A. (2014) 'The Erythrai Decrees Reconsidered: IG I^3 14, 15 & 16', in Matthaiou and Pitt (eds), 97–120.

Morris, I. (1994) 'Everyman's Grave', in Boegehold and Scafuro (eds), 67–101.

Most, G. W. (2015) 'Appendix', in G. W. Most and L. Ozbek (eds), 289–96.

Most, G. W. and L. Ozbek (2015) (eds) *Staging Ajax's Suicide*. Pisa.

Muecke, F. (1982), '"I know you – by your rags" Costume and Disguise in Fifth-century Drama', *Antichthon* 16, 17–34.

Mueller, M. (2010) 'Athens in a Basket: Naming, Objects, and Identity in Euripides' *Ion*' *Arethusa* 43, 365–402.

Mueller, M. (2016a) *Objects as Actors. Props and the Poetics of Performance in Greek Tragedy*. Chicago.

Mueller, M. (2016b) 'Dressing for Dionysus: Statues and Material Mimesis in Euripides' *Bacchae*', in Coppola, Barone and Salvadori (eds) 57–70.

Murnaghan, S. (2014) 'The Creation of Anachronism: Assessing Ancient Valor in Sophocles' *Ajax*', in J. Ker and C. Pieper (eds) *Valuing the Past in the Greco-Roman World*. Leiden, 199–218.

Neer, R. T. (2002) *Style and Politics in Athenian Vase-Painting, The Craft of Democracy, ca.530–460 B.C.E.* Cambridge.

Nelson, S. (2016) *Aristophanes and His Tragic Muse. Comedy, Tragedy and the Polis in the 5th Century Athens. Mnemosyne Supplements*. Leiden.

Oakley, J. H. (2003) 'Review of Neer, R. T. (2002) *Style and Politics in Athenian Vase-Painting, The Craft of Democracy, ca.530–460 B.C.E.* Cambridge', *AJA* 107, 509–10.

Oakley, J. H. (2004) *Picturing Death in Classical Athens*. Cambridge.

Oakley, J. H. (2009) 'Children in Athenian Funerary Art during the Peloponnesian war', in O. Palagia (ed.) *Art in Athens during the Peloponnesian War*. Cambridge, 207–35.

Ober, J. (1989) *Mass and the Elite in Democratic Athens*. Princeton, NJ.

Ober, J. (1994) 'Civic Ideology and Counterhegemonic Discourse: Thucydides on the Sicilian Debate', in Boegehold and Scafuro (eds), 102–26.

Oldfather, C. H. (1950) *Diodorus Siculus. Library of History, Volume V: Books 12.41–13*. Loeb. Cambridge, MA: Harvard University Press.

Olson, S. D. (1998) *Aristophanes* Peace. Oxford.

Olson, S. D. (2002) *Aristophanes* Acharnians. Oxford.

Olson, S. D. (2003) *Aristophanes* Peace. Oxford.

Osborne, R. (1997) 'Men without Clothes: Heroic Nakedness and Greek Art', *Gender & History* 9, 504–28.

Osborne, R. (1998) 'Sculpted Men of Athens: Masculinity and Power in the Field of Vision', in Foxhall and Salmon (eds), 23–42.
Osborne, R. (2008) JACT's *The World of Athens*. Second edition. Cambridge.
Osborne, R. (2010) 'Who's Who on the Pronomos Vase?', in Taplin and Wyles (eds), 149–58.
Ostwald, M. (1969) *Nomos and the Beginnings of the Athenian Democracy*. Oxford.
Ostwald, M (1986) *From Popular Sovereignty to the Sovereignty of Law*. Berkeley, Cal.
O'Sullivan, P. (2000) 'Satyr and Image in Aeschylus', *Theoroi*', *CQ* 50, 353–66.
Papadodima, E. (2013) 'The Battle of Marathon in Fifth-century Drama', *BICS* 124, 143–54.
Papadopoulou, T. (2008) *Euripides*: Phoenician Women. London.
Parker, R. (2008) 'Religion and the Athenian Empire', in P. Low (ed.) *The Athenian Empire*. Edinburgh, 146–58.
Parker, R. (2011) *On Greek Religion*. Ithaca and London.
Patronos, S. G. (2002) 'Public Architecture and Civic Identity in Classical and Hellenistic Ionia' PhD thesis, University of Oxford.
Patterson, C. (1994) 'The Case against Neaira and the Public Ideology', in Boegehold and Scafuro (eds), 199–216.
Petersen, W. (1910) *Greek Diminutives in –ION*. Weimar.
Petersen, W. (1913) *The Greek Diminutive Suffix –ισκο -ισκη-*. New Haven.
Phillips, D. J. (2003) 'Athenian Political History: A Panathenaic Perspective', in D. Phillips and D. Pritchard (eds) *Sport and Festival in the Ancient Greek World*. Swansea, 197–232.
Pickard-Cambridge, A. (1988; 1968 second edition rev. by J. Gould and D. M. Lewis) *Dramatic Festivals of Athens*. Oxford.
Podlecki, A. J. (1989) *Aeschylus, Eumenides*. Warminster.
Poe, J. P. (2000) 'Multiplicity, Discontinuity, and Visual Meaning in Aristophanic Comedy', *RhM* 143, 256–95.
Pownall, F. S. (2000) 'Shifting Viewpoints in Xenophon's *Hellenica*: The Arginusae Episode.' *Athenaeum* 88, 499–513.
Prag, A. J. N. W. (1985) *The Oresteia. Iconographic and Narrative Tradition*. Warminster.
Prag, A. J. N. W. (1991) 'Clytemnestra's Weapon Yet Once More', *CQ* 41, 242–6.
Prauscello, L. (2014) *Performing Citizenship in Plato's* Laws. Cambridge.
Pritchard, D. M. (2004) 'Kleisthenes, Participation, and the Dithyrambic Contests of Late Archaic and Classical Athens', *Phoenix* 58, 208–28.
Pritchard, D. M (2013) *Sport, Democracy and War in Classical Athens*. Cambridge.
Pritchard, D. M (2018) 'The Standing of Sailors in Democratic Athens', *Dialogues d'histoire ancienne* 44, 231–53.
Raaflaub, K. A. (2003) 'Stick and Glue: The Function of Tyranny in Fifth-century Athenian Democracy', in Morgan (ed.) 59–93.
Radley, A. (1990) 'Artefacts, Memory and a Sense of the Past', in D. Middleton and D. Edwards (eds), *Collective Remembering*. London, 46–59.

Raeburn, D. and O. Thomas (2011) *The Agamemnon of Aeschylus*. Oxford.
Reinke, A. (2019) 'Concepts of (Un)dressing in Greek Drama'. PhD thesis, University of Cambridge.
Revermann, M. (2006), *Comic Business: Theatricality, Dramatic Technique, and Performance Contexts of Aristophanic Comedy*. Oxford.
Revermann, M. (2013) 'Théâtre grec, outils comparatifs et analyse des objects scéniques', in Le Guen and Milanezi (eds), 35–49.
Rhodes, P. J. (1979) 'ΕΙΣΑΓΓΕΛΙΑ in Athens', *JHS* 99, 103–114.
Rhodes, P. J. (1981) 'Notes on Voting in Athens', *GRBS* 22, 125–32.
Rhodes, P. J. (1985) *The Athenian Empire*. Oxford.
Rhodes, P. J. (2004) 'Aristophanes and the Athenian Assembly', in D. L. Cairns and R. A. Knox (eds) *Law, Rhetoric and Comedy in Classical Athens*. Swansea, 223–38.
Rhodes, P. J. (2013) 'The Organization of Athenian Public Finance' *G&R* 60, 203–31.
Ricke, A. (2017) 'Making "sense" of Identity: Ethnicity, Nationalism, and the Sensory Experience of German Traditions in Brazil', *Journal of Contemporary Ethnography* 46, 173–202.
Rihll, T. (1995) 'Democracy Denied: Why Ephialtes Attacked the Areiopagus' *JHS* 115, 87–98.
Ringer, M. (1998) *Electra and the Empty Urn: Metatheatre and Role-Playing in Sophocles*. Chapel Hill.
Roberts, J. T. (2017) *The Plague of War: Athens, Sparta, and the Struggle for Ancient Greece*. Oxford.
Robertson, D. (1924) 'The End of the *Supplices* Trilogy of Aeschylus', *CR* 38, 51–3.
Roisman, H. M. and C. A. E. Luschnig (2011) *Euripides Electra*. Norman.
Roselli, D. K. (2011) *Theater of the People: Spectators and Society in Ancient Athens*. Austin.
Rosenbloom, D. (2012) 'Scripting Revolution: Democracy and its Discontents in Late Fifth-century Drama', in Markantonatos and Zimmerman (eds), 405–42.
Rosivach, V. J. (1988) 'The Tyrant in Athenian Democracy', *QUCC* 30, 43–57.
Ruffell, I. (2002) 'A Total Write-off. Aristophanes, Cratinus, and the Rhetoric of Comic', *CQ* 52, 138–63.
Rusten, J. (2019) 'The Phanagoria *chous*', in D. Braund, E. Hall and R. Wyles (eds), 59–81.
Samons, L. J. (1999) 'Aeschylus, the Alkmeonids and the Reform of the Areopagos', *The Classical Journal* 94, 221–33.
Sansone, D. (1978) 'The Bacchae as Satyr-Play?', *Illinois Classical Studies* 3, 40–6.
Schmidt, M. (1967) 'Dionysien' *Antike Kunst* 10, 70–81.
Schmitt-Pantel, P. (1990) 'Collective Activities and the Political in the Greek City', in O. Murray and S. Price (eds) *The Greek City-state from Homer to Alexander*. Oxford, 199–214.
Schwartzberg, M. (2010) 'Shouts, Murmurs and Votes: Acclamation and Aggregation in Ancient Greece' *Journal of Political Philosophy* 18, 448–68.
Seaford, R. (1981) 'Dionysiac Drama and the Dionysiac Mysteries', *CQ* 31, 252–75.

Seaford, R. (1994) *Reciprocity and Ritual. Homer and Tragedy in the Developing City-State*. Oxford Clarendon Press.
Seaford, R. (2001) *Euripides* Bacchae. Warminster: Aris and Phillips.
Seaford, R. (2003) 'Tragic Tyranny', in Morgan (ed.), 95–116.
Seale, D. (1982) *Vision and Stagecraft in Sophocles*. London.
Segal, C. (1980) 'Visual Symbolism and Visual Effects in Sophocles', *The Classical World* 74, 125–42.
Segal, C. (1981) *Tragedy and Civilization: An Interpretation of Sophocles*. Cambridge, MA.
Segal, C. (1997) *Dionysiac Poetics and Euripides'* Bacchae. Princeton.
Seidensticker, B. (1978) 'Comic Elements in Euripides' *Bacchae*', *AJPh* 99, 303–20.
Sells, D. (2019) *Parody, Politics and the Populace in Greek Old Comedy*. London.
Sguaitamatti, M. (1982) 'Attic White-ground lekythos Attributed to the Painter of New York 23.160.41', in H. Bloesch (ed.) *Greek Vases from the Hirschmann Collection*. Zurich, 84.
Shear, J. L. (2007) 'The Oath of Demophantos and the Politics of Athenian Identity', in A. H. Sommerstein and J. Fletcher (eds) *Horkos*. Exeter, 148–60.
Shear, J. L. (2012) 'The Tyrannicides, their Cult and the Panathenaia: A Note', *JHS* 132, 107–19.
Shirazi, A. (2018) 'The Other Side of the Mirror: Reflection and Reversal in Euripides' *Hecuba*', in Telò and Mueller (eds), 97–110.
Sicherl, M. (1977) 'The Tragic Issue in Sophocles' Ajax', *YCIS* 25, 67–98.
Sider, D. (1978) 'Stagecraft in the *Oresteia*', *The American Journal of Philology* 99, 12–27.
Silk, M. S. (1993) 'Aristophanic Paratragedy', in Sommerstein et al. (eds), 477–504.
Slater, N. W. (1985) 'Vanished Players: Two Classical Reliefs and Theatre History', *GRBS* 26, 333–44.
Slater, N. W. (2002) *Spectator Politics: Metatheatre and Performance in Aristophanes*. Philadelphia.
Slater, N. W. (2005) 'Nothing to do with Satyrs? *Alcestis* and the Concept of Prosatyric Drama', in G. W. M. Harrison (ed.), *Satyr Drama: Tragedy at Play*. Swansea, 83–101.
Slater, N. W. (2013) Euripides *Alcestis*. London.
Smertenko, C. (1932) 'The Political Sympathies of Aeschylus', *JHS* 52, 233–5.
Smith, A. C. (2005) 'Political Painters', *The Classical Review* 55, 341–4.
Smith, C. F. (1913) *Commentary on Thucydides Book 6*. Boston.
Smith, R. R. R. (2002) 'The Use of Images: Visual History and Ancient History', in T. P. Wiseman (ed.), *Classics in Progress: Essays on Ancient Greece and Rome*. Oxford, 59–102.
Sofer, A. (2003) *The Stage Life of Props*. University of Michigan Press.
Sommerstein, A. H. (1980) *Aristophanes* Acharnians. Warminster.
Sommerstein, A. H. (1981) *Aristophanes* Knights. Warminster.
Sommerstein, A. H. (1983) *Aristophanes* Wasps. Warminster.
Sommerstein, A. H. (1989a) *Aeschylus* Eumenides. Cambridge.

Sommerstein, A. H. (1989b) 'Again Klytaimestra's Weapon', *CQ* 39, 296–301.
Sommerstein, A. H. (2009a) *Aeschylus*. Oresteia: Agamemnon. Libation-Bearers. Eumenides. Loeb. Vol. 2. Cambridge, MA.
Sommerstein, A. H. (2009b) *Aeschylus Fragments*. Vol. 3. Loeb. London and Cambridge, Mass.
Sommerstein, A. H. (2010) 'Violence in Greek Drama', in id. *The Tangled Ways of Zeus*. Oxford, 30–46 [originally published in *Ordia Prima* 3 (2004) 41–56]
Sommerstein, A. H. (2016) '*Bacchae* and Earlier Tragedy', in D. Stuttard (ed.) *Looking at Bacchae*. London, 29–31.
Sommerstein, A. H., S. F. Halliwell, J. Henderson, and B. Zimmermann (1993) (eds), *Tragedy, Comedy and the Polis*. Bari.
Sotheby's (1993) *Greek Vases from the Hirschmann Collection*. London.
Sourvinou-Inwood, C. (1989) 'Assumptions and the Creation of Meaning: Reading Sophocles' *Antigone*' *JHS* 109, 134–48.
Sourvinou-Inwood, C. (1997) 'Medea at a Shifting Distance: Images and Euripidean Tragedy', in J. Clauss and S. Iles Johnston (eds.), *Medea: Essays on Medea in Myth, Literature, Philosophy and Art*. Princeton, 253–96.
Sourvinou-Inwood, C. (2003) *Tragedy and Athenian Religion*. Lanham, MD.
Sparkes, B. A. (1985) 'Aspects of Onesimos', in C. G. Boulter (ed.) *Greek Art, Archaic into Classical*. Leiden, 18–39.
Sparkes, B. A. (1988) 'A New Satyr-mask', in J. H. Betts, J. T. Hooker and J. R. Green (eds) *Studies in Honour of T.B.L. Webster*. Bristol, 133–6 with pl. 14.1.
Spivey, N. (1994) 'Psephological Heroes', in R. Osborne and S. Hornblower (eds), *Ritual, Finance, Politics. Athenian Democratic Accounts Presented to David Lewis*. Oxford, 39–52.
Squire, M. J. (2018) 'Embodying the Dead on Classical Attic Grave Stelai' *Art History* 41, 518–45.
Stanford, W. B. (1963) Ajax. London.
Stansbury-O'Donnell, M. D. (2006) *Vase Painting, Gender, and Social Identity in Archaic Athens*. Cambridge.
Stewart, E. (2017) *Greek Tragedy on the Move*. Oxford.
Storey, I. (1998) 'Poets, Politicians and Perverts: Political Humour in Aristophanes.' *Classics Ireland* 5, 85–134.
Taplin, O. (1977) *Stagecraft of Aeschylus*. Oxford.
Taplin, O. (1978) *Greek Tragedy in* Action. London.
Taplin, O. (1986), 'Fifth-Century Tragedy and Comedy: A Synkrisis.' *JHS* 106, 163–174.
Taplin, O. (1993a), *Comic Angels and Other Approaches to Greek Drama Through Vase-painting*. Oxford.
Taplin, O. (1993b) 'Do the "Phlyax Vases" have bearings on Athenian Comedy and the Polis', in Sommerstein et al. (eds.), 527–44.
Taplin, O. (2010) 'A Curtain Call?', in Taplin and Wyles (eds), 255–64.

Taplin, O. (2016) 'Aeschylus, "Father of Stage-Objects"', in Coppola, Barone and Salvadori (eds) 155–64.
Taplin, O. and R. Wyles (2010) (eds) *The Pronomos Vase and its Context*. Oxford.
Taylor, M. C. (2010) *Thucydides, Pericles, and the Idea of Athens in the Peloponnesian War*. Cambridge.
Taylor, M. W. (1991) *The Tyrant Slayers*. 2nd edition. Salem, NH.
Teague, F. (1991) *Shakespeare's Speaking Properties*. Lewisburg, PA.
Teegarden, D. A. (2014) *Death to Tyrants! Ancient Greek Democracy and the Struggle Against Tyranny*. Princeton.
Telò, M. (2010) 'Embodying the Tragic Father(s): Autobiography and Intertextuality in Aristophanes.' *ClAnt* 29, 278–326.
Telò, M. (2016) *Aristophanes and the Cloak of Comedy*. Chicago.
Telò, M. and M. Mueller (2018a) (eds) *The Materialities of Greek Tragedy*. London.
Telò, M. and M. Mueller (2018b) 'Introduction: Greek Tragedy and the New Materialisms', in Telò and Mueller (eds), 1–16.
Thalmann, W. G. (1978) *Dramatic Art in Aeschylus's* Seven Against Thebes. Yale.
Tod, M. N. (1946) *A Selection of Greek Historical Inscriptions*. 2nd edition. Oxford.
Torrance, I. (2007) *Aeschylus:* Seven Against Thebes. Bristol.
Torrance, I. (2011) 'In the Footprints of Aeschylus: Recognition, Allusion, and Metapoetics in Euripides', *AJPH* 132, 177–204.
Torrance, I. (2013) *Metapoetry in Euripides*. Oxford.
Trendall, A. D. (1959), 'Phlyax Vases', *BICS Supplement* 8, 1–77.
Trendall, A. D. (1988) 'Masks on Apulian Red-figured Vases', in J. Betts, J. Hooker, and J. R. Green (eds), *Studies in Honour of T.B.L. Webster*, vol. II. Bristol, 137–54.
Trendall, A. D. and A. Cambitoglou (1978) *The Red-Figured Vases of Apulia*. Oxford.
Trnka, S., C. Dureau, and J. Park (eds) (2013) *Senses and Citizenships: Embodying Political Life*. New York.
Tsirivakos, E. (1974) 'Iniochos technis tragikis', *Archaiologikon Deltion* 29, 88–94 with plates 48–53.
Tucker, T. G. (1901) *Aeschylus* Choephori. Cambridge.
Turner, J. C., P. J. Oakes, S. A. Haslam, and C. McGarty (1994) 'Self and Collective: Cognition and Social Context', *Personality and Social Psychology Bulletin* 20, 454–63.
van Wees, H. (2004) *Greek Warfare. Myths and Realities*. London.
van Wees, H. and G. F. Viggiano (2013) 'The Arms, Armor, and the Iconography of Early Greek Hoplite Warfare', in Kagan and Viggiano (eds.), 57–73.
Villacèque, N. (2007) '"Toi, spectateur de mes tourments": les adresses au public dans la tragédie grecque', *Cahiers du Centre Gutave Glotz* 18, 263–80.
Vlassopoulos, K. (2007) 'Free Spaces: Identity, Experience and Democracy in Classical Athens', *CQ* 57, 33–52.
Warr, G. C. W. (1898) 'Clytemnestra's Weapon', *CR* 12, 348–50.
Webster, T. B. L. (1948) 'South Italian Vases and Attic Drama', *CQ* 42, 15–27.

Weiberg, E. L. (2018) 'Weapons as Friends and Foes in Sophocles' *Ajax* and Euripides' *Heracles*', in Telò and Mueller (eds), 63–77.
Weilhartner, J. (2005) *Mykenische Opfergaben nach Aussage der Linear B-Texte*. Vienna.
Weiss, N. (2018) 'Speaking Sights and Seen Sounds in Aeschylean Tragedy', in Telò and Mueller (eds), 169–84.
West, M. L. (2006) 'Kings and Demos in Aeschylus', in D. Cairns and V. Liapis (eds), *Dionysalexandros*. Swansea, 31–40.
Whitehorne, J. (2005) 'O City of Kranaos! Athenian Identity in Aristophanes' *Acharnians*', *G&R* 52, 34–44.
Wiles, D. (2007) *Mask and Performance in Greek Tragedy*. Cambridge.
Wilkins, J. (2001) *The Boastful Chef, The Discourse of Food in Ancient Greek Comedy*. Oxford.
Williams, D. (1980) 'Ajax, Odysseus, and the Arms of Achilles', *Antike Kunst* 23, 137–45.
Wilson, N. G. (2015) *Herodoti Historiae Libri V–IX*. Oxford.
Wilson, P. (2000) *The Athenian Institution of the Khoregia: the Chorus, the City, and the Stage*. Cambridge.
Wilson, P. (2009) 'Tragic Honours and Democracy: Neglected Evidence for the Politics of the Athenian Dionysia', *CQ* 59, 8–29.
Wilson, P. (2010) 'The Man and the Music (and the Choregos?)', in Taplin and Wyles (eds), 181–212.
Winkler, J. J. (1990) 'The Ephebes' Song', in Winkler and Zeitlin (eds), 20–62.
Winkler, J. J. and F. Zeitlin (1990) (eds) *Nothing to do with Dionysus?* Princeton.
Winnington-Ingram, R. P. (1948) 'Clytemnestra and the Vote of Athena' *JHS* 68, 130–47.
Woodward, I. (2007) *Understanding Material Culture*. London.
Wright, M. (2013) 'Comedy versus Tragedy in *Wasps*', in E. Bakola, L. Prauscello, and M. Telò (eds), *Greek Comedy and the Discourse of Genres*. Cambridge, 205–25.
Wyles, R. (2007) 'The Stage Life of Costume'. London, PhD.
Wyles, R. (2008) 'The Symbolism of Costume in Ancient Pantomime', in E. Hall and R. Wyles (eds) *New Directions in Ancient Pantomime*. Oxford, 61–86.
Wyles, R. (2010) 'The Tragic Costumes', in Taplin and Wyles (eds), 231–54.
Wyles, R. (2011) *Costume in Greek Tragedy*. London.
Wyles, R. (2013) 'Heracles' Costume from Euripides' *Heracles* to Pantomime Performance', in Harrison and Liapis (eds), 181–98.
Wyles, R. (2014) 'Rethinking Violence in Greek Tragedy', *JCT* 29, 40–4.
Wyles, R. (2016) 'Staging in Bacchae', in D. Stuttard (ed.) *Looking at Bacchae*. London, 59–70.
Wyles, R. (2019a) 'The Power of Ajax's Sword', in D. Stuttard (ed.) *Looking at Ajax*. London, 55–65.
Wyles, R. (2019b) 'Greek Tragic Fragments with a Black Sea Setting', in Braund, Hall and Wyles (eds), 252–66.
Wyles, R. (2020) 'The Aeschylean Sting to *Wasps*' Tale', *CQ* 70.

Wyles, R. (forthcoming) 'Costume's comic and intertextual potential: the case of Philocleon's cloak', in N. Tsoumpra (ed.) *Costume in Aristophanes*. London.

Xanthaki-Karamanou, G. (2013). 'The Battle of Marathon as a "Topos" of Athenian Political Prestige in Classical Times', *BICS Supplement* 124, 213–21.

Yunis. H. (1996) *Taming Democracy: Models of Political Rhetoric in Classical Athens*. Ithaca and London.

Zeitlin, F. I. (1965) 'The Motif of the Corrupted Sacrifice in Aeschylus' *Oresteia*.' *TAPhA* 96, 463–508.

Zeitlin, F. I. (1966) 'Postscript to Sacrificial Imagery in the *Oresteia* (*Ag.* 1235–37)' *TAPhA* 97, 645–53.

Zeitlin, F. I. (1978) 'The Dynamics of Misogyny: Myth and Mythmaking in the *Oresteia*', *Arethusa* 11, 149–84.

Zeitlin, F. I. (1981) 'Travesties of Gender and Genre in Aristophanes' *Thesmophoriazousae*', *Critical Inquiry* 8, 301–27.

Zeitlin, F. I. (1985) 'Playing the Other: Theater, Theatricality, and the Feminine in Greek Drama' *Representations* 11, 63–94.

Zeitlin, F. I. (1989) 'Mysteries of Identity and Designs of the Self in Euripides' *Ion*' *PCPhS* 35, 144–97.

Zeitlin, F. I. (1994) 'The Artful Eye: Vision, Ecphrasis and Spectacle in Euripidean Theatre', in S. Goldhill and R. Osborne (eds) *Art and Text in Ancient Greek culture*. Cambridge, 138–96.

Zeitlin, F. I. (1996) *Playing the Other. Essays on Gender and Society in Classical Greek Literature*. Chicago.

Zuckerberg, D. G. (2014) 'The Oversubtle Maxim Chasers: Aristophanes, Euripides, and their Reciprocal Pursuit of Poetic Identity', PhD thesis, Princeton.

Zumbrunnen, J. (2012) *Aristophanic Comedy and the Challenge of Democratic Citizenship*. Rochester, NY.

Index

Aeschines
   Against Ctesiphon 64–5, 86
Aeschylus 4–6
   Agamemnon 39–40, 76–7, 79–83, 150, 153–8
   Choephori (=*Libation Bearers*) 48–9, 76–9, 83
   Eumenides 4–7, 35–47, 78, 157
   Oresteia 33, 35–43, 45–9, 75–83, 117, 134, 149–58
   Seven Against Thebes 84, 117
   Theoroi 135–8, 141–6
Agave 137–47
agency 4, 17, 41, 54, 94–6, 110–13, 127–31, 134–5
Ajax *see* Sophocles *Ajax*
Andocides
   On the Mysteries 59–60, 86
Apollo 36–9, 41, 50, 110
Areopagus court 36, 39–40, 42, 79
Arginusae, Battle of 14–15, 34, 50–1, 119–20
Aristogiton *see* tyrant slayers
Aristophanes
   Acharnians 4, 47, 100–5, 108–9, 138, 145, 152
   Amphiaraus 143
   Birds 10, 49–50
   Clouds 9
   Farmers 45
   Frogs 50, 108–9
   Knights 61–2, 134
   Lysistrata 57–8, 80, 107, 116, 118–19, 150
   Old Age 143
   Peace 9–10, 143
   Phoenician Women 119
   Thesmophoriazusae 99, 138, 144
   Wasps 45–8, 80, 100, 105–9, 152
Assembly 11–14, 53, 58, 123
Athena 2, 15–17, 32–42, 46, 62–3, 81–2
aulos player 129
axe 83, 153–8

ballot *see* voting urn and ballots
Boule 11–14, 53
Brygos painter cup
   British museum (1843, 1103.11) Fig. 2, 15–16
   Getty (86.AE.286) Figs. 12 and 19, 33, 90–3, 115–16

Callixeinus 14–15, 34, 51
chorus 3, 57–8, 79–80, 123–4, 132–4, 136
citizen right 3, 11, 13, 123–4
civic identity
   and collective activity 2–3, 13, 30, 34, 40, 110, 123–4, 127–9, 131–2
   and gender 32–3, 42–3, 49, 69–71, 81–3, 125, 132–4, 146–7
   and the ideal of participation 61, 123, 134, 225 n.4
   and the individual 4, 11, 34, 53, 67, 124
   and intergeneric dynamic 105, 109
   and judicial process 9–34, 115–16
   and performing 123–4, 131, 146–7
   problematization of 84–6, 94–6, 108–9, 115–16, 118–24, 127, 131–7, 149
   reaffirmed in crisis 2, 14, 34, 43, 59, 79, 82, 87, 109, 149
   and spectating 123–7, 132; *see also* communal gaze
Cleon 61–2, 107
Clytemnestra 76–83, 87, 143, 153–8
Comedy 4, 45–50, 57–8, 97–109, 118–19, 137–8, 143–5, 150–2
comic
   costume 58, 97–9, 127; *see also* phallus
   undercutting 45–7, 80, 97–104, 107–8, 137, 144
communal gaze 3, 13, 30, 40, 59, 63, 71–3, 78, 85–6, 89, 93–4, 125, 136, 146, 149
conjured image 90
contemporary resonance 39–44, 76, 84–6, 95–6, 100–4, 107–15, 150

Index

Cratinus
  Eumenides 45, 182 n.72
  Plutoi 45, 182 n.72
  Pytine 45
  Seriphioi 6, 137–8, 145

democracy 13–15, 32, 57–65, 86, 115–16, 123, 149
Demophantus' oath 14–15, 34, 59–60, 109–10, 115–18, 152
Dijon voting cup *see* Stieglitz painter cup
Diodorus Siculus 119–20
Dionysia (City or Great) 3, 53, 59, 63–5, 73, 78, 95, 109, 123–5
dramatic genre
  function 108, 124, 137–8, 144
  intergeneric dynamics of 1, 6, 80, 100–5, 118–19, 138, 141–4, 149
  self-definition of 6, 47–9, 80, 97–109, 118–19, 137–8, 142–4, 150

Ecclesia *see* Assembly
elite *see* status
Ephialtes 42, 79
Euripides
  Alcestis 97
  Bacchae 6, 137–47, 150–2
  Electra 6, 48–9, 150
  Ion 2, 6
  Orestes 109
  Phoenician Women 6, 109–21, 149, 152
  Suppliants 120
  Telephus 99–100

false preparation (dramatic technique) 93, 106, 156

gaze 125–9, 131–4, 141, 146; *see also* communal gaze
gender 28, 33, 42, 49, 69–71, 81–3, 125, 132–4, 146–7, 150–1, 156, 160 n.15, 216 n.60
genre *see* dramatic genre
glorification 16–17, 40–1, 67, 78, 129
grave *stele* 67–8, 132–4, 146

haptic 4, 91, 94–5, 151, 155
Herakleides Kritikos 123

Harmodius
  drinking song 54–60, 94, 106–7
  see also tyrant slayers
haunting (theatrical) 81, 83, 157
Heliastic oath 13, 41, 53
helmet 65, 69, 102–3, 218 n.86
Herodotus
  Histories 2, 33–4, 61, 71
Homer 84, 91
hoplite 3, 53, 61–5, 73–5, 84–6, 93–6, 102, 119, 134
hydria see voting urn and ballots

iconographic evidence
  dramatic exploitation of 91–3, 146–7, 150–1
  frontality in 127, 132, 141
  for mask 125–34, 137, 152
  relevant to *Ajax* 90–3, 151
  status of 1, 7, 91, 150–1
  for 'tragic' sword 97–100, 152
  for voting 15–33
identity *see* civic identity
ideology
  anxiety over its construction 30–2, 41, 87
  and comedy 105–9
  and drinking songs 54–7
  and festivals 53, 62–5, 123, 125
  and iconography 15–17, 28–30, 67
  and military service 61–2, 73
  and oaths 110, 117
  and objects 1–3, 5
  and ritual 73, 118
  and voting 11, 17
index (sign) 97, 99, 125
interperformative allusion 45–8, 97–109, 117–19, 137–8, 141–2, 145–6
intra-performative allusion 81–2, 102, 104, 157
isonomia 32, 54, 57

jurors 3, 9–36, 39–41, 44–7, 51, 84
justice *see* law court

kemos 44

ladling cups 45–8, 80, 100
Lamachus 102–4, 108, 143

law court 3, 6–7, 9–35, 39–40, 44–7, 49–51
Lenaea 50, 143, 224 n.1

Marathon, Battle of 33, 61–2, 71
mask
    agency 127, 129–31, 134–5
    dedication of 125, 134, 136, 141, 143–4
    frontality of (in art) 127, 132
    as generic marker 99, 124, 137–8
    horror of 125, 135, 143–4
    as prop 5, 134–47
    as symbol of civic identity 3–6, 123–34
    transformative power of 125, 127, 134, 137, 146–7
material culture 2–4, 151, 162 n.36
Menander 132
Metics 43, 76, 116, 151
mirroring 81, 106, 113, 127, 149, 157
mussel shell *see* voting urns and ballots
mythologization 15–17, 30, 41, 44, 75, 107

objects *see* props
Olbia 147
Orestes 76–81, 83, 153–4, 157

Paches 107–8
Panathenaea (Great) 3, 5, 43, 53, 62–3, 73, 95
parody
    of comedy 48, 145–6
    of tragedy 45–8, 97–109, 119, 137–8
pebble *see* voting urn and ballots
Pericles
    Citizenship law 175 n.101
    Funeral oration 3, 61
Persian wars 2, 33, 54, 61–2, 71
phallus 103–4, 106, 108–9, 127
'phlyax' drama 99
Phrynichus (*comicus*)
    Muses 50
playwrights
    competition between 47–9, 117–18, 137–8, 145–6
    debt between 43–4, 82–3, 117–18
    depiction of 132
Poseidon 136
Pronomos vase 131–2, 146
props
    counter-balancing of 81–2, 99, 105–6

    determinism of 97, 111–13, 117, 119
    dramatic life of *see* theatrical life of
    manufacture of 4, 36
    renegotiating meaning of 1, 6, 14, 51
    social life of 4–6, 9, 49, 102, 124–5, 138
    stage life of *see* theatrical life of
    stage presence of 36–7, 40, 50, 89–95, 97, 112–13, 155–6
    substitution of 45, 48–9, 80, 99–104, 150
    theatrical life of 4–6, 35–52, 75–122, 134–48
    see also mask, sword, voting urns and ballots

ritual
    perversion 84–6, 88–9, 93, 95, 118, 152
    see sphagia

satyr
    costume 129, 131
    drama 5–6, 44, 129–32, 135–7, 141–3, 146–7, 150, 165 n.56
scatological humour 101, 104, 108
shell *see* voting urn and ballots
shield 65, 67, 102, 104
Solon 2
Sophocles
    Ajax 6, 83–96, 105, 107, 117–18, 152
    Electra 82–3, 184 n.104
    Inachus 6, 44
spear 65, 67, 99, 113
sphagia ritual 3, 71–3, 83–96, 117–18, 152
staff *see* staves
stage image 58, 81, 83, 90–1, 101, 105, 117, 136–47, 151–2, 156
status 2, 27–8, 32, 42, 61, 65, 78
staves 21, 27, 79–80, 150
Stieglitz painter cup Figs. 3–11, 11, 17–34, 36, 41–2, 46–9, 81, 134
Strattis 119
sword
    in *Ajax* 83–96
    used by Clytemnestra 153–8
    display in festivals 62–5
    in hoplite iconography 65–71
    held by Orestes 197 n.15
    in *Oresteia* 76–83, 149, 153–8
    in *Phoenician Women* 109–22

in *sphagia* ritual 71–3
symbol of civic identity 7, 53–74, 109, 116–19, 152
and tragic violence 97–103, 112–13, 120
visibility in staging of Ajax's suicide 89–94
wielded by tyrannicides 54–8, 61, 107, 109
symbolism
mutability of 4, 6, 48–9, 82, 87, 107–9, 143–4, 149, 152
polyvalency 151, 155
renegotiation of 78, 87, 97–110, 144, 149–50

theatre
outside Athens 99–100, 127–9, 151–2
role in cultural discourse 33–4, 43, 82–4, 87, 97, 121, 149–50
Theseus 75
Thrasybulus (of Calydon) 60, 116
Thucydides
History of the Peloponnesian War 3, 59

tragedy 4–6, 35–44, 48–9, 75–97, 99–100, 109–21, 137–47, 149–58
tragic costume 137–9, 144–5
transposition 189 n.35
tyrannicides *see* tyrant slayers
tyranny 53–4, 58–62, 75–8, 82, 94, 106–7, 109, 113
tyrant slayers
comic allusion to 57–8, 80, 106–7, 118–19
political significance of 59–65, 71–3, 78–83
statue of 2–3, 53–9, 78, 82–3, 109, 150
and Theseus 75
tragic allusion to 76–83, 111–19, 152, 157

voting urn and ballots 9–34, 35–42

white-ground *lekythos* Fig. 17, 69–71, 104, 151
women *see* gender

Xenophon
Hellenica 14–15, 34, 51

www.ingramcontent.com/pod-product-compliance
Lightning Source LLC
Chambersburg PA
CBHW072132290426
44111CB00012B/1860